Empires of the Sand

EMPIRES OF THE SAND

THE STRUGGLE FOR MASTERY
IN THE MIDDLE EAST
1789–1923

EFRAIM KARSH AND
INARI KARSH

HARVARD UNIVERSITY PRESS

Cambridge, Massachusetts
London, England
1999

Library of Congress Cataloging-in Publication Data

Karsh, Efraim.
Empires of the sand : the struggle for mastery in the Middle East,
1789–1923 / Efraim Karsh and Inari Karsh.
p. cm.
Includes bibliographical references (p. -) and index.
ISBN 0-674-25152-0 (alk. paper)
1. Middle East—History—19th century. 2. Middle East—
History—20th century. I. Karsh, Inari. II. Title.
DS62.7.K37 1999
956'.015—dc21   99-28432

For Ro'i and Rachel

Contents

✦✦✦

Illustrations

Following page 68

Selim III. Reproduced by permission of the British Library.

Muhammad Ali. Reproduced from Duse Mohamed, *In the Land of the Pharaohs: A Short History of Egypt from the Fall of Ismail to the Assassination of Khalil Mahmud*, 2nd ed. (London: Frank Cass, 1968).

Sultan Mahmud II. Reproduced by permission of the British Library.

Ismail Pasha. Reproduced from Duse Mohamed, *In the Land of the Pharaohs: A Short History of Egypt from the Fall of Ismail to the Assassination of Khalil Mahmud*, 2nd ed. (London: Frank Cass, 1968).

Lord Dufferin. Reproduced from Archibald Forbes, *Czar and Sultan* (Bristol: Arrowsworth, 1894).

Minister of War Ahmad Urabi. Courtesy of the *Illustrated London News* Picture Library.

Battle of Tal al-Kabir. Courtesy of the Director, National Army Museum, London.

Sultan Abdul Mejid. Reproduced by permission of the British Library.

Osman Pasha's surrender to Tsar Alexander II. Reproduced from Archibald Forbes, *Czar and Sultan* (Bristol: Arrowsworth, 1894).

Sultan Abdul Hamid II. Courtesy of the *Illustrated London News* Picture Library.

Following page 198

Minister of War Enver Pasha. Reproduced from Henry Morgenthau, *Ambassador Morgenthau's Story* (Garden City: Double Day, 1918).

Minister of the Interior Talaat Pasha. Reproduced from Henry Morgenthau, *Ambassador Morgenthau's Story* (Garden City: Double Day, 1918).

Minister of the Navy Djemal Pasha. Reproduced from Henry Morgenthau, *Ambassador Morgenthau's Story* (Garden City: Double Day, 1918).

ILLUSTRATIONS

The Gallipoli campaign. Reproduced from John Masefield, *Gallipoli* (London: William Heinemann, 1917).

Surrender of the British expeditionary force. Courtesy of the Director, National Army Museum, London.

The Armenian genocide. Reproduced from Henry Morgenthau, *Ambassador Morgenthau's Story* (Garden City: Double Day, 1918).

Sheikh al-Islam. Reproduced from Henry Morgenthau, *Ambassador Morgenthau's Story* (Garden City: Double Day, 1918).

Sharif Hussein of Mecca. Photograph courtesy of the Imperial War Museum, London (IWM Q59888).

Ibn Saud. Courtesy of the *Illustrated London News* Picture Library.

Triumphal entry into Aqaba. Photograph courtesy of the Imperial War Museum, London (IWM Q59193).

Chaim Weizmann. Courtesy of Weizmann Archives, Israel.

Prime Minister Eleutherios Venizelos. Reproduced from "Mr. E. Venizelos' Great Speech on the Balkan Crisis" (London: George Vellonis, 1913).

The Hijaz delegation to the Paris Peace Conference. Photograph courtesy of the Imperial War Museum, London (IWM Q55581).

Cairo Conference, March 1921. Courtesy of the Trustees of the Liddell Hart Centre for Military Archives, King's College London.

Emir Abdullah Ibn Hussein. Courtesy of the Middle East Centre, St. Antony's College, Oxford.

Mustafa Kemal (Atatürk). Courtesy of the *Illustrated London News* Picture Library.

Lausanne Peace Conference. Courtesy of the *Illustrated London News* Picture Library.

Maps

Empires of the Sand

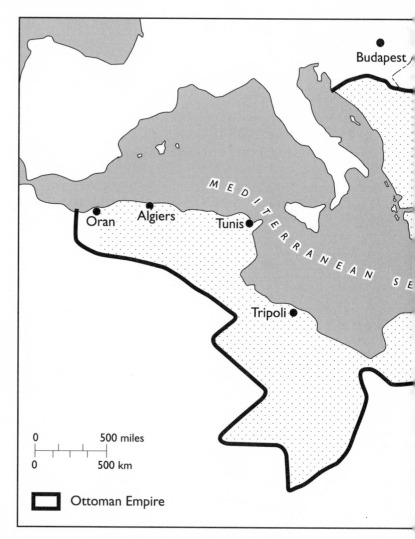

The Ottoman Empire in the late eighteenth century

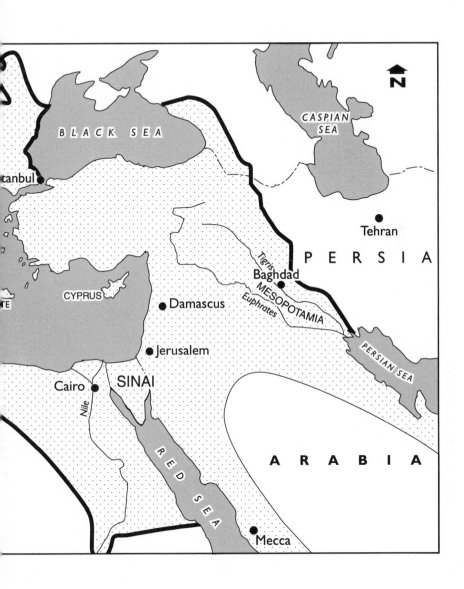

INTRODUCTION

"If war erupts, we will win," Iraqi Foreign Minister Tariq Aziz told U.S. Secretary of State James Baker during their meeting in Geneva on the eve of the 1991 Gulf War. There was no fear in Baghdad of the looming confrontation, he said, and the Americans were deluding themselves into believing that Iraq would confront Arab forces on the battlefield. "Their leaders might tell you that they would fight on your side," said Aziz,

> but when a war breaks out between an Arab and Muslim country on the one hand, and foreign powers such as the United States, Britain, and other foreign nations on the other, combatants will not keep in mind that they will be fighting to vindicate UN resolutions . . . The soldier in our region does not fight only when ordered to do so. Indeed he fights out of convictions . . . Against the backdrop of your ties with Israel, I would like to tell you in all sincerity that if you initiate military action against an Arab country, you will be faced with hostile sentiment in the region, and in many Muslim states as well.[1]

This is not what happened. Many Arab and Islamic regimes had no compunction about fighting shoulder to shoulder with the "infidel" West to liberate Kuwait from the Iraqi occupation. Yet Aziz's buoyant prediction echoes the general belief in the existence of a deep schism, if not a "clash of civilizations," between Middle Eastern and Western nations. To some this is only the latest manifestation of the millenarian struggle between Christianity and Islam. To others it is a more recent phenomenon stemming from Western imperialist intervention in the Middle East during the nineteenth and twentieth centuries.

According to this conventional wisdom, having made the declining Ottoman Empire "a field for [their] economic, political and military activities,"[2] the European powers—Britain, France, Russia, and Italy—used the Turks' entry into the First World War "to fall upon the carcass" and carve the defunct Muslim Empire into artificial entities, in accordance with their imperial interests and in complete disregard of the indigenous peoples' yearning for political unity.[3] By way of doing so they duped the naive and well-intentioned Arab nationalist movement into a revolt against its Ottoman suzerain, only to cheat it of the fruits of its struggle and to break the historical unity of this predominantly Arab area, thus sowing the seeds of the endemic malaise plaguing the Middle East to date.[4]

However intriguing, this presentation of modern Middle Eastern history as an offshoot of global power politics fails to provide an adequate analytical framework for understanding the struggle for mastery in the region, ignoring as it does the main impetus behind regional developments: the local actors. Twentieth-century Middle Eastern history is essentially the culmination of long-standing *indigenous* trends, passions, and patterns of behavior rather than an externally imposed dictate. Great-power influences, however potent, have played a secondary role, constituting neither the primary force behind the region's political development nor the main cause of its notorious volatility. Even at the weakest point in their modern history, during the First World War and in its immediate wake, Middle Eastern actors were not hapless victims of predatory imperial powers but active participants in the restructuring of their region.

Thus, for example, not only did Hussein Ibn Ali of the Hashemite family—the sharif of Mecca and perpetrator of the "Great Arab Revolt"—succeed in inducing Britain to surrender to his family substantial parts of the collapsing Ottoman Empire; he also drove British officialdom to seriously entertain the notion of destroying that empire. As late as June 1915, nearly a year after the outbreak of the First World War, and a short while after reluctantly acquiescing in Russian and Italian territorial gains at Ottoman expense, British policymakers were still amenable to the continued existence of Turkey-in-Asia, as evidenced by the recommendations of an interdepartmental committee, headed by Sir Maurice de Bunsen of the Foreign Office, that regarded the preservation of a decentralized and largely intact Ottoman Empire as the most desirable option. Four months later, the British high commissioner in Egypt, Sir Henry McMahon, had been sufficiently alarmed by Hussein's false claims to accept his main territorial demands, albeit in a highly equivocal fashion. McMahon's promises would have a considerable impact on the course and outcome of great-power negotiations on the future shape of the Middle East, as did the ability of the Zionist movement to exploit the war to harness British support to its national cause, to have this support endorsed by the international community and incorporated into the League of Nations Mandate for Palestine, and to cling tenaciously to these achievements in the following decades.

Above all, the chain of events culminating in the destruction of the Ottoman Empire and the creation of the modern Middle East was set in motion *not* by secret diplomacy bent on carving up the Middle East, but rather by the decision of the Ottoman leadership to throw in its lot with Germany. This was by far the single most important decision in the history of the modern Middle East, and it was anything but inevitable. The Ottoman Empire was neither forced into the war in a last-ditch bid to ensure its survival, nor maneuvered into it by an overbearing German ally and an indifferent or even hostile British policy.[5] Rather, the empire's willful plunge into the whirlpool reflected a straightforward imperialist policy of territorial aggrandizement and status acquisition. Had the Ottoman leaders chosen to remain aloof, as they certainly could have, given the Entente's eagerness to buy Ottoman neutrality, they would most likely have been able to keep their empire. That they turned a deaf ear to continuous British, French, and Russian pleas for neutrality evidenced their determination to reverse the Ottomans' prolonged decline and revive their imperial glory.

European-Ottoman relations were nothing like the hunter-prey relationship that characterized, for example, the "Scramble for Africa." Rather, they were a delicate balancing act of manipulation and intrigue among fellow imperialists—Ottomans and Europeans alike—in which all parties sought to exploit regional and world affairs to their greatest advantage: an interaction among actors of markedly uneven power and status, but among fellow imperialists nevertheless. Notwithstanding its internal weakness and inferiority to its European counterparts, the Ottoman Empire managed to stay in this intricate game of European power politics for a surprisingly long period of time, and even to outlive (if by a slim margin) its two formidable imperial rivals: the Habsburgs and the Romanovs.

This success was due in part to the unique circumstances of nineteenth-century Europe. Those were the high days of imperialism. The Ottomans were an empire among empires, and, apart from their strategic, economic, and political interest in Ottoman survival, the European powers were loath to knock a fellow empire out of existence lest they rock the Continental imperial order. Hence, contrary to the conventional wisdom, the era preceding the collapse of the Ottoman Empire, or the Eastern Question, as it was commonly known, was *not* an extended period "during which European powers slowly picked the Ottoman Empire to pieces," but one during which they shored up the Muslim Empire.[6]

This is not to say that the Europeans did not encroach on Ottoman territories—one has only to recall the French occupation of Algeria (1830) and Tunisia (1881) and the Italian conquest of Libya (1911–1912)—but this was nibbling at the edges of the empire and had little effect on the Ottoman edifice. The only substantial great-power infringement on Ottoman territorial integrity—the British occupation of Egypt in 1882—was born of chance, not design; as such it was a demonstration of great-power immersion in an undesirable regional crisis that it had done little to create and over which it exercised little control. Had Sultan Abdul Hamid II not mismanaged the Egyptian crisis on a grand scale, British intervention would have been readily averted. Had he seized his opportunities after the invasion, a quick British withdrawal from Egypt might well have ensued.

Nor was the Ottoman Empire a passive spectator of European events. It was certainly "sick," and seriously so, but it would not just lie down and die. Instead, it would do whatever it took to survive, be that skillfully pitting its enemies against one another or using European support to arrest, and if possible reverse, domestic disintegration and external decline. A landmark of Ottoman reliance on "infidel" support against fellow Muslims was crossed in the 1830s, when the great powers saved the Muslim Empire from certain destruction at the hands of one of its imperialist subjects, Egypt's Governor Muhammad Ali. Similarly, it was Britain and France, later joined by Sardinia, that bailed out the Ottomans from their ill-conceived "holy war" (jihad) against Russia, triggering in the process what came to be known as the Crimean War of 1854–1855. When in the 1870s the Ottomans were confronted with a general revolt in their Balkan provinces that culminated in a full-fledged Turco-Russian war, it was yet again the great powers that redressed the Ottoman setbacks and kept the clinically dead Muslim Empire alive. The same scenario was repeated as late as 1913, when Istanbul was about to be overrun by a war coalition of the Balkan states seeking an end to the Ottoman imperial presence in Europe once and for all, only this time it was Russia that played a leading role in securing Ottoman survival.

This symbiotic relationship was to become a regular feature of twentieth-century Middle Eastern politics. There has been no "clash of civilizations" between the Middle East and the West in the past two centuries, but rather a pattern of pragmatic cooperation and conflict. For all their religious, nationalistic, and anti-imperialist rhetoric, local states and regimes have had few qualms about seeking the support and protection of the "infidel" powers they have been vilifying—against fellow Arabs or Muslims—be it for the promotion of an imperialist order or for the protection of their national existence. Just as the Ottoman Empire used the great European powers to gain a long lease on life, so Sharif Hussein fought alongside the British "infidels" against his Muslim suzerain to promote his imperialist ambitions, and his great-grandson, King Hussein of Jordan, repeatedly relied on British, American, and Israeli support to prop up his crown. Just as Egyptian President Gamal Abd al-Nasser, who had built his reputation on standing up to "Western imperialism," introduced large numbers of Soviet troops into Egypt when confronted with an unmanageable Israeli threat, so Ayatollah Ruhollah Khomeini, the high priest of radical Islam, was not deterred from acquiring weapons from the "Great Satan" by way of saving the Islamic Republic. Even Saddam Hussein managed to survive his eight-year war against Islamic Iran through heavy reliance on Western and Soviet military and economic support, only to forget this fact and face the restoration of Kuwaiti statehood by a Western-Arab-Muslim war coalition.

The origins of Ottoman reliance on Western support for imperial survival can be traced back to the late eighteenth century. By then the

Ottoman Empire—at its peak one of the largest powers on earth, stretching from the Persian Gulf to Morocco and from the Caspian Sea to Vienna—had become but a pale shadow of its former glorious self. In the Treaty of Carlowitz, signed on January 26, 1699, the empire was forced, for the first time in its history, to cede extensive lands to the "infidel." In the Treaty of Kuchuk Kainardji, of July 21, 1774, it acquiesced in the transformation of Russia into a predominant naval power in the Black Sea, hitherto an Ottoman lake. A few years later Russia came still closer to the Ottoman capital of Istanbul when it annexed the Crimean Peninsula—a longtime Ottoman-Islamic possession.

Yet these setbacks, humiliating as they were, did not imperil the Ottoman Empire's very existence. Not so Napoleon Bonaparte's imperial ambitions. In 1798 Napoleon invaded Egypt, the Ottoman Empire's foremost Afro-Asian province; the following year he was knocking on the gates of Acre, in northern Palestine. And as a new century dawned, and a new direct bid for European mastery was launched, Napoleon even toyed with the idea of destroying the Ottoman Empire altogether. But this was not to be. Confronted with lethal threats to his empire, Sultan Selim III turned to the European powers for help and was saved. It is here that our story begins.

Part One

IMPERIAL SUNSET

I

RIDING THE
NAPOLEONIC STORMS

*T*he French Revolution was a nightmare for the European monarchies, but for the Ottoman Empire it was a blessing in disguise. While its enemies were tied up elsewhere, Istanbul was granted a precious respite to gather forces. For Sultan Selim III, who ascended the throne in 1789, the very same year that the cry for "Liberté, Légalité, et Fraternité" reverberated throughout Europe, the message ran loud and clear: "Modernité." The young sultan was determined to acquire the best in Western technology and know-how in order to save his empire from external and internal threats alike. Not only did he establish permanent embassies in the major capitals in an attempt to incorporate the Ottoman Empire into the European political and diplomatic milieu, but he also turned to France, which he held in great esteem, for help in creating the "New Order," Nizam-i Jedid, for his men in arms.[1]

This honeymoon soured, however, following the appearance of a brilliant young Corsican general who spread the revolution right to the Ottoman doorstep. In 1797, following a string of shining victories in Italy, Napoleon Bonaparte dictated peace to Austria in Campo Formio, rendering France for the first time in history a direct neighbor of the Ottoman Empire. In May of the following year Bonaparte, together with some thirty-eight thousand troops and an impressive cohort of scientists and scholars, set sail to conquer Egypt.

The invasion fell upon the Egyptians like a bolt out of the blue. Scarcely aware of the revolutionary fervor in Europe in general and of Bonaparte's military ambitions in particular, the Mamluk beys, who were the effective rulers of Egypt under nominal Ottoman suzerainty, responded with contempt and disbelief: "Let the Franks come; we will crush them beneath our horses' hooves."[2] Soon enough they swallowed their words. Confronted with a far superior army, the Mamluk forces proved a poor match for their French adversaries. On July 21, 1798, the remnants of Mamluk resistance were crushed in the Battle of the Pyramids, just outside Cairo.

As the French tricolor was hoisted beside the Ottoman flag throughout the country, the bewildered Egyptians realized that they had acquired a new foreign master. They nicknamed Bonaparte al-Sultan al-Kabir, and the general, elated over his conquest, went out of his way to present himself, or for that matter all Frenchmen, as men of the Prophet. "In the name of Allah, the Merciful, the Compassionate. There is no God but Allah," ran a French appeal to the Egyptian religious authorities, "tell your nation that the French are also faithful Muslims."[3]

Sultan Selim was not impressed. Although Bonaparte went to great pains to present the invasion as a gallant attempt to save the Ottoman Empire from the claws of the unruly Mamluks, Selim preferred to choose his own would-be saviors. Having no intention to remain a passive spectator to the occupation of his lands, he promptly declared a jihad against the infidel French invaders. Meanwhile, he arranged for other infidels, namely, Britain and Russia, to defend his Islamic order.

Discussions began as early as July 1798. Britain felt its imperial lifeline to India threatened, while Russia feared a French attack on its southern flank. In September, for the first time ever, the Russian Black Sea fleet crossed the Turkish Straits to the Mediterranean to join forces with its Ottoman counterpart. Soon afterward negotiations produced a historic secret military alliance between the Muslim Empire and the Christian Powers: on January 3, 1799, the Ottomans joined forces with Russia, and two days later with Britain.[4]

Before long this coalition squeezed the French out of the region. Forced to live under intolerable conditions, Bonaparte's men were cured of any romantic notions of an Egyptian "noble savage." They realized that in the eyes of the Egyptians they remained unwelcome "Nazarene" plunderers. Worse, they were deserted by their own leader—who had to return to France—and their retreat became a humiliating affair. By 1802 Sultan Selim's territories had been fully recovered, with France even becoming a guarantor of his imperial order. The dark cloud of Bonaparte's ambitions over the Ottoman horizon had disappeared.

Or had it? As France and Britain renewed hostilities in the spring of 1803, Istanbul was teeming with European diplomats vying to win the Ottomans over to their cause. Even Bonaparte, eager to tie Russia down in the Balkans, went out of his way to convince the Ottoman Empire to join his anti-Russian coalition. Yet he was playing an unscrupulous double-game: at the same time that his envoy was pleading with the sultan, Bonaparte's agents were still fomenting sedition in various quarters of the Balkans and charting options for occupation should that become a possibility. Bonaparte even approached Tsar Alexander I with the suggestion that they partition the Ottoman Empire, only to be turned down.[5] In October 1804 Russia joined Austria in guaranteeing the integrity of the Ottoman Empire; the following year the two countries joined Britain in its war against France.

Not surprisingly, the question of a renewed anti-Napoleonic coalition in the Middle East loomed large. No sooner had Selim indicated his willingness to conclude an alliance with Russia than both London and St. Petersburg agreed to join him. In the Treaty of Defensive Alliance of September 1805, Russia vowed to defend the integrity of the Ottoman Empire against France and its "projects of aggrandizement," while the Ottomans promised to join the anti-Napoleonic coalition and, most desirably for Russia, to facilitate the passage of Russian warships in the Turkish Straits.[6]

For his part Napoleon toiled tirelessly to draw the two Middle Eastern empires—the Ottoman and the Persian—into his anti-Russian axis. "Are you blind to your own interests—have you ceased to reign?" he asked the sultan:

> If Russia has an army of 15,000 men at Corfu, do you believe that it
> is directed against me? Armed vessels have the habit of hastening to
> Constantinople. Your dynasty is about to descend into oblivion . . .
> Trust only your true friend—France.[7]

In the summer of 1806 Napoleon sent General H. L. Sebastiani as ambassador extraordinary to Istanbul to convince the Porte to cancel all special privileges granted to Russia, to open the Turkish Straits exclusively to French warships, and, above all, to join France in a war alliance against Russia. In return, Napoleon promised to help the sultan suppress an anti-Ottoman rebellion in Serbia and to recover lost Ottoman territories, particularly the Crimean Peninsula, whose capture by Catherine the Great was still a painful thorn in the Ottomans' side. "It is my mission to save your empire, and I put my victories at our common disposal," he wrote to Selim.[8]

The French emperor was preaching to the converted. Having signed the Treaty of Defensive Alliance, Selim began to have second thoughts. He was willing to sup with the Russian "devil" in 1799, and yet again in 1805, to protect his imperial possessions, but he had neither forgiven Russia's past seizure of Ottoman lands nor forgotten its ominous threat to his empire. Nor had Selim's basic admiration for France diminished following Napoleon's Middle Eastern adventure and his European expansion. Now that the French were going from strength to strength—defeating the Austrians in Austerlitz (1805) and routing the Prussians in Jena and Auerstadt (1806)—the sultan was reconsidering his priorities. Perhaps, after all, Napoleon was the answer to the Ottomans' imperial predicament. Perhaps he really could enable the Ottomans to regain their lost possessions.

Hence, Selim refused to ratify his 1805 agreement with Russia, let alone renew the alliance with Britain. In February 1806, after two years of equivocation, he recognized Napoleon as emperor.[9] And, to Russia's detriment, the sultan also stipulated that Russian warships could pass through the Turkish Straits only after a formal request, a euphemism for the *de facto* closure of the waterway.

Tsar Alexander was enraged. On September, 8, 1806, the Russian ambassador to the Porte, Andrei Italinsky, issued a warning to Selim to abide by his treaty obligations with Russia and, moreover, to renew the alliance with Britain. His country had a 90,000-strong army at the Dniester, the ambassador intimated. Whether this force would be used in support of the Ottoman Empire or against it was up to the sultan. These pressures were reinforced by the British, who demanded that Istanbul end its flirtation with France and allow Russian warships to pass through the straits. When Selim failed to comply, eloquently explaining that the straits could not be opened to Alexander's vessels of war owing to the Ottoman obligation of neutrality, the Russians invaded the Danubian Principalities of Moldavia and Wallachia in November 1806. To sweeten the pill for the sultan, the tsar presented the invasion as a temporary move to protect the Ottoman Empire against Napoleon, promising to withdraw his troops from the Ottoman provinces as soon as Istanbul respected its treaty obligations.

Selim would not budge. On December 24, 1806, he ordered Italinsky to leave Istanbul; three days later he declared war on Russia. This in turn put the Ottoman Empire on a collision course, not only with St. Petersburg, but also with London. In no time the British ambassador to the Porte, Charles Arbuthnot, was pressuring Selim to expel Napoleon's envoy, declare war on France, cede the Danubian Principalities to Russia, and surrender the Ottoman fleet, together with the forts on the Dardanelles, to Britain. To underscore the seriousness of these demands, a British squadron, commanded by Admiral John Duckworth, entered the Dardanelles on February 19, 1807, destroyed an Ottoman naval force in the Sea of Marmara, and anchored opposite Istanbul.

Selim kept his nerve. Having secretly mobilized his forces, he rebuffed the British ultimatum and opted for a military alliance with France, "our sincere and natural ally." This shook the British, who suddenly realized the vulnerable position of their naval forces in the straits. To escape encirclement, Duckworth sailed back to the Mediterranean, but not before suffering humiliating losses.

Routing the British forces, however, was meager consolation to Selim, whose hopes of recovering lost Ottoman territories "from the yoke of Russian domination" were continually thwarted. The ill-prepared and poorly equipped Ottoman army proved no match for its Russian adversary. By the time Selim declared war on Russia in December 1806, the latter had already advanced as far as Bucharest; shortly afterward Russia was in complete control of Wallachia and Bessarabia. In the summer of 1807 the Russian fleet blockaded the mouth of the Dardanelles and crippled the Ottoman navy in two major encounters: the Battle of the Dardanelles (May 22) and "the Russian Trafalgar" (July 1). Military aid from France was too little too late to save the day.

To make matters worse, the sultan made a tragic blunder on the domestic front. Taking advantage of the departure of his elite fighting force, the Janissaries, for the battlefront, he sought to establish a new, more efficient fighting force along European lines. This triggered a violent response from all those who feared that Selim's "Frankish manners" would undermine their vested interests, including those Janissaries who remained in Istanbul, the reactionary party in the Divan, and the religious authorities, the *ulema*. The Janissaries overturned their soup kettles as a sign of revolt, and before long the sultan was replaced by Mustafa IV "in the interest of the House of Osman." Selim, having warned his successor off too many reforms, reportedly sought to poison himself, but Mustafa grabbed the chalice from his lips. Selim retreated to palatial imprisonment. But the days of Ottoman trouble were far from over.[10]

In one crucial respect Mustafa continued, and even accelerated, his predecessor's policy: the French connection. At the time of his ascendancy, Franco-Ottoman negotiations were at a stalemate, with the French demanding a permanent offensive alliance directed against both Russia and Britain, and the Ottomans insistent on a defensive alliance against Russia for no longer than three years. To break this deadlock Mustafa agreed to accommodate the French position, sending his new foreign minister, Halet Efendi, to Paris. Halet offered to continue the war against Russia and Great Britain, but demanded French guarantees for the restoration of Ottoman territories, first and foremost the Crimea, in the framework of a final peace treaty.[11]

By now, however, the French war strategy had gone full circle. Having defeated Russia in Friedland in June 1807, Napoleon no longer needed an Ottoman alliance. Instead, he performed a spectacular diplomatic feat by reaching out to the Ottoman archenemy, Alexander I, in an attempt to harness him to France's struggle against England.[12] The tsar, for his part, war-weary and saddled with food and supply shortages in his army, was willing to desert England. In a historic meeting between the two emperors in the German town of Tilsit, on July 7, 1807, a secret agreement was struck. Napoleon abandoned his alliance with the Ottomans and undertook to force them into a settlement with Russia; in return, Alexander recognized the French conquests and agreed to hand back the Danubian Principalities to the Porte and to leave the Ionian Islands and Dalmatia to France. Failing the conclusion of a Russo-Ottoman peace, France would join the war against the Ottomans and make arrangements to divide their European colonies, leaving only Istanbul and the province of Rumelia to the sultan. When Alexander requested the cession of the Ottoman capital to Russia, Napoleon reputedly gave an adamant response: "Constantinople? Never!"

As rumors of Tilsit reached Istanbul, a feeling of betrayal crept in despite French assurances. Yet, assessing that Ottoman interests would be better served under a victor's umbrella, the sultan announced his intention to sign an alliance with France and expressed readiness to make peace with Russia. This, in turn, allowed France to mediate an armistice between Russia and the Ottoman Empire on August 24, 1807, in accordance with the Tilsit Treaty: Russia agreed to evacuate Moldavia and Wallachia within thirty-five days, while Ottoman forces were to move south of the Danube.

Only the Ottomans kept their end of the bargain. Because he was reluctant to relinquish control over the principalities, the tsar refused to ratify the armistice agreement under the pretext that his representative lacked the authority to sign it. Moreover, in his second meeting with Napoleon in September 1808, Alexander cemented a secret deal whereby Moldavia and Wallachia would be given to Russia. Apart from the principalities, Napoleon guaranteed the integrity of all Ottoman possessions. The question of partitioning the Ottoman Empire, which Napoleon had occasionally toyed with in the past, was dropped from the agenda.

Napoleon's failure to secure Russia's compliance with the armistice agreement confirmed the Ottomans' fears of betrayal, pushing them into British arms.[13] On January 5, 1809, the Ottoman Empire and Britain concluded the Dardanelles Treaty of Peace, Commerce, and Secret Alliance, which terminated "every act of hostility" between the two countries. The Porte restored extensive British commercial and legal privileges in the empire—or the Capitulations, as they were called. In secret articles, Britain promised to protect the integrity of the Ottoman Empire against the French threat, both with its own fleet and through weapons supplies to Istanbul. Last but not least, Britain committed itself to helping secure a Russo-Ottoman peace treaty that would restore the "complete integrity of Ottoman Dominions."[14]

Under these circumstances the new ruler of the Ottoman Empire, Sultan Mahmud II, who had ascended to the throne after the deposition of Mustafa, was in no mood for adventurism. When approached by Napoleon in early 1812 with proposals for a secret alliance, he declined. The temptation was powerful indeed—restoration of the Danubian Principalities and the Crimea—but the attendant cost was exorbitant: enforcement of the Continental Blockade against Britain and support for a French invasion of Russia. Besides, there was a bitter sense of *déjà vu* in Istanbul. Had Napoleon not promised all these things before, only to renege on his promises at the first opportunity? Rather than embark on an uncertain bear hunt with a dubious partner, Mahmud preferred to tame the beast on his own: he began direct negotiations with Russia.

For their part the Russians were showing greater flexibility. Confronted with the ominous threat of a French invasion, they were willing to remove the main stumbling block to Russo-Ottoman peace: the question of Moldavia and Wallachia. Hence, in the Treaty of Bucharest, signed on May 28, 1812, the principalities were returned to the Ottoman Empire under their traditional autonomy, together with all Russian gains north of the Black Sea and in the Caucasus. In return, Russia received Bessarabia, with its boundary on the Pruth River, and the Ottomans agreed to respect a measure of autonomy for Serbia.[15]

When in the following month Napoleon declared war on Alexander and invaded Russia, Mahmud was beside himself with rage. Regretting his haste to sign the agreement, he dismissed his grand vizier and had his peace negotiators beheaded. Yet he did nothing to reverse the situation. Notwithstanding the loss of Bessarabia, the Treaty of Bucharest was unquestionably an Ottoman victory, in which a vastly inferior power skillfully exploited a window of opportunity to impose most of its terms on a superior neighbor.

As the final curtain dropped on the Napoleonic upheavals, the Ottomans could count their blessings. While the greatest powers on the Continent collapsed in succession, and vast territories were overrun by Napoleon's armies, the Ottomans managed to weather the storm almost unscathed, despite their domestic degeneration and external weakness.

The Ottomans' survival was due in great part to the empire's fortunate geopolitical location, on the fringes of the Continent; but to no small measure it was the product of Ottoman political acumen. For while their peripheral position spared the Ottomans the need to take the brunt of Napoleon's main onslaught, their direct contiguity to the Russian and the Habsburg empires, and their control of the Turkish Straits, made them targets of Napoleon's imperial designs—first through his invasion of the Middle East in 1798, and then through his plans to dismember the Ottoman Empire. At the same time, this strategic location increased great-power interest in Ottoman goodwill and friendship and afforded the empire more room to maneuver.

Indeed, on several occasions during these turbulent years the Ottoman Empire found itself in the enviable position of having too many, rather than too few, options. Simultaneously courted by Russia, Britain, and France, Selim opted for the French connection, in a surge of imperialist greed. Although this proved a cardinal mistake, leading to the loss of the Danubian Principalities to Russia and to Napoleon's Tilsit betrayal, the Ottomans managed to rebound, and in grand style. In 1809 they regained British guarantees to their territorial integrity, and by 1812 they had recouped the Danubian Principalities. Last but not least, despite its alliance with Napoleon, the Congress of Vienna (1815), which reconstituted the Continent after the Napoleonic Wars, recognized the Ottoman Empire as essential to the European status quo. This was a spectacular achievement for an empire that not only had been defeated on the battlefield but could hardly contain its possessions.

2

THE GREEK TINDERBOX

*N*apoleon, the would-be master of Europe, ended his days, lonely and despondent, on the tiny Atlantic island of Saint Helena. His territorial acquisitions were undone by the victorious powers, and stability was restored to a war-torn Continent. But for the Ottoman Empire the trouble was just beginning. The external threat posed by Napoleon had been removed, but the ferment stirred by the Napoleonic upheavals had spread like wildfire throughout the Balkans. The message was loud and clear: Ottoman rule was an incubus.

Particularly disturbing for the Ottomans was the growing national awareness of the Greeks. This cosmopolitan and polyglot community was perhaps the most privileged and prosperous of the Ottoman Christian subjects, enjoying a high degree of autonomy and achieving pride of place in the empire's administrative and commercial life—to the bitter resentment of other Balkan nationalities. As far as the Ottomans were concerned, there was no conceivable reason for this group to bite the hand that fed it.

Yet it was precisely this prominence that allowed the Greeks to translate their national aspirations into facts on the ground. Their rising level of literacy and increasing interaction with Europe; their commercial contacts with Russia and the Western European powers; their skillful merchant marine; their military experience; and their growing self-consciousness all combined to lay the groundwork for a Greek national awakening.[1]

In 1814 three members of the Greek merchant colony founded a secret society, Philiki Etairia (Friendly Society), in Odessa. The society's aim was to establish a large Greek-dominated empire along the lines of the Byzantine Empire in the Balkans with Constantinople as its capital. The group saw its opportunity in February 1821 and declared a revolt against the empire. The plan was to invade Moldavia and join forces with local rebels. A strong impetus to the uprising was provided by the belief that Russia would throw its weight behind this momentous act—an expectation not wholly unrealistic given the widespread support for the Greek cause in Russia. Because of both an affinity with its co-religionists and the desire to strengthen its position in the Balkans, Russia styled itself as a champion of Orthodox Christianity, skillfully fanning the flames of Greek discontent.

Yet Tsar Alexander I was also the head of the Russo-Austro-Prussian Holy Alliance, committed to the preservation of the conservative order in Europe. In this capacity, he viewed the uprising as the worst of all evils: chaos. To allow the forces of revolution and disorder to prevail over a fellow empire was to let the genie of the French Revolution out of the bottle. Thus he angrily turned down the rebels' pleas for support, and their leader, Alexander Ypsilantis, a general in the Russian army who had served as the tsar's aide-de-camp, was unceremoniously dismissed from his post. By May 1821 the tsar had convinced his partners in the Holy Alliance to join him in strong condemnation of the revolt, going so far as to inform the Ottomans of his support for the quick suppression of the uprising.[2] Britain and France delivered a similar message to the Porte, though for completely different reasons: the two countries viewed Ottoman power as the only barrier to Russian expansionism in the Mediterranean and were loath to weaken Istanbul in any way.

Yet again the Ottoman Empire was the direct beneficiary of great-power preoccupation with the European balance of power; and yet again it exploited this fortunate position to the fullest: in June 1821 the rebellion was crushed and Ypsilantis fled to Habsburg territory, only to end up in an Austrian dungeon.

This defeat, nevertheless, did not eliminate Greek national aspirations. Even before the collapse of the Philiki Etairia revolt, a new popular uprising, with its sights set on Greece rather than on the entire Balkans, had been spreading from the Morea in the south to the mainland and the Greek Islands. Rebels captured several naval centers and established their own war fleet. In January 1822 a National Assembly convened at Epidauros, adopted a constitution, elected Alexander Mavrokordatos as the first president of the Hellenic Republic, and issued a Declaration of Greek Independence: "The Greek nation calls Heaven and Earth to witness that in spite of the frightful yoke of the Ottomans, which threatened it with destruction, it still exists."[3]

To the sultan, the declaration was a treacherous Orthodox-Christian act, inspired by Russia. As far as he was concerned, the Greeks were a subject people, had always been, and would always be. The notion of an independent state on a par with the Ottoman Empire was not only an unspeakable affront to Ottoman-Muslim dignity but also a subversive ideal that could undermine the very foundations of the Islamic Empire: "Whereas it has become a sacred duty upon all and every member professing the Mahomettan Faith, from first to last to form themselves in one body . . . the encouragement of such idle reports [that is, nationalist sedition] would, God forbid, be a means of operating with those very purposes which are peculiar to the infidel race, and be the cause of rendering dissension permanent among the Mussulmans: which is unworthy of man professing the true Faith . . . We are true believers, and all in strict union together."[4]

Before long, the Ottoman-Greek confrontation deteriorated into an endless exercise in violence, rife with atrocities on both sides, though in Europe it was Ottoman brutality that received attention. Almost immediately the Greek rebels embarked on wanton massacres of Muslims, culminating in the decimation of the population of Tripolitsa in October 1821. The Muslims responded with ferocious attacks on Greek quarters in the towns of Asia Minor. In Istanbul itself, Mahmud shocked all of Christendom, especially Orthodox Russia, by having the Venerable Patriarch Gregorius V publicly hanged at dawn on Easter Day.[5] It mattered not that Gregorius had preached restraint to his congregation and had denounced the Philiki Etairia uprising in no equivocal terms; as far as the sultan was concerned, the patriarch, as the head of the religious community *(millet),* was the guarantor of Orthodox loyalty. Having failed this test, he was to pay the ultimate price.

Despite their military superiority and the deep rifts within the Greek community, which by 1823 had culminated in civil strife, the Ottomans failed to subdue the uprising. Thus Sultan Mahmud II was gradually pushed to a desperate move: requesting help from an unruly subject, Egypt's Governor Muhammad Ali Pasha, who was promised the Island of Crete for his services. The ambitious viceroy agreed and sent his eldest son, Ibrahim Pasha, to crush the Greek revolt. This the latter did with great enthusiasm, sending a bag of rebels' ears to Istanbul to prove his efficiency. Ibrahim was then ordered to move against the Greek mainland, after Muhammad Ali had extracted further concessions from Mahmud. By early June 1827 the Greek garrison in Athens had been forced to surrender.

These developments put the European powers in a quandary. They were all exhausted by the Napoleonic wars and wary of a conflagration that could undermine the integrity of the Ottoman Empire, thereby setting in motion a wider disintegration of the European order. Thus they ignored desperate Greek pleas for support, considering the revolt a nuisance "beyond the pale of civilization," to use the words of the Austrian chancellor, Prince Clemens von Metternich.[6]

This aloofness, nevertheless, created a discrepancy between popular sentiment and official foreign policy. An unprecedented wave of sympathy, drawing on recollections of antiquity and liberal values, swept the Continent. For Europeans, the Greek uprising was a heroic struggle by the descendants of Pericles and Aristotle to liberate themselves from the yoke of Ottoman captivity. Everything Greek—history, art, and literature—was the word of the day. Now that the revolt seemed to be collapsing, the European chancelleries were reluctantly edging in the direction of the popular will. Even Tsar Alexander, who had initially condemned the uprising, became increasingly exasperated with the continuation of the conflict, which not only imperiled his interests as the head of the conservative status quo and leader of the Orthodox Christians, but also damaged Russia's Mediterranean trade. This exasperation escalated into harsh anti-Ottoman rhetoric following Alexander's demise and his succession by Nicholas I, a champion of Orthodoxy and a skeptic of European cooperation. On March 17, 1826, Nicholas sent an ultimatum to the sultan with a long list of demands, most notably the immediate evacuation of the Danubian Principalities. If the Porte did not comply within six weeks, hostilities would ensue.

This alarmed George Canning, the British foreign secretary, who feared a war in which "Russia would gobble up Greece at one mouthful and Turkey at the next."[7] His cousin, Stratford Canning, was quickly

sent to Istanbul to find out what kind of agreement short of independence would be acceptable to the Ottomans and the Greeks, while
the duke of Wellington visited St. Petersburg to ascertain the Russian
position. On April 4, 1826, Russia and Britain concluded the Protocol of
St. Petersburg, in which they proposed that Greece remain an autonomous dependency of the Ottoman Empire, paying an annual tribute to
the sultan. The document provided for mediation between the Porte and
the Greeks, but also laid the groundwork for the signatories' intervention, either jointly or separately, in the event that Ottoman-Greek agreement proved unfeasible.[8]

For a while the conflict seemed to be abating. Devastated by Ibrahim's
repression, the Greeks clung to the accord and pleaded for mediation.
Likewise, surprisingly, Mahmud seemed to reach out for the olive
branch, agreeing to accept Nicholas's ultimatum. Appearances were deceiving, however. The sultan's change of heart had little to do with the
Greek situation. He desperately needed a respite to put his house in
order: to launch a series of long-overdue domestic reforms, not least the
formation of a new and better military force—a factor that would also
bring him the much-desired victory over the rebellious Greeks.

Reforming the military was in itself a monumental task, and Mahmud
never forgot how Selim III's "Frankish manners" had sealed his cruel fate
at the hands of the Janissaries. Hence, while the Hatt-i Sherif (imperial
rescript) of May 28, 1826, proclaiming the formation of the new army
effectively revived Selim's Nizam-i Jedid, it carefully refrained from any
allusions to this ill-fated force; instead, it was eloquently wrapped in
praise for Sultan Suleiman the Magnificent. The question that now
remained on everyone's lips was how the Janissaries would react.

Sure enough, on June 15 the Janissaries once again rose in rebellion.
Only this time Mahmud made sure that they rattled their soup kettles
for the last time. After eliminating these fierce warriors who had fought
to establish the Ottoman Empire in the first place, he created in their
place a new army, known as the Mansure-i Muhammadiye, or the victorious Muhammedan soldiers.

On October 7, 1826, having initiated major changes, the sultan thought
it best to join Russia in the Convention of Ackerman, which contained
significant Ottoman concessions. These included the restoration of the
autonomous rights of the Danubian Principalities and the institution of
similar rights for Serbia. Russia's right to new possessions in the Caucasus

and to free commercial navigation in all the domestic waterways of the Ottoman Empire was similarly recognized.[9]

Tactical considerations aside, there was no love lost between Mahmud and Nicholas. As the mood in Istanbul was turning against the agreement, perceived as blatant interference in the internal affairs of the Muslim Empire, the sultan sought to demonstrate who was Greece's legal master: in June 1827 he sent allied Ottoman and Egyptian forces to recapture Athens. Neither Mahmud nor Muhammad Ali would stop fighting with victory so close at hand.

This maneuvering alarmed the European countries, which feared the all-out destruction of the Greeks. The Russian foreign minister, Count Karl Nesselrode, threatened that unless the Ottomans backed down, Russia would take independent action, while Britain and France ordered a naval blockade between the Dardanelles and Egypt until the sultan retreated. In July 1827 France joined Britain and Russia in the Treaty of London, which called for an immediate end to hostilities.[10]

Like its precursor, the Protocol of St. Petersburg, this accord stipulated Greek self-rule under Ottoman suzerainty. The great powers agreed to guarantee the peace between the Ottoman Empire and the Greek rebels, pledging not to seek any advantages for themselves in the arrangement. The sundering of the Ottoman Empire seemed to be in nobody's interest. At the same time, the treaty made it eminently clear to both belligerents that the European powers would no longer tolerate the continuation of hostilities. He who rejected an armistice would face strong retribution; only to everybody's surprise, this came sooner rather than later.

On October 20, 1827, allied naval forces entered Navarino Bay, where an Ottoman-Egyptian fleet was anchored. An exchange of fire ensued, turning the bay into a scene of general confrontation. Within three hours the European vessels had destroyed sixty ships and killed eight thousand soldiers. By sunset, the bay had become a graveyard for the Ottoman-Egyptian fleet.

The news of Navarino reverberated throughout the Middle East and the West. While the Greek rebels and average Europeans rejoiced unabashedly, both the Western governments and the Porte were shocked. Most humiliating was the fact that the Ottoman fleet had been sunk by friendly powers during a time of peace. In protest, the Porte broke off diplomatic relations with Britain, France, and Russia, renounced the Convention of Ackerman, and on December 18, declared Holy War.

The Russians picked up the gauntlet. In January 1828, Nesselrode proposed that the allies enter the Turkish Straits and dictate peace "under the walls of Seraglio," the sultan's palace.[11] Russian money poured into Greece to aid the rebels, and the Russian commander in the Mediterranean was ordered to support the Greeks with arms. This muscle-flexing failed to impress the sultan, and in May 1828 a Russian contingent crossed the Pruth River and began advancing southward, while another force moved along the eastern coast of the Black Sea to eastern Anatolia, defeating the Ottoman forces in Kars in July 1828. The Ottomans fought with unexpected tenacity, despite a worsening plague and food shortages resulting from an Allied naval blockade. But with the Janissaries and the navy gone, and the Mansure army still at an embryonic stage of development, they were no match for the superior Russian army. On August 19, 1829, the key city of Adrianople fell without a single shot. By early September, the tsar's cavalry units were less than forty miles from Istanbul. Hysteria spread throughout the city. The sultan pleaded for peace.

Surprisingly enough, Nicholas was willing to lay down his arms. For all his impressive successes, the tsar's position was more precarious than it appeared. Of the one hundred thousand Russian soldiers who began the campaign, a mere fourteen thousand reached Adrianople. The rest were dying of various diseases—particularly dysentery and pestilence—at such a frightful pace that they could neither advance nor retreat. Were the war to continue, the scales might be tipped in the Ottomans' favor without their having to fight at all.

But even if Russia were to retain the upper hand, the Western nations would never tolerate the disintegration of the Ottoman Empire for fear that this would jeopardize the stability of Europe and the Middle East. Indeed, unaware of the tsar's uncertain military position, Britain and France were showing growing signs of alarm at the prospective doom of the Ottoman Empire. Their ambassadors to the Porte urged the Russians to halt further advances and encouraged the Porte to call the British and French Mediterranean squadrons into the Dardanelles, should the need arise to protect Istanbul. On September 9, 1829, Nicholas instructed his commander-in-chief to conclude peace. Five days later, on September 14, 1829, Russia and the Ottoman Empire signed the Treaty of Adrianople.

The document reaffirmed the Convention of Ackerman and granted Russia several additional territorial acquisitions, including the Danube Delta, Georgia, and eastern Armenia. A massive war indemnity was imposed on the Ottoman Empire; Russia was granted free passage through the Turkish Straits for its merchant vessels, and Russian subjects were to have complete freedom of trade in Ottoman lands under the exclusive jurisdiction of their own consuls. A new system of administration was established in the Danubian Principalities, to be supervised by Russia, while the privileges already enjoyed by Serbia were to be implemented in other areas on its borders as well. Last but not least, the treaty obliged the sultan to accept the London Protocol of March 22, 1829, and to grant the Greeks autonomy.[12]

This was a heavy political and economic blow to Mahmud, who could ill afford further loosening of the disaffected Balkans or additional financial burdens on his fragile economy. But his troubles did not end there. The Treaty of Adrianople and the disastrous Ottoman military performance had produced a fundamental change of heart in the West: judging from the state of disorganization in the Ottoman Empire, it no longer made any sense to keep the Greeks under their tottering suzerain. Even London, the sultan's staunchest supporter, deemed it best to opt for an independent Greece—lest the Ottoman Empire disintegrate "from its own inherent causes of decay."[13]

Under the circumstances, the sole consolation for the sultan was the fact that the British pushed to keep the new Greek state as small as possible for fear that the new entity might become a Russian satellite. The Austrian prime minister, Prince Clemens von Metternich, who was arranging a loan to Istanbul to ease the Ottoman indemnity, shared this position. Russia, for its part, while still supportive of keeping Greece an Ottoman tributary with generous frontiers, made it clear that it would not resist the idea of a smaller independent Greece. The sultan, seeing no choice but to comply, gave his reluctant consent to the idea, provided that the frontier of Greece be reduced. Greek wishes were totally ignored.

The way was thus paved for an international conference in London, whose protocol of February 3, 1830, declared that "Greece shall form an independent State."[14] Greece's new government was to be a monarchy, and its territorial integrity was guaranteed by Britain, Russia, and France. In deference to the Ottoman desire to reduce the frontiers, the northern border of the new kingdom was to be bound by the Zitouni-Aspropotamos line pushed down almost to the Gulf of Corinth, and the Greek islands, excluding Crete and Samos.

But it would take two more years, a bitter civil war in which the elected Greek president, Count John Capodistrias, was murdered, and yet another great-power intervention before Greek independence would be sealed. On May 7, 1832, Britain, France, Russia, and Bavaria signed a convention that named Prince Otto of Bavaria the king of Greece, delineated the Greek border at the Arta-Volos line, and provided a much-needed loan for the new monarch, who arrived in Athens in February 1833.

Thus ended the Greek saga. After a decade of bloodshed and mayhem, an independent Greece, a sovereign nation among nations, had come into being. Few had anticipated this outcome, apart perhaps from the rebels themselves; but then the new nation was a far cry from the imperialist vision cherished by many champions of the Greek cause, for most "Hellenes" still remained under foreign rule.

Nevertheless, this was a truly revolutionary development for the Ottoman Empire, signaling the first loss of territory to the rising force of nationalism. It was also a caustic humiliation for Sultan Mahmud II, who remained resentful toward the great powers, Britain included. But he had only himself to blame. Unlike in the turbulent days of Napoleon, when the Ottoman Empire had skillfully manipulated European anxieties over its survival to protect the empire's territorial integrity, this time the sultan had overplayed his hand. His desperate efforts to prevent the loss of lands, culminating in Muhammad Ali's brutal suppression of the Greek revolt, were perfectly understandable from an imperial point of view, yet they ended in further Ottoman fragmentation, as the great powers were, reluctantly, forced to make a stand for Greece. But even worse was to come.

3

MUHAMMAD ALI'S
IMPERIAL DREAM

$\mathcal{W}$hen the Ottomans sought European help, first against the
French incursion into the Middle East and then against the general
Napoleonic upheavals, they were responding to an acute external threat
to their empire. But their perennial weakness did not disappear with
Napoleon's downfall, and the Ottomans would yet again seek European
support for the preservation of their imperial possessions. They did so
with varied success during the Greek uprising, and then again shortly
afterward—when confronted with a new lethal threat to their empire.
Only now they were crossing another threshold: they were using
"infidel" Europe to suppress a Muslim challenger, who, for his part,
sought to harness great-power support to his imperialist cause.

This time the threat came from the ambitious and able governor of
Egypt, Muhammad Ali Pasha, who aspired to nothing less than the
substitution of his own empire for that of the Ottomans. Interestingly
enough, the man who would be known as the "founder of modern
Egypt," and whose family would rule that country for well over a century, was neither a native of the land nor a speaker of its language. Born
in 1769 in the Macedonian town of Kavalla, Muhammad Ali began his
career as a small tobacco dealer. At the turn of the century he was

appointed second-in-command of a small force of irregulars from his hometown and sent to Egypt to participate in the Ottoman campaign against Napoleon. Taking part in the disastrous battle of Abu Qir, he was driven to the sea but was saved from drowning by a British ship. Two years later he returned to Egypt to take command of the Albanian regiment there.[1]

The Napoleonic invasion left Egypt in chaos, with the Ottoman governor and the Mamluk beys vying to reassert their shattered authority. For Muhammad Ali, however, this adversity presented a great opportunity. Instrumentalist *par excellence,* he supported the Mamluks in driving the Turkish governor out of Cairo, only to turn against them later and oust his main rival, Khusrau Pasha. In May 1805 Muhammad Ali was appointed governor of Egypt. Six years later, having carefully consolidated his power base, he dealt the death blow to the Mamluk establishment: on March 1, 1811, he gathered the Mamluk beys and hundreds of their soldiers to his Cairo citadel, ostensibly to celebrate the investiture of his son, Ahmad Tusun Pasha, with the command of an Arabian expedition, only to slaughter them to a man. Those who were fortunate enough to miss the "celebration" were hunted down and killed.

"I was born the same year as Napoleon," Muhammad Ali liked to boast, and in many ways he was deeply inspired by the Corsican general. Napoleon's military ingenuity was a model for the pasha, with his insatiable thirst for military knowledge. No less important, Bonaparte's imperial ambitions and the scientific efforts that had accompanied his invasion of Egypt convinced Muhammad Ali of the indispensability of science and technology for empire-building.

Having secured his domestic front with the massacre of the Mamluks, Muhammad Ali, in the spirit of Napoleon and with the aid of European know-how and expertise, embarked on his long, arduous, and ambitious program of modernization. He began to tear down traditional structures that had been part of Egyptian life from time immemorial, and his land, tax, industrial, religious, and educational reforms seemed nothing short of a revolution to his Egyptian subjects. But above all, Muhammad Ali set out to improve the Egyptian army. The pasha sought to utilize for his own advantage the many promising French officers left idle after the collapse of the Napoleonic Empire.

A ruthless single-mindedness fed by a growing imperial appetite underlay the impressive and extremely costly endeavor. Every change and innovation was geared toward one paramount goal: rendering Muhammad Ali's power supreme. His aim was to establish a completely new Egypt—a modern centralized state with a prosperous economy and the most effective fighting force in the entire Middle East. With this mighty tool the pasha hoped to free himself of Ottoman control, and then rekindle Islamic glory and don the mantle of the House of Osman. In his own words:

> I am well aware that the [Ottoman] Empire is heading by the day toward destruction, and that it will be difficult for me to save her. And why should I seek the impossible . . .? On her ruins I will build a vast kingdom . . . up to the Euphrates and the Tigris.[2]

These ambitions did not escape Istanbul, where the fear was steadily growing that "Muhammad Ali aims to control the Sultanate." As early as 1806 the Porte attempted to transfer Muhammad Ali to the pashalik of Salonika. Later it was reported that the sultan sent a Georgian slave girl (ostensibly a gift) to poison Muhammad Ali.

For his part Muhammad Ali sought to counteract the sultan's machinations by turning to the West. On several occasions between 1808 and 1812 he sought to tempt the British and the French with offers of alliance, but to no avail. The European war was still raging and both powers were assiduously indulging the Ottomans. Muhammad Ali thus made a tactical decision. While playing coy to the West, he would consolidate his position under the guise of overflowing loyalty and obeisance: he would prove to Sultan Mahmud II that he was indispensable.

The pasha did not have to wait for long. In 1812 he was ordered by the sultan to reconquer the Hijaz, the westernmost part of the Arabian Peninsula that was the birthplace of Islam, from the Wahhabis. Established by a theologian and jurist from the central Arabian quarter of Najd, by the name of Muhammad Ibn Abd al-Wahhab (1703–1791), this puritan militant sect preached a return to the "unspoiled" Islam of the seventh century, rejecting all subsequent accretions of belief and custom. Buoyed by the adoption of Wahhabism by the Najdi emir, Muhammad Ibn Saud, the movement not only established domination over most of central Arabia, including the Holy Cities of Mecca and Medina, but also extended its power and influence in the direction of the Fertile Crescent. In 1801 the Wahhabis raided the holy Shi'ite town of Karbala, in Iraq, murdering and pillaging wherever they could, and seven years later they reached as far north as Damascus and Aleppo. All Ottoman attempts to suppress the Wahhabis had come to naught, but now the sultan—seeing ample advantages in pitting two threats against each other—found an effective muscle in the form of Muhammad Ali. Between 1811 and 1818 the pasha occupied most of the Hijaz, including the Holy Cities, driving the Wahhabis back to their original base in Najd. Ostensibly he was acting on behalf of his suzerain; in fact he was enhancing his own prestige and keeping his mutinous troops, who were far from happy with his military reforms, away from Egypt. In 1818 the Egyptian forces completed the occupation of Najd and stormed its capital, Dar'iyya. The Wahhabi emir, Abdullah Ibn Saud, was sent to Istanbul to be beheaded. As a token of his "appreciation," the sultan instigated a revolt against Muhammad Ali in Cairo.

But the pasha was as determined as his suzerain. He suppressed the disorder and set his sights on a new venture: the conquest of the Sudan. By extending his rule along the Red Sea coast down to Ethiopia, and controlling the estuaries of the Nile, which provided Egypt with its livelihood, Muhammad Ali hoped to consolidate his political and commercial base. He was, moreover, lured by reports of the existence of alluvial gold, which he hoped would boost the Egyptian economy, depleted by the Arabian campaigns. Last but not least, Muhammad Ali hoped to tap into the Sudan's slave trade in order to recruit large numbers of black slaves for his new European-style fighting force, al-Nizam al-Jadid.

Alas, these great expectations failed to materialize. Although Ismail, Muhammad Ali's third son, brought his father new territorial acquisitions at the price of his own life, his was a hollow victory. The alluvial gold turned out to be more of a mirage than a miracle. So did Muhammad Ali's vision of a new substantial body of fighters. While the Egyptian forces in the Sudan found themselves bogged down in an inhospitable country, the thousands of slaves shipped to Egypt died by the score. The pasha had no choice but to introduce general conscription to build his al-Nizam al-Jadid, an army consisting of native Arabic-speaking Egyptians.

But no setback could dampen the indomitable Muhammad Ali. By now he was building up his navy in the hopes of using the Greek revolt to his own advantage. Not that the pasha harbored any personal grudge against the Greeks. To the contrary, many of his own associates were Greek and his merchant navy was manned by scions of this great seafaring nation. But once again, Muhammad Ali's approach was determined not by his personal like or dislike, but rather by his single-minded instrumentalism. He saw the uprising as a political trump card that would weaken the sultan and divert his attention from Egypt. He also anticipated, and rightly so, that sooner or later Istanbul would be forced to request his help to suppress the uprising. This, in turn, would allow him to extract a high price for his services. Hence, he cynically permitted Philiki Etairia to operate in Egypt.

Initially Muhammad Ali's plan worked well; Sultan Mahmud's eagerness for his support brought the pasha substantial territorial gains in Crete and the Greek mainland. But with Ibrahim's brutal suppression of the revolt drawing the reluctant European powers into the picture, Muhammad Ali's early gains were rapidly undone. He lost his navy in the Battle of Navarino of 1827 and was forced into a hasty evacuation of the Morea to escape the surrender of his land forces. Yet another quest for gain and glory ended in a military disaster, economic catastrophe, and political ignominy.

Briefly it seemed that the sultan had finally managed to contain his ambitious pasha. But this was merely a lull in the storm. To Muhammad Ali the Greek episode was the last straw. He felt that the price of Ottoman decline had been paid by him—with exorbitant interest—and he was determined to change the future "rules of the game" with his thankless suzerain. He also realized the perils of alienating the European powers, and was careful not to repeat this mistake.

Indeed, as early as 1829 Muhammad Ali conspired with the French consul-general in Egypt to conquer, with the aid of the French, Tripoli, Tunis, and Algeria—officially part of the Ottoman Empire, though *de facto* independent. In return for its help France was to receive part of the Tunisian coast. Nothing came of this plan, however, because Muhammad Ali and the French failed to agree on the terms of the operation. Nor did the sultan fall for the pasha's trap and grant him a *firman* over these areas, despite Muhammad Ali's emphatic claims that such a move would greatly enhance the sultan's Islamic prestige and ease his empire's economic plight by wiping out the stubborn menace of piracy and improving tax collection. Not least, London signaled its disapproval of the Franco-Egyptian plans in no uncertain terms. As the British consul-general in Egypt issued a final warning, Muhammad Ali swiftly declared that he had already said no to the French.

But by now Muhammad Ali was ready for his real imperial bid: the conquest of the sultan's Levantine lands, from Gaza in the south all the way to Asia Minor. Through this move Muhammad Ali hoped to kill several birds with one stone: to strengthen his position against a hostile master whose suzerainty he deeply resented; to reap abundant economic gains in the form of wood, silk, tobacco, soap, olives, and cotton; and, above all, to establish himself as the real power broker in the Middle East and a true successor to the Ottoman Empire.

The timing of the campaign seemed perfect. Still reeling from the Greek humiliation, Sultan Mahmud was consumed with the consolidation of his power base and the modernization of his administration. He had to curb the power of the *ulema;* to suppress the wealthy beys who had risen against his abolition of the feudal land system; and to rebuild the armed forces after the destruction of the Janissaries in 1826.

It was a Sysiphean task indeed. With the Ottoman economy ill-equipped to deal with the rising cost of a Westernized style of living, disorder and corruption rife among reformist ministries, and traditional moral values breaking down, the ruling institutions and the public at large were disorientated. Under the age-old order there had been an accepted code of loyalties. Now, all of a sudden, this fabric was torn asunder and replaced by a new set of institutions, alien to officialdom and subjects alike.[3]

Muhammad Ali found a handy excuse to exploit this situation: the refusal of the governor of Acre, Abdullah Pasha, to return some six thousand *fellahin* who had fled Egypt to escape Muhammad Ali's conscription and taxes. At the end of October 1831, Ibrahim's fifty-thousand-strong army moved northward, taking in rapid succession Gaza, Jaffa, Jerusalem, and Haifa, and laying siege to Acre. After several months of stubborn resistance, the impregnable town that had successfully stood up to Napoleon Bonaparte fell to Ibrahim on May 27, 1832. A fortnight later Damascus was captured.

The sultan responded to this threat by declaring war on Muhammad Ali and appointing another governor in his place. In July 1832 Ottoman forces confronted the Egyptians, only to suffer two humiliating defeats: first in Homs and then in the Beylan Pass between Antioch and Alexandretta. The Levant was Muhammad Ali's. Anatolia—the heartland of the Ottoman Empire—lay ahead.

After a few months of futile attempts by Muhammad Ali to translate his son's battlefield victories into political gains, Ibrahim resumed his advance. On December 21, 1832, he won an astounding victory over a numerically superior Ottoman force in Koniah, in central Asia Minor. A month later he reached Kutahia, less than two hundred miles from the Ottoman capital, where he received his father's order to stop. Muhammad Ali's imperial dream seemed within reach.

Soon after his initial successes Ibrahim had urged some of the Ottoman pashas in the Levant "to join the Orthodox Moslems who were anxious to free Islam from the Christian practices which had been imposed upon it by Sultan Mahmud."[4] Now that his appetite had grown with the Koniah exploit, Ibrahim was ready to march on Istanbul and deal the sultan a *coup de grâce*. "Although it is clear that [the Ottomans] will be able . . . to make peace in their favour," he wrote to his father on his way from Koniah to Constantinople,

> It would seem to the incompetent mind of Your humble servant that as long as the accursed Sultan Mahmud continues to exist this question can not be brought to a truly acceptable close . . . Accordingly we should endeavour to expel this accursed individual and to seat the heir-apparent on the throne of the Ottoman Sultanate, in accordance with our previous policy. By taking these steps it may be possible to arouse our Islamic people.

Keenly aware that it was his excesses that had led to the Greek debacle, Ibrahim sought to allay his father's fears of Western intervention. "Even should [the European powers] not be pleased with our course," he reasoned, "they will nevertheless be unable to block it. And when they learn of it subsequently, they will not be able to alter what has become a *fait accompli.*"[5]

Ibrahim's analysis seemed to be based on solid ground. France, the Ottomans' traditional ally, had not only displayed sympathy to Muhammad Ali, but also exploited the sultan's predicament to occupy Algeria in 1830. Nor did the British government show any inclination to intervene, given its preoccupation with its own approaching parliamentary elections. The sultan's repeated offers of an Anglo-Ottoman alliance were rebuffed.

What Ibrahim failed to take into account, though, was that desperation breeds the oddest of allies. In his plight the sultan turned to the *bête noire* of the Ottoman Empire: Russia and Tsar Nicholas I. This was not a request the tsar had expected, yet it was one he could not refuse. Not only did Ibrahim's advances threaten the privileges granted to Russia by a succession of favorable treaties with the Porte since 1774, but Muhammad Ali was viewed as a dangerous source of international instability. Were the Ottoman Empire to collapse because of the ambitions of the Egyptian viceroy, a great-power struggle was certain to ensue right in Russia's backyard. Besides, it was better to deal with the devil one knew, particularly since Muhammad Ali's past behavior gave rise to the belief that an empire under his leadership would be far less benign a neighbor than the familiarly weak Ottoman Empire. Hence, on February 20, 1833, a Russian naval squadron entered the Bosphorus and anchored opposite the Ottoman capital as a shield against the approaching Egyptian forces. The tsar declared that his forces would not withdraw until Ibrahim recrossed the Taurus Mountains southward.

Now, as if awakening from a deep sleep to an unexpected disaster, both France and Britain raised their voices in protest against what they feared would turn into a Russian domination of the Ottoman Empire. The new French ambassador to the Porte, Admiral Roussin, launched a fierce campaign to break the Russo-Ottoman alliance, threatening to leave Istanbul if Russian troops were permitted to land in the straits area. When his ultimatum had no effect, Roussin signed a convention with the Porte in which he guaranteed that Muhammad Ali would make peace on the condition that he receive the provinces (velayets) of Damascus and Tripoli and the administrative districts of Acre, Jerusalem, and Nablus. To back its words with deeds, France threatened, together with Britain, to blockade Alexandria if Ibrahim did not withdraw to the Levant. In return the Ottoman government promised to "renounce all kinds of foreign assistance that it had considered necessary in the circumstances."[6] The Russians would have to evacuate their forces from Ottoman territory.

The Russians did not immediately depart. On the contrary, on April 5, 1833, they landed a task force near Istanbul, to be reinforced two weeks later by a naval squadron in the straits. This convinced Muhammad Ali and Ibrahim that the occupation of Istanbul was no longer possible, and that they had better strike a deal with the sultan. In the Peace of Kutahia, signed on May 5, 1833, Muhammad Ali and Ibrahim received the governorships of Crete and the four Syrian provinces of Aleppo, Tripoli, Damascus, and Sidon, for which they were to pay annual tribute, and were granted the right to collect taxes in Adana, in Asia Minor. Ibrahim retreated behind the Taurus and the Russians withdrew from the Bosphorus.

While the Peace of Kutahia saved the Ottoman Empire from imminent doom, the dictation of peace terms by a defiant subject was thoroughly humiliating for Sultan Mahmud II, who remained deeply suspicious of Muhammad Ali's intentions. His response was to conclude a treaty of defensive alliance with Russia, known as the Treaty of Hunkar-Iskelesi. Signed on July 8, 1833, the treaty provided for mutual "aid, and the most efficacious assistance . . . [in] the common defense of their dominions against all attack." In a separate and secret article, however, Russia absolved the Ottoman Empire of the obligation to come to its aid in the event of an attack, confining Ottoman support in such circumstances to preventing "any foreign vessels of war [from entering the Turkish Straits] under any pretext whatsoever."[7]

At the relatively low cost of closing the straits to belligerent warships—in itself no real concession but rather reaffirmation of an old obligation that had generally been observed—the sultan managed to buy his fledgling empire an insurance policy against Muhammad Ali. No less important, he rekindled dormant anxieties over the survival of the Ottoman Empire, thus rallying the European great powers behind his cause yet again.

While Russia went out of its way to prove that Hunkar-Iskelesi "does not impose on the Porte any burdensome condition nor cause it to commit to any new engagement," the British foreign secretary, Lord Palmerston, viewed the agreement as giving Russia a free hand to partition or destroy the Ottoman Empire at its whim.[8] He therefore offered the Ottomans military support and empowered his ambassador to the Porte, John Ponsonby, to summon the British Mediterranean squadron to the Turkish Straits at the sultan's request, to prevent a possible Russian seizure of Constantinople. Prussia, for its part, dispatched a military contingent to Constantinople in 1834 under the leadership of Helmut von Moltke to help Ottoman military reforms.

Muhammad Ali's attempts to exploit British fears over Hunkar-Iskelesi by portraying his 150,000-strong army as the most effective barrier to Russia's expansionism in the Middle East proved unsuccessful. Unfortunately for the Egyptian pasha, he was dealing with the formidable Lord Palmerston, one of Britain's great nineteenth-century politicians who would fight tooth and nail for Ottoman integrity as the best guarantor of Britain's own interests. To Palmerston, Muhammad Ali was nothing but "an ignorant barbarian," a ruthless tyrant whose unbridled ambitions had pushed the sultan into Russia's arms, thereby threatening Britain's routes to India. Palmerston denounced the pasha's offers of an alliance—in return for which he requested British recognition of his independence—as sanctioning "rebellion and usurpation against a sovereign who is in alliance with His Majesty" and warned the pasha off any attack on the sultan.[9]

Shielded from his rebellious subject by the European powers, the sultan was planning his revenge. In 1833 he sought to attack Ibrahim, but was dissuaded by Palmerston, who feared the consequences of yet another crushing defeat for the Porte. A year later Mahmud tried to capitalize on a revolt in Palestine, which he had helped instigate, to invade the Levant, but he backed down when he realized how displeased the great powers were with this move.[10] When the sultan sent a personal emissary to London in 1836 to gain British support for an attack on Muhammad Ali, he returned empty-handed to Istanbul. More than anything else, Palmerston feared that the renewal of hostilities would provide Russia with a pretext to impose its domination over the Ottoman Empire, thereby undermining the European balance of power. Thus, it was not only Mahmud II's enthusiasm that Palmerston sought to dampen but also that of his own ambassador to Constantinople, Ponsonby, an incurable Russophobe who constantly urged the sultan to take on the Egyptian pasha.

Ponsonby was preaching to the converted. With his health deteriorating by the day, Mahmud's greatest fear, if not personal obsession, was that he might die before crushing his enemy. Having failed to convince Britain to join the Ottoman Empire in an offensive alliance against Muhammad Ali, he rebuffed Palmerston's offer of a defensive alliance and ordered his forces into the Levant—only to suffer yet another crushing defeat by Ibrahim in the Battle of Nazib, northeast of Aleppo.

On July 1, 1839, a week after his latest humiliation, Sultan Mahmud II was pronounced dead. His frail health had finally betrayed him—it is said that Mahmud drank himself to death out of unbearable pain. He was succeeded by his eldest son, sixteen-year-old Abdul Mejid, far too young a leader for the trying times. And while Ibrahim's latest victory and Mahmud's death were still on everybody's lips, the Ottoman fleet appeared at Alexandria: not to attack the city, but rather to defect to the Egyptian pasha! The Ottoman Empire had lost its sultan, its army, and its navy. Once again it seemed that nothing could stop the Egyptian advance on Istanbul.

In what had by now become an instinctive Ottoman reflex—seeking European aid and protection against an internal threat—Abdul Mejid implored the great powers to strike a deal with Muhammad Ali on his behalf, with the provision that the Levant not be surrendered to the pasha. To his horror, the new sultan soon realized that France had broken ranks with the European powers and sided with Muhammad Ali. Having occupied Algeria in 1830, France now sought to exploit the crisis to consolidate its imperial foothold in North Africa. France did not participate in the collective pledge of support for the Ottoman Empire that was issued by the great-power ambassadors in Istanbul in July 1839, and when the Ottoman fleet defected to Egypt, France refused to pressure Muhammad Ali to return it. Even more alarming from Abdul Mejid's point of view, France now declared that the pasha's victories entitled him to concessions from the Porte. To Prime Minister Adolphe Thiers and his cabinet, formed in February 1840, this seemed the natural course of action given Muhammad Ali's military superiority over the sultan.

It was left for Britain, then, to act as the sultan's savior. Alarmed by the magnitude of Muhammad Ali's latest exploits; fearful of Russian intervention in the straits under the Treaty of Hunkar-Iskelesi; and startled by the behavior of the French, Palmerston was determined to keep the Ottoman Empire intact, come what may. On June 25, 1839, the British Mediterranean fleet had been ordered to block all sea lanes between Egypt and the Levant, so as to ensure the immediate suspension of hostilities. A month later Palmerston ordered Ponsonby to call the British fleet to the Dardanelles if the Russians should enter the Bosphorus.[11] But this instruction was soon suspended when the British, alarmed at French support for Muhammad Ali, reached a temporary rapprochement with Russia.

Eager to drive a wedge between Britain and France, Nicholas in September 1839 sent a special Russian envoy, Baron E. P. Brunnow, to London to reach an agreement with the British government. Brunnow offered to establish a great-power collective security system that would resolve the dispute between Muhammad Ali and the sultan and guarantee Ottoman integrity. To allay British apprehensions over Hunkar-Iskelesi, he suggested that the treaty not be renewed in 1841, when it was due to expire, and agreed that the closure of the Dardanelles to military navigation be made a principle of European public law. Given that

Russia would be acting as "the representative of Europe," Brunnow argued, Britain had no reason to fear Russian naval intervention on the sultan's behalf. With this logic amenable to Palmerston, in January 1840 the two countries, together with Austria and Prussia, prepared a draft proposal for the resolution of the Ottoman-Egyptian dispute.

The sultan was delighted. He urged the powers to undertake collective action to resolve the crisis and informed them of his readiness to grant Muhammad Ali the hereditary possession of Egypt if he would relinquish all his gains. The pasha's response was dismissive: he would be willing to return the Ottoman fleet only if he could keep all his conquests.[12]

This condition was totally unacceptable to the negotiating powers in London. Were Muhammad Ali, with French backing, to corner the sultan, this would not only damage great-power interests, but also result in public humiliation they could not afford. In no time the London powers expressed their dismay at Muhammad Ali's proposals and pressured the sultan to stick to his guns. They did not have to try hard. Abdul Mejid had no intention of accepting the pasha's "outrageous" demands. Aware of Muhammad Ali's growing predicament in the Levant—in June 1840 the Muslims and Druzes of Mount Lebanon joined forces with the Christians in a popular uprising against Ibrahim—the sultan was becoming increasingly confident of his ability to squeeze the pasha of most of his gains. On July 15, 1840, the Ottoman Empire, Britain, Russia, Austria, and Prussia signed a series of agreements. In the main treaty, the London Convention for the Pacification of the Levant, the great powers pledged to protect the Porte against "all aggression" by Muhammad Ali and "to unite their efforts," including the resort to armed force, to coerce the pasha into complying with that arrangement.[13] In a separate act attached to the main convention, Muhammad Ali was offered the hereditary vice royalty of Egypt and, for his lifetime, the title of the pasha of Acre and the administration of the southern part of Syria. Were he to fail to accept these lifetime concessions within ten days after their communication, they would be withdrawn; were he to procrastinate for a further ten days, he would lose the hereditary tenure of Egypt as well.

Either way, Muhammad Ali was to remain an Ottoman subject, and his army and navy, part of the Ottoman armed forces. The Ottoman fleet, needless to say, had to be surrendered to its lawful owner. In a separate protocol the powers agreed that, if necessary, action could be taken against Egypt even before the ratification of the principal convention. In return for great-power protection, the Porte declared explicitly that the Turkish Straits would be closed to all foreign warships.[14]

Not surprisingly, France condemned the agreement and encouraged Muhammad Ali to stay his course. The French consul in Egypt was particularly confident of the pasha's ability to resist pressure, even an armed attack by the European powers. This, in turn, emboldened Muhammad Ali and drove him to a dangerous game of brinkmanship. He ignored the ten-day limit set by the allies, demonstratively preparing his army for the resumption of hostilities. When the twenty-day deadline had almost expired, the pasha offered to accept the second alternative as a tactical ploy to buy more time, yet he refused to confirm this acceptance by the immediate release of the Ottoman fleet.[15]

He paid dearly for his gamble. On September 2, 1840, the Ottoman Divan decided that should Muhammad Ali persist in his rebellious ways, he would be declared an enemy of Islam. Five days later news arrived in Egypt that the sultan had stripped the pasha of all his offices.[16] Far more seriously, the great powers proved ready to back their strong words with equally harsh deeds. On September 11, 1840, the British fleet subjected Beirut to heavy bombardment, while Ottoman troops, commanded by Omer Pasha, a Croatian-turned-Muslim, and supported by British and Austrian marines, attacked Muhammad Ali's forces in Lebanon. On October 4, the port of Sidon fell; the following day Emir Beshir II, the most powerful warlord in Mount Lebanon and Ibrahim's close ally, bowed to the inevitable and recognized the sultan as his sovereign. On October 10, Muhammad Ali's troops were defeated at Beit-Hannis by the British admiral, Charles Napier, and soon afterwards Beirut surrendered. Acre followed suit on November 4. Ibrahim's lines of communication had been cut, and he had no choice but to begin a humiliating retreat to Egypt.

When Napier's fleet appeared in Alexandria on November 15, Muhammad Ali understood that the game was over. He might have considered fighting on had France rendered him the same kind of support that the sultan had received from his European allies. But French promises of support turned out to be a hollow reed. In October 1840 France rejoined the pro-Ottoman great-power consensus, and the embittered pasha was not inclined to risk the future of his dynasty by taking on the combined power of Europe. On November 27, Muhammad Ali and Napier signed a convention on the evacuation of the Levant and the restoration of the

Ottoman fleet, on condition that the pasha be recognized as the hereditary governor of Egypt. By February 1841, Ibrahim's forces had returned
to Egypt.

Nearly four months later, on June 1, 1841, the sultan issued a *firman*
that made the government of Egypt hereditary in Muhammad Ali's
family within the Ottoman Empire. Clearly reflecting a master-subject
relationship, the *firman* offered the pasha power in a well-defined framework: succession in Egypt was to be "in a direct line, from the elder to
the elder, in the male race among the sons and grandsons"; the pasha
would pay an annual tribute to the sultan; his army would be limited to
eighteen thousand men in peacetime; and the building of warships without explicit Ottoman permission would be forbidden.[17]

Thus ended the international crisis triggered by Muhammad Ali and
his son Ibrahim. After a decade of war and violence, of expansion and
contraction, the most lethal internal challenger ever to threaten the
Ottoman Empire had been confined to his domain, his imperial dream
shattered. Having dominated most of the Middle East for more than a
decade, the pasha had to content himself with remaining the sultan's
servant in his Egyptian pashalik. For an imperialist like Muhammad Ali,
this was a bitter pill to swallow.

Muhammad Ali's failure did not stem from his miscalculation of the
regional balance of forces: his military superiority over the sultan was
never in question, and he was perfectly capable of dealing his suzerain
the mortal blow. Nor was it due to the widespread resentment of his rule
in the Levant, which undercut all possible pretences of "liberating" the
Arabs from Ottoman oppression: Muhammad Ali was perfectly capable
of suppressing any local rising. Rather, the pasha's critical mistake lay in
his underestimation of the lengths to which the Ottomans would go to
keep their empire intact.

Not that this should have come as a surprise. After all, the sultans had
used the most unlikely "infidel" saviors during the Napoleonic wars, and
Muhammad Ali himself was indulging Britain and France in an attempt
to gain their acquiescence in his imperialist dream. Yet the ablest of
leaders have their blind spots, and the sultan's appeal to Russia, which
Muhammad Ali had apparently failed to anticipate, fostered a wave of
European concern over Ottoman stability that the pasha could not stem.

There was strong European opposition to the substitution of the
unknown and potentially militant House of Muhammad Ali for the
familiar and enfeebled House of Osman. With the exception of France,

which used the crisis to expand at the expense of the Ottoman Empire and for a brief while seemed unperturbed by the prospects of Ottoman collapse, the great powers showed no inclination to use the sultan's plight to expand their imperial possessions. Even Russia, clearly interested in a foothold on the Turkish Straits, did not wish to see its southern neighbor go down. Yet again the sultan had managed to enlist European help in the fight to save his ailing empire.

4

LOSING EGYPT

$\mathcal{M}$uhammad Ali's imperialist dream did not die with him in August 1849; it only changed in scope and substance. Whereas his grandson and successor, Abbas I (1848–1854), would have nothing to do with the pasha's domestic reforms and external ambitions, those next in line, Said (1854–1863) and Ismail (1863–1879), sought to follow in Muhammad Ali's footsteps. Neither of them measured up to their forefather's military genius and political ambition, but Said toyed with the idea of an independent and internationally prominent Egypt, and Ismail even with the imperialist dream.

Keenly aware of international constraints, Ismail neither attempted to substitute his empire for that of the Ottomans, as Muhammad Ali had done, nor took up arms against his suzerain. Rather, he sought to loosen the sultan's grip over Egypt through manipulation and bribery. In the end, not only did Ismail fail to lead Egypt to independence, let alone to the coveted regional preeminence, but his imperialist dream drove the country to financial ruin and internal turmoil. Far worse, his ambition implicated Egypt in the tangled web of great-power interests, fears, and greed. As a result, the country found itself substituting Britain for the Ottoman Empire as its effective imperial master.

The seeds of change were sown in November 1854, when Said Pasha, Muhammad Ali's youngest son, who had just ascended the throne, granted Ferdinand de Lesseps, a former French diplomat, a ninety-nine-year concession to dig a sea-level canal from the Mediterranean to the Red Sea port town of Suez. Muhammad Ali had vehemently opposed the idea of a canal lest it hopelessly entangle Egypt in world affairs and prevent it from gaining independence. Said, conversely, viewed the project as an ideal means to sever Egypt from Istanbul, both physically and politically, and to transform the country—and of course himself—into a key international player, courted by the European powers.

Although Said had anticipated official Ottoman opposition to the digging of the canal, he was nevertheless taken aback by the widespread hostility to the idea. In Egypt itself, members of the ruling family, politicians, bureaucrats, and merchants alike feared the ruin of the prosperous overland route between the Mediterranean and the Red Sea. This fear was fully shared by Britain, for whom the Egyptian route had become an essential link with India. Until the early 1830s, travel from London to Bombay via the Cape of Good Hope took several months; the establishment of steamship services between Britain and Alexandria, and between Suez and Bombay, cut transit time to a mere month. This route was further improved in the 1850s by the completion of railway lines from Alexandria to Cairo, and from Cairo to Suez.

A canal linking the Mediterranean with the Red Sea could of course shorten travel time between Britain and India still further, but it could also kill the overland route and create competition for Britain's highly profitable trade with Asia. The fact that the canal had been conceived of and dug by a Frenchman, and was hugely popular with the French public, made it suspect to the British from the outset. The lukewarm response of the French government, then an ally of the Ottoman and British empires in the Crimean War, to the idea did little to allay Prime Minister Palmerston's suspicions. To him the canal was not only a new manifestation of an age-old French plot to reassert its hegemony in Egypt and to undermine Britain's shortest route to India; it was also a major threat to the integrity of the Ottoman Empire, which Britain was determined to uphold. To make sure that the canal would not be constructed, Palmerston pressured the sultan not to ratify the concessions to de Lesseps.[1]

The odds were stacked against them, but Said and de Lesseps stayed their course. When in November 1858 the Suez Canal Company went public in Paris, Said subscribed to approximately one-quarter of the 400,000 public shares; another 210,000 were taken by ordinary Frenchmen, who were driven by strong patriotic and anti-British sentiments.

Before long the French government was closing ranks with its constituents. The Crimean War became past history and Napoleon III saw no reason to continue appeasing the Ottoman Empire and Britain. Instead, the ferocity of British opposition to the canal galvanized official French support for the project; if the idea was anathema to London, surely there was something in it for France. This was the message de Lesseps had been waiting for. On April 25, 1859, he announced the commencement of work on the canal. The sultan's refusal to ratify the canal concessions was conveniently overlooked; a joint ultimatum by the sultan and Said, who for a moment lost his nerve, was similarly ignored. Instead, de Lesseps talked Said into a large purchase of additional shares, bringing the pasha's personal holding to 177,642 shares.

Said's death in January 1863 and his succession by Ismail, son of Ibrahim Pasha, Muhammad Ali's illustrious son, did not slow the canal project. On the contrary, the ambitious and indefatigable Ismail moved doggedly to gain the sultan's seal of approval for the idea. He was successful in March 1866, and three years later, on November 17, 1869, the Suez Canal was opened with great pomp.

This was a shining victory for Ismail. Legions of foreign dignitaries flocked to Egypt from across the globe to share his greatest moment, among them French Empress Eugenié, who opened the canal. Only the sultan was conspicuously missing from the guest list. This was no coincidence. Like his immediate predecessor, Ismail believed that the road to Egyptian independence and glory passed through Suez; now he had a golden opportunity to demonstrate to the entire world where his Egypt stood *vis-à-vis* the Ottoman Empire. It was widely rumored that Ismail had planned to use the ceremony to declare Egypt's independence, but had only been dissuaded from doing so by the European consuls in Cairo.

In reality Ismail wanted much more than independence. His dream was to transform Egypt into a modern imperial power, towering over its neighbors and rivaling the Ottoman Empire for status and influence. The canal was one dimension of his ambition; reform and modernization were the other. The tireless Ismail left no stone unturned. The administration, the legal and military systems, industry and agriculture, infrastructure and education, all were thoroughly overhauled, and a semiparliamentary body, the Chamber of Deputies, was established. Foreign merchants and industrialists were invited to settle in Egypt and play an active role in its development; American officers were commissioned to reorganize the Egyptian army. During Ismail's reign the number of foreigners in Egypt swelled from a few odd thousand to some one hundred thousand. Ismail surrounded himself with Christian advisers, most notably Nubar Pasha, a talented Armenian of strong pro-European inclinations. "Egypt is no longer in Africa, it is in Europe," Ismail boasted.[2]

This was taking reality up a peg. Egypt was indeed transformed into a Europe-in-Africa of sorts, but in Africa it stayed, and not in the mere geographical sense. Europe was the role model for Ismail, but the Black Continent was the object of his imperial dream. In 1869 Ismail asked Sir Samuel Baker, the celebrated British explorer, to restore order in the Sudan, which had been occupied by Muhammad Ali. By the time he retired from Ismail's service in 1873, to be replaced by Colonel Charles Gordon, a fellow Englishman, Baker had acquired a new province for his master—Equatoria. Meanwhile, the American chief-of-staff of the Egyptian army, General Charles Stone, was busy extending Ismail's control southward, to Abyssinia (Ethiopia) and Somalia.

Thus, by the mid-1870s a vast Egyptian empire had come into being, extending from the Mediterranean in the north to Lake Victoria, and from the Indian Ocean in the east to the Libyan desert. Like his fellow European imperialists, Ismail portrayed his territorial rapacity as a civilizing mission, a "white man's burden" of sorts. "The prerequisite for this [civilization and prosperity] lies in the subjects' acquisition of the sciences," he wrote to his governor in the Sudan. "So that they can excel in them and be always disposed to love of the homeland, and eager to obtain the wealth of excellence and progress in knowledge and the arts."[3]

But the imperialist dream did not end in Africa. The lure of the sultan's Asiatic lands was too great to be ignored. By now collaboration with the "infidels" against one's Muslim suzerain had become routine, and Ismail had no compunction about flirting with the idea of a joint Arab-Slav revolt against the Ottomans. His co-conspirator was the Russian ambassador to Istanbul, General Nikolai Ignatiev, a paragon of pan-Slavism. In 1869 the two reached a verbal understanding by which Russia, Egypt, and Montenegro would help the Arabs and Slavs against the Ottoman Empire. This was followed a year later by a draft treaty providing for Russian and Egyptian military support for a joint Arab–

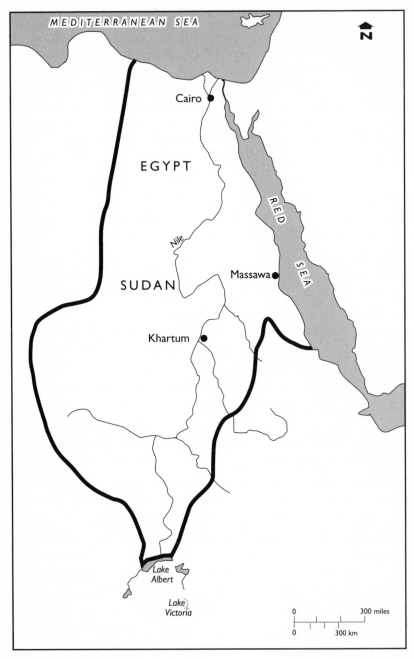

Ismail's African empire

Southern Slav uprising; in the event of war between Turkey and Russia, Egypt was to remain neutral.

Alas, nothing came of the deal. In January 1875 the pan-Slav general Rostislav Fadeyev arrived in Egypt to prepare the country for war against Turkey; a year later he left, disheartened by Ismail's refusal to heed his advice. When the Balkan powderkeg exploded in the mid-1870s, Ismail remained impervious to Ignatiev's pleas for intervention; instead, when war broke out in the spring of 1877 between the Ottoman and the Russian empires, he sent thirty thousand troops to help his suzerain.

There were several reasons for Ismail's equivocation. Once news of the secret flirtation had leaked, the pasha was confronted with an Anglo-French ultimatum to forgo his imperialist plans. Besides, most of the Egyptian army was tied up in Ismail's African venture, which slowed its reorganization and modernization; to judge by its poor combat performance, particularly in the Abyssinian War (1875–1876), this force was in no position to fight the Ottoman army. With the passage of time Ismail began to suspect (and correctly so) that his interlocutor was acting on his own, behind the backs of Tsar Alexander and his chancellor, Prince Alexander Gorchakov. Finally, as ambitious as he was, Ismail would not take on the Ottoman Empire. A military expedition in Black Africa was one thing; confrontation with the largest Muslim power on Earth quite another.

Here indeed lay the main difference between Ismail and his father and grandfather. Ibrahim and Muhammad Ali were hardened men of the sword, willing to fight their way to an empire; Ismail would rather buy his. Fortunately for him, the Ottoman Empire was heading toward financial ruin owing to the excesses of the avaricious Sultan Abdul Aziz, and Ismail resolved to exploit this predicament to the fullest. In no time he developed the habit "of making [periodic] visits to Constantinople, carrying away with him each time, by judicious payments, some shred of the sovereign rights of the Porte. These visits became a regular source of income and emolument to the Palace and all its myrmidons."[4] Through gifts, bribery, and flattery Ismail managed to win what Muhammad Ali had failed to obtain by the sword.

As early as 1863, less than a year after his accession, Ismail was accorded a great honor: an official visit by the sultan, the first of its kind since the Ottoman conquest of Egypt in 1517. Three years later, in May 1866, Ismail managed to revise the existing succession rules that had assigned the oldest surviving male of the ruling family as successor to the throne; now Ismail extracted a royal *firman* establishing succession by primogeniture, from father to eldest son. He was also granted permission to enlarge his army from eighteen thousand to thirty thousand troops. Apart from the customary bribery, these concessions cost Ismail a near doubling of the annual tribute to the Porte, from £400,000 to £750,000. The following summer, in June 1867, Ismail won an important victory: he was allowed to substitute the Persian title of khedive (ruler suzerain, or sovereign) for that of vali (governor). Precisely six years later these gains were reaffirmed and expanded by a new *firman,* issued in return for more than £1 million in bribes and an increase in the annual tribute from £1.7 million to £3.2 million. Apart from the old privileges, Ismail was granted the hereditary governorship of the strategic Red Sea ports of Sawakin and Massawa, as well as complete administrative and financial independence. No less important, he was allowed to increase his army and navy without prior approval of the Porte, and to conclude nonpolitical treaties and loan agreements with foreign countries and banks.

By now, however, Ismail was beginning to realize that buying one's way to an empire was no less hazardous than taking it by force. Muhammad Ali had managed to bring the Ottoman Empire to the verge of destruction, only to see his gains wrested from him by the great powers. Ismail posed no such threat to his suzerain, which allowed him to build an African empire and to weaken Ottoman control over Egypt without alarming the Porte or the European chancelleries. Yet Egypt was not strong enough to bear the full weight of its ruler's imperial dreams. The construction of the Suez Canal, the ambitious reform programs, the African ventures, and the lavish payments heaped on the sultan all began to take their toll. On his accession Ismail had inherited a public debt of £3 million; by the mid-1870s this had risen to £90-£100 million, £68 million of which was in short-term foreign loans. Nearly half the borrowed sum was required to service the national debt, which was growing at the terrifying rate of £7 million per year. A dramatic increase in international demand for Egyptian cotton in the mid-1860s stemming from the American Civil War and the temporary incapacitation of the American cotton industry, as well as stringent measures to slash the domestic debt (some £15 million of the total indebtedness), proved of little help. The khedive's imperial dream had firmly set Egypt on the road to financial ruin.

In 1875, in a desperate bid to salvage his economic position, Ismail sold his shares in the Suez Canal Company to the British government for

£4 million, slightly above their nominal value. When this proved to be nothing more than a drop in the ocean, the khedive approached Britain for financial advice. But when the British investigator, Stephen Cave, recommended that the Egyptian national debt be reorganized and the khedive's financial activities placed under international supervision, Ismail refused to comply. Instead he set up a special commission in May 1876, with representatives from Britain, France, Italy, and Austria, to control the servicing of the debt. When this failed to create international confidence in Egypt's financial strength, Ismail, who had meanwhile suspended payment of interest on his loans, was forced to accept tighter foreign supervision over his finances. In October 1876 a British and a French controller were appointed to supervise Egyptian revenue and expenditure in what came to be known as the Dual Control.

But this was no panacea. Ismail once again bowed to foreign pressure. On August 30, 1878, he instructed the Armenian Nubar Pasha to form a cabinet with the participation of European ministers: Sir Rivers Wilson of Britain as the minister of finance, and M. de Blignières of France as the minister of public works. This was humiliating for both Ismail and his imperial master in Istanbul. For the first time in modern history the Ottoman Empire had to sanction official European participation in the running of one of its Afro-Asian provinces, and not a mere province, but the largest and most important of them all. This was particularly galling to the new sultan, Abdul Hamid II, who took great pride in his Islamic credentials. Egypt, of course, came under brief Napoleonic occupation; but this was a flagrant, transient violation of Ottoman sovereignty, which the Porte had resisted to the best of its ability. Now the encroachment was requested by the lawful ruler of Egypt and threatened to become a permanent arrangement.

The moment of truth had thus caught up with Ismail. At a stroke the would-be empire-builder had been reduced to a constitutional monarch under direct European control. Popular discontent was growing by the day. Wherever they turned, Egyptians encountered Western influences, be it the way the upper classes and the officialdom dressed, or the religious missions that mushroomed throughout the country. Egyptians resented the higher salaries paid to foreigners, their higher standard of living, and the extensive ex-territorial privileges enjoyed by the large foreign colony under the Ottoman system of Capitulations (even after the establishment of Mixed Courts in 1876, foreigners could still evade the Egyptian tax and legal systems). Once Ismail had put Europeans in his cabinet, passions reached the boiling point. The khedive was seen as a foreign stooge.

Ismail bided his time. He had accepted the diminution of his powers under great duress, but he was determined to reverse this humiliating setback at the first available opportunity. This came (probably with a little help from the khedive himself) on February 18, 1879, when Nubar Pasha and Rivers Wilson were attacked in Cairo by a crowd of officers who were enraged over arrears in their salaries. The two were dragged from their carriages, beaten up, and locked up in the Ministry of Finance. Ismail dashed to the scene, cheered by the huge crowd outside the ministry. Tense and somber, yet evidently reveling in this show of public support, he briskly stepped into the building. Having reassured the officers that their demands would be met, he told them to release the prisoners, which they begrudgingly did. Slowly the mob besieging the building began to disperse.

The incident rocketed Ismail's popularity to new heights and convinced him to strike while the iron was still hot. To Egyptians, the Christian Nubar, who had risen to extraordinary political prominence and obtained great personal wealth under Ismail, was a humiliating reminder of their growing subordination to the West; this made him dispensable to his benefactor. On February 19, the day after the Cairo incident, Ismail removed Nubar from the premiership and replaced him with his own son, Tawfiq Pasha. On April 7 he dismissed Wilson and de Blignières and ordered the anti-European nationalist Sharif Pasha to form a new government.

This was a personal victory for Ismail. In one fell swoop he recouped his lost powers and recast his beleaguered image. Forgotten was his responsibility for both Egypt's massive debts and the strong foreign presence on its soil. Yesterday's "western stooge" had been transformed into a national savior, extricating his country from the claws of foreign predators; the great Europeanizer was now fanning the flames of xenophobia. Personal survival and national fortunes had been inextricably linked, and Ismail was steadily raising the stakes in the hope that his bluff would not be called.

But it was. When on April 22 Ismail granted the Chamber of Deputies control over Egypt's finances, in defiance of the great powers, Britain and France demanded the khedive's resignation. He refused and sent a special emissary to the sultan in an attempt to bribe his way out, but to no avail. On June 26, 1879, Ismail received a telegram from his suzerain addressed "to the ex-Khedive." That same evening Tawfiq Pasha, Ismail's son, acceded to the throne. Soon afterward Ismail was exiled to Naples. His imperial dream had turned into a nightmare.

If Abdul Hamid hoped that Ismail's dismissal would relieve him of his Egyptian headache, he was thoroughly disillusioned. For a while the situation seemed to calm down as Tawfiq substituted the pro-Ottoman Riad Pasha for Sharif Pasha as prime minister and suspended the activities of the Chamber of Deputies. To ease great-power fears over the Egyptian debts, he allowed two European financial controllers to sit in his cabinet, though they had no voting rights. He also decreed the formation of an International Commission of Liquidation and agreed to abide by the Liquidation Law, promulgated in July 1880. This brought Egypt's finances under tight European control and generated an air of optimism among its creditors, but not for long. Ismail's unsavory bequest was too heavy for his young, lackluster son to shoulder. The treasury was empty, the people disgruntled, and the military rebellious. Anti-Western sentiments, together with pan-Islamic agitation, turned popular opinion against international financial control and the landed Turco-Circassian aristocracy. The imperial dream had brought the country to the verge of an explosion.

The military was at the cutting edge of this public discontent. Even during Ismail's reign Egyptian officers had grumbled over the privileged status of the Turco-Circassian military elite. When Tawfiq appointed a Circassian general, Osman Rifqi, as the minister of war and charged him with restructuring the armed forces, all repressed anger burst out. In January 1881 a group of officers handed the khedive a petition criticizing Rifqi's policies and demanding his dismissal. Their leaders were arrested and put on trial the following month, but as they were being court-martialed their troops raided the building and secured their release. The khedive was terrified. He fired Rifqi and appointed one of the mutineers, Colonel Mahmud Sami al-Barudi (himself a Circassian), as the minister of war.

But the moving spirit behind the officers, and the real winner of their defiant stand, was Ahmad Urabi Pasha (1841–1911). The son of a village sheikh, he was taken for military service at the age of fourteen, rising meteorically to reach the rank of lieutenant-colonel by 1860. When his promotion ground to a halt owing to Ismail's cultivation of the Turco-Circassian elite, Urabi joined the widening club of frustrated officers.

Though poorly educated and of less than brilliant military talents, he had an imposing figure and peasant authenticity that made him *primus inter pares* among his fellow officers. Now that the khedive's arm had been publicly twisted, Urabi was rapidly establishing himself as a popular hero, the leader of a widespread coalition comprising provincial notables and chamber deputies alongside the officers.

Intoxicated by his newly gained power and fearing a backlash by the khedive, who seemed to be recuperating from the February debacle, Urabi brought things to a head. On September 9, 1881, shortly after Barudi had been replaced by a member of the royal family, Urabi handed the new minister of war a strong message. "I, together with the officers and men, have ascertained that an order has been issued by your Excellency to the third Regiment of Infantry to proceed to Alexandria," he wrote.

> And inasmuch as such an order is intended to disperse the military power with a view of revenge upon us, and as we cannot deliver ourselves up to death, we hereby give notice to your Excellency that all the regiments will assemble today at 9 o'clock, Arabic time, in the Abdin Square for deciding this question . . . No regiment will march in obedience to the orders given by your Excellency until ample security be given for the lives and interests of ourselves and our relatives.[5]

Urabi made good on his promise. Appearing in front of the royal palace, sword in hand, at the head of a large throng of troops, he presented the khedive with three demands: to dismiss the cabinet, to reactivate the Chamber of Deputies, and to restore the army to the authorized limit of thirty thousand. After some haggling through the British consul in Alexandria, Sir Charles Cookson, who stood in for Consul-General Sir Edward Malet, on leave in London, the khedive gave in. The cabinet was disbanded and the former prime minister Sharif Pasha, dismissed by Tawfiq two years earlier, formed a new cabinet, with Barudi reinstated as the minister of war. The Chamber of Deputies, suspended since Tawfiq's accession, was to resume its activities at the end of December 1881. The officers relaxed; the threat of khedival reprisal had been removed. It was their turn to call the shots.

The confrontation in Cairo caused some concern in London and Paris, but no undue alarm. The liberal leader William Ewart Gladstone, who in

April 1880 had succeeded his lifelong rival, Benjamin Disraeli, as Britain's prime minister, was scarcely aware of the Egyptian imbroglio, having divested his energies in the resolution of a Boer uprising in the Transvaal and the pacification of Irish restiveness. When his foreign secretary, Lord Granville, informed him of the events in Egypt, Gladstone hoped the episode would resolve itself without external interference. Should worse come to worst and extraneous force be required, the Ottoman Empire, in its capacity as Egypt's suzerain, was the obvious candidate. In any event, no British or French intervention should be contemplated "unless ships be needful for *bona fide* protection of subjects." The moment he heard Granville's reassurance that "there seems to be a lull in Egyptian affairs, and I do not think it impossible that it may last," the prime minister breathed a sigh of relief. Meanwhile, Edward Malet visited Istanbul on his way back to Egypt and tried to convince the sultan to reassert his authority over the country in case of further deterioration.[6]

Gladstone's hopes for a quick diffusion of the Egyptian crisis were shared by his French counterpart, Jules Ferry, who feared that France's tenuous grip over Tunis, occupied in April 1881, could be further weakened by the spread of nationalist fervor. But in November 1881 the French premiership passed to Léon Gambetta, perhaps the most flamboyant and unpredictable of French politicians, for whom imperialism was the key to the restoration of French greatness. He viewed the occupation of Tunis as an important milestone on this path, and he rejected Ottoman intervention in Egypt lest the precedent be repeated in Tunis. If Egypt were to fall again under the sway of an imperial power, that power should be France, not Turkey or Britain.

As the scheduled reopening of the Egyptian Chamber of Deputies approached amid rumors that the officers were seeking to topple Prime Minister Sharif Pasha, the gap between Gambetta and Gladstone gradually narrowed. The former advocated a joint action to save the khedive, the latter a careful balancing act short of physical intervention. Gambetta insisted on keeping the sultan out of the picture, whereas Gladstone insisted on his active involvement. The outcome of these conflicting preferences was the Anglo-French note of January 8, 1882, expressing support for the khedive and implying the possibility of a joint action on his behalf.

This was a high-risk bluff. Intervention was the last thing on Gladstone's mind. As a sworn anti-imperialist he was bent on reducing Britain's overseas commitments, not increasing them. Moreover, he had no intention of allowing the Egyptian irritant to distract Britain from its real problem: Ireland. Restiveness on the island was rife, the Irish Land Act prepared by Gladstone fractured his cabinet, and the prime minister's thoughts could not be further removed from Egypt. His sole concern in the Egyptian crisis was the maintenance of stability, and he hoped that the joint note would settle the problem without actual intervention; at the very least, it would preempt a unilateral French action without damaging Anglo-French relations. Personally he harbored no hostility toward Urabi and his fellow nationalists. On the contrary, as a self-styled champion of small nationalities, Gladstone was sympathetic to their cause, and deemed their demand for greater control over Egypt's finances as quite reasonable. "I am not by any means pained, but I am much surprised at this rapid development of a national sentiment and party in Egypt," he wrote to Foreign Secretary Granville:

> The very ideas of such a sentiment and the Egyptian people seemed quite incompatible. How it has come up I do not know: most of all is the case strange if the standing army be the nest that has reared it . . . "Egypt for the Egyptians" is the sentiment to which I should wish to give scope: and could it prevail, it would[,] I think[,] be the best, the only good solution of the "Egyptian Question."[7]

This, however, was not how the Anglo-French note looked in Cairo. "Sir Edward Malet must really think we are children who do not know the meaning of words," Urabi blustered at his friend and sympathizer, the poet Wilfrid Blunt, who conveyed to him the consul-general's assurance that Britain had no intention of intervening in Egypt. "It is the language of menace. There is no clerk in this office who would use such words with such a meaning."[8]

Indeed, the Anglo-French note achieved the opposite effect of that intended. Rather than stabilize the situation, it set in motion a chain of events that would culminate in Britain's involvement in Egyptian affairs in ways undesired by Gladstone. Since his appointment as prime minister in September 1881, Sharif had been trying to appease the khedive, on whom he had been imposed, the Urabist officers, who had instated him, the Chamber of Deputies, which pushed for greater powers, and the anxious Europeans. As the officers and the chamber closed ranks in an attempt to tighten their control over the national finances at the expense of the European controllers, Sharif found himself increasingly cornered. After the great-power note, he was painted as protector of foreign interests in Egypt. On February 2 he tendered his resignation. Barudi became prime minister; Urabi was promoted to a major-general and made minister of war.

From here the situation snowballed. Comfortably calling the shots from his new office, Urabi pressured Barudi to dismiss the European members of the cabinet and to bring the chamber under his control. To consolidate his own power base, he embarked on a wholesale promotion of officers of Egyptian origins. This drove the Turco-Circassian military elite into a rearguard action. Some left the country under protest, others allegedly conspired to assassinate Urabi and his comrades. Whether or not this threat was real, Urabi took no chances; he spent his nights in the well-protected Abdin barracks, and his mother confided to a British friend that she was keeping her son's drinking water under lock and key to prevent him from being poisoned. In a thorough purge of political opponents, some forty officers, including the former minister of war, Osman Rifqi, were stripped of their ranks and privileges and exiled to the Sudan. When the khedive commuted their sentences, Urabi refused to comply and pushed Barudi to convene the Chamber of Deputies, which had already adjourned for the year, to gain its support. Tawfiq condemned the move and Barudi resigned on May 15. Though left without a prime minister, Urabi and the rest of the ministers refused to resign. Rumors of plots and counterplots spread through the capital.[9]

In their eagerness to resolve the situation without committing themselves to Egypt's occupation, England and France took yet another high risk. On May 19, an Anglo-French naval squadron arrived off Alexandria in a show of support for the khedive. Six days later the president of the Parliament was handed an ultimatum demanding the dismissal of the cabinet, the temporary exile of Urabi, and the retirement of his closest associates, colonels Ali Fahmi and Abdel Al Hilmi, into the interior of Egypt.

Like the Anglo-French note of January 1882, this was a hastily contrived and ill-conceived compromise. While the new French prime minister, Charles de Freycinet, who at the end of January 1882 replaced Gambetta, sustained his predecessor's militant line, Gladstone vehemently opposed direct intervention in Egypt. Instead, he advocated an international effort, with active Ottoman participation, to resolve the Egyptian crisis by peaceful means. As Freycinet would hear nothing of the sort, the British prime minister saw no choice but to accept the French proposal for a naval show of force[10]

As in January 1882, the Anglo-French action backfired. The Egyptian cabinet resigned in protest and the khedive was all too happy to accept this move. This nevertheless brought him under harsh nationalist criticism, and he backed down in fear. On May 27, Urabi was reinstated as the minister of war and Tawfiq retreated to Alexandria, closer to the great-power gunboats. Westerners fled Egypt by the thousands. Impending disaster was in the air.

Tensions exploded on June 11–12 in the form of ferocious anti-Christian riots in Alexandria, in which 50 Europeans and 250 Egyptians were killed. In one account the riots were incited by Tawfiq in an attempt to discredit Urabi and the army; another account put the blame on Urabi, whose security forces did little to contain the raging mob. The truth, however, is that the arrival of the naval squadron off Alexandria had unleashed widespread anti-Western sentiments that had been brewing in Egypt since Ismail's day. Urabi might well have been fighting for his political survival, but his actions had generated a huge nationalistic wave; initially he might not have been anti-Western, but the Anglo-French muscle-flexing had made the temptation of an extremist stance irresistible. Urabi's open defiance and his immediate reinstatement by the khedive were taken by Egyptians as a sign of their imminent deliverance from foreign subjugation. To them Urabi was not only a national hero who would restore "Egypt for the Egyptians," but also al-Wahid, the "only one" in living memory who dared to rise against the ruling elites and foreign powers alike.[11]

The Alexandria riots caused a general uproar in London. There was widespread indignation at the killing of European subjects and exasperation with members of the government for allowing themselves to be humiliated by a local leader. Yet Gladstone held his ground against an increasingly militant cabinet, and his restraint received an unexpected boost from the French prime minister, who had lost his nerve following the Alexandria riots and acquiesced in the British view that the reassertion of Ottoman sovereignty over Egypt might be the least of all evils. An international conference thus convened in Constantinople on June 23 to discuss the Egyptian situation, with the participation of Britain, France, Austria-Hungary, Germany, Russia, and Italy. There was only one fly in the ointment: the sultan would not join them.

From his palace in Istanbul Abdul Hamid followed with horror the events that were unfolding in Egypt. Three years earlier he had removed

Ismail in the hope of stabilizing the situation and restoring Ottoman control over Egypt; now the country seemed to be moving toward even greater catastrophe. The financial situation had not improved, only attracted tighter foreign control. Egyptian nationalism had not subsided, only risen to unprecedented peaks. The presence of a strong man at the helm augured the possible revival of the Egyptian imperial dream. Under the weak and indecisive Tawfiq this was a virtual impossibility; under a powerful and greedy Urabi, the "Ismail Syndrome" could well recur. Repeated pleas of innocence from the Urabists did little to quiet Abdul Hamid's suspicion. He urged Tawfiq to crush the mutineers and, if possible, "to give Urabi [poisoned] coffee." When he gradually realized that the khedive was not up to the job and that the officers enjoyed far wider support than he initially assumed, Abdul Hamid decided to remain on the sidelines in the hope that mutual exhaustion would eventually force the rival camps to request the restoration of Ottoman authority in Egypt. When in September 1881 Tawfiq invoked his position as the sultan's official representative in Egypt and demanded the dispatch of twenty Ottoman battalions to his rescue, Abdul Hamid declined; all he was willing to do was to send a five-member commission to Egypt to investigate the situation. Having heard the commission's opinion that events in Egypt posed no threat to his imperial order, the sultan persevered in his inaction.[12]

It was only the arrival of the Anglo-French naval task force in the region that shook the sultan out of his passivity. Early in June 1882 Abdul Hamid sent a delegation to Egypt, headed by one of his generals, Dervish Pasha, to try to bring the conflict to a swift conclusion. Dervish was instructed to effect a reconciliation between the khedive and his nemesis; if this proved impractical, he was to disband the Chamber of Deputies, dismiss Urabi and send him to Istanbul, and "arrest one by one the authors of the troubles." This was of course an impossible task, and Dervish quickly found himself playing both ends against the middle. He simultaneously urged Tawfiq to quash the rebels and incited the Urabists to escalate their struggle, showering both parties with promises of support. To sow discord among the great powers, he pretended to seek the advice of the German, Italian, and Austro-Hungarian consuls-general.[13]

When the crisis defied all attempts at resolution and shot to new heights following the Alexandria riots, the sultan panicked. On Friday afternoon, June 23, 1882, a few hours after the opening of the Constantinople conference that Abdul Hamid had failed to attend for fear of being labeled a "Western lackey," Reshid Bey, the sultan's private secretary, called on the British ambassador to Istanbul, Lord Dufferin. His master was possessed by the greatest fear and hatred for France, he said, and desired to come to an understanding with Britain about Egypt to the exclusion of France. Would Her Majesty's government be prepared to sign a bilateral treaty whereby England would be given the exclusive control and administration of Egypt, with the sultan reserving for himself only those rights of suzerainty that he possessed at the time?[14]

Dufferin was stunned. Up to that very moment, Abdul Hamid had been violently opposed to international intervention in the Egyptian crisis. He had denounced the Anglo-French note of January 1882 and the two countries' subsequent show of naval force. Now all of a sudden Britain was being offered possession of Egypt! The shift was simply too dramatic to be true. Perhaps the sultan was playing his habitual game of divide and rule in an attempt to drive a wedge between England and France? Besides, military intervention in Egypt, not to speak of its physical occupation, was still anathema to Gladstone and the majority of his ministers. Without much ado, Dufferin declined the offer. "Britain's principal aims are the maintenance of the sultan's existing rights and of the *status quo*," he said:

> We not only accept the sultan's sovereignty in Egypt as a fact, but regard it with benevolence. We have but two interests in Egypt— the freedom of the Suez Canal and such a satisfactory jurisdiction of Egyptian internal affairs as to preclude any power from finding an excuse to meddle with them.

In these circumstances, concluded Dufferin, "if the sultan were to hand over Egypt to us as a gift, with all Europe consenting, I doubt whether the British government would accept such a burden and responsibility."[15] Reshid was evidently disheartened. He pleaded with Dufferin to convey the request promptly to his superiors, and to hand the official reply in person to the sultan. This came within a day. Gladstone and Granville found the idea so absurd as to dismiss it without consulting their fellow ministers. "We wish to see the sultan's sovereignty maintained without any limitation excepting those which have been conceded by the Firmans," wrote Granville to Dufferin:

> Our wish for the present is that the Sultan should by sending troops support the authority of the Khedive, free His highness from

the risk of the continuance or renewal of the military pressure which has been exercised against him, and restore the normal *status quo*. Our desire for the future is that this state of things should continue without excluding safe improvement of internal Administration, but with entire exclusion of preponderating influence of any single power.[16]

Confronted with Britain's refusal to occupy Egypt on his behalf, the sultan continued to equivocate. On June 28, he conferred a high decoration on Urabi; a couple of days later Dervish Pasha was at loggerheads with the minister of war and it was intimated that his delegation had better leave the country. When on July 6 the international conference requested that Ottoman troops be sent to Egypt, the sultan refused, against the view of his ministers; even a desperate offer by the venerated war hero Osman Pasha to go to Egypt, if only as the head of a battalion, failed to do the trick. Four days later Abdul Hamid changed his mind again: he would join the conference the following day and would propose "a satisfactory solution [to] the Egyptian question."

While the Constantinople Conference was progressing inconclusively, developments on the ground sucked the reluctant British cabinet into the Egyptian marsh. Like Frankenstein's monster turning against its maker, the Anglo-French squadron assumed a life of its own, in ways unforeseen by its senders. Once the squadron was in place, the question of how to protect it was raised in earnest. On May 31, the commander of the British squadron, Admiral Beauchamp Seymour, reported that the Egyptians were raising earthworks in Alexandria and requested that three more ships be added to his force. At the sultan's demand, work on these forts was suspended on June 6, but was recommenced a few weeks later. On July 1, Seymour reported that Urabi was allegedly planning to trap the allied fleet by sinking stone barges in the channel. Two days later he was instructed by the Admiralty to tell the military governor of Alexandria that "an attempt to bar the channel will be considered an act of war" and that if work was resumed on the fortifications, or further guns mounted, he would "destroy the earthworks and silence the batteries."

On July 5 the cabinet met to approve these demands. After a heated debate members reached a compromise whereby Seymour would issue his ultimatum but would land no forces in the canal to destroy the fortifications, as demanded by several ministers. This Seymour did the following day, only to receive the Egyptian governor's emphatic denial of both the mounting of guns and the continuation of work on the fortifications. When Seymour reported the continued mounting of guns despite the governor's reassurance, the cabinet met again on July 8 to approve a second ultimatum to the Egyptians. By now the sultan had declined the international request for the dispatch of Ottoman forces to Egypt, while France had decided to pull its forces from the naval squadron and was assiduously working to undercut the British position by negotiating a separate deal with Urabi. Without much fanfare Seymour was authorized to reissue the ultimatum if works on the fortifications resumed. The realization that Britain was on the verge of war in Egypt, however limited that war might be, hardly sank in. British leaders were confident that "the explosion of one or two shells will send all the earthworks to glory, and there will be an end for the moment of the matter."[17]

On July 9 Seymour reported the resumption of work on the fortifications, and the mounting of two guns on Fort Silsileh. The following morning he informed the foreign consuls in Alexandria that he had just issued an ultimatum and would "commence action twenty-four hours after, unless the forts on the isthmus and those commanding the entrance to the harbour are surrendered."

Seymour had overstepped his authority. The cabinet had approved the destruction of the fortifications, not their capture. It had never intended involvement to include a physical occupation that could embroil Britain in a costly adventure and entail adverse international implications. The irritated Gladstone demanded to know by what authority Seymour had issued his ultimatum. Once the prime minister was told that unless the fortifications were surrendered Urabi could carry on for weeks while pretending to comply with the British demand, he accepted Seymour's logic. The admiral was promptly instructed to change the wording of the ultimatum to "temporary surrender for the purpose of disarmament." To the Egyptian cabinet, nevertheless, these linguistic intricacies mattered little. On July 10, they rejected the ultimatum. The following morning Alexandria came under heavy bombardment from Seymour's forces.[18]

Contrary to British expectations, the shelling failed to bring Urabi down. Instead, he called a general conscription and declared a holy war against Britain. Alexandria was put to the torch as a raging mob indulged in a spree of killing and pillaging. When the khedive dismissed Urabi, the latter countered with a religious ruling (*fatwa*) signed by three al-Azhar sheikhs, which deposed the khedive on grounds of betraying Islam by inviting foreigners to occupy Egypt.

This unexpected resilience put Gladstone in a quandary. What had been grudgingly approved as a brief and limited operation was rapidly developing into a massive undertaking, the consequences of which were difficult to predict. Yet he felt that there was no way back. The most powerful empire on earth could not afford to be publicly humiliated by the subject of a much weaker empire. The job had to be completed, preferably under a great-power mandate; however, as Gladstone told the House of Commons on July 22, "if every chance of obtaining cooperation is exhausted, the work will be undertaken by the single power of England."[19]

This indeed seemed to become a distinct possibility. Fearing a unilateral British intervention, de Freycinet re-donned his activist mantle and agreed to a joint Anglo-French occupation of the canal zone. But when the proposal was put to the French Chamber of Deputies on July 29, it was decisively defeated. Attempts to harness Italy to the protection of the canal and to convince the Constantinople conference that Britain had no desire to occupy the canal indefinitely all came to nought. This made the sultan Britain's only hope. As the official suzerain of Egypt and the caliph of the largest Muslim empire, the sultan could at the very least give the operation a much-needed air of legitimacy; in the best-case scenario, his support for the suppression of Urabi could exempt Britain from the need to occupy Egypt, something that was still anathema to Gladstone. After all, if Abdul Hamid was prepared to allow Britain to rule Egypt on his behalf, why should he be averse to the far-less-dangerous option of a joint Anglo-Ottoman expedition?

On July 12, while gunfire still reverberated throughout Alexandria, Gladstone dined with the Ottoman ambassador to London, Musurus Pasha. The British action had cleared the way for the dispatch of Ottoman troops to Alexandria, he argued, and the sultan had a great opportunity at hand; the Ottoman Empire had unwittingly stumbled across "a supreme moment, which . . . it was still possible to use for good; but time was precious, and this opportunity would probably be the last." The ambassador concurred with Gladstone's assessment and expressed his confidence that the sultan would agree to send the requested troops, provided that he was not to act as a representative of Europe. The prime minister responded that to the best of his knowledge, the idea of the sultan being a *mandataire* had not been entertained. What was of critical importance for the mission's success, however, was that there should be unity of purpose.[20]

The ambassador's optimism was well placed, if largely premature.

Even more than Gladstone, Abdul Hamid now dreaded the adverse implications of an Urabist victory. For him it was not a question of lost prestige or a mere strategic setback; it was a matter of life and death, and he knew that Britain was the only power capable of helping him stop the chain reaction caused by Urabi's nationalist surge. But much as they needed each other, the Ottoman and British empires could not overcome mutual prejudice and distrust. At the end of July, the Ottoman delegates to the Constantinople Conference informed their European counter-parts of the sultan's agreement to send forces to Egypt, but insisted that foreign troops evacuate the country upon the arrival of the Ottoman forces. The British government welcomed the offer but demanded pre-cise details of the planned intervention: the number of troops the sultan intended to send, the date of their likely departure, and their proposed disposition. As a guarantee that Ottoman forces would not join with Urabi against the khedive, the British insisted that the sultan "should at once, and before the dispatch of his troops, issue a proclamation uphold-ing Tawfiq Pasha and denouncing Urabi as a rebel." Ottoman officials were quoted as saying that "the only reason for sending Turkish troops to Egypt would be to drive the English away." While this assertion might have been designed to neutralize domestic opposition to the impending intervention, it raised suspicions in London of the sultan's real in-tentions.[21]

Nor did Abdul Hamid's erratic negotiating style, with its constant change of tack in accordance with the latest advice he received from his coterie, buy him any friends in London. Particularly influential was the xenophobic Sheikh Abu al-Huda al-Sayyadi, an Arab from the province of Aleppo who arrived in Istanbul in 1878 to establish himself as Abdul Hamid's Rasputin. He worked indefatigably to obstruct an agreement with "infidel" Britain and warned the sultan of the (alleged) backlash such an accord would cause among Muslim communities. The Ottoman representatives to the talks, Said and Assim Pashas, thus found them-selves in the unenviable position of trying to make sense of the contra-dictory instructions given to them. On August 18, they finalized a draft convention with Lord Dufferin, only to have it thrown back at them the following day by the sultan. Even the issue of provision of donkeys and mules for the expedition became a bone of contention when the sultan suspended the delivery of these beasts of burden, purchased in Asia Minor, and arrested their drivers; nearly a week of unremitting pressure from Dufferin was required to end this bizarre episode.

The most frustrating aspect of the talks was the sultan's evasiveness over the condemnation of Urabi. On September 3, after months of procrastination, Abdul Hamid gave his consent to the immediate issuance of the condemnation, apparently removing the last obstacle to the signing of an Anglo-Ottoman convention. But when Dufferin read the official proclamation in the morning papers three days later, his heart sank. In a blatant repudiation of the agreed draft, the sultan had changed the wording on some material points. Enraged at "such an inconceivable act of bad faith," Dufferin refused to sign the convention or to accept the Porte's apologies. It was only on September 15, after another round of futile negotiations, that Abdul Hamid decided to bring matters to conclusion. He invited Dufferin to his palace, and for eleven hours he haggled with the ambassador over the amendments he wished to introduce in the convention and the proclamation.

At 1:15 A.M. Dufferin's young secretary and brother-in-law, Arthur Nicolson, who waited with him for the sultan's reply, observed "the sinister figure of the sultan's astrologer [Abu al-Huda] creeping across the anteroom toward his master's room." Half an hour later Said and Assim returned to their British interlocutors: "His Majesty was unable to approve the compromise agreed to and further discussions [will] be required."[22]

It was nearly three o'clock when the distraught Dufferin arrived at the embassy. There, to his surprise, he was handed a ciphered telegram from Granville stating that a British force under the command of Sir Garnet Wolseley had routed Urabi's army in Tal al-Kabir, some sixty miles from Cairo, and that in view of this victory "Her Majesty's Government contemplated shortly commencing the withdrawal of the British troops from Egypt, and presumed that, the emergency having passed, the sultan would not now consider it necessary to send troops." Three days later, on September 18, Dufferin was instructed to inform the sultan, "in the most courteous terms," that Britain was dropping the negotiations of the military convention.[23] The sultan had lost yet another golden opportunity to reassert his suzerainty over Egypt.

The British invasion of Egypt provides a vivid illustration of the limits of great-power control over Middle Eastern dynamics. The invasion was neither a premeditated act of imperial aggrandizement nor an attempt to sunder the Ottoman Empire. Rather, the largest empire on Earth found itself on a slippery slope too late to prevent the slide. Policymakers in

London were unaware of the simmering Egyptian crisis until it exploded in their faces; even then they chose to handle the situation haphazardly, through hastily contrived half-measures, and to focus on more pressing problems, notably the Irish question. It was only after the khedive and the sultan had miserably failed to put their house in order, and after cooperation with France had proved counterproductive, that the British cabinet reluctantly intervened in Egypt.

Nor did Britain wish to disrupt the evolution of Egyptian nationalism. On the contrary, Gladstone was sympathetic to the nationalists, as was his Egyptian envoy, Edward Malet. Even Auckland Colvin, a member of the Dual Control of the Egyptian debt and an arch-proponent of intervention, was well disposed toward the nationalists. "The liberal movement now going on should, I think, in no wise be discouraged," he wrote. "It is essentially the growth of the popular spirit, and is directed for the good of the country, and it would be most impolitic to thwart it."[24] That all three eventually supported the khedive and opposed Urabi had less to do with the latter's nationalist pretensions than with his growing image as a threat to the integrity of the Ottoman Empire in general, and to Britain's primary interests in Egypt in particular: continued international financial control, deemed essential for Egypt's economic recovery; exclusion of the preponderant influence of any single power; and, above all, the security of the Suez Canal.

In an ironic twist of history Britain, the chief opponent of the construction of the canal, had become its main beneficiary. British trade through the canal accounted for approximately 80 percent of Britain's total trade, and the waterway quickly established itself as the country's foremost imperial line to India. Yet this did not breed any desire to occupy Egypt. Quite the reverse; even a quintessential imperialist like Prime Minister Benjamin Disraeli considered the maintenance of Ottoman integrity, of which Egypt was a key component, the most effective bulwark against Russian expansionism. Hence his unyielding stand against Russia in its 1877–1878 war with Turkey and his tireless efforts during the Berlin Congress to limit Russia's territorial gains; and hence his decline of Bismarck's repeated suggestions that Britain seize control of Egypt.[25]

Gladstone had even less interest in Egypt as an imperial conquest. Loathing everything his predecessor had stood for (he could not even bring himself to attend Disraeli's funeral), Gladstone had systematically censured Britain's growing economic stake in Egypt. Yet as is often the case with pious moralists who fail their principles the moment they reach power, Gladstone discovered the gap between ideals and reality too wide to bridge. In 1877 he dismissed the possible closure of the canal as a minor irritant that could at worst delay communication with India by three weeks; in September 1882 he claimed that "apart from the Canal we have no interest in Egypt which would warrant intervention."[26] Once the Egyptian question became one of whether to support those who for all their many imperfections came closer to his ideals, or the player who, quite wrongly, seemed to offer stability over the long term, Gladstone opted for the latter. With no premeditation or design, this sworn anti-imperialist managed to accomplish what his avowedly imperialist precursor had carefully avoided: entangling Britain in the largest and most enduring imperial acquisition in the Middle East.

While portraying the Egyptian venture as an undesirable burden passed on to him by Disraeli, Gladstone recognized the irony in the situation. On August 10, 1882, he had stated that an indefinite occupation of Egypt would be "at variance with all the principles and views of Her Majesty's Government, and the pledges they have given to Europe, and with the views, I may say, of Europe itself."[27] Now that Egypt had inadvertently come under British occupation, it became a hot potato that had to be disposed of before scorching the prime minister's palms. As early as September 14, a day after Urabi's crushing defeat, Gladstone outlined his ideas for an Egyptian settlement. British forces were to be withdrawn as soon as possible and Egypt set on the road to self-rule. Egyptian military and police forces were to be reorganized, self-governing institutions developed, and the privileges enjoyed by the Europeans, such as exemption from taxation, terminated. The sultan's suzerainty over Egypt would be retained, albeit on a more restricted basis: he would still receive tribute, but he would not nominate the Egyptian ruler or command the service of Egyptian troops. The conduct of the canal company was to be reviewed, and the possible neutralization of the canal discussed.

Dufferin was accordingly instructed to inform the sultan that "Her Majesty's Government contemplated shortly commencing the withdrawal of the British troops from Egypt." In a circular to the great powers on January 3, 1883, Granville promised that Britain would withdraw from Egypt "as soon as the state of the country, and the organization of proper means for the maintenance of the Khedive's authority, will admit of it." This promise was to be repeated sixty-six times between 1882 and 1922, when Egypt became an independent state.[28]

For years the British cabinet was operating on the idea that Britain would withdraw quickly from Egypt—to no tangible effect. One reason for the delay was Britain's insistence that any withdrawal be preceded by the resolution of a host of problems: the reassertion of khedival authority, freedom of navigation in the Suez Canal, Egypt's financial insolvency, the legal status of foreign residents in Egypt, and the reorganization of Egyptian internal administration, to mention just the most prominent items on the agenda. On November 7, 1882, Lord Dufferin was sent out to recommend measures for the quick reorganization of Egypt; his gloomy conclusion was that "for some time to come, European assistance in the various Departments of Egyptian administration will be absolutely necessary." Lord Northbrook, who embarked on a similar mission two years later, reached the same conclusion. "No one can be more opposed to the annexation of Egypt, or to any step in this direction, than I am," he wrote. "But I may have to recommend that we . . . remain in Egypt for a term of three to five years, with the consent and at the request of the sultan if possible."[29]

Withdrawal was also held back by a series of indigenous developments over which Britain had little control. Foremost among them was a popular uprising in the Sudan, led by Muhammad Ahmad Ibn Abdullah, a young sufi sheikh of humble origins who styled himself as the Mahdi, the Messiah. In the summer of 1881 he began spreading his revolutionary message from the Island of Abba, 150 miles south of Khartum; he preached a holy war to expel the Turkish (that is, Egyptian) and Christian occupiers from the Sudan, and to restore Islam's lost glory. As he went from strength to strength, defeating successive Egyptian attempts to subdue him, the Mahdi assumed superhuman qualities in the eyes of his followers. In November 1883 he annihilated a ten thousand–strong Egyptian contingent headed by the British general William Hicks, with light losses to his own forces. Two years later, on January 26, 1885, Khartum was overrun after a prolonged siege and savaged by the raging mob. General Charles Gordon, who had been sent to the Sudan a year earlier to curb the uprising, was killed on the steps of his palace. His head was chopped off and sent to the Mahdi. Sudan was the Messiah's. London was shocked to the core, the Liberal government swept from power.

How could British forces evacuate Egypt, with its strategic waterway and Red Sea ports, before the "savage" of the Sudan had been tamed?

Abdul Hamid's erratic behavior and clumsy attempts to manipulate great-power divergencies to his advantage were an equally formidable impediment to British withdrawal. Wavering among anger at Britain's occupation of Egypt, eagerness to see its quick departure, and reluctance to incur the military and financial consequences of Egypt's reincorporation into Ottoman structures, the sultan could not make up his mind regarding the best course of action. When in May 1887, after two years of arduous negotiations, an Anglo-Ottoman convention was signed providing for British withdrawal within three years but giving Britain and the Ottoman Empire the right to re-enter Egypt in certain circumstances, Abdul Hamid would not ratify it. France and Russia were threatening that ratification would give them the right to occupy Ottoman provinces and to leave only after the conclusion of a similar convention; France might do so in the Levant, Russia in Armenia. No less important, a fierce battle for the sultan's heart raged in the palace. Kamil Pasha, the grand vizier, and Rajib Bey, Abdul Hamid's private secretary, pleaded with their imperial master to ratify the convention and warned him of Russia's expansionist designs. They were countered by a strong anti-British lobby, headed by Riza Pasha, Russia's "man in the palace," and Dreyssé Pasha, France's foremost champion in the royal court. Supported by the sultan's favorite mystic, Abu al-Huda, who had played a pivotal role in obstructing Anglo-Ottoman collaboration in 1882, the rejectionists gradually won the upper hand. On May 26, 1887, an extremely gracious and cheerful Abdul Hamid met the British ambassador, Sir William White; he lauded the newly signed convention and urged the ambassador to work for its quick implementation. A week later the sultan was adamant that the agreement be amended in certain important respects, most notably that Britain be forbidden to re-enter Egypt unless invited by the Porte.

The pro-ratification faction seemed to be shrinking in fear. The ministers, who had only limited access to the sultan, dared not speak their mind; a spell of forty-eight hours in jail disciplined Rajib Bey and drove the timid Kamil Pasha to change his tune. The former grand vizier Said Pasha, who had negotiated the convention at its initial stage, kept his distance; when asked by Abdul Hamid for his opinion, he answered that he required more time to study the subject, with which he was only vaguely acquainted. On July 15, the long-suffering British negotiator Sir

Henry Drummond Wolff left Istanbul empty-handed. When Abdul Hamid attempted to renew the negotiations, he was informed by Lord Salisbury, who in June 1886 had succeeded Gladstone as prime minister, that "so long as the Sultan was so much under the influence of other advisors as to repudiate an agreement which he had himself so recently sanctioned, any fresh agreement would obviously be liable to meet with the same fate as the late Convention."[30]

This was Abdul Hamid's last chance to regain Egypt, and he dropped the ball. But he had only himself to blame. Five years earlier he had missed at least two critical junctures in which he could have halted the sliding of this prized province from his hands. On July 6, 1882, he declined an international request to dispatch an Ottoman force to Egypt that could have averted the British bombardment of Alexandria five days later; in the following months he failed to sign an Anglo-Ottoman convention that could have preempted a unilateral British occupation. Now that he compounded his earlier mistakes by failing to ratify the 1887 convention, Britain could claim a clean conscience. It had displayed a good-willed and cooperative approach but had been let down. Given that Abdul Hamid was so undeserving of trust, Britain had no choice but to remain in Egypt for as long as was required to get the country going again. What had begun as a brief and decisive military action in 1882 had turned into a long occupation that was to have a profound impact on the making of the modern Middle East.

Selim III, the modernizing sultan of the late eighteenth century, established a longstanding pattern of Ottoman reliance on "infidel" support for imperial survival.

The imperial ambitions of Muhammad Ali (above), Egypt's governor, brought the Ottoman Empire to the verge of destruction and drove Sultan Mahmud II (right) to seek European support against his rebellious Muslim subject.

Sultan Mahmud II

In his eagerness to follow in the footsteps of his illustrious grandfather, Muhammad Ali, Ismail Pasha (above) brought Egypt to financial ruin. As the crisis deepened, Sultan Abdul Hamid II asked the British ambassador to Istanbul, Lord Dufferin (right), to arrange for British control over Egypt. Dufferin rejected the request.

Lord Dufferin

Minister of War Ahmad Urabi came to personify local resentment of growing European interference in Egyptian affairs. His defeat in the Battle of Tal al-Kabir (September 1882) ended Egyptian hopes for greater freedom and ushered in a far longer period of British rule in Egypt than originally conceived.

Battle of Tal al-Kabir

Having effectively ignited the Crimean War, Sultan Abdul Mejid skillfully used the European powers to emerge as the main victor in the conflict.

The extraordinary Ottoman resistance under the leadership of Osman Pasha in the Battle of Plevna (1877) kept the Russians out of Istanbul but failed to prevent the loss of most of Turkey-in-Europe at the Congress of Berlin the following year. Here Osman surrenders to Tsar Alexander II.

After thirty-two years on the throne, during which he saw the loss of most of the Ottoman Empire's European provinces, Sultan Abdul Hamid II was effectively removed from power by the Young Turk Revolution of July 1908. Here the aged sultan, watched by his subjects, travels from his palace to restore the constitution, which he had suspended in 1876.

5

OUT OF EUROPE

*T*he loss of Egypt, however traumatic, did not threaten the foundations of the Ottoman imperium. The occupation of the sultan's prized territory resulted not from internal stagnation, European expansionism, nor even an indigenous imperialist challenge in the manner of Muhammad Ali's. Rather, the wound was self-inflicted by the empire's own master. Had Sultan Abdul Hamid not utterly mismanaged the Egyptian crisis, the British occupation could have been averted.

Not so in the European lands of the Ottoman Empire, where the advent of nationalism challenged the very existence of the multiethnic empire. Unleashed by the French Revolution and fueled by the Napoleonic upheavals, nationalism had already wrested Greece from the Ottomans in the early 1830s, and the nationalist eruptions of 1848 that quickly spread from Paris to engulf the entire Continent further loosened the Ottomans' grip over their European possessions. In the Danubian Principalities of Moldavia and Wallachia, revolutionaries confronted the ruling landowners with the demand to end their repressive oligarchic control. In June 1848 a newly established Wallachian government, in which the revolutionaries were represented, adopted a constitution that abolished feudal rights and social distinctions and declared an independent Romania, comprising the two principalities.

The Ottomans were not the only ones threatened by these developments. No imperial chancellery in Europe wished nationalism to triumph over a fellow empire, not even an Islamic one. The Habsburgs were beset by their own nationalistic fervor, which resulted in the effective severance of Hungary from their rule for most of 1848 and forced the emperor to flee Vienna. The Russians, who had enjoyed considerable influence in the principalities since 1829, when these had been rendered autonomous under Ottoman suzerainty, were greatly alarmed by the surge of Romanian nationalism, which was no less directed against them than against the Ottomans. In July 1848, having secured the sultan's approval, Tsar Nicholas I sent his troops to put down the Danubian insurgencies on Turkey's behalf.

Ottoman consent, to be sure, was half-hearted at best. Russia's longstanding influence in the Danube basin had been a thorn in the side of the Ottomans, and Sultan Abdul Mejid had little trust in the purity of Russia's intentions. When Russia kept its forces in the principalities after the suppression of the nationalist surge, justifying its presence by the treaties of Kuchuk Kainardji (1774) and Adrianople (1829), the sultan's suspicions rose sharply. In September 1848 he sent his forces to Wallachia, ostensibly to collaborate with the Russian army against the revolutionaries but actually to forestall the imposition of Russian hegemony there. Then, in the spring of 1849, after the Russians helped the Habsburgs to reassert their control in Budapest, the sultan refused to surrender the leaders of the Hungarian rebellion who sought asylum within the Ottoman Empire. The withdrawal of the Russian and Austrian ambassadors from Istanbul did little to impress the sultan. On September 17, 1849, Russo-Ottoman diplomatic relations were severed and the specter of war loomed large. Although Russia and Austria were the first to back down, affording the sultan a glowing diplomatic success, the crisis left an air of hostility and distrust that made war between the Ottoman and the Russian empires over the principalities seemingly inevitable.

The spark that ignited this war was not long in coming, though it emerged from a somewhat unexpected quarter: the Holy Land. Since the mid-eighteenth century the Latin monks had neglected their duties as custodians of the Holy Places, and the Greeks had gradually stepped into their shoes, with the blessing and support of Russia—the self-styled champion of all Orthodox Christianity. For a while this development posed no serious problem, but in the mid-nineteenth century everything changed abruptly. During Christmas 1847, the season of goodwill, Latin and Greek monks were hitting each other with candlesticks at the Church of the Nativity in Bethlehem.

The confrontation was a direct result of French politics, or more precisely of the ambitions of Louis Napoleon, Napoleon Bonaparte's nephew and the president of France, who in December 1852 made himself emperor by a *coup d'état*. Inspired by his great uncle, the French leader was determined to restore France's grandeur, including its pivotal role in the Middle East. To obtain Church support for his ambitious designs, Napoleon III, as the new emperor came to be known, sought to strengthen France's Catholic position in the Holy Land by demanding the restoration of French privileges that had been granted in a concession made in 1740.

This demand enraged Tsar Nicholas. Apart from his profound resentment of Catholic encroachment on Greek Orthodox rights, he also viewed the surge of French interest in the Holy Land as a reflection of Napoleon's real and most sinister intention: to subvert the conservative order in Europe. Before long Russia and France were locked in a fierce competition for custody over the Holy Shrines in Jerusalem, Bethlehem, and Nazareth, and in a no-less-bitter feud over the sultan's favor. When in December 1852 Abdul Mejid settled the dispute in favor of France, giving the Catholics the key to the Church of the Nativity, Nicholas viewed the decision as a denial of the religious rights of the Orthodox subjects of the Ottoman Empire, who, under the Treaty of Kuchuk Kainardji (1774), had been placed under Russian protection.[1] Even worse, the Ottoman Empire seemed to be falling under the sway of the "revolutionary" French, something that would threaten not only direct Russian interests, but also the entire balance of power in the Middle East and Europe. Was Napoleon III not deliberately plotting the destruction of the Ottoman Empire so as to prove a worthy namesake of his famous ancestor?

To check this alarming development, the tsar approached Britain. Encouraged by the forming of a cabinet by his favorite politician, Lord Aberdeen, with whom he had enjoyed a meeting of minds in the past, Nicholas initiated a series of conversations with the British ambassador to St. Petersburg, Sir George Hamilton Seymour, in the early months of 1853. He told the ambassador of his fear that the fall of the Ottoman Empire was a foregone conclusion and that Britain and Russia should therefore reach a general understanding about what was to be done "when the Bear dies" or, more important, about "what shall not be done upon that event taking place." "We have on our hands a sick man—a very sick man," Nicholas said, coining the phrase that was to become the standard metaphor of the Eastern Question. "It will be, I tell you frankly, a great misfortune if, one of these days, he should slip away from us, especially before all necessary arrangements were made."[2]

Politely yet firmly the ambassador rejected the tsar's prognosis. "We have no reason to think that the Sick Man (to use your Majesty's expression) is dying," he said. "For myself, I will venture to remark that experience shows me that countries do not die in such a hurry." The tsar stuck to his guns. "If your Government has been led to believe that Turkey retains any elements of existence, your Government must have received incorrect information," he argued.

> Eager as we all are for the prolonged existence of the [Sick] Man . . . we cannot resuscitate what is dead; if the Turkish Empire falls, it falls to rise no more; and I put it to you, therefore, whether it is not better to be provided beforehand for a contingency, than to incur the chaos, confusion, and the certainty of a European war, all of which must attend the catastrophe if it should occur unexpectedly, and before some ulterior system has been sketched.[3]

Time and again Nicholas tried to convince Seymour that he was acting out of concern over French aggressiveness, and that he had no premeditated territorial designs on the Ottoman Empire:

> You know . . . the dreams and plans in which the Empress Catherine was in the habit of indulging; these were handed down to our time; but while I inherited immense territorial possessions, I did not inherit those visions, those intentions if you like to call them so. On the contrary, my country is so vast, so happily circumstanced in every way, that it would be unreasonable [for] me to desire more territory or more power than I possess; on the contrary, I am the first to tell you that our great, perhaps our only danger, is that which would arise from an extension given to an empire already too large.[4]

This professed innocence failed to impress Seymour. Rather than take Nicholas's proposals for what they were—contingency planning by a status quo power trying to preempt a detrimental development—the ambassador viewed the tsar as a devious leader who sought to do to the Ottoman Empire what his predecessor Catherine the Great had done to Poland, namely, "to reduce her to vassalage and make her existence a burden to her" so as to end the empire's independent existence and fall upon its carcass. Seymour's superiors in London were in general less suspicious of Nicholas's ulterior motives, yet they would not cede him the understanding he wanted. They reassured the tsar that Britain had no territorial ambitions in the Ottoman Empire, Istanbul in particular, and promised not to take any steps toward the dissolution of this empire without first communicating with Russia. In the meantime, Russia was advised to exercise "the utmost forbearance toward Turkey" and to avoid any peremptory demands or military pressures on the Porte.[5]

To Nicholas this position was simply not good enough. If Britain was not willing to read the writing on the wall, Russia would have to save the Ottomans from the French on its own. Rattling his saber, the tsar mobilized two army corps and sent his special envoy, Prince Alexander Menshikov, to Istanbul to undo the Catholic gains and, better still, to extract a formal agreement placing the Orthodox subjects of the Ottoman Empire under a Russian protectorate.

This was pushing the line too far. Though prepared to nullify the religious concessions to France, the sultan would hear nothing of the second part of the Russian demand, which amounted to the subordination of some ten million Ottoman subjects, mainly in the Balkans, to Russian rule.[6] Her Majesty's government was no less appalled by the Russian demand. Britain had urged the Porte to accommodate Russia on the question of the Holy Places because it thought the tsar had a point in this respect; because it shared Nicholas's fear of French imperialism; and because it wanted to avoid a Russo-Ottoman confrontation. Yet Whitehall was unwilling to see the Ottoman Empire reduced to a Russian satellite. Even Prime Minister Aberdeen, perhaps the most sympathetic to Nicholas among cabinet members, found the Russians' latest demand "unreasonable."

The Porte, buoyed by the British position, informed Menshikov of its readiness to make some minor concessions as a token of goodwill, but ruled out any formal recognition of a Russian protectorate over the Ottoman Orthodox. On May 21, 1853, Menshikov left the Ottoman capital empty-handed. Six days later diplomatic relations between the two empires were severed and the sultan was confronted with an ultimatum: unless he accepted Menshikov's demands within eight days, Russia would invade the Danubian Principalities. Britain responded by moving its Mediterranean squadron toward Besika Bay, outside the Dardanelles, to be followed by the French fleet a week later. With Russian armies amassing in the Balkans and French and British naval forces deployed outside the straits, the key to war and peace on the Continent was unwittingly placed in Ottoman hands.

The Porte exploited its new power to the fullest. When on August 1, 1853, a great-power compromise proposal known as the "Vienna Note" was announced, urging the sultan to grant the Orthodox Church all privileges enjoyed by members of other Christian rites and to make no changes in the position of his Christian subjects without the consent of Russia and France, the tsar gave his positive reply within four days. The sultan, in contrast, equivocated for three weeks before rejecting the Vienna Note. To some contemporaries this was a gratuitous reaction that bore the signature of the British ambassador to Constantinople, Lord Stratford de Redcliffe, as Stratford Canning had become. Yet for all the ambassador's influence in the Porte, which had bought him the unofficial title of Sultan Stratford, the Ottomans' rejection reflected their perennial fear of further weakening their already waning authority in the Balkans. As seen from Istanbul, the note gave Russia and France effective control over the Ottoman Christians, something no imperial power in its right mind could afford, without providing any guarantees against Russian expansionism, notably the evacuation of the Danubian Principalities. And as if to confirm these Ottoman fears, on September 7 the Russian foreign minister, Count Nesselrode, argued that the Vienna Note had given Russia control over the Ottoman Orthodox, including the right to intervene militarily on their behalf.[7]

This was the last straw for the sultan. Even before the enunciation of the Vienna Note the Ottoman Empire had been moving toward war. Now with fear of Russia's military presence in the principalities combined with exasperation at its bullying over the issue of the Orthodox Christians, anti-Russian sentiments were running high in Istanbul. It mattered not that war was something the ailing Ottoman economy could ill afford. The *ulema,* in a state of agitation over Menshikov's mission, urged Abdul Mejid to draw the Sword of the Prophet from the cupboard and declare jihad. The arrival in Istanbul, on August 12, of a strong Egyptian fleet, bearing some thirty-five thousand troops, rocketed war fever to new heights. This was indeed an ironic twist of history. Merely two decades after Russian forces had landed in the straits to save the fledgling Ottoman Empire from Muhammad Ali's imperialist bid, now Egyptian forces sent by the pasha's grandson, Abbas Pasha, were protecting Istanbul against Russian aggression.

Even Britain, which had initially hoped to persuade the Ottoman Empire to accept the Vienna Note, found itself swept in the direction of war. Nesselrode's interpretation of the Vienna Note, denounced by Foreign Secretary Clarendon as "violent," made Britain (and France) deeply suspicious of the tsar's real intentions. On September 23, without consulting any other members of the cabinet, Aberdeen and Clarendon agreed to a French proposal to send the British and French squadrons still deployed at Besika Bay through the Dardanelles—in violation of the 1841 Convention.

The unexpected escalation awakened Nicholas to the gravity of the situation. At the end of September he met with Austrian Emperor Franz Joseph at Olmütz, Bohemia, in a last-ditch effort to prevent war. He tried to win over the emperor with talk of partitioning the Ottoman Empire, offering the western Balkans to Austria. At the same time he struck an exceptionally conciliatory tone toward Turkey. He dissociated himself from Nesselrode's "violent interpretation" and agreed to give the Porte guarantees against Russian aggression. Moreover, he abandoned his refusal to consider any amendments to the Vienna Note and claimed that his only goal was to ensure the religious status quo of the Ottoman Orthodox. Above all, Nicholas expressed readiness to evacuate the principalities once his conditions were met. Surely, this would cause the Ottomans to back down.[8]

Nicholas's concessions came too late. Istanbul was firmly set upon a showdown. Emboldened by the arrival of the Egyptian contingent, and attentive to the increasing militancy of his subjects and his cabinet alike, the sultan stepped over the brink. On September 25, the Ottoman Grand Council solemnly decided to wage a holy war against Russia, and the decision was ratified by the sultan four days later. On October 4, the official declaration of war was conveyed to Russia with the demand that it withdraw from the principalities within a fortnight. When Russia refused, an Ottoman force commanded by Omer Pasha, who had proved his mettle in the campaign against Muhammad Ali in Lebanon, crossed the Danube, while other forces confronted the Russians in Erzerum and Kars, southeast of the Black Sea.[9]

Whereas Omer managed to check the Russian advance along the Danube, which was to become a source of great pride for the Ottomans, the sinking of a sizeable Ottoman flotilla near the Black Sea fort of Sinope was a far-less-heartening development. St. Petersburg celebrated this decisive, if secondary, victory by holding elaborate balls. "By destroying the Turkish squadron in Sinope you have added a new glorious chapter to Russian naval history," Nicholas wrote to Admiral Nakhimov, the mastermind behind this success.[10]

Suddenly the Ottoman Empire found itself in the all-too-familiar situation of having to seek European support to save itself from itself. The empire had taken on more than it could handle, and now it once again needed external help. In no time the Porte was pleading with Britain and France for "active efforts" on its behalf.[11]

Across the Continent the Ottoman-Russian war was received with dismay. The Western powers were exasperated with the Ottomans for starting the conflict and feared an uncontrollable escalation. On December 5, 1853, representatives of the four powers convened yet again in Vienna, promulgated a peace proposal that called upon the tsar to respect Ottoman territorial integrity and to avoid weakening the sultan's authority over his Christian subjects, and urged the sultan to abide by his earlier commitments to protect those subjects. On December 11 the Russian ambassador to Vienna, Baron Peter von Meyendorff, delivered the tsar's acceptance of the collective proposal. But as the European chancelleries sighed with relief over the imminent suspension of hostilities, news of the Battle of Sinope reached the Continent and turned the tables on them.

Why this military encounter, which did not decide the Russo-Ottoman war or put Ottoman existence in jeopardy, was to have such a profound impact on the course of European history remains a mystery. The annals of history are filled with events that have been blown out of proportion, and the greater the event, still greater the clamor. When the Ottoman cabinet was told of the Sinope debacle, their immediate reaction was one of complete aloofness; when news of the "massacre of Sinope" reached London and Paris, thousands of miles away from the scene of events, the public cried out for war.

On January 4, 1854, the British and French fleets sailed up from the straits into the Black Sea to protect the Ottoman Empire. The following month Russia broke off diplomatic relations with the two Western powers, and on March 12, following Russia's rejection of an ultimatum to withdraw from the principalities, Britain and France signed a treaty of military aid with the Porte, thereby committing themselves to defend the Ottoman Empire against Russia. When Nicholas responded by sending his troops across the Danube, Britain and France declared war on Russia on March 28. The Crimean War had begun.

From the Russian standpoint, the war could not have been more inopportune. Whereas the Ottoman Empire was aligned with Britain and France, and from January 1855 with Sardinia as well, Russia found itself in complete isolation. Its partners in the Holy Alliance, Austria and Prussia, not only remained glaringly aloof, but even pressured Russia to evacuate the principalities. To make things worse, on June 14, Foreign Minister Reshid Pasha and the Austrian internuncio to the Porte, Baron von Karl Ludwig Bruck, concluded a treaty that transferred Ottoman sovereign rights in the principalities to Austria for the duration of the war and allowed Austria to occupy these areas. If disorder were to break out in Herzegovina and Albania, Austria should capture them, too. With one brilliant feat of diplomacy, Turkey had transformed Austria from a formal, albeit reluctant, ally of Russia into a *de facto* adversary. This was a contingency for which Nicholas had not braced himself. On June 29, he begrudgingly agreed to evacuate the principalities on condition that Austria prevent Britain and France from filling the void. A month later a full-fledged Russian withdrawal was under way.

This put the Western powers in a quandary. They had gone to war to prevent Ottoman imperial possessions in Europe from falling under Russian influence, something that seemed detrimental both to the continued existence of the Ottoman Empire and to the European balance of power on the whole. Now that Russia was pulling out of the principalities, this *raison d'être* was valid no more. But the war machine had been put into full gear, and British forces were advancing on Odessa from the west. Should the fighting continue, a new political and strategic logic would have to be devised without delay.

This is indeed what happened, with Austria's unwitting help. In an attempt to capitalize on its success and bring the war to a swift conclusion, on August 8 Vienna announced Four Points for the establishment of a Russo-Ottoman peace. These called for the substitution of a European guarantee for the special Russian rights in the principalities and in Serbia; free navigation in the Danube; revision of the 1841 Straits Convention "in the interests of the balance of power in Europe"; and renunciation of Russia's claim to a protectorate over the Orthodox subjects of the Ottoman Empire, whose security would be entrusted to the Porte.[12]

Had Russia accepted this plan, the ability of the Western powers to wage war would have been seriously jeopardized. As things were, Nicholas chose the road of rejection. His armies had only begun fighting, and Nicholas was in no mood for compromise over what he viewed as an act of Austrian duplicity. So furious was the tsar with the Four Points that Nesselrode had to use all his influence to dissuade him from declaring war on Austria.[13]

This rejection provided the allies with the rationale they sought to continue the war against Russia. From containment of Russian encroachments on Turkey-in-Europe, the war had developed into a collective effort to destroy Russian naval power in the Black Sea "in the interests of the balance of power in Europe," as stipulated by the third of the Four Points. In September 1854 fifty thousand British and French troops, augmented by a seven thousand–strong Ottoman force, landed on the Crimean Peninsula and advanced to lay siege on Sebastopol.

After an auspicious start for the allies, fighting was reduced to a protracted siege around Sebastopol that neither the allies nor the Russians were able to tilt in their favor. Suffering on both sides was tremendous, with more lives lost to raging epidemics and biting snowstorms than to actual fighting. So depleted were allied ranks that in February 1855 the Ottomans signed an agreement to provide twenty thousand additional troops and supplies to assist the war effort.

The tsar, too, became increasingly disillusioned with the unwinnable war. On November 29, 1854, he officially accepted the Four Points, only to find that this would no longer satisfy the allies. It was only after Nicholas's sudden demise, on March 2, 1855, and the accession of his son, Alexander II, that the allies agreed to start talking.

The assumption was that the thirty-seven-year-old new tsar would be more inclined toward a settlement than his father had been. This, though, was not the case. In the peace conference that convened in Vienna on March 15, 1855, Alexander reaffirmed Nicholas's acceptance of the Four Points; but when the question of the Russian Black Sea fleet was taken up, in accordance with point three, Alexander would not budge. He was willing to make peace, but he insisted that since Russia had not been defeated, its sovereignty in the Black Sea should not be restricted. Rather than accept a dishonorable peace, Alexander declared, Russia was ready to continue the war against all Europe. Lord Palmerston, who on February 6 had become prime minister following the fall of the Aberdeen government, was prepared to pick up the gauntlet, as was Napoleon III.

On June 4, 1855, negotiations broke down, leaving it for the guns to have their say.

Three months later, on September 8, the Allies stormed Sebastopol after 349 days of siege. This was undoubtedly the pinnacle of the campaign and a most appropriate note on which to end the war. Yet the Western powers continued fighting, as if possessed by an unconquerable impulse; only now they shifted their military operations to the Baltic Sea, a region that had nothing to do with the war's original objectives, and added Sweden to the anti-Russia coalition. For its part Russia continued to press the Ottomans from the Caucasus. Advancing from Circassia, Russian forces managed to seize Bayezid and threaten the key Ottoman fortress of Kars. The Ottoman garrison was able to hold out for six months, but eventually surrendered in late November 1855, having been starved of food and ammunition. Anatolia lay open to a Russian thrust. But at this point "General Winter" interceded and brought Ottoman-Russian fighting to a close.

With fighting at a standstill, the old and by now familiar pattern of Austrian diplomacy was resumed. Under Vienna's guidance the Ottoman Empire, Britain, and France drafted a peace proposal in line with the Four Points, which was submitted to Russia on December 15. To Alexander this seemed a peace without honor, yet he was in no position to bargain. Russia was in a hopeless situation: militarily defeated, politically isolated, and economically bankrupt. On January 15, 1856, the Russian Crown Council accepted the peace proposal unconditionally.

"For most of the Powers the Crimean War had been an indecisive engagement," wrote the British historian A. J. P. Taylor, in what represents the standard judgment of this conflict.[14] Perhaps so, but this interpretation overlooks the real winner of the war: the Ottoman Empire. It was the Ottomans who had triggered a war they could not afford, only to harness the great powers to their cause. Moreover, on earlier occasions when they had been saved from impending doom, such as Muhammad Ali's imperialist bid, the Ottomans had had to plead for help from an unquestioned position of inferiority. This time, though in a similar predicament, they effortlessly convinced the Europeans to fight their war, for the chain of events they had set in motion did the work for them. Consequently, the Ottoman Empire fought the Crimean War as a full-fledged member of a great-power coalition, rather than as the protected party it actually was. This equality was formally institutionalized by the

Congress of Paris, during which the Ottoman Empire not only gained a collective guarantee for its security but was effectively introduced into the prestigious great-power club.

The Treaty of Paris, signed by the great powers and the Ottoman Empire on March 30, 1856, provided for the removal of the Russian military presence from the principalities and the restoration of Ottoman suzerainty over them (Moldavia even regained southern Bessarabia, seized by Russia in 1812). Russia also renounced its protectorate over Serbia, returned the Transcaucasian fortress of Kars to Turkey, and agreed to the neutralization of the Black Sea. Although this last provision meant that the Ottoman Empire, and not only Russia, could not maintain warships or naval arsenals in the Black Sea, there is little doubt as to who was to be protected from whom. Indeed, according to the treaty, the great powers guaranteed "the independence and the territorial integrity of the Ottoman Empire" and pledged not to interfere "either collectively, or separately, in the relations of His Majesty the Sultan with his subjects, nor in the internal administration of his Empire."[15]

But if the Ottomans hoped that they had managed to bottle the nationalist genie and arrest the steady contraction of their European empire, they quickly realized that even this high-water mark of diplomacy contained all the makings of future disaster, not least by encouraging secession in the Danubian Principalities.

When reinstated under Ottoman suzerainty, these provinces were accorded a series of new privileges, including the right to have their own administration and their own militias. Most important, a freely elected and fully representative assembly (Divan) was to be set up in each principality. A great-power commission would then sound out both assemblies to determine the national aspirations of the Romanian people and report its findings to a great-power conference that would determine the final status of the principalities.

The Ottomans had few illusions about where Romanian national sentiments lay, and thus they spared no effort to ensure that these would not prevail. Having fought Russia to keep the principalities in its empire, the Porte was loath to lose them through the ballots, particularly since this democratic procedure was totally alien to Ottoman thinking and practice. When the first elections in Moldavia were held in July 1857, the Ottoman authorities rigged them and managed to produce a majority vote against the unionist party, in flagrant contravention of popular will.

This triggered an international crisis. At the Paris Congress the great powers had already diverged over the future of the principalities, and these divisions only deepened in its aftermath. The idea of a unified Romanian state embracing the two principalities was anathema to Austria, which feared a dangerous domino effect in its own Romanian population in Transylvania and Bukovina. Britain was initially well disposed to unification, but was eventually overcome by its perennial suspicion of Russia—and France—and stuck to its longstanding policy of maintaining Ottoman territorial integrity. The championship of Romanian nationalism was thus left to Napoleon III, who had his own grand vision of the national reorganization of the Continent. He was supported by Sardinia and Prussia, both of which were interested in the weakening of Austria, the main obstacle to their own plans of unification, and by Russia, which sought to end its international isolation, to punish Austria for its "misconduct" during the Crimean War, and to drive a wedge between the French and the British war allies.

Once it became clear that the Ottomans were defying the Treaty of Paris by rigging the Moldavian elections, France demanded that they immediately annul the results. When they refused, France severed its diplomatic relations with the empire, to be followed by Russia, Prussia, and Sardinia. To prevent the situation from getting out of hand, in August 1857 Queen Victoria met Napoleon III in the Isle of Wight, where the two monarchs reached a compromise over the principalities. Britain agreed to the annulment of the elections and promised to advise the Porte in this vein; France undertook to opt for a "broad administrative union" of the principalities rather than their full unification. This understanding convinced the sultan to soften his position and to hold new elections in September 1857.[16] These resulted in a landslide victory for the unionists, both in Moldavia and in Wallachia. The following month the newly elected assemblies met in Bucharest and Jassy respectively, and voted to unify the principalities into a single state, governed by a foreign prince and subject to Ottoman suzerainty.

This was not what Victoria and Napoleon had intended, and they acted quickly in response. In May 1858 representatives of the great powers convened in Paris to draft a convention for the principalities; after three months of arduous deliberations they achieved their goal. The convention kept the principalities separate, but not completely so. Each was to have its own lifetime ruler *(hospodar)*, yet the same person could be simultaneously elected by the two national assemblies. Each was to have its own militia, yet these were to be two parts of a unified army. Finally, each was to have its own legislative and executive institutions, yet a jointly appointed commission was to administer, with limited powers, common affairs of the two principalities.

In January 1859 the Moldavian assembly elected a native boyar, Colonel Alexandru Cuza, as their *hospodar,* and a month later the Wallachian Divan followed suit in the election of Cuza. Although such a dual election was clearly not excluded by the 1858 Convention, the Ottoman Empire and Austria immediately voiced their opposition. Yet there was little they could do. At the end of April 1859 war broke out between Austria and Sardinia, and a week later France joined the Italians. This prevented Austrian involvement in the principalities and allowed Cuza, supported with French arms and war matériel, to consolidate his position. In May the sultan reluctantly accepted a British face-saving tactic and recognized Cuza as the lifetime *hospodar* of Moldavia and Wallachia, but insisted that this did not imply acceptance of the principalities' unification and that the assemblies in both provinces would continue their parallel coexistence.

By now, however, Cuza's appetite was rapidly growing. This unlikely ruler, who reputedly preferred Jamaican rum to public affairs, was rapidly establishing himself as the architect of a modern Romanian state. In December 1860 Cuza extracted an Ottoman *firman* on the fusion of the assemblies into a single body, though only for the duration of his personal rule. With this amalgamation completed in February 1862, a Romanian national state with Bucharest as its capital had effectively come into being, albeit under the unassuming title of the United Principalities of Wallachia and Moldavia.

This arrangement was barely tolerable to the sultan. He resented the fact that the principalities were slipping from his control and feared that the Romanian example would set a dangerous precedent for national movements throughout the Ottoman Empire. Hence, when Cuza was toppled in a military coup in February 1866, the Porte quickly used this development to undo Romanian unification and restore the loose association between the principalities, as envisaged by the 1858 Convention. Russia backed the Ottoman position. Britain gave its lukewarm approval. None wished to see Austria fill the void left by Cuza's downfall and set its sights on the principalities.

The Romanian nationalists, though, had their own plans. Immediately after Cuza's downfall they offered the throne to Prince Philip of Flanders, the younger brother of King Leopold I of Belgia. When he declined, owing to French pressure, the provisional government held a tightly controlled plebiscite that elected Prince Charles Hohenzollern-Sigmaringen, a cousin of the king of Prussia, ruler of Romania. In May 1866 Charles arrived in Romania, to be accorded formal recognition by the great powers two months later. In October the sultan was forced to bow to the inevitable and give Charles his official investiture. Yet it was evident to both parties that this was to be a temporary arrangement. Charles had no intention of remaining an Ottoman subject for the rest of his life, not even by title. In the following decade he was to work assiduously to eradicate the remnants of Ottoman suzerainty over Romania and to render the country truly independent. Fortunately for him, his struggle converged with a string of uprisings across the Balkans that would leave most of the region, and not only Romania, free of Ottoman imperial domination.

The Balkan powder keg was sparked by a peasant uprising that erupted in July 1875 in the small town of Nevesinje, in the province of Herzegovina, at the southwestern extreme of the Ottoman Empire in Europe. It was a desperate act by the Christian peasantry against their repression by both the Ottoman authorities and the local Muslim landowners. But these socioreligious grievances were considerably exacerbated by militant notions of pan-Slavism, propagating the unification of all Slavs in a Russian-dominated federation ruled from Constantinople, and its Serbian and Montenegrin offshoots, which sought to expel the Ottomans from the Balkans and establish a unified South Slav state dominated by Serbia, or alternatively, Montenegro.

In this volatile atmosphere the uprising spread rapidly to immerse Herzegovina and the neighboring province of Bosnia in wholesale massacres of Muslims. "Dead bodies were lying in various corners unburied; and we noticed the head of a boy in one of the streets blackening in the sun," reported the British consul in Sarajevo, William Holmes, following a visit to Nevesinje:

> A little Turkish girl was brought to us, wounded in the throat, and we were told that an insurgent was on the point of cutting off her head when she was snatched from him . . . as far as could be ascertained some fifty or sixty persons perished on both sides during the attack [on the previous day].[17]

Ottoman efforts to suppress the insurrection led to a vicious cycle of reprisals and counter-reprisals, and before long the turmoil in Bosnia-

Herzegovina was reverberating throughout the region. In Serbia and Montenegro nationalist passions were flying high. In the Macedonian port town of Salonika, foreign consuls were murdered. An abortive revolt in Bulgaria in September 1875 invoked the Bosnian insurrection as "the spark which will set the whole Balkan Peninsula in flames . . . [and will] lay the Turkish monarchy in ruins."[18]

In their plight the Ottomans approached the Europeans for support. Could the Western powers "seek out the insurgents and make them understand that they cannot expect help from any foreign Power, nor from the neighbouring Principalities, and that, if they have any complaint to make against the local administration, they have only to send their confidential agents before the Extraordinary Commissioner of the Sublime Porte?"[19]

This plea fell on receptive ears. Memories of the Crimean War were still vivid, and none of the powers was eager to be drawn into the Ottoman quagmire yet again. With Ottoman strategic importance for British imperial interests rising dramatically following the opening of the Suez Canal in 1869, the charismatic prime minister Benjamin Disraeli dreaded anything that could destabilize the ailing empire. Like Palmerston, he harbored little trust for the Russian bear. Viewing the uprising as a corollary of Russian imperialism, he urged the sultan to bring it to an immediate end.

Disraeli's suspicions were overblown. It is true that the Russian ambassador to the Porte, General Nikolai Ignatiev, was a sworn pan-Slavist whose indefatigable machinations bought him the unflattering title of "the evil spirit of Russian diplomacy." Yet the ideals of pan-Slavism were revolting to Tsar Alexander II and Chancellor Gorchakov: not only because they marred Russia's relations with the great powers, but also because of their revolutionary potential. Were the insurrection in Bosnia and Herzegovina to spread further, it could spell disaster for the entire Continent. The best course of action, therefore, was for Russia, Austria, and Germany, who had just formed the League of the Three Emperors (Dreikaiserbund), to collaborate in ending the revolt both by supporting the Porte and by preventing the neighboring provinces of Serbia and Montenegro from intervening.[20]

This outlook was shared by the Habsburg Empire. There were of course expansionist elements in Vienna, the military leadership in particular, who advocated the occupation of Bosnia and Herzegovina to compensate for Austria's Italian losses and to arrest its growing Magyarization (in 1867 the Austrian Empire officially became Austria-Hungary, or the Dual Monarchy) through the incorporation of a significant Slav population. Yet these expansionist tendencies were largely neutralized by the Habsburg foreign minister, Count Julius Andrássy, who viewed the preservation of Ottoman integrity in the Balkans as the key to regional stability.

Chancellor Otto von Bismarck, the "strong man" of Europe after Prussia's victory over France in September 1870 and the constitution of the German Empire four months later, sided with his allies in the Three Emperors' League. Having little interest in the fate of the Ottoman Empire, he was concerned only with preventing the uprising from escalating into a general war that could threaten Germany's newly gained preeminence. He was not averse to the preservation of Ottoman integrity, but he did not preclude the partition of Turkey-in-Europe either, should this be the only way to prevent a world war. What counted was Germany.

Even France, the foremost champion of nationalism, showed little sympathy for the insurgents. Istanbul was up to its neck in debt—£200 million bearing an annual interest of £12 million, as against £22 million in annual revenues. Sultan Abdul Aziz, who in the summer of 1861 succeeded his brother Abdul Mejid to the throne, was avaricious even by Ottoman standards. His lavish entertaining and his palaces cost him a fortune, as did his insatiable appetite for military acquisitions. This diverted vital funds from works of public utility and forced the sultan to begin borrowing from Europe. On October 6, 1875, the Porte declared that it was no longer able to meet its financial obligations. As Turkey's primary creditor, France was far more interested in salvaging its financial investments in the ailing empire than in improving the wretched conditions of the Bosnian-Herzegovian Christian peasantry.

On December 30, 1875, Andrássy announced a reform package designed to quell the insurrection in Bosnia-Herzegovina. When the initiative led to a sharp escalation in the fighting—having been accepted by the Porte but rejected by the rebels—the Three Emperors' League prepared yet another peace proposal in May 1876. This, too, was quickly nullified by events. In the spring the Bulgarians revolted in the Balkan Mountains, supported by Serbia and émigré revolutionaries. The Ottoman authorities responded heavy-handedly, and the uprising deteriorated into a bloodbath. Massacres of Bulgarians and destruction of villages by Turkish irregulars and equally gruesome atrocities by the rebels became common. By June the Porte had suppressed the uprising, only to be confronted with Serbian and Montenegrin declarations of war.

For a short while it seemed that the Ottoman imperial order in the Balkans was over. The Serbian and Montenegrin revolt was no spontaneous and poorly organized insurrection as in Bosnia-Herzegovina; it was a carefully planned revolt by the two most powerful South Slav nations (Serbia even boasted a 150,000-strong army), imbued with aspirations to create a powerful new empire in the Balkans. Yet the Ottomans had no intention of "packing their bags" and leaving. The graver the threat to their empire, the harsher their response became. Although Montenegro scored some initial successes in Herzegovina, Serbia was soon brought to its knees. Its large army proved a paper tiger; even the able leadership of General Mikhail Cherniaev, a Russian war hero and a dedicated pan-Slav who arrived to command the Serbian campaign without official permission, could not save the day. The droves of ill-disciplined pan-Slav volunteers from Russia proved a liability rather than an asset. Rumors of a Serbo-Russian alliance, setting off alarms in Istanbul, turned out to be baseless. Not only had Russia *not* been consulted on the war, but it would not support the insurgents and made it eminently clear that if Serbia committed aggression against the Ottoman Empire, Russia would abandon it to its fate. At a meeting on July 8, a week after the Serbian declaration of war, Gorchakov and Andrássy decided not to intervene in the new conflict and agreed that none of the belligerents would be allowed to reverse the *status quo ante bellum* in the event of victory. This meant that the main Serbo-Montenegrin war objective—the creation of a large South Slav empire—could not be achieved.

Capitalizing on this international aloofness as well as the disorder in the rebels' camp, the Ottomans pressed forward. In September 1876 they routed the Serbian army not once but twice. Belgrade lay ahead.

In an attempt to prevent the expansion of the conflict, Britain proposed holding an international conference in Istanbul. Fearing an unwieldy entanglement in the Balkans, the great powers quickly agreed; the Ottomans refused. Only when confronted with the stark choice between a conference and a Russo-Ottoman war—this time without British support—did they relent. Yet the Ottomans had no intention of being pressured into a solution. On the morning of December 23, 1876, as the first plenary session of the Constantinople Conference commenced, the capital was rocked by salvoes of guns. Without further ado the Ottoman representative, Safvet Pasha, rose to his feet. "Gentlemen," he told the startled delegates. "The cannon that you hear across the Bosphorus notifies the commencement of the promulgation by His Majesty the Sultan of a Constitution guaranteeing equal rights and constitutional liberties to all the subjects of the Empire alike." "In the presence of this great event," came the final bombshell, "I think our labours have become superfluous."[21]

These were not empty words. In an act of defiance, the new constitution declared the Ottoman Empire "an indivisible whole" and rejected the detachment of even a single part "under any pretext whatever." When the great powers presented their proposals to the Porte on January 15, 1877, warning that rejection would lead to the adjournment of the conference, the sultan's answer was a predictable "no." On January 20, the conference broke up.

Ottoman intransigence continued. Two months later the sultan rejected yet another Russo-British peace initiative. The London Protocol, as the joint venture was called, urged the Porte to pursue its own program of reform in the Balkans, but under international supervision and subject to possible international sanctions. The Porte refused. Such demands, it argued, not only contradicted the spirit and letter of the 1856 Treaty of Paris but imperiled the territorial integrity of the Ottoman Empire at a time when it was struggling "for [its] very existence." The sultan was certainly committed to reforming his empire, but only in a way that would "unite all the populations of the Empire into one single body politic." Any exclusive privileges "for Bosnia, Herzegovina and for localities inhabited by Bulgarians" were a recipe for disaster.[22]

To add insult to injury, the Porte declined a Russian request that it send a special ambassador to St. Petersburg to discuss the question of mutual disarmament. This was the last straw for Tsar Alexander II. On April 24, 1877, he declared war on the Ottoman Empire.

Why did the Ottomans choose to defy international will and risk war with their powerful neighbor to the north? There were several reasons. Drunk with their Serbian exploits, the Ottomans were in no mood for compromise with the defeated "renegades." No matter what the circumstances were or what London professed, the Ottomans were convinced that fear of Russia would push Britain to their aid. But the underlying cause of Ottoman obstinacy was to be found in the personality of the new sultan, the thirty-five-year-old Abdul Hamid II, who, on August 31,

1876, replaced his half-brother, Murad V, on the throne. Notwithstanding his pledges of reform, which had helped him to gain power in the first place, Abdul Hamid was imbued with pan-Islamic ideals: religious conservatism, not Western-type reforms, was for him the key to restoring imperial glory. Suspicious to the point of paranoia, the new sultan lived in constant fear of domestic conspiracies and foreign machinations. He surrounded himself with an elaborate system of spies and double agents, going so far as to have all the water pipes in Yildiz Palace disinterred under his own watchful eyes and replaced with new ones, running close to the surface, to ensure that any attempt to use them for subversive purposes would be instantly detected.

Exacerbated by these psychological pressures, Abdul Hamid's near-messianic commitment to the preservation of Ottoman Islamic order was to have a profound impact on the domestic and foreign affairs of the empire for more than three decades. In the turbulent months of 1876 and 1877, it undermined the international efforts toward a peaceful resolution of the Balkan conflict and landed the Ottoman Empire in yet another costly war it could ill afford.

Had the sultan accepted the London Protocol, or even the Russian disarmament initiative, war might well have been averted. As things stood, Alexander's patience was running thin. Much as he detested pan-Slavism and appreciated the economic costs of war, the tsar felt that the Porte had systematically aborted all efforts to resolve the Balkan conflict by peaceful means, leaving Russia no choice but to resort to arms.

On the brighter side of the picture, Alexander could clearly see the potential fruits of victory: restoration of Bessarabia, ceded to Moldavia by the Treaty of Paris, and reassertion of Russia's leading position in the Balkans. This would drive the final nail into the coffin of the Paris Treaty, something the tsar had passionately desired for two decades. Moreover, through its intransigence the Porte had robbed itself of international goodwill. Russia's partners in the Three Emperors' League, Austria-Hungary and Germany, were benevolently neutral; France and Italy remained aloof. Even Britain, the foremost champion of Ottoman integrity, conducted itself with considerable circumspection. Not that Disraeli would not move more aggressively against Russia if given the chance, but his divided cabinet clung to the principle that Britain should not embroil itself in a war without a Continental ally, and Disraeli failed to secure such an alliance.

Under the circumstances, all that Disraeli could do, despite Queen

Victoria's staunch support for his views, was to try to deter Russia from occupying the straits and Constantinople. On June 6 he instructed the British ambassador, Sir Henry Layard, to convince the sultan to request the dispatch of a British naval force to Constantinople and the capture of Gallipoli by British troops. Later that month, when Russian forces crossed the Danube, the British fleet was ordered into Besika Bay. On July 21, the cabinet decided to declare war in the event of a permanent Russian occupation of Constantinople.

This fear proved premature. To everybody's surprise, the Sick Man of Europe fought with great tenacity. In the Caucasus the Ottomans managed to check the Russian advance and even to regain much of the lost territory. In the main theater of war, the Danube, the uninterrupted string of Russian successes was abruptly ended in July 1877 in the small Bulgarian town of Plevna, where the Ottomans defeated two consecutive Russian offensives. The elated Abdul Hamid conferred the title of *ghazi* on Osman Pasha, the hero of Plevna, and Muhtar Pasha, the defender of the Caucasus.

These successes nevertheless failed to save the day. By January 1878 the Russians were knocking on the capital's gates, and the terrified sultan was losing his nerve. The conviction that Britain would never allow the Ottoman Empire to fight Russia on its own had played an important role in Abdul Hamid's readiness to risk war with Russia. Disraeli's assurances to the Ottoman ambassador in London, Musurus Pasha, Layard's sympathetic attitude, and the widespread public support in Britain for the Turkish cause, all kept the Ottomans hopeful of British intervention throughout the war. Yet when their war machine collapsed after the fall of Plevna, the Ottomans began looking elsewhere for support. At the end of November the Porte asked Bismarck to use his good offices with Russia to cease hostilities, but to no avail. On December 13, 1877, three days after the fall of Plevna, the Porte pleaded with the signatories to the 1856 Treaty of Paris to mediate an end to the war. It even took the desperate step of suggesting to Franz Joseph that Austria-Hungary take Bosnia. The emperor refused, yet he became sufficiently alarmed to warn the tsar that peace with the Ottoman Empire was a matter that only Europe as a whole, and not Russia alone, could decide.

The sultan, however, had no intention of allowing his empire to die. He would save it, and his throne, come what may; and if this meant acceptance of a Russian dictate, so be it. On January 31, 1878, an armistice agreement was signed in Adrianople. Two months later, on March 3, these conditions were institutionalized in the Peace Treaty of San Stefano.

The architect of San Stefano was none other than Ignatiev, and the treaty bore the hallmarks of his pan-Slav thinking. An autonomous Greater Bulgaria, embracing the whole of Macedonia and part of western Serbia, was created in the vast territory between the Black Sea and the Aegean. This area was to remain under Ottoman suzerainty, but would be ruled by an elected prince and have its own governing institutions and a national militia. Ottoman forces were excluded from the newly established state, which was to remain under Russian military occupation for two years. Romania, Serbia, and Montenegro gained full independence, together with some territorial acquisitions. The main beneficiary of this arrangement was Montenegro, which nearly tripled its size, but Romania and Serbia were adequately compensated for the territorial adjustments they were forced to make. The Ottoman Empire, already financially in dire straits, was to pay Russia a war indemnity of 310 million rubles, and to introduce reforms in Bosnia-Herzegovina and Armenia. Russia received southern Bessarabia and part of Armenia comprising Kars, Ardahan, Bayezid, and Batum. The straits were to remain open during both war and peace "to merchant vessels of neutral states arriving from or destined for Russian ports."[23]

This marked the worst Ottoman setback since the 1699 Treaty of Carlowitz, when for the first time the empire was forced to surrender territory to "infidel" Europe as a defeated power. Not that there had not been significant setbacks ever since. The Treaty of Kuchuk Kainardji (1774) involved territorial concessions to Russia, which subsequently emerged as a Black Sea power; the Treaty of Adrianople (1829) loosened the Ottoman grip over the Danubian Principalities. But San Stefano went much further than that. It was the beginning of the end for Turkey-in-Europe. The Ottomans had been virtually squeezed out of the Balkans, retaining only a tenuous foothold there through their official suzerainty over Bulgaria and Bosnia-Herzegovina and a small strip of Thrace.

This was precisely what Ignatiev intended. To him San Stefano was the realization of a lifetime ambition; on his gravestone he had only three words carved: "Peking" (from which he had extracted territorial and economic concessions in 1859–1860) and "San Stefano." To the great powers, however, the treaty was a vindication of Russian expansionism, which they were determined to check. As early as March 6, three days after San Stefano, Foreign Minister Andrássy issued invitations for a great-power gathering to be held in Berlin, and three months later, on June 13, 1878, the congress opened in the German capital.

Boasting an impressive gallery of statesmen, the Berlin Congress was the last of the spectacular nineteenth-century great-power gatherings, such as the congresses of Vienna and Paris, that had shaped the destiny of Europe. But behind the splendor and pomp raged a relentless tussle for power and territory. Ostensibly the congress was about the rectification of the Treaty of San Stefano; effectively it was a jockeying for position in the newly carved Balkans.

A particularly hard battle was fought over the future of Greater Bulgaria, where Britain and Russia found themselves hopelessly polarized. It was only Disraeli's willingness to bring things to a head that eventually forced the Russians to back down; at one point he even ordered his special train to be prepared for departure. He was supported by the congress's willful president, Chancellor Bismarck.

Greater Bulgaria was thus divided into three parts. Bulgaria proper, one-third its San Stefano size and completely severed from the Aegean, was to become an autonomous principality tributary to the sultan; the area of Eastern Rumelia, south of the Balkan Mountains, was placed under a Christian governor and made semiautonomous; Macedonia was to return to direct Ottoman rule. For its part Russia received southern Bessarabia and the Asiatic territories of Kars, Ardahan, and the port of Batum on the Black Sea. The independence of Romania, Montenegro, and Serbia, proclaimed in San Stefano, was reaffirmed. Montenegro nearly doubled its territory, and in 1881 it received access to the Adriatic with the acquisition of the port of Dulcigno. Romania was deprived of southern Bessarabia (in blatant violation of its agreement with Russia prior to the war), but received as consolation the poorer, non-Romanian territory of Dobrudja and the Danube Delta. Greece set its sights on Thessaly, Epirus, Crete, and part of Macedonia, but had to content itself with Thessaly and part of Epirus.

As for Bosnia and Herzegovina, the forgotten cause of the entire crisis, they were to be occupied by Austria-Hungary, which was also to garrison the strategic *sanjak* (district) of Novibazar, between Serbia and Montenegro. For all intents and purposes these provinces had been severed from the Ottoman Empire, yet Andrássy—the foremost champion of Ottoman integrity in Europe—could not bring himself to admit this fact in public; in deference to Ottoman remonstrations he agreed to a declaration that the occupation was provisional and that the sovereign rights of the sultan should not be infringed. Even after the congress he continued to allude to the eventual return of these provinces to Ottoman rule.

The Ottomans watched with horror this wholesale partitioning of their European empire but were powerless to arrest the avalanche. Their delegation to Berlin had been amateurishly prepared. They had been given verbal instructions on some key points—such as the subversion of Greater Bulgaria and the restoration of Batum—but were kept in the dark throughout the negotiations about the vicissitudes in the Porte's position. Nor could Sultan Abdul Hamid's choice of representatives have been worse. True, the chief negotiator, Caratheodory Pasha, was an efficient foreign official who won the respect of his peers, but his timidity and the muddled instructions he received from Istanbul prevented him from playing any meaningful role in the talks. The second delegate, the minister in Berlin, Sadullah Bey, was a miserable alcoholic who drank himself to death shortly after the congress. The third representative, Mehmet Ali Pasha, was a deserter from the Prussian army who had converted to Islam and had risen to military prominence in the sultan's service. The idea of dealing with such a person could not be more repugnant to Bismarck, who treated the Ottoman representative with downright contempt. "If you think the Congress has met for Turkey, disabuse yourselves," he said. "San Stefano would have remained unaltered, had it not touched certain European interests."[24]

It is true that none of the Balkan peoples was given gentler treatment than the Ottomans. Bulgaria was dismembered without being heard; the Bosnians and Herzegovinians, whose grievances had sparked the conflict to begin with, were kept out of Berlin; Serbia, Montenegro, and Romania were allowed to present their case to the congress but not to participate in its deliberations; and Greece, as an independent state, was admitted to the congress but was made to understand that its claims mattered little. "At Potsdam there are mosquitoes—here there are minor powers," wrote the patronizing Salisbury to his wife. "I don't know which is worse."[25]

Yet the Balkan peoples had all been imperial subjects who had just made, or were about to make, their debut as independent players (and some of them would not even reach this stage); the Ottoman Empire was a power among powers, master of a vast empire stretching over three continents. The fact that the Ottomans received the same treatment as those minor powers could only mean one thing: thanks to Sultan Abdul Hamid, the Ottomans' brief tenure in the prestigious club of the European great powers was over. As in the early 1850s, the unbridgeable gap between the Ottoman desire to keep its European provinces and the wishes of the indigenous populations to rid themselves of this imperial domination resulted in the all-too-familiar cycle of violence and bloodshed. Now, as then, the Ottomans' imperial impulse drove them to provoke their major challenger, Russia; only now the sultan's paranoia and gross miscalculation of the international balance of power and interests immersed the Ottoman Empire in a catastrophic war that led to the virtual loss of its European provinces. The boundaries of the future Middle East were thus moved eastward, making it an essentially Asian-African geographical expression.

6

THE YOUNG TURKS
IN POWER

$\mathcal{N}$o sooner had the Balkan states made their debut on the international scene than they began setting their imperialist sights on the empire of their former master. King Ferdinand of Bulgaria cherished the dream of occupying Constantinople and reviving the glory of the medieval Bulgarian empires; King Nicholas of Montenegro hoped to establish his dynasty as the leader of the South Slavs; while the charismatic Greek prime minister, Eleftherios Venizelos, was an ambitious empire-builder who saw war as a useful tool to accomplish the "Great Idea"—the incorporation of all areas of Greek settlement in the eastern Mediterranean into a single empire with its capital in Constantinople.

In the spring of 1912 Serbia and Bulgaria signed political and military agreements stipulating *inter alia* that they would join forces in the event of war, including war against the Ottoman Empire. These agreements were complemented on May 29 by a Greco-Bulgarian agreement for mutual assistance against the Ottoman Empire. And with Montenegro concluding defensive alliances with Bulgaria and Serbia several months later, a Balkan League came into being with the explicit aim of waging war against the Ottoman Empire. Indeed, the Montenegrin-Bulgarian agreement obliged Montenegro to initiate hostilities with the Ottomans by September 20, 1912, and Bulgaria, within a month of the outbreak of a Montenegrin-Ottoman war.

To camouflage their expansionist designs and put the Ottomans on the defensive, the Balkan states adopted a handy rallying cry: the need for reform in Macedonia. Denying any ulterior motives and ignoring Ottoman readiness to execute certain reforms, they capitalized on a string of violent incidents in Macedonia in the summer of 1912 to question the Ottoman Empire's ability to rule the province. On October 8, King Nicholas of Montenegro declared war on Turkey, to be followed a week later by the three other Balkan states. In an ultimatum to the Porte they demanded not only Macedonian autonomy and "radical reforms" throughout Turkey-in-Europe, but also the complete decentralization of the Ottoman Empire and "confirmation of ethnical autonomy of the nationalities of the Empire, with all its consequences." And to eliminate the slightest chance of compliance with the ultimatum, the Balkan states insisted that the Ottoman Empire disband its army and fully compensate them for the costs of their own mobilization.[1]

This was too much for the Ottoman Empire, and on October 17, 1912, it declared war on Serbia and Bulgaria. "In view of orders for general mobilization in Bulgaria, Serbia and Greece, Turkey has no alternative but to defend herself," stated Acting Foreign Minister Gabriel Efendi Noradounghian. "But the Government [considers the] attack absolutely unprovoked in view of the fact that [the] general program of [the] present Government was one of reform not only in European provinces of Turkey but in Asia Minor."[2]

This was not the first challenge confronted by the Young Turks, a revolutionary group that seized power in Istanbul in July 1908 and nine months later had Sultan Abdul Hamid deposed by the Ottoman Parliament. Not only did they lose Bulgaria (which declared its independence) and Bosnia-Herzegovina (officially annexed to Austria-Hungary) within months of coming to power, but in 1911–1912 they were forced to surrender their last North African foothold—Tripolitania and Cyrenaica (or today's Libya)—to Italian imperialism. But then the former provinces had already been effectively severed from Ottoman control in 1878, while the latter had only been under nominal Ottoman rule, with control concentrated in the hands of the Sanusis, a puritan order that was established in the mid-nineteenth century and preached a return to the ways of early Islam. In contrast, the imperialist ambitions of the independent Balkan states put the very existence of the Ottoman Empire at stake.

By the time the Balkan War was over, in May 1913, the Ottoman Empire had lost all its remaining European dominions apart from Istanbul and a narrow strip of land along the straits. Had the Balkan armies pressed their victories to their natural conclusion, Constantinople might have readily been overrun, thus setting in motion a process of general disintegration. That this doomsday scenario failed to materialize was due to the same factor that had systematically prevented Ottoman collapse throughout the nineteenth century: the European great powers. Had these powers been interested in falling upon the carcass and dismembering the Ottoman Empire, they could have easily done so at this point—as indeed they could have done on several past occasions. Instead, they tried to forestall a general Balkan conflagration, and when war nevertheless broke out, they played a key role in ending it and preventing a total Ottoman collapse.

This desire to keep the Ottoman Empire alive had nothing to do with altruism. Fearful lest their own empire not survive the demise of the Ottoman "Sick Man" and the advent of national states, the Habsburgs were bent on curbing the surge of Balkan nationalism in general, and Serbian nationalism in particular. Germany, a close ally of both the Habsburg and the Ottoman empires, had no desire to see their Balkan position jeopardized. For its part Britain dreaded both upsetting the Balkan status quo and antagonizing its vast Muslim population in India; indeed, in mid-October 1912 a Muslim rally was held in Karachi to thank "His Britannic Majesty's Government for endeavouring to avert [an] unjust attack of Balkan States upon Turkey and [we] trust it will stand by Turkey."[3] Even Russian agitation, which had an inflammatory effect on Balkan nationalism, was directed against Austria-Hungary for its annexation of Bosnia-Herzegovina rather than against the Ottoman Empire. Tsar Nicholas II and his top foreign policy advisers, Prime Minister Vladimir Kokovtsov and Foreign Minister Sergei Sazonov, had no desire to see a general explosion in the Balkans; if there was one single reason they would go to war, it was to prevent the fall of Constantinople to Bulgaria, not the destruction of the Ottoman Empire.[4]

For their part the Young Turks capitalized on great-power concerns to gain yet another lease on life. As early as October 10, 1912, two days after the Montenegrin declaration of war, the Porte approached Austria-

Hungary with the suggestion that "if the Powers stop Bulgaria from going to war, the Ottoman Empire would place in the hands of the Powers the execution of the reforms that are necessary." Later that month Kamil Pasha, the president of the High Council of State and a sworn Anglophile, asked Britain to take the lead in ending the war, arguing that this would greatly enhance its prestige in the Muslim world. Before the month was over, he made yet another appeal, this time as a newly appointed grand vizier, stating that "Turkey will at any moment be prepared to [deal] with [the] Great Powers but not with the Balkan states."[5]

As their armies stumbled from one catastrophe to another, the Ottomans quickly changed their tune. Now they were prepared to talk peace with the Balkan states, albeit through great-power mediation, and to authorize the admission into the Bosphorus of one warship from each power at the request of their respective ambassadors, in order to reassure European subjects living in Turkey. "The Turks are vanquished and they acknowledge it," the Ottoman ambassador to London, Tewfiq Pasha, told Foreign Secretary Sir Edward Grey.

> Why not have a cessation of hostilities and prevent further bloodshed? We are pressed to receive without any delay the support and intervention of the powers to bring about the immediate cessation of the advancement of the Bulgarian troops, to end the hostilities and to enter peace negotiations to reach a peace.

By November the Bulgarians were knocking at the gates of Istanbul, and Ottoman anxiety was intensifying. "If the King of the Bulgarians and troops would stop at San Stefano a catastrophe might be averted," warned the Ottoman foreign minister on November 4, 1912, "but if they persisted in entering the capital the Government and Sultan would have to leave, possibly for Broussa."[6]

Three days later he was more confident, informing the great powers that "the Sultan and the Imperial Princes have decided not to leave their palaces; Ministers will also remain in their departments, and we have all decided to die at our posts." Yet he reiterated his warning that "Constantinople is the seat of [the] Caliphate, and Mussulmans number 650,000 against 350,000 non-Mussulmans; we are thus going straight towards a catastrophe."[7]

It was some time before the European powers fully realized the severity of the situation, but by the end of October 1912 there was real concern for the survival of the Ottoman Empire. The French government urged the great powers to work together in "absolute disinterestedness" to bring about the cessation of hostilities, while Russian Foreign Minister Sazonov called for a great-power ultimatum to prevent the fall of Adrianople. When his proposal failed to produce results, Sazonov offered to mediate between the warring parties and warned the Balkan League not to march on Constantinople. "Russia would regard any attempt made by another Power to take permanent possession of [Constantinople and its environs] as a *casus belli,*" he cautioned; these areas "must either remain Turkish or become Russian."[8]

Whereas Bulgaria quickly reassured Russia that it had "no intention of retaining Constantinople," the Ottomans remained wary. Even if its professed lack of interest in an indefinite occupation of Constantinople was genuine, Bulgaria still did not rule out the city's temporary retention as a bargaining chip in the peace negotiations, something that was totally unthinkable for the Turks. Hence, on November 5, the Ottoman foreign minister asked the European powers to mediate the terms of peace, and six days later the American ambassador to Constantinople was asked to assume this role should the Europeans fail to do so.[9]

At this point, the focus of international diplomacy shifted to London, where peace negotiations began on December 16, 1912. It was evident to all that the regional order established by the Berlin Congress was now dead, but how precisely it was to be recast was far more controversial. The Balkan allies insisted that the Ottoman Empire cede all its European possessions and the Aegean Islands, while the Ottomans were adamant about retaining the provinces of Edirne (Adrianople) and Albania, which, they insisted, were to be rendered autonomous under great-power administration, and Macedonia, which was to become autonomous under the rule of a member of the Ottoman family. The Ottomans also refused to cede the Aegean Islands, but agreed to submit to a great-power decision on Crete.

In the following months the great powers would use a carrot-and-stick approach to narrow the gaps between the belligerents and bring about the much-desired peace agreements. In January 1913 Grey devised a compromise whereby the Ottoman Empire would retain only those European parts of Eastern Thrace that lay south of a line drawn from Midye on the Black Sea to Enez (Enos) where the Maritsa flows into the Aegean. This proposal would eventually form the basis of the settlement that ended the war, but not before another round of hostilities was allowed to run its course. The new leadership in Istanbul, which seized power in a violent *coup d'état* on January 23, 1913, sought to demonstrate its patriotism by restarting war against the Balkan states, only to find itself decisively defeated and having to plead for great-power support. On March 28, the seventeen thousand Ottoman troops in Adrianople surrendered to a joint Bulgarian-Serbian army. Three days later Sazonov threatened Bulgaria yet again with military intervention should it threaten the Chatalja lines, on the outskirts of Constantinople. By May 30, Grey's proposal had been incorporated into the Treaty of London, which terminated the Balkan War.

Though the Ottomans managed to exploit the schisms within the Balkan League to regain some of their lost territories (for example, Adrianople and part of Thrace) in what came to be known as the Second Balkan War, the Balkan debacle resulted in recriminations and searches for scapegoats, both at the popular level and within the regime. Blaming Europe, Russia in particular, for this recent disaster, Muslims in various parts of the Ottoman Empire vented their anger on Christians, who, by virtue of their religion, were seen as sympathizing with Europe.

For their part the Young Turks were anxious to prove that the setbacks reflected not the inadequacy of their policies but rather their less-than-perfect application. Their initial ticket to power had been the destruction of Hamidian despotism; hence their 1908 revolution had ushered in an unprecedented spell of political liberties, notably the reactivation of both the 1876 Constitution and the first elected Ottoman Parliament in more than thirty years. But then had come the backlash. In their political naïveté the Young Turks had viewed the Constitution and Parliament as an instant panacea that would cure all Ottoman ills rather than as the first step on the long road to recovery. Nor had they realized that the ideals of equality and fraternity they sought to instill had been anathema to many Ottoman subjects whom they had purported to serve. A multiethnic and multidenominational empire can be viable over the long term only if its constituents share a genuine national vision, which neither the nineteenth-century Ottoman reforms (the Tanzimat) nor the 1908 revolution managed to create.

The Young Turks, awakening to these stark realities, concentrated control of the Ottoman Empire in the hands of their nationalist, anti-liberal faction, the Committee of Union and Progress (CUP), whose road to restored glory was far more akin to that of the deposed sultan than to the ideal that had propelled the entire revolutionary process: constitutionalism. The original pledges of freedom, equality, and decentralization were emptied of any real substance as all political life was streamlined to the will of the CUP. Parliament became a rubber stamp, elections were controlled, opposition—real or imaginary—was suppressed. Past allies in the revolutionary struggle became potential threats that had to be crushed, and national and ethnic movements were made illegal. The death penalty was exercised on a wider scale than during the days of Hamidian despotism.

Like Abdul Hamid, the CUP toyed with the ideal of pan-Islam as a means to arrest fragmentation and restore past glory; but unlike the ill-fated sultan, they relegated religion to a secondary place, making Turkish nationalism, Turkism, the primary vehicle for their imperial dreams. The logic behind this policy was clear and straightforward: since the Turks were the superior and most reliable element of the Ottoman Empire, with no subversive secessionist tendencies, their national reinvigoration was the only key to imperial success.

Before long Turkish nationalism expanded into Pan-Turanism, an imperialist ideology propagating the unification of all Turkic-speaking peoples within the mythical entity of "Turan," that vast landmass stretching from China to the Balkans. The chief theoretician of this ideology was Mehmet Ziya, alias Ziya Gökalp (d. 1924), a sociologist, poet, and essayist from southeastern Anatolia. According to Gökalp, the Turks were an ancient nation with a glorious past and superior qualities that, regrettably, had never fulfilled its potential for greatness. Indeed, "the sword of the Turk and likewise his pen have exalted the Arabs, Chinese, and Persians" rather than his own people: even the Ottoman Empire represented the interests of a cosmopolitan ruling class rather than that of the Turkish nation. Now the time had come for the Turkish nation to realize its manifest destiny. To achieve this it needed only "to turn back to [its] ancient past" and follow in the footsteps of its illustrious forefathers—Attila, Genghis Khan, Tamerlane, and Hulagu. As a first step in this direction, the Ottoman Turks would Turkicize the entire empire, whereupon their closest relatives, the Azerbaijanis of Russia and Persia, would be included in a pan-Turkish state. Eventually this national expansion would unite all Turkic peoples of Asia and Europe into one nation. As Gökalp put it in his famous poem, "Turan," in what became the motto of pan-Turanism: "The land of the Turks is not Turkey, nor yet Turkestan. Their country is the eternal land: Turan."[10]

In line with this philosophy the CUP launched a sustained effort to instill a common national sentiment in all Turks—and to force Turkification on all non-Turkish subjects of the Ottoman Empire. Through relentless centralization and repression the empire would indeed become one. Turkish nationalists espoused reforms to "purify" the Ottoman identity and established special institutions to fight for the "Turkish race and language." All signs of non-Turkic national expression were regarded as treason, and the nationalist societies as a grave threat to Ottoman unity that had to be eradicated, by law or by force. Dissident Albanian and Macedonian national groups were suppressed and Armenians attacked. Zionist activities in Palestine were curbed, the powers of Arab chieftains curtailed, and the tiny Arab political and cultural societies purged.

Now that the Ottoman Empire had been defeated by its former Balkan subjects, these pan-Turanist notions, spiced with pan-Islam and Ottoman loyalism, were increasingly seen as "the only way of saving Turkey from the complications which threatened on every side, building up her strength and giving her true place among nations."[11] And the distance between recognition of the need for restoring the Ottoman "true place among nations" and the advent of self-styled "saviors" on the political stage was very short indeed.

On January 23, 1913, some two hundred CUP members, headed by Enver Pasha, the hero of the Libyan War, staged a violent *coup d'état* that came to be known as the "Raid on the Sublime Porte": the minister of war was shot, and the grand vizier and the entire cabinet forced to resign. Absolute power would rest in the hands of a radical CUP triumvirate—Enver Pasha, who would become the minister of war; Talaat Pasha, the minister of the interior, and Djemal Pasha, the minister of the navy—complemented by the grand vizier, Said Halim, himself a CUP member. The rest of the Ottoman ruling institutions—the government, the Parliament, and the sultan—were made to dance to the tunes of the triumvirate. The Ottoman Empire had been transformed into a military dictatorship. Its fate had unwittingly been sealed.

Part Two

DEMISE
OF THE
"SICK MAN"

7

THE OTTOMAN ROAD TO WAR

*F*ar from restoring lost glory and venturing to new imperial heights, the Young Turks found themselves presiding over the most humiliating setbacks in Ottoman history. The Balkan wars ended half a millennium of Ottoman imperialism in Europe and wrested a sizeable portion of the empire's territory and some 20 percent of its population. This setback was particularly traumatic, not only because Turkey-in-Europe was the most desirable part of the empire, whose loss threatened the Ottomans' very existence, but also because it was effected, not by the great powers, but by former subjects, the newly independent Balkan states.

Desperate times called for desperate measures. The task of redeeming Ottoman glory fell to the triumvirate who had effectively taken the reins of power after the January 1913 *coup d'état:* Enver, Talaat, and Djemal Pashas. The three men viewed the Ottoman setbacks as a direct outcome of an "undecided and vacillating policy," and were resolved to restore the empire's "true place among the nations" through "an active foreign and domestic policy."[1] Agents were sent to foment unrest in the Balkans, Macedonia in particular, so as to entice the great powers into measures that would restore the area to Ottoman rule; attempts were made to sow divisions among the Balkan states by weaving a tangled web of Ottoman alignments with former enemies. In January 1914 a secret Turco-Bulgarian defensive treaty was agreed upon, kindling rumors of a joint plan to establish a corridor to the Adriatic through either Albania or Montenegro.[2] The Ottomans' attempts to forge an alliance with their Greek nemesis (with the possible participation of Romania) were far less successful, as the two parties failed to overcome their differences, not least over the future of the Aegean Islands, whose seizure by Greece during the Balkan wars was one of the bitterest pills for the Porte to swallow.[3]

The primary vehicle for imperial resurgence was to be military might, and the role model for emulation was Japan, the rising power of the Far East that in 1905 inflicted a devastating defeat on the Russian Empire. By way of transforming the Ottoman Empire into the "Japan of the Near East," the triumvirs turned to the European powers for military support. In France they placed orders for six destroyers and two submarines, as well as for French naval expertise. From Britain the Ottomans ordered two formidable warships of the new dreadnought class—*Reshadieh* and *Sultan Osman I,* and in the summer of 1912 a British advisory mission was deployed within the Ottoman navy, headed by Rear Admiral Sir Arthur Henry Limpus—a personal friend of the first lord of the Admiralty, Winston Churchill.

For the reorganization of their ground forces the Young Turks turned to Germany. A small number of Prussian officers had advised the Ottoman army since the mid-1830s, and their presence was expanded and institutionalized in 1882, with the arrival of a military delegation headed by Major-General Otto Köhler, who was succeeded three years later, upon his death, by Baron Colmar von der Goltz. Having been profoundly humiliated during the Balkan wars, the Ottoman Empire asked Berlin to reorganize and supervise its shattered forces. The latter complied and a German delegation, headed by Lieutenant-General Otto Liman von Sanders, a recently ennobled fifty-eight-year-old divisional commander, arrived in Istanbul late in 1913.

Of the triumvirs who dominated the Ottoman political scene, Enver has been the least studied and appreciated. Either because of his relative youthfulness (he was nine years younger than Djemal and seven years younger than Talaat), or because he left no published memoirs (unlike his two partners), or, most likely, because his imperialist inclinations do

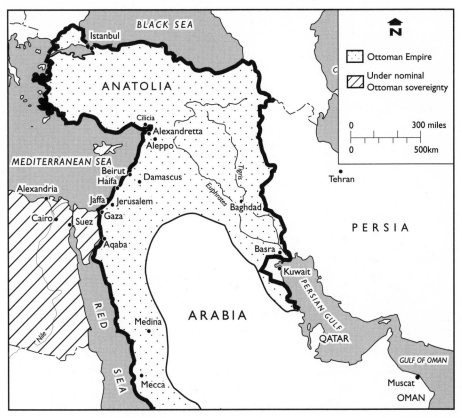

The Ottoman Empire on the eve of the First World War

not fit the conventional historical narrative blaming the European powers for drawing the Ottoman Empire into the First World War, Enver's influence on the fateful decision that condemned the Ottoman Empire to destruction has been largely overlooked. Yet it was Enver who played the key role in plunging the empire into its most catastrophic misadventure ever. His actions were motivated *not* by a sense of anxiety or fear but by pure expansionist greed. His was an unwavering conviction that Germany would be the winner of any European war and that alignment with that country would allow the Ottoman Empire not only to recoup its European losses but also to go on the offensive: to expand its territory at Russia's expense.

The man who would lead his empire to destruction was born in Istanbul on November 22, 1881, to a low-ranking civil servant. Having graduated from the Military Academy, Enver was posted as staff captain to the Third Army in Macedonia (in September 1906 he was promoted to the rank of major), where he spent three years in military operations against Macedonian guerrillas, and where he was won over to the Young Turks' cause. In June 1908 he escaped with a group of followers to the Macedonian hills, thereby fomenting the Young Turk revolution of July 23, 1908. At the age of twenty-six, Enver was already a revered revolutionary hero.

In the autumn of 1911 Enver resigned his post as military attaché in Berlin, which he had held since 1909, to fight in the Libyan War. This he did with great valor, rocketing his national reputation to new heights as the military leader who stood up to the Italians. In June 1912 he was promoted to lieutenant-colonel and three months later, despite the CUP's fall from power in the summer of 1912, he was appointed governor *(mutassarif)* of the *sanjak* of Benghazi.

By now Enver's sense of self-importance and indispensability was growing by the day. He referred to Benghazi as "his kingdom," printing money bearing the signature of "the savior of Libya."[4] Indeed, it was not long before Benghazi became too small for the ambitious warrior, who now set his sights on nothing less than the reins of Ottoman power. Exploiting the acute trauma attending the setbacks of the First Balkan War, on January 23, 1913, Enver led the raid on the Sublime Porte that reinstated the CUP after a brief spell out of power. Although this putsch failed to halt the chain of external defeats suffered by the Ottomans—on March 24, Adrianople fell to the Bulgarians—Enver salvaged his reputation by leading the Ottoman counteroffensive in the Second Balkan War that turned the tables on Bulgaria and restored Adrianople to Ottoman rule in July 1913.

Yet again Enver found himself basking in nationwide adulation, and he took full advantage of his revered status. On January 4, 1914, he was promoted two ranks to major-general and appointed minister of war in the Unionist cabinet of Grand Vizier Said Halim Pasha, the grandson of Muhammad Ali of Egypt. Two months later Enver married Emine Nadjiye Sultan, the niece of the reigning monarch, Mehmed V. The war hero had become related to the sultan-caliph.

But even this celebrated status and a fortuitous marriage failed to curb Enver's insatiable ambition. A dedicated pan-Turkist (he was *inter alia* the patron of the Turanian youth movement), Enver aspired to nothing less than the restoration of Ottoman glory in the manner of Suleiman the Magnificent, a new imperial order in which he would occupy pride of place. He had no intention of being a fool in the service of a puppet sultan who would reap the fruits of his toil. He even went so far as to secure the appointment of Hairi Bey, who had consistently denounced the caliphate as a source of corruption and obscurantism, to the highest religious post, sheikh el-Islam.

Germany was the power on which Enver pinned his hopes for imperial regeneration. Its military prowess and efficiency had captured his imagination from an early stage, and to Germany he turned once Europe had been thrown into disarray following the assassination of the Austro-Hungarian heir apparent, Archduke Francis Ferdinand, in Sarajevo on June 28, 1914. As far as Enver was concerned, the gathering storm over the Continent created a unique opportunity for the Ottoman Empire to recoup its European losses, provided that it aligned itself with the right great power. While Europe was still reeling from the assassination, Enver reportedly made his first secret overture to Berlin for an alliance; soon afterward he informed the governor of Basra that the Ottoman Empire was ready to help Germany in return for assistance received during the Balkan wars, and that German arms were on their way to Basra—to be followed by thirty-two secret German emissaries, including officers, to preach jihad both within and beyond the boundaries of the Ottoman Empire. A few weeks later Enver ordered the governor to "arrange [Basra] for speedy mobilization" and informed the vali of Najd, Abd al-Aziz Ibn Saud, that the German officers were being dispatched "so that they may put your troops in order quickly."[5]

At the same time Enver gathered his associates around him: Minister of the Interior Talaat Pasha, the most powerful man in Turkey after Enver; Said Halim Pasha, the grand vizier and foreign minister, who was under Enver's spell; and Halil Bey, the president of the Senate. In secret deliberations, held at the grand vizier's villa on the Bosphorus, the four decided to make simultaneous overtures to the German and Austro-Hungarian ambassadors for a military alliance, while keeping the rest of the Ottoman cabinet in the dark.

On July 20 Enver, Talaat, and Said Halim met the Austro-Hungarian ambassador to Istanbul, Johann Margrave von Pallavicini. They warned him that the Triple Entente, especially Russia, was hard at work engineering an Ottoman-Greco-Romanian alliance, and that only a bold Austrian move could preempt such a development: "This was Austria's last chance to restore its prestige as a great power in the eyes of both

Turkey and the Balkan peoples. Not only Bulgaria but also Romania and Turkey would unflinchingly ally with the Triple Alliance should Austria teach Serbia a proper lesson." Pallavicini was duly impressed.[6]

Two days later, on July 22, Enver approached the German ambassador, Baron Hans von Wangenheim. He told him that "the majority of the committee, headed by the Grand Vizier, Talaat, Halil, and himself, did not wish to become Russian vassals and were convinced that the Central Powers were militarily stronger than the Entente and would triumph in the event of a world war." This in turn meant that "the present Turkish Government was eager to associate itself with the Central Powers and would decide, with a heavy heart, in favor of a pact with the Triple Entente only if spurned by Germany."[7]

Wangenheim sought to deflect Enver's enthusiasm. He was not convinced that the Ottoman Empire required an alliance. Was the Porte aware that the proposed association could jeopardize the Ottomans' economic recovery? Did they consider the far-reaching political implications of such a move and its attendant military risks? As the weakest member of the Central Powers, the Ottoman Empire would be exposed to Russian retribution; not even an Ottoman-Bulgarian bloc would remove such a threat or be of real value to the Central Powers unless it included Romania as well. But such a possibility was not in the offing.[8]

Wangenheim's skepticism of Turkey's value as an ally was shared by his superiors in Berlin, Foreign Minister Gottlieb von Jagow, and Prime Minister Theobald von Bethmann Hollweg, as well as by influential members of the military, who referred to the Ottoman army as the "Sorgenkind," or problem child.[9] Yet they were confronted with a formidable coalition advocating the virtues of an Ottoman alliance, notably Marine Minister Grand-Admiral Alfred von Tirpitz, Undersecretary of State for Foreign Affairs Arthur Zimmerman, and General Liman von Sanders. Above all, Kaiser Wilhelm himself was keen to see the Ottoman Empire join his team. "A refusal or a snub would result in Turkey's going over to Russo-Gallia, and our influence would be gone forever," he angrily responded to Wangenheim's lukewarm reception to the Ottoman overtures. "Wangenheim must express himself to the Turks, on the issue of an alignment with the Triple Alliance, with unmistakably plain compliance, receive their desires, and report them! *Under no circumstances whatsoever can we afford to turn them away.*"[10]

Wangenheim was thus peremptorily ordered to accept the Ottoman offer of an alliance, and he dutifully complied. Secret negotiations were resumed in Istanbul, and on July 28 the grand vizier made a formal alliance proposal to Wilhelmstrasse. This called for an offensive and defensive alliance against Russia that would pave the way for the Ottoman Empire's incorporation into the Central Powers. The treaty was to be activated in the event of both a Russian attack on either Turkey, Germany, or Austria-Hungary, and an attack by Germany or the Triple Alliance on Russia. Germany would leave its military mission in the Ottoman army for the duration of the war. In return, the Ottoman Empire would place its Supreme Military Command and the actual command of one-fourth of its army under the German mission.[11]

The kaiser's acceptance of the proposal came within hours. The Habsburg Empire had just declared war on Serbia, and Wilhelm was determined to draw the Ottoman Empire into what increasingly appeared an inevitable war with Russia. "His Majesty has agreed to the proposal of the grand vizier," Prime Minister Bethmann-Hollweg cabled to Wangenheim on July 28, with the modification that if the Austro-Hungarian-Serbian conflict failed to develop into a German-Russian war, the alliance would no longer apply.[12]

This qualification, however, was wholly unacceptable to the Ottomans. They insisted on an alliance that would "protect Turkey from all possible consequences attending its association with Germany" and would ideally last for a seven-year period; but as a means of last resort they would be prepared to settle for a treaty that would run "only" until the end of 1918.[13] Yet again the Germans complied, and on August 2, 1914, , Wangenheim and Said Halim affixed their signatures to the secret alliance treaty. The Ottoman Empire pledged to wage war against Russia in the event of the latter's military intervention in the Habsburg-Serbian conflict, and to give the German mission "an effective influence over the general conduct of the army, in conformity with what has been agreed upon directly by His Excellency the Minister of War and His Excellency the Chief of the Military Mission." For its part Germany pledged "by force of arms if need be, to defend Ottoman territory in the event it should be threatened."[14]

Given that Germany was already in a state of war with Russia on August 2, it expected its new ally to abide by its treaty obligations and declare war on Russia. On August 4, Foreign Minister Jagow informed Wangenheim that Britain might declare war on Germany within the day and emphasized that "a Turkish declaration of war on Russia this very day if possible appears to be of the greatest importance." Helmut von

Moltke, the chief of the Prussian general staff, who had previously dismissed the Ottoman military as insignificant, went a step further: he demanded immediate Ottoman action not only against Russia, as stipulated by the treaty alliance, but also against the other members of the Entente (something that was not required by the agreement), notably the initiation of insurrections in Egypt and India.[15]

This was not to be. To Berlin's deep dismay, on August 3, Turkey mobilized its forces and proclaimed an armed neutrality.

The proclamation was phony. The underlying principle of neutrality is complete and unqualified impartiality on the part of the nonbelligerent, and its abstention from any action favoring one of the combatants. This precludes *ipso facto* participation in bilateral and multilateral alliances, let alone those entailing military obligations. Through its treaty with Germany, the Ottoman Empire had effectively transformed itself into a belligerent in the Continental conflict, though this fact was not fully recognized for some time because of the agreement's secretive nature.

For Enver, however, the proclamation provided the breathing space necessary to prepare for the Ottoman entry into the war: to complete the reorganization and rearming of the military; to dispel remaining apprehensions within the cabinet, whose members were largely unaware of the secret Ottoman-German alliance; to sway public opinion in the direction of the Central Powers, and to convince the Turks, still reeling from the Balkan wars, that another war would be in their interest; to ensure the most favorable regional arrangement in the Balkans; and to buttress the fledgling Ottoman economy. Above all, the feigned neutrality allowed Enver to extract material and political benefits simultaneously from Germany, which was eager to see the immediate implementation of the secret agreement, and from the Entente, which was keen to keep the Ottoman Empire out of the war.

An unexpected event provided an early boost to Enver's machinations: on August 3 the British requisitioned the two warships the Ottomans had ordered from them—the *Sultan Osman* and the *Reshadieh.* And while this decision had nothing to do with anti-Ottoman sentiments— First Lord of the Admiralty Churchill was among the most pro-Ottoman members of the British cabinet, yet he would not risk allowing such powerful vessels to leave home territory on the eve of an all-European war—the requisitioning fell into Enver's lap like a ripe plum. To the Ottomans the vessels were a source of great national pride. They embodied the burning ambition to regain the Aegean Islands from Greece, and the government had turned their purchase into a national mission: children were urged to donate pocket money, women to sell their hair to raise funds for the ships. Once the news broke that the ships would not be coming, a virulent anti-British propaganda campaign was launched, largely inflating German victories in the war. The kaiser was portrayed not only as the greatest friend of the Ottomans, but also as the pious protector of Islam—"Hadji Wilhelm." As Halil Bey, the president of the Senate and Enver's close associate, put it: "France and Russia will have to give way before the German army . . . England will not be able to get at the German fleet." Should the Entente be victorious, "Turkey would be . . . at the mercy of Russia, and England would not be able, even if it wished, to prevent its present ally, Russia, from consummating its traditional policy of the destruction of Turkey." In contrast, "if Germany and Austria were victorious, there would be a better chance of Turkey being supported and allowed to exist and develop itself."[16]

This position was rapidly becoming the received view within the cabinet. Contrary to the conventional wisdom, there was no real pro-Entente faction inside the government; the vast majority of Ottoman leaders—and not just the four who engineered the secret alliance: Enver, Talaat, Said Halim, and Halil—were pro-German from the outset. The most prominent pro-British cabinet member, Minister of Finance Djavid Bey, and the influential minister of the navy Djemal Pasha, wrongly considered pro-French, were instantly won over to the secret alliance and sworn to confidentiality when on August 1 Enver informed them of the imminent British requisitioning of the ships. (Enver had learned of the requisitioning from the Ottoman ambassador to London, Tewfiq Pasha). The grand mufti, the minister of justice Ibrahim Bey, and the minister of education Shukri Bey also expressed their support for the alliance.

This pro-German disposition notwithstanding, the cabinet was still divided over certain critical issues. While most ministers wished to join Germany in war against Russia, they had no desire to fight Britain and France. Some saw the German option in more defensive terms than others, some advocated a longer waiting period before going to war. No one had any intention of being drawn into the war on Germany's terms, not least Enver himself.[17]

Having secured Germany's commitment to defend the Ottoman Empire, Enver skillfully exploited Germany's eagerness to bring Turkey into the war to extract substantial material and political gains from the kaiser. Even before the conclusion of the secret agreement Ottoman negotiators had devised a list of six far-reaching demands, requiring Germany to support the abolition of the Capitulations, the longstanding economic, legal, and political concessions enjoyed by Europeans in the Ottoman Empire; to facilitate the conclusion of agreements with Bulgaria and Romania; to forgo a peace agreement so long as Ottoman territory remained under enemy occupation; to guarantee the restoration of the Aegean Islands to Turkey if Greece were to join the Entente; to secure the eastern Ottoman frontiers so as to establish a link with the Muslim peoples of Russia; and finally, to see that the Ottoman Empire was adequately compensated at the end of the war.

These far-reaching demands were eventually left out of the negotiations in order to facilitate the conclusion of the Ottoman-German treaty. Once the agreement was in hand, however, the Ottoman negotiators immediately tried to improve on its conditions, by presenting their demands to Wangenheim on August 3. Of the six demands the ambassador accepted one: Germany would avoid making peace before the withdrawal of all enemy forces from Ottoman territory. But three days later he relented and accepted all the demands *en bloc,* including the most imperialist of them all, namely, that the Ottoman Empire share the war spoils at Russia's expense. The reason for this concession was quite simple. The German Mediterranean squadron, commanded by Admiral Wilhelm Souchon, was steaming toward Istanbul, chased by a superior British force, and Berlin was anxious to have its ships enter the safe haven of the Dardanelles.

On August 1 Wangenheim and von Sanders had requested the squadron, in particular the formidable cruiser *Goeben* and its smaller sister *Breslau,* following a secret conference with Enver, who for his part instructed the Ottoman military authorities to keep the straits—closed to warships by virtue of the 1841 London Convention—open for the arrival of the German vessels.[18] Yet once these vessels came under British threat, the Ottomans tried to make the most of the German plight. On August 4, the grand vizier told Wangenheim that since granting asylum to the two cruisers would expose the Ottoman Empire to grave risks, the ships would have to remain outside the straits for the time being. Two days later Said Halim was more "conciliatory." The Ottomans had decided to allow the ships into their territorial waters, he said, but they expected a

German *quid pro quo* in the form of acceptance of the six demands. The ambassador saw no choice but to comply: the British were breathing down Souchon's neck and any delay in opening the straits could mean annihilation for the German squadron. Four days later, in the evening hours of August 10, the *Goeben* and the *Breslau* arrived outside Istanbul. Enver's joy was overflowing: "To us a son is born!"[19]

The ships, though, had not yet exhausted their usefulness for the Ottomans. As a neutral power and a signatory to the XIII Hague Convention of 1907 concerning the Rights and Duties of Neutral Powers in Maritime War, the Ottoman Empire was obliged either to return the German ships to international waters within twenty-four hours, or to intern them along with their crews for the duration of the war.[20] To get around this obligation, on August 9 the grand vizier made the following proposal to Wangenheim: the Ottomans would take possession of the ships and would pretend to have paid Berlin for them. This would put a shiny legal gloss on the ships' continued presence in Ottoman waters—in full military preparedness.

The Germans' angry response to this proposal did not dissuade the Ottomans. On the same day that the ships arrived in Istanbul, Wangenheim was summoned to the Sublime Porte. Ignoring his own role in introducing the squadron into the straits, and the exorbitant price exacted for this concession, the grand vizier reprimanded the ambassador in front of the entire cabinet for the "premature arrival" of the vessels, which he alleged put the Ottoman Empire at great peril. He then reiterated the proposal for a fictitious purchase of the ships. When the ambassador declined the offer yet again, the Porte dropped a bombshell, publicly declaring that the Ottomans would purchase the two German warships for the alleged price of eighty million marks. On August 16, Djemal Pasha received the *Goeben* and the *Breslau,* renamed *Yavuz Sultan Selim* and *Medilli,* into the Ottoman fleet.

The Germans were flabbergasted, but they complied. The Ottoman Empire was too precious an ally to alienate over such an issue. Besides, despite their formal incorporation into the Ottoman navy, the cruisers remained with their German crews. Not least, coming on the heels of the British requisition of the two dreadnoughts, the bogus purchase of the German ships was immensely popular with the Ottoman public and rocketed German prestige to new heights. The Germans could hope that their effective control of the ships, their closer association with the

Ottoman navy (on September 24 Souchon was officially made commander of this force), and their burgeoning popularity would expedite the Ottoman entry into the war.

These hopes were eventually vindicated, but not before Enver further exploited German vulnerabilities. The mobilization had placed an unbearable strain on the crumbling Ottoman economy, and on September 30 the Porte appealed to Germany for a loan of five million Turkish pounds (T£) in gold, only to be thoroughly disappointed. Berlin was willing to lend Turkey the requested sum, Undersecretary Zimmerman told the Ottoman ambassador to Berlin, Mukhtar Pasha, but only after the Ottomans had entered the war; until then, Turkey would have to content itself with an advance payment of T£250,000.

This was not what Enver had expected, and on October 9 he called on Wangenheim. The pro-war faction in the cabinet was about to prevail, he argued, and the army was fully prepared. The only obstacle to the Ottoman entry into the war was financial: the Turks could not assume such a demanding undertaking without being certain of Germany's financial commitment. Two days later Enver paid yet another visit to the ambassador, this time with Talaat, Djemal, and Halil. The four reaffirmed their commitment to war and promised to allow Souchon to attack Russian targets the moment the German government deposited T£2,000,000 in Istanbul.

These meetings did the trick. On October 12, a shipment of T£1,000,000 in gold left Germany on its way to Istanbul, to be followed five days later by a second shipment of T£900,000. This was manna from heaven to Enver. With German credit he could immediately see to the upkeep of the army and have forces ready to go into action. The doubting voices within the cabinet would be silenced once and for all. As the shipments arrived in Istanbul in record time, Enver made his move. On October 21, 1914, he prepared the Ottoman war plan, which was immediately submitted to German imperial headquarters. The opening blow was to be directed at the Russian fleet by Admiral Souchon, who, in turn, would blame Russia for the incident. The Ottoman army would then initiate "defensive operations" in Transcaucasia (to be expanded later to an offensive against Russia's southern flank), while an expeditionary force would advance against Egypt. The German chief of the general staff, General Erich von Falkenhayn, immediately gave his seal of approval.[21]

The die was cast. On October 25, Enver ordered Souchon to "attack the Russian fleet at a time that you find suitable." Four days later, in the predawn hours of October 29, Ottoman torpedo boats attacked Russian warships in Odessa, while the *Goeben* and the *Breslau* attacked Sebastopol.

The attack had an electrifying effect on the Ottoman government. The antiwar faction was thrown into disarray. On October 30 Enver, Djemal, and Talaat convened an extraordinary session of the CUP, which came out in strong support of an immediate entry into the war. The prevailing view within the CUP was that the Ottoman Empire's continued adherence to neutrality would be extremely dangerous, since at the end of the war Russia might attempt to occupy the Bosphorus and the Dardanelles.

In a sudden loss of nerve, the grand vizier insisted that Russia be given an apology. Enver dutifully obliged—but in a manner that defeated the vizier's intention. The Porte apologized to St. Petersburg but put the blame for the attack on Russia: despite being provoked by Russia, ran the "apology," the Ottoman Empire was prepared to settle the matter amicably by making all necessary concessions. Not surprisingly, this was too much for the Russians to digest, and they contemptuously dismissed the "apology" and an attendant offer to investigate the incident. Nothing less than the dismissal of all German personnel from the Ottoman military would be acceptable to Russia. This Istanbul rejected. On November 4, Russia declared war on the Ottoman Empire; Britain and France followed suit the next day.

The Ottomans picked up the gauntlet. On October 31 the cabinet had already defined its imperialist war objectives in no uncertain terms: "the destruction of our Muscovite enemy, in order to obtain thereby a natural frontier to our empire, which should include and unite all branches of our race."[22] Now that Russia had declared war on the Ottoman Empire, the cabinet reaffirmed the inevitability of war. The dissenting ministers, headed by Djavid Bey, left the cabinet. A declaration of war was quickly drafted by Enver, Djemal, and Talaat (who temporarily took over the Ministry of Finance), together with their close associates, and overwhelmingly approved by the chamber and the Senate. On November 11 the sultan, in his capacity as caliph, declared holy war against Russia, Britain, and France. Enver could rejoice: the Ottoman Empire had joined the Great War.

8

THE ENTENTE'S ROAD TO WAR

*N*early a century after the catastrophic blunder that led to the destruction of what had been the longest reigning empire on earth, culpability is still apportioned to the European powers. Rarely is the dogged effort of Enver and his accomplices to align themselves with Germany taken for what it was: an imperialist bid for territorial expansion and restoration of lost glory. Instead, the Ottoman Empire is generally viewed as the hapless victim of either the "forceful and clever German diplomacy" that "persuaded and maneuvered" the Young Turk government "into taking such a perilous gamble," or Austrian pressure, "it being the object of Austria to control Ottoman ambitions in the Balkans by tying the Porte into the Triple Alliance." Still another theory holds that the coldness of the Entente drove the isolated and spurned Ottoman Empire to look for its place in the sun. "The Unionists who seized power in January 1913," runs this last theory, "felt betrayed by what they considered was Europe's anti-Turkish bias during the Balkan wars, and therefore they had no faith in Great Power declarations regarding the Empire's independence and integrity." Hence, when their attempts to secure formal alliances with the Entente were declined, they had no choice but to throw in their lot with Germany.[1]

This received wisdom could not be further from the truth. Far from "betraying" the Ottoman Empire during the Balkan Wars, the European powers saved the tottering empire from certain destruction at the hands of its former subjects. Even Russia, Turkey's longstanding nemesis, made no attempt to exploit the war for its own territorial aggrandizement; rather, it was Russia's tough warnings that halted the Bulgarians at the gates of Istanbul.

Nor did these powers turn their backs on the Ottoman Empire in the wake of these wars, let alone abandon their longstanding interest in its continued existence. True, following the 1908 Young Turk Revolution Britain declined several invitations to explore an Anglo-Ottoman alliance and Turkey's inclusion within the Entente (the last such attempt was made in June 1913). But this had nothing to do with vanished interest in Ottoman integrity; rather, it reflected Britain's belief that under the circumstances such an alliance would be counterproductive, and that the best way to ensure Ottoman territorial integrity was through a great-power declaration or treaty. In the words of Foreign Secretary Grey: "We cannot revert to the old policy of Lord Beaconsfield; we have now to be pro-Turkish without giving rise to any suspicion that we are anti-Russian." Indeed, in the summer of 1913 Britain and France agreed "that a partition into spheres of influence was not possible, for this would first of all lead to an intervention on the part of [powers other than] those of the Triple Entente, which must then lead to a partition of Turkey, which would bring about a crisis this time without any hope of preventing a war." Hence, it was "necessary to support Turkey to a certain degree," and by means supported by all the great powers. A few months later the British, Russian, and German emperors all agreed "on the necessity of preserving the Turkish Realm in its present form."[2]

But if Britain discouraged Turkey's timid explorations of a bilateral alliance, its partners in the Triple Entente did not. Close scrutiny of the alliance overtures the Ottomans allegedly made prior to the First World War—to Russia in May 1914 and to France two months later—would quickly dispel any notion of rejection. In the former case it was Turkey, rather than Russia, that aborted its own timid overture; in the latter case there is no hard evidence that a concrete alliance proposal was ever made.

The overture to Russia was made by Talaat during a courtesy visit to the Livadia Palace in the Crimea. The third of its kind since 1879, when Abdul Hamid institutionalized the habit of sending a delegation to pay homage to the tsar at his summer resort, this visit had no specific political aim, let alone the exploration of an Ottoman-Russian alliance. Indeed, apart from the customary pleasantries and reassurances to his guests, Talaat evaded any serious discussion of concrete foreign policy issues, "pleading complete ignorance of everything relating to foreign politics."[3]

It was only on the last day of the visit, after a dinner on the sultan's yacht, anchored at Yalta, that Talaat bent down to the Russian foreign minister, Sergei Sazonov, seated next to him. "I have to make you a very serious proposal," he whispered in his ear. "Would the Russian government care to conclude an alliance with Turkey?"

Sazonov was taken by surprise. "Why did you leave this proposal until the last moment, when you had so many opportunities to make it before?" he asked. Talaat ducked the question. There was obviously no time to discuss it now, he said; he was simply interested in the foreign minister's view regarding the feasibility of such an alliance. Sazonov was forthcoming. Although the proposal took him completely by surprise, he did not reject the idea in principle; but such an important matter required a very serious discussion. The Russian ambassador to Istanbul, Mikhail Nikolaevich de Giers, would be returning to his post in three days, and he would instruct him to discuss the issue with the Ottoman authorities. On this note the conversation ended amicably, leaving Sazonov puzzled yet hopeful of the unexpected potential opening.

Later that evening Sazonov told Giers of Talaat's proposal, which neither he nor the other Russian guests on the sultan's yacht had heard. The ambassador was astonished at the proposal and the manner in which it had been made, yet he deemed it worth pursuing and promised Sazonov that he would "explore the question thoroughly" on his return to Istanbul.

When he reported back to St. Petersburg some time later, however, Giers was profoundly disillusioned. "It would be useless to expect a continuation of the conversation on the subject of an alliance with Russia so unexpectedly introduced by the Turks," he argued. "The Young Turk Cabinet, frightened at the boldness of its own proposal[,] had evidently decided to abandon the plan contemplated by Talaat."[4]

This was scarcely surprising. Giers's original bewilderment at the casual manner in which the proposal had been made was fully warranted. Talaat had not shared his plans to make an overture with his partners in Istanbul let alone received their blessing. Indeed, in his memoirs Talaat makes no mention of the entire episode.

It is highly improbable that this glaring omission reflects Talaat's exasperation with "Sazonov's indifference" to his proposal, as claimed by a Turkish apologist.[5] In his attempt to exonerate the Ottoman leadership from the disastrous decision to enter the war on the losing side, Talaat has accused the Entente of boxing Turkey into a corner by turning their backs on the Ottomans prior to the war; what could have underscored this accusation better than a blatant Russian rebuff of a desperate Ottoman plea for alliance? Yet rather than making this concrete accusation, Talaat himself states in his memoirs that the Ottoman leadership was *already* overwhelmingly pro-German at the time of the Balkan wars (that is, more than a year before the bizarre overture to Russia), and that it had *already* made an abortive bid for an Ottoman-German alliance months earlier. This, in turn, casts Talaat's move in a different light: in this scenario his overture to Russia is seen as a shrewd attempt to kindle German and Austro-Hungarian apprehensions over Turkey's future course, so as to enhance its strategic and political value in their eyes. Indeed, the Austrian ambassador to Istanbul, Johann Margrave von Pallavicini, was sufficiently aggravated by the visit to ring the alarm bells in Vienna of Turkey's imminent fall into Russia's lap.

As for the alleged overture to France, there is no evidence whatsoever that it was ever made, and the only mention of its existence is in Djemal Pasha's memoirs. In Djemal's account, during his meeting with Pierre de Margerie, the director of political and commercial affairs in the French Foreign Ministry, he offered his interlocutor a straightforward *quid pro quo:* support for the Ottoman demand for the Aegean Islands in return for Turkey's incorporation into the Entente, which was shrewdly presented as benefiting the Entente far more than Turkey:

> The Ottoman Government says to itself: "The object of the policy of France and England is to forge an iron ring around the Central Powers." That ring is closed except in the south-west . . . If you want to close your iron ring once and for all, you must try to find some solution of this question of the islands between us and the Greeks. You must take us into your Entente and at the same time protect us against the terrible perils threatening us from Russia. If you support us in our upward striving, you will soon have a very faithful ally in the East![6]

Djemal claims to have received a noncommittal response from de Margerie, who promised to forward the proposal to the other members of the Entente yet seriously doubted whether they would lend their support to the idea. This "convinced" Djemal and his colleagues of the Entente's unreliability and paved the way for the Ottoman-German secret agreement of August 2.

Interestingly enough, de Margerie's report of the meeting makes no mention whatsoever of the alleged alliance proposal. De Margerie makes some general observations about Djemal's reference to the need for Turkey "to orient its policy toward the Triple Entente" and to reach a rapprochement with both the Balkan states and the Entente (something which de Margerie did by no means discourage), but these did not amount to an alliance proposal. Far from it. De Margerie's report leaves no doubt that Djemal's primary, indeed exclusive, concern throughout the meeting was the restoration of the Aegean Islands to the Ottoman Empire, not the extraction of an alliance. There was nothing in Djemal's demeanor remotely reminiscent of the hubris surrounding Ottoman indispensability for the encirclement of Germany, presented in his memoirs. Instead, Djemal went out of his way to reassure his interlocutor of Turkey's genuine interest in the peaceful resolution of the islands question and of the attendant gains of such a development for the Entente, namely, the creation of a Balkan coalition well disposed to the Entente.[7]

Djemal's memoirs were written in the wake of the First World War and the collapse of the Ottoman Empire with the clear aim of exonerating himself from responsibility for this calamity. It was with this goal in mind that he generated the claim of an alliance proposal. Furthermore, even in Djemal's own account the visit was initiated by the French before the Sarajevo assassination, when the specter of a European war did not loom large. It was conceived as a goodwill visit by the Ottoman minister of the navy to view the naval maneuvers of the Fourteenth-of-July celebrations, with no specific objective in mind beyond the demonstration of Ottoman-French affinity. Had the French deemed the visit to be of any practical value, Djemal would have been given an audience with René Viviani, the French premier and foreign minister, rather than with de Margerie.

All this means that by the outbreak of the First World War the Ottoman Empire was scarcely the rejected and isolated international player it is commonly taken to be. Rather, it was in the enviable position of being courted by the two warring camps—one wishing its participation in the war (the Central Powers), the other desiring its neutrality (the Triple Entente). The fact that an alliance with the Entente had never been given serious consideration by the Porte, at least not by those who mattered most—Enver, Talaat, and their close associates—was not for want of options. Apart from their admiration for Germany and their conviction that it would ultimately be victorious, the Entente had less to offer by way of satisfying this group's imperialist ambitions: even the allure of Egypt was secondary to Enver's designs on Russia and the Balkans.

Hence, the outbreak of the war gave rise to a cat-and-mouse game between the Ottoman Empire and the Entente Powers. Though effectively a belligerent by virtue of its secret treaty with Germany, the Ottoman Empire pretended neutrality, while steadily bracing itself for war. To the Entente, neutrality seemed the natural and preferable course of action; by staying out of trouble, the Sick Man of Europe could well prolong his precarious existence, while sparing them the headache of diverting their energies to a secondary, if potentially marshy, arena. They wanted the Ottomans to remain neutral and were willing to ignore growing evidence that they were anything but, and none more so than their three ambassadors to the Porte: Mikhail Nikolaevich de Giers of Russia, Sir Louis Mallet of Britain, and Maurice Bompard of France.

Even when they learned of the existence of an Ottoman-German agreement, within a week of its signature, the Entente Powers continued to delude themselves: they not only failed to explore the real essence of this alliance or exploit it as a *casus belli,* but also acted as if it did not exist and as if Ottoman neutrality could be indefinitely secured for the right price.

The Ottomans did not fail to exploit this self-delusion. On August 3, a day after personally signing the secret alliance treaty with Germany, Grand Vizier Said Halim assured Ambassador Giers and British Charge d'Affaires Henry Beaumont (Mallet was on vacation in England) of Turkey's strict neutrality. He presented the mobilization as primarily motivated by fear of a surprise Bulgarian attack: actually, with German help, Turkey and Bulgaria were frantically negotiating a secret alliance treaty, which was signed three days later, on August 6, by Talaat and the Bulgarian prime minister, Vasil Radoslavow. As for the presence of German military advisers in the Ottoman army, Said Halim was dismissive: "Retention of the German military mission meant nothing and had no political significance. He regarded them as Turkish employés who were doing good work, and, as they had offered to remain, it would have been ungracious to refuse."[8] This was yet another lie: it was Turkey, rather than Germany, which insisted that the mission remain on Ottoman soil in the event of war.

Similar reassurances were passed on by the Ottoman ambassador in

London, Tewfiq Pasha, to Foreign Minister Grey, and by Enver himself to Ambassador Giers. The Entente need not fear Germany's influence in Constantinople, the minister of war claimed: "Turkey only follows her own interests."[9]

This was not the end of Enver's deception. On August 5 he approached the Russian military attaché in Istanbul, General Leontiev, with a staggering proposal: the Ottoman Empire was prepared to enter into a military alliance with Russia, committing Ottoman forces to the Russian war effort in return for the restoration of the Aegean Islands and Western Thrace to Ottoman control.

The proposal was clearly bogus. Apart from providing a handy cover-up for the concentration of Ottoman forces in Thrace, in accordance with Enver's agreement with Liman von Sanders, it was made with the full knowledge of the German embassy in Istanbul and with the close cooperation of the Bulgarians, who were a day away from an alliance with Turkey against the pro-Entente Balkan states. Indeed, on the same day that Enver saw Leontiev, the Bulgarian ambassador to Istanbul played his own game of deception with Giers. "The moment has come for Bulgaria to return to the Russian orbit of influence and join with the other Balkan states," he claimed, "but we want guarantees that we will not be attacked by Turkey." To underscore the sincerity of the alleged Bulgarian fears of Turkey, the ambassador made "a rather transparent allusion" to the existence of an Ottoman-German "understanding" directed against Russia.

Giers was duly impressed. He suspected that Turkey and Bulgaria had been discussing possible collaboration with Germany and Austria. He even recognized that an Ottoman-German understanding might have been reached, though he deemed it to be of no immediate import owing to the poor operational state of the Ottoman army. Yet he remained totally unaware of the real essence of the Ottoman-German secret alliance or of the imminent Ottoman-Bulgarian treaty. In his view, Turkey and Bulgaria were free agents, seeking to strike the best possible deal, and it was in Russia's best interest to prevent them from drifting into the German orbit.[10]

Sazonov agreed with the ambassador's diagnosis, but not with his prognosis. He felt that the Ottomans' military weakness would prevent them from entertaining any expansionist thoughts, which, in turn, would give Russia wide latitude in its dealings with Constantinople. When on August 9 Giers reiterated his plea for an immediate deal with

Turkey following yet another phony overture by Enver, Sazonov instructed him to keep the Ottoman option open while discouraging the Turks from intervening: "While maintaining the friendliest tone with the Turks, try to convince them that actions on their part which do not receive our sanction will jeopardize all of Asia Minor, whose existence we, in alliance with France and England, hold in our hands, while they are not in a position to harm us."[11]

Two days later Sazonov was far more alarmed. The Entente Powers were wholly unprepared for the entry of the *Goeben* and the *Breslau* into the Bosphorus. Unaware that it was the Ottomans who were actually calling the shots, they misinterpreted this development as reflecting Germany's growing domination over the Ottoman Empire, which was bound to implicate the Turks in the Great War. Needless to say, the Ottomans made no effort to disabuse the Entente of this misperception but rather capitalized on these fears to divert attention from their own imperialist agenda and to harness the Entente's sympathy to their cause: since Turkey was the harmless underdog, bullied by Germany to forsake its strict neutrality, it was to be helped out of the German's embrace, not leaned upon.

The front man in this campaign of disinformation, admirably orchestrated by Enver, was Grand Vizier Said Halim, whose sincerity was generally taken for granted by the Entente's ambassadors to Istanbul. Different tunes were sung to different ears. To the British and the French the Ottomans complained of Russia's imminent aggression; to the Russians they sustained their false interest in an alliance. As late as mid-August Enver was laying down his conditions for such an alliance, including the cession of Western Thrace and the Aegean Islands to Turkey, as well as Russian commitment to fight any Balkan state that would take on Turkey, not least Bulgaria.[12]

Coming at a time when the Ottoman Empire had successfully blackmailed Germany into accepting its territorial designs on Russia, secretly aligned itself with Bulgaria against other Balkan states, incorporated the *Goeben* and the *Breslau*, with their German crews, into the Ottoman fleet, and removed Admiral Limpus and his mission from their positions in the Ottoman navy, these proposals were nothing short of an elaborate smoke screen. And yet the Entente, though vaguely aware of the existence of Ottoman-German and Ottoman-Bulgarian understandings, would not read the writing on the wall. Rather, they stubbornly subscribed to the misperception of Turkey as a hapless victim that could still be extricated from the claws of the Germans.

On August 15 Sazonov conveyed his ideas to London and Paris. Were the Ottoman Empire to abide by its declared neutrality and commence military demobilization as proof of its sincerity, the Entente would guarantee its integrity and ensure that the peace treaty would give the Ottomans possession of all German concessions in Asia Minor. The following day, having heard of Enver's latest conditions for an alliance, Sazonov agreed to raise the reward still higher and to restore Lemnos Island, just opposite the straits, to Ottoman control. The British and the French ambassadors to St. Petersburg were asked to canvass their governments for a tripartite declaration that would guarantee Ottoman integrity and its "economic emancipation from Germany," provided that the Turks "engaged to adopt [a] strictly neutral attitude during the war."[13]

This is indeed what happened. Both Britain and France were amenable to the preservation of the Ottoman Empire, and were even willing to consider certain concessions to the Ottomans in the Aegean Islands, though not in a way "that meant injury to Greece." As early as August 7, Grey had disavowed any intention of "injuring Turkey," emphatically denying Ottoman allegations of a British plan to alter the status of Egypt. When a week later Churchill sent a personal letter to Enver to warn him of the folly of allying with Germany, Grey inserted an unequivocal reassurance: "If Turkey remains loyal to her neutrality, a solemn agreement to respect the integrity of the Turkish Empire must be a condition of any terms of peace that affect the near East."[14] Now that Sazonov had suggested a tripartite declaration to the same effect, Grey gave his immediate consent. "As soon as French and Russian Ambassadors are similarly instructed," he wrote to Beaumont on August 16, "you are authorised to declare to [the] Turkish Government that if Turkey will observe scrupulous neutrality during the war[,] England, France, and Russia will uphold her independence and integrity against any enemies that may wish to utilise the general European complication in order to attack her." Two days later, he reassured the Ottoman ambassador to London, Tewfiq Pasha, that his empire's territorial integrity "would be preserved in any conditions of peace which affected the Near East, provided that she preserved a real neutrality during the war." On the same day, August 18, Ambassadors Mallet, Giers, and Bompard gave Said Halim the tripartite guarantee of Ottoman territorial integrity in return for Ottoman neutrality. Five days later, at the request of the grand vizier and Djavid Bey, the Triple Entente put this pledge in writing.[15]

The significance of this proposal cannot be overstated. The Entente Powers effectively offered the Ottoman Empire a defense pact—and at no price at all. True, they were unwilling to accommodate Ottoman expansionist ambitions, but then they asked nothing of the Turks beyond their staying out of the war; and they were prepared to reward this neutrality with the ultimate prize: imperial survival. And this was not all; there were additional gains being offered, to which the Young Turks attached great importance, most notably revision of the Capitulations regime. When on August 19 Djavid Bey urged the Entente to support the abolition of the Capitulations, the response was rather sympathetic. Sazonov agreed to examine the issue, suggesting the establishment of an Anglo-French commission to prepare a scheme of judicial and prison reforms; Russia would go along with whatever recommendation the commission made. Similarly, Grey instructed Mallet to inform the Ottoman government that, in return for certain indications of its neutrality, such as the repatriation of the German crews of the two cruisers, the Entente would agree "with regard to the Capitulations, to withdraw their extra-territorial jurisdiction as soon as a scheme of judicial administration, which will satisfy modern conditions, is set up."[16]

Since the Ottoman leadership had no real interest in an alliance with the Entente, having already made their deal with Germany, they made no effort to seize the rope thrown to them. Instead, they continued their policy of speaking peace while laying the groundwork for war. This was an increasingly difficult task, as the expanding magnitude of Ottoman war preparations did not evade the Entente's eyes. Yet the Ottomans unflinchingly denied all accusations of misconduct.

The most vivid demonstration of such duplicity was afforded, perhaps, by the question of the *Goeben* and the *Breslau*. The incorporation of the two German-manned warships—which retained their position in the German Imperial Navy—into the Ottoman navy made a mockery of the idea of neutrality and gave the Entente a clear *casus belli*, had they actually wished to attack Turkey. Yet the Ottomans never strayed from the lie that the ships had been properly purchased and that their German crews would be leaving any minute. The Allies, for their part, were prepared to give them the benefit of the doubt.

With Britain the Ottomans even found a handy guilt button that they never tired of pressing: the Admiralty's requisitioning of the two dreadnoughts on August 3. The purchase of the *Goeben* and the *Breslau* was a result of Britain's detention of the *Sultan Osman,* the grand vizier told Beaumont on the day of the bogus sale. Turkey needed the cruisers as a bargaining chip in the negotiations over the Aegean Islands, and their purchase was in no way directed against Russia. A week later, on August 18, Said Halim reiterated this lie, and in a more forceful manner, to Ambassador Mallet, who had meanwhile returned from his vacation in England. He argued that "seizure of Turkish ships building in England by His Majesty's Government had caused the whole crisis," adding that,

> as almost every Turkish subject had subscribed towards their purchase, a terrible impression had been made throughout Turkey, where British attitude had been attributed to [an] intention to assist Greece in aggressive designs against Turkey. [The] Turkish population would have understood if Great Britain had paid for the ships, or if she had promised to return them when the war was over; but as it was it looked like robbery.

On the same day Mallet heard the same story from Enver. Public hostility toward Britain would be halted immediately, the minister of war promised, if the British government declared that it would eventually return the requisitioned ships and pay an indemnity for their seizure.[17]

These complaints were fantastically untrue. The Bank of England had already refunded the Ottoman down-payment on the ships (worth some £648,000) on August 7, and the British government had promised due compensation for the loss of the ships upon their requisition, but these facts were concealed from the Ottoman public by their own government.

Yet the British were willing to give Enver and Said Halim what they wanted in order to keep the Ottoman Empire out of the war. "I deeply regretted [the] necessity for detaining Turkish ships because I knew the patriotism with which the money had been raised all over Turkey," Churchill wrote to Enver on August 19:

> As a soldier you know what military necessity compels in war. I am willing to propose to His Majesty's Government the following arrangement:
> (1) Both ships to be delivered to Turkey at the end of the war after

being thoroughly repaired at our expense in British Dockyards; (2) if either is sunk we will pay the full value to Turkey immediately on the declaration of peace; (3) we will also pay at once the actual extra expense caused to Turkey by sending out crews and other incidentals as determined by an arbitrator; (4) as a compensation to Turkey for the delay in getting the ships we will pay £1,000 a day in weekly instalments for every day we keep them, dating retrospectively from when we took them over.[18]

Had the Ottomans really been interested in recompense for their ships, they could have readily accepted this offer (which was also conveyed to Djemal Pasha and Said Halim). All that was asked of them in return was to observe a strict neutrality and to remove the German crews of the *Goeben* and the *Breslau* from their territory—something the Ottoman government had pretended to desire in the first place. But this was not to happen. The British had unwittingly called the Ottoman bluff. Enver would not accept Churchill's message, making himself unavailable to the British ambassador under the guise of a diplomatic illness; and when the Ottoman crews who were to have manned the two requisitioned ships arrived in Istanbul on August 22, he used the occasion to turn public opinion against Britain.

This was a double blow to Britain: until then the Ottomans had feigned a lack of adequate replacements as a means to retain the German crews, but they claimed that once the Ottoman officers and men from England arrived they would be dismissed. Still the British were willing to turn the other cheek. On August 25, Grey instructed Mallet to pass a personal message from King George V to the sultan, expressing "deep regret at the sorrow caused to the Turkish people by the detention of the two warships" and promising to "restore them to the Ottoman Government at the end of the war, in the event of the maintenance of a strict neutrality by Turkey without favour to the King's enemies."[19]

This royal pledge had no impact whatsoever. The Ottomans continued to criticize Britain's refusal to compensate them for the ships, while the Germans not only showed no sign of removing their crews from Turkey but also poured in fresh reinforcements, together with consignments of weapons and ammunition. On August 23, Mallet reported the arrival of twenty-eight German officers in Turkey; three days later another ninety German sailors passed through Sofia on their way to Istanbul, to be followed on August 28 by a five hundred–strong German contingent; most of these troops were deployed in fortifications along the Dardanelles. Reports from Cairo told of subversive Ottoman activities in India, Yemen, Libya, and Egypt, and of military deployments in an apparent intention to attack Egypt in the event of war.[20]

By September there were nagging doubts in the Allied chancelleries regarding Turkey's ability to stay its course. Military circles in Russia viewed the Ottoman mobilization as geared toward war, and they demanded adequate preparations to meet this threat. Several British ministers, notably Winston Churchill and the chancellor of the Exchequer, David Lloyd George, maintained that the Ottoman Empire was about to join the Central Powers and that the Entente should work toward establishing a Balkan League that would not only contain Turkey but also move against Austria-Hungary. On September 2, the British cabinet decided to extend financial aid to both Romania and Serbia, and "to sink Turkish ships if they issue from the Dardanelles." The following day the British decided that the two Indian divisions, then on their way to Europe, would be held for a few days in Egypt "as a warning to the Turks to keep quiet."[21]

These moves, nevertheless, signaled no general shift of strategy. The overriding concern of Prime Minister Herbert Asquith, Foreign Secretary Grey, and the minister of war, Lord Horatio Herbert Kitchener, remained unchanged: to keep the Ottoman Empire out of the war. Even those who advocated a harsher line did so primarily out of the conviction that "a kind word and a gun" would carry more weight with the Porte than "just a kind word." The Russians were even less keen than the British to see a slide toward war, as Sazonov repeatedly informed his allies and the Ottomans; early in September he responded negatively to a British inquiry about whether Russia would join in an attack on Turkey. As for the French, having just checked the German advance on Paris, they were as keen as ever to keep Turkey out of the war.

The hope that Turkey might remain neutral was reinforced by the encouraging messages of the Entente's ambassadors to Istanbul. They did not shy away from warning the Ottomans, at times in the most uncompromising language, of the folly of their joining the war. Nor were they blind to the gathering storm over the Ottoman horizon.[22] Yet, on the whole, the three ambassadors judged the situation as anything but hopeless and urged their governments to "go on as long as possible without provoking a rupture." When at the end of August the *Goeben* seemed poised to enter the Black Sea, the ambassadors advised the Entente not to act against Turkey, "as time is on our side." Early in September they were still willing to hear the reassurances of Halim, Djemal, and Djavid that "nothing will induce them to side actively with either belligerent and that they will not go to war with anyone." Even Enver's pledge that he was "determined not to go to war" was not dismissed out of hand. The general feeling among the Entente Powers was that the situation was improving and that "a current has set in" against any Ottoman adventure.[23]

This hopefulness was vividly illustrated by the Entente's response to the Ottomans' unilateral abolition of the Capitulations. Though aware for quite some time of Istanbul's intention to make this move, and well disposed toward revising the Capitulations regime, the Entente Powers were caught off guard by the Ottomans' September 9 announcement of the imminent abolition. So was Germany, despite its recent secret pledge to support such action. In an extraordinary move all great-power ambassadors to Istanbul, including the German and the Austro-Hungarian, addressed identical notes to the Sublime Porte disputing the legality of the Ottoman decision and threatening that "in the absence of [an] understanding arrived at before 1st October [when the abolition was to take effect] between [the] Ottoman Government and our respective Governments, we cannot recognise executory force after that date of a unilateral decision of [the] Sublime Porte."

This left the door open to a mutually agreed upon formula for reforming the Capitulations, which the Entente was eager to arrange. "Principal card in the hands of peace party is abolition of Capitulations, but they are realising great difficulties in the way of abolition of judicial Capitulations, and would be ready to defer discussion of that question if they could obtain immediately consent of the three Powers for abolition of fiscal and commercial treaties," Mallet reported on September 15. "My French and Russian colleagues are pressing me to join them at once in agreeing to this, and I concur with them in thinking that we should no longer delay. If we hesitate peace party will lose their influence and their heads, and throw in their lot with extremists."

The following day he received the green light from London. "I am disposed to point out to the Turks that, if they maintain neutrality, what we have already said to them holds good, and we shall be prepared to consider reasonable concessions about Capitulations," Grey wrote, "but that their conduct with regard to the German officers and crews is most irregular, and they must not expect concessions from us while this continues." Similar messages were dispatched from St. Petersburg and Paris to ambassadors Giers and Bompard.

Even when the Ottomans rendered the question wholly academic by effecting the abolition of the Capitulations on October 1, as initially planned, the Entente Powers did precious little. Indeed, as late as October 9, Grey was still willing to offer the Ottoman Empire a compromise, including full most-favored-nation status on a mutual basis, acceptance of a "commercial treaty on modern lines to remain in force for at least fifteen years," and "specific customs tariff equivalent on average to 15 percent *ad valorem,* duty on no single article to exceed 25 percent *ad valorem.* "[24]

This deference was all the more extraordinary given that by this time the Ottoman Empire had taken several critical steps closer to war: on September 20, at long last, the German cruisers entered the Black Sea, and four days later Rear-Admiral Wilhelm Souchon, commander of the German Mediterranean squadron, was appointed the commander of the Ottoman navy. On September 27, the Ottomans closed the straits to international shipping in violation of the 1841 treaty regulating navigation in this waterway. Russia lost its only ice-free link with the West, and could only be supplied through the lengthy and dangerous northern route to Archangel.

Still the Allies continued their indulgence. Giers viewed the entry of the German ships into the Black Sea with stoic indifference, as if it were not his own country that stood to be attacked by these ships: he expressed confidence that no incident would ensue and proposed to ignore the whole thing. Mallet was more wary, but only slightly so. On September 16, he had received the strongest assurances to date from both Said Halim and Talaat that they had no intention of sending the *Goeben* into the Black Sea, and three days later he heard the same message from Halil Bey. Yet when the hollowness of these pledges became apparent within days, Mallet refused to see the Ottomans' subterfuge for what it was, viewing this episode as reflecting the cabinet's lack of control over "the minister of war and the Germans." Grey was willing to go along with this:

> We do not want to precipitate a conflict with Turkey and are not contemplating a hostile act by our fleet against her. But the Turkish Government must not suppose that because we have not taken any

hostile action against Turkey we regard her present attitude as consistent with obligations of neutrality . . . Constantinople is in fact under German control. We have ample ground, if we desired, for protesting against the present state of things as [a] violation of neutrality; in the hope that the peace party will get the upper hand we have not hitherto taken action, but the Grand Vizier should realise that his party must succeed soon in controlling the situation and bringing it within the limits of neutrality.[25]

The Ottomans were unimpressed. On September 27 they closed the straits and blamed Britain for their action. Earlier that day a British squadron, lying outside the Dardanelles since the arrival of the two German cruisers in early August, had stopped and turned back an Ottoman destroyer venturing out of the straits. This, the grand vizier told the three ambassadors, gave rise to fears of an imminent British attack and caused the abrupt closure of the straits. He reassured Mallet that the Turkish government "would never make war upon Great Britain," and claimed that "if His Majesty's Government will move the fleet a little further from the entrance to the Dardanelles, the Straits will be reopened."

Grey was prepared to give the Ottomans the benefit of the doubt. "It is the Germans who keep the Straits closed, to the great detriment of Turkey," he cabled Mallet. "If you concur, you may point out to the Turks that the British fleet will move away as soon as the German officers and crews leave and the Turkish navy ceases to be under German control. We should then have no fear of hostile action on the part of the Turks."[26]

This stance was still based on the general misperception, shared by the three ambassadors and their respective governments since the outbreak of the Great War, that the Ottoman Empire was a hapless captive of German machinations, and was therefore to be offered a helping hand out of its undesired entanglement. Even at this advanced stage of the crisis, despite the abundant evidence to the contrary, the Entente Powers could not bring themselves to acknowledge the imperialist aspirations of the leading group in Istanbul. They were increasingly aware that the "Turks are possibly less blind to their interests than is generally supposed," and that they were possibly exploiting the situation to extract the maximum gains from Germany, but they misinterpreted these facts as reinforcing Ottoman reluctance "to go all lengths with Germany." The Entente also occasionally caught glimpses of the Ottoman mindset: following a meeting with Enver on October 5, for example, the British military attaché concluded that "his Excellency had ambitious schemes in the Arab world and in Egypt"; yet the Entente continued to underestimate Enver's real influence and to believe that it was the Germans who masterminded most of Turkey's more militant moves, such as the closure of the straits and anti-British incitement among Arabs and Muslims. Thus they saw the situation as far rosier than it actually was, allowing Enver and his associates to continue their game of deception, and sustaining the hope, punctured by recurrent fears, that given the necessary support and barring Allied mistakes, the "peace camp" would eventually carry the day.[27]

As late as mid-October 1914, Mallet estimated that it was the Germans who were behind the increasingly threatening Ottoman military posture vis-à-vis Egypt, and that "probably [the] Government as a whole have little control over these activities, but do not disapprove of them." Enver was still mistaken for a "willing tool of [the] Germans," and Talaat for a strong opponent of war.[28] The truth was, of course, precisely the opposite. By that time Enver and Talaat had already reached the point of no return in their imperialist odyssey, having promised Germany that they would initiate hostilities the moment a large consignment of German gold arrived in Istanbul to shore up the fledgling Ottoman economy against the effects of war.

The Entente Powers got wind of this shipment on October 16, as part of it crossed Bulgaria en route to Istanbul, and a week later they were already aware of its real magnitude. The Russians were the first to grasp the detrimental implications of this German enterprise. On October 20, Sazonov told Britain that he expected an Ottoman declaration of war within a few days; Giers assessed that unless Turkey planned a last-minute betrayal of Germany, the possibility of which he could not completely exclude, it would wage war on Russia on receipt of the first half of the T£4 million worth of German gold.[29]

Mallet was far more sanguine. "Danger of attack on Russian Black Sea fleet is not perhaps so great as my Russian colleague seems to think," he cabled to London on October 23. In his view, Germany had tired of enticing Turkey into an attack on Russia and had subsequently turned its attention to Egypt and to the incitement of Ottoman religious fanaticism against Britain. But even in this arena Germany's success was far from assured:

I do not expect that they will make regular war but we shall have raids and attempts on the part of Turks and Germans to create trouble in underhand and perhaps equally dangerous ways. Pamphlet which consul at Beirut reports as likely to be smuggled into Egypt may be one which I have seen here of a religious character and in nature of incitement to Holy War . . . If Egyptian campaign proves a failure, Turks will tire of it.

Grey concurred. Without much ado he instructed Mallet to disabuse the Porte of the notion that a military move against Egypt would in some way be different from an act of war against Russia: violation of the Egyptian frontier would threaten the international Suez Canal, which Britain was "bound to preserve," and would place Turkey "in a state of war with three allied Powers." Should this happen, Grey stated firmly, "it will not be we but Turkey that will have aggressively disturbed the *status quo.*"[30]

Mallet remained hopeful against all odds. "It is clear that an expedition against Egypt is now uppermost in [the] minds of Enver, Talaat, and Djemal, and that they are making every preparation to this end," he cabled to Grey on October 27. "I learn, however, that there is considerable opposition in the Committee, where the majority are said to be opposed to war. I cannot vouch for the accuracy of this news, but it seems to be fairly authentic." Shortly afterward he was even more confident. "It is now clear that, with [the] exception of [the] Minister of War, [the] Turkish Government are seeking to temporize," he began yet another telegram underscoring Enver's isolation within the Ottoman leadership and the opposition of such leading figures as Talaat and Halil to war, at least not before the spring of 1915. At the end of the telegram he noted, as if for the record, that the Ottoman-German fleet "has, in point of fact, today gone into [the] Black Sea, so it is impossible to forestall what is in store." Yet he did not seem to trust his own judgment. On October 29, the very day that Ottoman and German warships attacked Russia, Mallet assessed that "the Turks wish to gain time with the Germans, and we may succeed in spinning out the situation for some months."

Grey was no more aware than his ambassador of the imminent explosion. At a time when the Ottoman fleet was about to attack Russian ports in the Black Sea, and when some two thousand armed bedouins had crossed the Egyptian frontier and begun advancing toward the Suez Canal, the foreign minister was troubled by reports on the impending movement of four Ottoman gunboats from the Mediterranean port of Alexandretta. "You should warn Turkish Government," he instructed Mallet on October 28, "that, as long as German officers remain on *Goeben* and *Breslau* and Turkish fleet is practically under German control, we must regard movement of Turkish ships as having a hostile intention, and, should Turkish gunboats proceed to sea, we must in self-defence stop them."

He was looking in the wrong direction. As the *Goeben* and Ottoman gunboats attacked Russia's Black Sea ports, the unwitting Mallet was protesting to the grand vizier over the bedouin incursion into Egypt. Even at this late stage Said Halim feigned innocence, claiming to have instructed the minister of war that on no account should he allow the movement of any forces across the frontier: "If it were true, he would give immediate orders for recall of Bedouins, but he did not believe [the] accuracy of the information."[31]

The Ottoman attack on Russia, which the Entente (with the partial exception of St. Petersburg) had so miserably failed to predict despite the numerous warning signs, ended at a stroke months of self-delusion and wishful thinking. War in the Middle East was inevitable—or was it?

The Entente *still* hoped that war was avoidable. Although the incident was a blatant act of aggression that could have constituted a perfectly legitimate *casus belli* against the Ottoman Empire, the Entente kept its cool. Repudiating the absurd Ottoman apology, in which the Turks blamed Russia for the attack and offered to settle the manner amicably, Sazonov gave the Porte one last chance to avert war: the immediate dismissal of all German military officers in the Ottoman army and navy. London and Paris followed suit. The hopeful Mallet pleaded with his superiors to exercise the utmost restraint, for there was still a chance that the anti-German faction within the Ottoman government would prevail. But he was instructed by Grey to warn the Porte that unless the Turks promised within twelve hours to divest themselves "of all responsibility for these unprovoked acts of hostility by dismissing the German military and naval missions, and fulfilling their often repeated promises about the German crews of the *Goeben* and [the] *Breslau*," he would have to ask for his passport and leave Istanbul with the staff of the embassy.[32]

The Entente was asking for the impossible. The Porte had attacked

Russia not with the intention of averting war but rather in the hope of triggering it. For months Enver and his powerful group had been patiently preparing the Ottoman Empire for what they saw as a historic chance to reach new imperial vistas, and they were not going to let this golden opportunity slip from their grasp. On October 31 Giers left Istanbul, to be followed a day later by Mallet and Bompard. On November 3, on Churchill's instructions, British warships, assisted by two French ships, bombarded the outer forts of the Dardanelles. A day later Russia declared war on the Ottoman Empire, and Britain and France soon followed suit. The Entente Powers had been drawn into a war against their will.

9

THE LUST FOR GLORY

*G*reed rather than necessity drove the Ottoman Empire into the First World War. Its war aim was to realize the imperialist vision of the powerful minister of war Enver Pasha: a tangled web of grievances and revanchist hopes geared toward reassertion of Ottoman imperial glory and unification of the Turkic peoples within an expanded empire. This in turn meant the destruction of Russian power, as overtly stated in the Ottoman proclamation of war;[1] the liberation of Egypt and Cyprus from British occupation; and, last but not least, the taming of the Balkan states, especially Greece, and the recovery of Turkey's lost territories in Europe, first and foremost Macedonia and Western Thrace. Military planning envisioned the extension of the Ottoman frontier all the way to the Volga River, and as late as the autumn of 1916, more than two years after the outbreak of the Great War, Ottoman officers in the Levant were still talking openly of an intended march on India via Iran and Afghanistan.[2]

Although Germany constituted the key to Enver's grandiose goals, this by no means made Ottoman strategy hostage to Germany's whims. Just as he had exploited German anxieties in order to extract handsome

returns for entering the war, Enver had no intention of allowing Ottoman dependence on German support to deflect his war aims. High
military policy was decided by him and his colleagues: none of the
German officers exercised authority over Ottoman forces other than that
explicitly delegated to them by Enver; and Liman von Sanders, whom
Enver held in low esteem at best, was even informed that any supplies
from Germany would be distributed by Enver himself—and no one else.

Thus the objective balance of power between the two war allies was
scarcely reflected in the actual relationship between them. Quite the
reverse; in line with their long-standing practice of using their perennial
weakness as a lever for extracting concessions from powerful allies, the
Ottomans exploited their setbacks in the First World War to attract
ever-growing material and economic support from Germany, which for
its part acceded to "all Turkish demands in the hope that when peace
came to be negotiated, the Ottoman Government would voluntarily
[forgo] them."[3]

That the Ottoman Empire was more adept than Germany at using
pressure and manipulation to achieve its goals was evidenced by the
numerous instances in which the former managed to prevail over its
reluctant senior partner. Thus, for example, during the negotiations on
the renewal of the Ottoman-German Treaty of Mutual Alliance in the
autumn of 1917, the Ottomans secured the reiteration and expansion of
the original German war pledges, notably the abolition of the Capitulations system and a commitment both to avoid a separate peace treaty and
to accord the Ottoman Empire vast territorial gains in Thrace, Macedonia, and Transcaucasia. Similarly, when in the summer of 1917 Enver
set out to establish a special 120,000-strong new army, code-named
Yilderim ("Thunderbolt"), the Germans agreed to assign 6,500 of their
own troops to this force, despite their great reluctance to divert any
forces from the main theater of war in Europe. Last but not least, the
Germans resented Enver's foray into Transcaucasia following Russia's
departure from the war in the wake of the October 1917 Revolution.
They were particularly opposed to his encroachments on Georgia, with
which they concluded a political and economic treaty granting them
virtual control of its resources, and to his interference in Iran, which, in
the German view, prevented the perennial anti-British and anti-Russian
sentiments there from developing into a straightforward alliance with
Germany. Despite the Germans' dissatisfaction with Ottoman strategy,

however, all their attempts at influence came to nought, for Enver saw Transcaucasia as the natural preserve for the implementation of his imperial pan-Turanian dream, and he was not about to give it up.

At the outbreak of the war, the Ottoman armed forces consisted of some 600,000 troops, grouped into thirty-eight divisions and three armies. The largest of these, the 250,000-strong First Army, comprising five army corps, was based in the European parts of the empire for the defense of Istanbul and the straits. The Second and Third armies, each 125,000-strong, were deployed respectively along the Asian shore of the Sea of Marmara and in Transcaucasia, along the Russian border. Yet another 100,000 troops, scattered across the empire's Arabic-speaking provinces, were incorporated into a Fourth Army shortly after the outbreak of war and placed under the command of the minister of the navy Djemal Pasha.[4]

Once war was declared, the Suez Canal was earmarked as the primary target for an offensive. However, since the Ottomans were in no position to launch the attack despite their frantic preparations during the last months of 1914, von Sanders proposed an invasion of the Ukraine from Odessa. This, however, was not to the liking of Enver, who hoped to win a rapid victory in Transcaucasia, which was defended by a mere eight Russian divisions. Such a venture would not only satisfy the Ottoman yearning for revenge and recovery of lost territories, particularly the strategic fortress of Kars, but would also open the door to Ottoman incursions into the Russian Caucasus, and possibly the Ukraine or Central Asia. The Turanian dream would receive a vital boost.

For a while Enver's strategy seemed to be well conceived, as the Third Army scored a string of successes. The elated Enver decided that it was time to strike immediately while the Russians were still licking their wounds, and he would personally assume command. Ignoring von Sanders's warning of the merciless winter conditions in Transcaucasia, he packed his bags and hurried to the Third Army's headquarters in Erzerum.

At the end of December, Enver led his men on the offensive near the town of Sarikamish, some sixty miles northeast of Erzerum. He hoped to overwhelm the Russians with a bold strike, but there was no surprise, no rapid advance. The Russians had exploited the lull in the fighting to improve their defenses and reorganize their forces, while the Ottoman troops were not ready for winter. Fought under snowy conditions, the

Battle of Sarikamish turned out disastrous for the Ottomans. The Third Army lost more than 80,000 men within a matter of days: nearly 90 percent of those participating in the fighting. As the Russians crossed the joint border and began advancing on Erzerum, Enver escaped by the skin of his teeth, arriving in Istanbul in early January 1915. Anxious to hide the magnitude of his defeat, he ordered a blackout on news from the front and quickly blamed the debacle on the lack of German support.

While Enver was immersed in his Transcaucasian misadventure, Djemal was charting his own path to glory. A member of the triumvirate who had effectively run the Ottoman Empire since 1913, the minister of the navy resented his transfer from the capital in November 1914 to command the Fourth Army. He was fully aware that this move reduced his powers in comparison with the other two members of the collective leadership, Enver and Talaat, and he used his "geographical sphere of domination" as a springboard for a political comeback. He ruled the Levant as if it were his own personal preserve, often in disregard of the central government's instructions, using Islam as a means to whip up pro-Ottoman sentiments among his largely Arabic-speaking subjects.

Djemal saw the attack on the Suez Canal as a potential personal coup, a golden opportunity to outshine Enver and to regain his central place in the national leadership. He reiterated his determination to die rather than fail "to rescue Egypt, the rightful property of Islam, from the hands of English usurpers"; and he spared no effort to shape the Ottoman units in the Levant and Mesopotamia into a coherent fighting force that would wrest Egypt from Britain. As he told Ambassador Bompard, the Ottoman leadership felt about Egypt as deeply as "the French did about Alsace-Lorraine."[5]

On the night of February 2, 1915, Djemal, at the head of a twelve thousand–strong force, attacked the Suez Canal, only to suffer an ignominious defeat. Not only did the sandstorm on which he had pinned his hopes for a tactical surprise suddenly die down, but Lieutenant General Sir John Maxwell, a guardsman who in September 1914 had taken command of the British forces in Egypt, anticipated the Ottoman attack and deployed his forces accordingly. On February 3, within hours of launching his attack, Djemal had already ordered a general retreat. To cover up his shame, he immediately congratulated his patriotic men for having successfully carried out an "offensive reconnaissance against the Canal." When Djemal's German head of operations, Kress von Kressenstein, asked what happened to his heroic promise to die rather than return empty-handed from Egypt, he was bluntly quieted.[6]

Ironically, the Ottoman setbacks in Transcaucasia and Suez set in motion a chain of events that was to culminate within months in a catastrophic Allied attack on the Dardanelles, thus allowing Enver to redeem his tarnished prestige and to bask momentarily in the glory he so coveted.

For the Entente, the Ottoman entry into the war was an unwelcome expansion of the conflict. However, as fighting on the Western front degenerated into a bloody and futile stalemate, some prominent British policymakers, notably First Lord of the Admiralty Churchill and Secretary of War Kitchener, suggested throwing the Central Powers off balance by striking at their Achilles' heel—"The Sick Man of Europe." By way of achieving this goal the Easterners, as the proponents of a Middle Eastern campaign were dubbed, advanced three possible courses of action:

- a landing in the Gulf of Alexandretta with a view to cutting the railroad between Syria and Anatolia, thus forestalling an Ottoman attack against Egypt and encouraging the Arabic-speaking subjects to break with their suzerain;
- dispatch of a force to Salonika strong enough to bring Greece and Bulgaria into the war on the Entente's side; and, finally,
- an attack on the Dardanelles and the landing of a force to take Istanbul.

Before long the Dardanelles option reigned supreme over the other two. While the Salonika and Alexandretta landings were complex amphibious operations necessitating large numbers of ground forces, the attack on the straits was seen as a predominantly naval gambit requiring only modest ground forces. Also, the French were adamantly opposed to a British landing in the Levant, for fear that this would jeopardize their future position there, while an attack on the Dardanelles generated no such anxieties. Above all, a successful naval attack on Istanbul could deliver the knock-out blow to the Ottoman Empire with all its attendant consequences: diverting significant Russian forces from Transcaucasia to the main theater of war in Europe; securing the logistical naval lifeline between the Western Allies and Russia; curtailing German influence in the Middle East and the Balkans and inducing the uncommitted Balkan states to enter the war on the side of the Entente; and, finally, consolidating Britain's position in Egypt and Mesopotamia.

Enter Enver's Transcaucasian offensive. In an attempt to relieve the Ottoman pressure, on December 27 the Russian commander-in-chief, Grand Duke Nicholas, made a direct appeal to Kitchener for an immediate action against the Ottomans "at their most vulnerable and sensitive point." The secretary of war complied, promising to effect a show of force against the Ottomans, albeit of a minor nature. Had the two allies recognized the real situation on the ground, the entire episode would have been averted altogether; indeed, the Russians withdrew their request within days, having learned of Enver's defeat at Sarikamish. By now, however, the situation had acquired a life of its own. Once committed to helping its ally, the British government saw no reason to renege on its word. Besides, since the failure of Djemal's Suez campaign, Kitchener and some other cabinet members had reached the conclusion that the moment had come to move the ball to the Ottomans' court. Admiral Sir Sackville Carden, the commander of the Aegean fleet, was accordingly ordered to prepare a naval campaign in February 1915 against the Gallipoli Peninsula, on the western tip of the Strait of Dardanelles, with Istanbul as its ultimate objective. On February 19, the admiral launched his attack and four days later occupied the Island of Lemnos, some fifty miles southwest of Gallipoli. But when Carden's successor, Admiral John de Robeck, tried to force the Dardanelles on March 18, he was in for an unpleasant surprise. With German help the Ottomans had thoroughly mined the waterway and mounted heavy artillery on the surrounding hills. In no time six British and French battleships were sunk, forcing de Robeck to effect a hasty withdrawal.[7]

This was a critical mistake whose disastrous consequences would plague Allied war strategy for many months to come. Had de Robeck stayed his course he might have forced the straits, for Ottoman resources had been strained to the extreme. As the admiral was the first to blink, the Ottomans were given a vital breathing space that Enver exploited to the fullest. He quickly brought reinforcements from Syria and deployed them around Istanbul to defend the city against a possible Russian attack, and he formed an entirely new army of six divisions for the defense of the Dardanelles—the Fifth Army—which he placed under the command of Liman von Sanders.

For their part, the Entente Powers had by now been disabused of the idea of knocking the Ottoman Empire out of the war through a naval operation alone. On March 11, General Sir Ian Hamilton, a sixty-two-year-old officer with a distinguished record of service in India, the Sudan, and South Africa, was appointed to command this force, and within a fortnight he had finalized his plan for a combined naval and ground attack on the Gallipoli Peninsula. Though a far cry from the original Dardanelles plan, whose main attraction lay in its operational simplicity and limited scope, Hamilton's plan was approved. On April 24, de Robeck's formidable fleet set to sea and the following day landed large forces on the Gallipoli Peninsula, only to run into unexpectedly tough Ottoman resistance. It was only after several days of fierce fighting and heavy naval bombardments that the Allies managed to establish precarious bridgeheads on the peninsula. All attempts to make further advances broke against the uncompromising Ottoman resistance, with the attacking forces suffering heavy losses; on May 12, the British warships *Goliath,* *Triumph,* and *Majestic* were sunk. On top of this, the scorching summer heat and the poor supply of drinking water exacted a heavy toll on the Allies, with chronic diarrhea and other sickness debilitating their operational capabilities and dampening their morale.

By now Churchill had been made to pay the price of failure and resign his cabinet post, but his strategic vision remained largely intact. Eager to bring the Gallipoli campaign to a swift conclusion, the newly formed Dardanelles Committee decided on June 7 to send three more divisions to the area; six more divisions were to follow shortly. The idea was to deal the Ottoman Empire a *coup de grâce* through a landing in Suvla Bay, on the western side of the peninsula, followed by a rapid advance on the Narrows, the eastern entrance of the Dardanelles, thus opening the door to a naval attack on Istanbul. Instead of being their finest hour, however, Suvla drove the final nail into the Allies' coffin. In five days of fierce fighting, from August 6 to August 10, the Ottomans, under the able leadership of the young and dashing Brigadier Mustafa Kemal, appointed field commander by von Sanders, managed to hold their ground. The Entente sustained 18,000 casualties; another 20,000 sick and wounded had to be evacuated.

A last-ditch attempt by Hamilton to save the day cost the British a further 5,000 casualties and the commander his job. On October 28, Hamilton was replaced by General Sir Charles Munro, who recommended the evacuation of the peninsula. By early 1916 the Entente forces had been withdrawn from Gallipoli.

British casualties in the campaign, including 90,000 evacuated sick, amounted to 205,000, which, with the addition of 47,000 French casualties, brought the Allied total to 252,000, or half the troops sent to Gallipoli, against the officially admitted Ottoman losses of 251,000.[8] Yet despite their heavy casualties, the Ottomans were elated. They had wiped out the ignominy of the Transcaucasian and Suez campaigns; kept the Black Sea closed to Allied navigation; remained poised for a move against either Russia or Egypt; and improved their logistical lifeline to Germany with Bulgaria's entry into the war in mid-October on the side of the Central Powers. And while Mustafa Kemal, and of course Liman von Sanders, were the real heroes of Gallipoli, much of the credit was taken by the CUP leadership, first and foremost by Enver.

Even while the Entente Powers were resigning themselves to the inevitability of disengaging from Gallipoli, they were slouching toward yet another painful setback in Mesopotamia. In a battle near Ctesiphon, twenty miles south of Baghdad, on November 22–23, 1915, the Sixth Anglo-Indian Division under Major General Sir Charles Townshend, a seasoned officer with a distinguished record of service in India and the Sudan, was decimated by a well-entrenched Ottoman force. After sustaining 4,600 casualties, nearly half the division's effective strength, Townshend began withdrawing to the small town of Kut al-Amara, on the Tigris River, which he had occupied the previous month. By the time it arrived in Kut on December 3, there was little left of the Sixth Division as a coherent fighting force.

This is not how things had looked on November 6, 1914, when the Sixth Division first landed in the Shatt al-Arab, the confluence of the Tigris and the Euphrates rivers at the head of the Persian Gulf, shortly after the Ottoman Empire's entry into the war. Easily rebuffing an ill-prepared Ottoman attack, the British Expeditionary Force, under the command of Lieutenant General Sir Arthur Barrett, captured the port town of Basra, Mesopotamia's primary gateway to the Persian Gulf. The town of Qurna, some fifty miles north of Basra, was secured shortly thereafter.

By the spring of 1915, the expeditionary force, or "Force D," as it was known, had expanded to a corps of two divisions and was placed under the command of Lieutenant General Sir John Nixon, an ardent polo player whose impetuosity was matched only by his lust for glory. Viewing his new appointment as a ticket to posterity, especially in light of the disastrous Gallipoli campaign, Nixon set his sights on nothing short of the ultimate Mesopotamian prize: Baghdad; and with the support of Sir

Percy Cox, the chief political officer of the expedition and formerly the resident in the Persian Gulf and secretary of the Foreign Department in India, he managed to win permission for a limited campaign against the town of Amara, seventy miles further up the Tigris. On June 3 Amara fell to Townshend's force, and the elated Nixon immediately sent his second division to occupy Nasiriya, some one hundred miles north of Basra on the Euphrates River. Once the town was captured, on July 25, the entire velayet of Basra had come under British occupation.

In this euphoric atmosphere, Nixon did not find it difficult to secure permission for a continued drive northward, and on September 29, Townshend's Sixth Division entered the town of Kut al-Amara, ninety miles north of Amara and a mere one hundred miles south of Baghdad. By now the magnitude of the Gallipoli debacle was becoming increasingly evident, and Nixon's appetite was insatiably wetted: on October 3, he let it be known that he was perfectly capable of taking Baghdad.

This seemed to many a dangerous overextension that could put the entire Mesopotamian campaign at peril. Yet Nixon's overflowing optimism, buttressed by the eloquence of Cox and Sir Arthur Hirtzel, the political secretary in the India Office in London, carried the day. The capture of Baghdad, they argued, would be a momentous event akin only to the fall of Istanbul; by contrast, halting the campaign at the height of its success would not only be an operational mistake but would mortally injure British prestige in Iran, Afghanistan, and the Arabic-speaking provinces of the Ottoman Empire, already tarnished by the Gallipoli debacle. On October 29, a special interdepartmental committee, headed by Sir Thomas Holderness, the permanent undersecretary of the India Office, approved the drive on Baghdad and the transfer of two Indian divisions from France for that purpose. Three days later Prime Minister Herbert Asquith told Parliament that "General Nixon's force is now within measurable distance of Baghdad. I do not think that in the whole course of the War there has been a series of operations more carefully contrived, more brilliantly conducted, and with a better prospect of final success."[9]

What the euphoric prime minister failed to perceive was that Nixon's forces were hopelessly overextended; that the two divisions, destined to leave Marseilles on December 10, would not be available for action in northern Mesopotamia before the end of the year; that the Baghdad garrison had been reinforced by some twenty thousand Turks, more seasoned fighters than the Arab-based Ottoman units hitherto encountered by Nixon; and that the Ottoman commander defending Baghdad, the forty-two-year-old Nurredin Pasha, was a first-rate warrior with extensive combat experience. The only one who seemed to have grasped the magnitude of the lurking catastrophe was Townshend, but his remonstrations against an immediate advance on Baghdad were unceremoniously brushed aside by Nixon (who later claimed that no such objections had ever been made). Being the professional soldier he was, Townshend kept a stiff upper lip and led his division into battle, only to find his worst fears realized: a crushing defeat and a prolonged and tortuous siege in the town of Kut.[10]

By the time Townshend's forces surrendered to the Ottomans on April 28, 1916, after 143 days of siege, the Mesopotamian campaign had ground to a complete halt. In January Nixon was replaced by Lieutenant General Sir Percy Lake, the chief of the general staff of the Indian army, yet all subsequent attempts to relieve the besieged force failed miserably. As Townshend's men were marched hundreds of miles to Anatolia, where most of them would perish in Ottoman labor camps, the War Cabinet took direct control of the Mesopotamian campaign, subordinated the Indian army to the Imperial War Office, and settled in for a period of stabilization and consolidation.

The Entente's setbacks in Gallipoli and Mesopotamia were bright rays of light in the otherwise cloudy Ottoman horizon. But the main boost to Enver's imperial dream came not from the battlefields of the Middle East but from the earthquake that convulsed Turkey's northern neighbor: the Russian revolutions of 1917. As early as March 1917, after the overthrow of the tsar and the formation of a revolutionary government under Alexander Kerensky, the five hundred thousand–strong Russian army in Transcaucasia went into rapid disintegration. Seven months later, following the Bolsheviks' seizure of power in what came to be known as the October Revolution, Russia left the war and on December 15, 1917, signed an armistice with Germany in the Polish town of Brest-Litovsk. The Ottoman Empire was a direct beneficiary of this agreement, regaining the provinces of Kars, Ardahan, and Batum, lost during the Russo-Ottoman War of 1877–1878.

This was not good enough for Enver. Prior to the Revolution he would have settled for the Transcaucasian status quo, however unfavorable, given the wretched state of the Ottoman forces there. But not anymore. Now that his dream of a vast pan-Turanian empire was becoming a reality at long last, the retrocession of lost territories, a pipe dream only a few months earlier, would not suffice: Turkey had to incorporate the entire Transcaucasian landmass into its empire, up to the Iranian and the Afghan borders. In their negotiations with the "Transcaucasian Federation"—a loose association formed in the wake of the Russian Revolution by the three main ethnic groups in Transcaucasia, the Armenians, the Georgians, and the Azerbaijanis—the Ottoman made demands that went far beyond the territorial limits of Brest-Litovsk. They now included Alexandropol and its environs, the Trans-Georgian Railway, and free use of all Transcaucasian railways for as long as the Ottoman Empire was at war with the Entente. When these onerous terms were declined, the Ottomans overran the Armenian city of Alexandropol and began advancing on the Caspian oil city of Baku. Shortly afterward, on June 4, 1918, the Treaty of Batum was concluded between the Ottoman Empire, on the one hand, and the Georgians, Armenians, and Azerbaijanis on the other. Georgia was permitted to retain the Black Sea port of Batum, while Armenia was to cede significant parts of its territories to the Ottoman Empire.

By now Enver had created his Army of Islam, which comprised volunteers from the newly occupied Transcaucasian territories: Tartars, Azeris, Ajars, and other Transcaucasian Muslims. Commanded by Nuri Pasha, Enver's brother, this force was to operate alongside the regular Ottoman army, its first task being the occupation of Baku. On September 14, after heavy Ottoman shelling, an Anglo-Indian force under Brigadier General Lionel Dunsterville, which had arrived in Baku a few weeks earlier, fled the city to the curses of the local population; so did many Armenians. The next day the Ottomans entered the city and for the next forty-eight hours indulged in an orgy of slaughter and pillage, particularly of the Armenians. In the words of an eyewitness to the horrendous fate befalling this community:

> We heard cries of women and children and we heard single shots. Rushing to their rescue I was obliged to drive the car over the bodies of dead children. The crushing of bones and strange noises of torn bodies followed. The horror of the wheels covered with the intestines of dead bodies could not be endured by the colonel and

the *asker* [adjutant]. They closed their eyes with their hands and lowered their heads. They were afraid to look at the terrible slaughter. Half mad from what [he] saw, the driver sought to leave the street, but was immediately confronted by another bloody hecatomb.[11]

As so often in the past, the price of Ottoman imperialism was paid for by its national minorities.

10

GENOCIDE IN ARMENIA

*T*here is no such thing as an egalitarian empire. The imperial notion, by its very definition, posits the domination of one ethnic or national group over another. This can range from outright repression to "enlightened despotism," but there is never a doubt as to who the master and the subject are; and whenever things fail to go the master's way, there is little doubt who will pay the price.

The fate that befell the Ottoman minorities during the First World War, especially the more nationally aware among them, affords a vivid illustration of this unsavory side of the imperial mindset. Nationalism had long posed the gravest threat to the integrity of the Ottoman Empire and had consequently been met with intense violence on the part of the Turks. It was the struggle for national liberation that squeezed the Ottoman Empire out of its European colonies during the nineteenth and early twentieth centuries in an orgy of bloodletting and mayhem, as the Muslim Empire vied to keep its reluctant subjects under its domination. And it was the lack of a similar national awakening in the empire's Asiatic provinces that accounted for the survival of Turkey-in-Asia and for the lesser violence there. The Young Turks saw the First World War as a golden opportunity to restore lost territories and incorporate new lands and national groups into their empire. When these imperialist dreams were defeated in the snowy mountaintops of Transcaucasia and the sand dunes of Sinai, the newly organized national movements in Turkey-in-Asia, especially the Armenians', had to foot the bill for their suzerain's failures.

By the second half of the nineteenth century, the Armenian population of the Ottoman Empire totaled approximately two million, three-quarters of whom resided in so-called Turkish Armenia, namely, the velayets of Erzerum, Van, Bitlis, Sivas, Kharput, and Diarbekir in Eastern Anatolia. The rest, or about half a million Armenians, were equally distributed in the Istanbul-Eastern Thrace region and in Cilicia, in southwestern Asia Minor.[1] As a result of Russian agitation, European and American missionary work, and, not least, the nationalist revival in the Balkans, a surge of national consciousness within the three Armenian religious communities, Gregorian, Catholic, and Protestant, began to take root. In the 1870s Armenian secret societies sprang up at home and abroad, developing gradually into militant nationalist groups such as the Huntchakian and the Dashnaktsutiun. Uprisings against Ottoman rule erupted time and again; terrorism became a common phenomenon, both against Turks and against noncompliant fellow Armenians. Nationalists pleaded with the European chancelleries to enforce Ottoman compliance with the 1878 Berlin Treaty, which had obliged the Porte to undertake "improvements and reforms demanded by local requirements in the provinces inhabited by the Armenians, and to guarantee their security against the Circassians and Kurds." But the great powers were reluctant to weaken the Ottoman Empire in any way, and Sultan Abdul Hamid made the best of this reluctance. In a brutal campaign of repression in 1895–1896, in which between one hundred thousand and two hundred thousand people perished and thousands more fled to Europe and America, Armenian resistance was crushed and the dwindled population bullied into submission.

But not for long. Armenian nationalism continued to breathe under the embers; visions of Greater Armenia became more liberating than ever. By 1903 a vicious circle of escalating violence was under way yet again, and rebels engaged in dialogues with Ottoman exiles on joint measures to overthrow the sultan. On July 21, 1905, during the Friday prayers, Abdul Hamid narrowly escaped an assassination attempt by a group of nationalists.

With the painful memories of the 1895–1896 massacres fresh in their minds, the Armenians shared the general enthusiasm of the Empire's non-Muslim minorities at the overthrow of Abdul Hamid and the ascendancy of the Young Turks. And like the rest of their non-Muslim counterparts, they were quickly disillusioned with the new regime. As early as the spring of 1909, less than a year after the Young Turks Revolution, thousands of Armenians were massacred in the Cilician city of Adana. Although the authorities disassociated themselves from this atrocity, with Enver even delivering the eulogy for the murdered, a new cycle of massacres soon swept across Ottoman Armenia. At the same time, years of cultural repression attending the CUP's policy of Turkification, including a ban on the public use of the Armenian language, rekindled nationalist sentiments, with the yearning for an independent Armenian state growing ever stronger. These aspirations gained a fresh impetus as a result of the First Balkan War, when the Ottoman Empire was decisively beaten by its former subjects. Bulgarian Armenians formed a volunteer unit to fight the Ottomans, while Russian Armenians urged their government to raise the "Armenian Question" with the Ottoman authorities. Even some Ottoman Armenians were sufficiently enthused to approach the great powers with wild schemes of national liberation. In March 1913, for example, the British consul in Aleppo reported to Ambassador Lowther in Istanbul that certain leading Armenians were toying with the idea of occupying Adana and establishing a small principality there with access to the sea. The scheme was to be implemented by Armenian troops who had fought in the Bulgarian army during the Balkan War. The following month some Armenians asked Britain to occupy Cilicia, from Antalya to Alexandretta, and to internationalize Istanbul and the straits as a means of "repairing the iniquity of the Congress of Berlin." At about the same time, a committee of the Armenian National Assembly, the governing body of the Apostolic Ottoman Christians, submitted to the Russian Embassy in Istanbul an elaborate reform plan for Ottoman Armenia.[2]

The Russians picked up the gauntlet. Styling themselves as champions of the Armenian cause, they demanded that the Turks implement far-reaching reforms in Ottoman Armenia. The crux of these was the unification of the six Armenian velayets into a single province under an Ottoman Christian or European governor, in which each nationality would be allowed cultural and administrative autonomy.

Needless to say, these demands reflected no genuine interest in the

Armenian cause: at a time when Russia was insisting on extensive reforms for the Ottoman Armenians, it was denying its own Armenians those very rights. Indeed, by resurrecting the Armenian Question, the Russians sought to gain the maximum influence in Ottoman Armenia so as to forestall both possible German penetration of Transcaucasia and the region's slide into anarchy. In the words of Foreign Minister Sazonov: "A revolt of the Armenians in the velayets of Asia Minor, bordering upon Transcaucasia, was always possible in view of the intolerable conditions of life there. Such a rising threatened to set fire to our own border provinces."[3]

In the end the Ottoman government accepted a Russo-German proposal, worked out in February 1914, which provided for the creation of two Armenian provinces, one incorporating the Sivas, Erzerum, and Trebizond velayets, and the other the velayets of Van, Bitlis, Kharput, and Diarbekir. Each of the provinces was to be administered by a European inspector-general appointed by the great powers; by May the first two inspectors-general, a Norwegian and a Dutchman, assumed their posts.

This was the situation in Ottoman Armenia at the outbreak of the Great War. The February 1914 reforms had fallen far short of Armenian aspirations, partitioning the region into two separate entities instead of creating a unified province and diluting Armenian proportional strength in these new creations. Yet for all their imperfections they contained the most far-reaching concessions the Armenians had managed to extract from their suzerain, and most of them were eager to preserve these gains come what may. Hence, when the Ottoman Empire entered the war, the Armenians immediately strove to demonstrate their loyalty: prayers for an Ottoman victory were said in churches throughout the empire, and the Armenian patriarch of Istanbul, as well as several nationalist groups, including the Dashnaktsutiun Party, announced their loyalty to the Ottoman Empire and implored the Armenian people to perform their obligations to the best of their ability.

Not all Armenians complied with this wish. In its congress, held in the Romanian town of Constanza shortly before the outbreak of war, the Huntchakian Party vowed to fight the Ottoman Empire. Scores of Ottoman Armenians, including several prominent figures, crossed the border to assist the Russian campaign. Others offered to help the Entente by other means. In February 1915, for example, Armenian revolutionaries in the Cilician city of Zeitun pledged to assist a Russian advance on the area provided that they were given the necessary weapons; to the British they promised help in the event of a naval landing in Alexandretta. The rebels made a similar offer to the British ambassador to Bulgaria, Sir H. Bax-Ironside, in March 1915.[4]

Although these activities were an exception to the otherwise loyal conduct of the Ottoman-Armenian community, they confirmed the standard Ottoman stereotype of the Armenians as a troublesome and treacherous people. These views were further reinforced by Enver's crushing defeat in Sarikamish and the later setback in northern Iran, where an expeditionary force that occupied Iranian Azerbaijan in January 1915 under the command of Halil Pasha, Enver's uncle, was forced out by the Russians several months later. In both instances (non-Ottoman) Armenians were implicated in the Russian war effort, but particularly galling to Enver was the mass participation of Russian Armenians in the Battle of Sarikamish, which dealt a devastating blow to his pan-Turanian dreams. That Enver would not forget.

Not that Enver required a special reminder of the need for a drastic solution to the Armenian Question. As the largest nationally aware minority in Asiatic Turkey, the Armenians were naturally seen as the gravest internal threat to Ottoman imperialism in that domain; and with Turkey-in-Europe a fading memory and Turkey-in-Africa under Anglo-French-Italian domination, the disintegration of Turkey-in-Asia would spell the end of the Ottoman Empire, something that neither Old nor Young Turks would accept.

Before long the Ottoman Armenians were subjected to the ultimate punishment inflicted on rebellious Middle Eastern populations since Assyrian and Babylonian times: deportation and exile. First the Armenians had to be rendered defenseless; then they were to be uprooted from their homes and relocated to concentration camps in the most inhospitable corners of Ottoman Asia. The Armenians' towns and villages would then be populated by Muslim refugees, their property seized by the authorities or plundered by their Muslim neighbors.

Whether or not the Young Turks had a premeditated genocidal master-plan, something that contemporary Ottoman leaders and latter-day Turkish academics would persistently deny, is immaterial. It must have occurred to the Young Turk leadership that the destruction of such a pervasive national movement would inevitably entail suffering on an enormous scale, and that the forceful relocation of almost an entire people to a remote, alien, and hostile environment amid a general war was tantamount to a collective death sentence. In the end, whatever their initial intention, the Ottomans' actions constituted nothing short of genocide.[5]

The first step in this direction was taken shortly after Sarikamish, when the Armenian soldiers in the Ottoman army were relegated to "labor battalions" and stripped of their weapons. Most of these fighters-turned-workers would never get the opportunity to labor for their suzerain: they would be marched out in droves to secluded places and shot in cold blood, often after being forced to dig their own graves. Those fortunate enough to escape summary execution were employed as laborers under the most inhuman conditions.

At the same time, the authorities initiated a ruthless campaign to disarm the entire Armenian population of all personal weapons. This sent a tremor throughout Armenia: the 1895–1896 massacres had been preceded by similar measures, and most Armenians had no illusions regarding the consequences of surrendering their arms while their Muslim neighbors were permitted to retain theirs. Nonetheless, the community's religious and political leaders persuaded their reluctant flock to do precisely that in order to avoid harsh retaliation by the government. But even this was not a simple task. The authorities demanded that the Armenians produce a certain number of weapons regardless of the actual number of arms bearers, thus putting the Armenians between a rock and a hard place: those who could not produce arms were brutally tortured; those who produced them for surrender, by purchase from their Muslim neighbors or by other means, were imprisoned for treachery and similarly tortured; those found to have hidden their arms were given an even harsher treatment.

With the Armenian nation rendered defenseless, the genocidal spree entered its main stage: mass deportations and massacres. Having "cleared" Cilicia of its Armenian population by the autumn of 1915, the authorities turned their sights to the foremost Armenian concentration: the velayets of Eastern Anatolia. First to be "cleared" was the zone bordering on Van, extending from the Black Sea to the Iranian frontier and immediately threatened by Russian advance; only there outright massacres often substituted for slow deaths along the deportation routes or in the concentration camps of the Syrian desert.

The main executioner of this dreadful spree was Djevdet Pasha, the brother-in-law of Enver who, in February 1915, was made governor of

Van. A sadist known throughout Armenia as the "horseshoer of Bashkale" for his favorite pastime of nailing horseshoes to the feet of his victims, Djevdet inaugurated his term in office by slaughtering some eight hundred people—mostly elderly men, women, and children. By April the death toll had already grown to ten thousand, and in the following months the population of the Van zone would be systematically exterminated. In the western and northwestern districts of Ottoman-Armenia, depopulated between July and September, the Turks attempted to preserve a semblance of deportation, though most deportees were summarily executed after starting on their journey. In the coastal towns of Trebizond, for example, the authorities sent Armenians out to sea, ostensibly on deportation, only to throw them overboard shortly afterward. Of the deportees from Erzerum, Erzindjan, and Baibourt, only a handful survived the initial stages of the journey.

The Armenian population in Western Anatolia and in the metropolitan districts of Istanbul was somewhat more fortunate, as many people were transported in (grossly overcrowded) trains for much of the deportation route, rather than having to straggle along by foot. In Istanbul deportations commenced in late April, when hundreds of prominent Armenians were picked up by the police and sent away, most of them never to be seen again; some 5,000 "ordinary" Armenians soon shared their fate. Though the majority of the city's 150,000-strong community escaped deportation, Armenians were squeezed from all public posts, with numerous families reduced to appalling poverty. Deportations at Ankara began toward the end of July; at Broussa, in the first weeks of September; and at Adrianople, in mid-October. By early 1916 scores of deportees, thrown into a string of concentration camps in the Syrian desert and along the Euphrates, were dying by the day of malnutrition and disease; many others were systematically taken out of the camps and shot.[6]

Independent estimates of the precise extent of the Armenian genocide differ somewhat, but all paint a stark picture of a national annihilation of unprecedented proportions. In his official report to the British Parliament in July 1916, Viscount Bryce calculated the total number of uprooted Armenians during the preceding year as 1,200,000 (half slain, half deported), or about two-thirds of the entire community. Johannes Lepsius, the chief of the Protestant Mission in the Ottoman Empire who had personally witnessed the atrocities and had studied them thoroughly, put this total at a higher figure of 1,396,000, as did the American Committee for Armenian and Syrian Relief, which computed the number of deaths at about 600,000 and of deportees at 786,000. And Aaron Aaronsohn, a world-renowned Zionist agronomist who set up the most effective pro-Entente intelligence network in the Middle East during the First World War, estimated the number of deaths between 850,000 and 950,000.[7]

The Ottoman authorities tried to put a shiny gloss of legality on their genocidal actions. The general deportation decree of May 30, 1915, for example, instructed the security forces to protect the deportees against nomadic attacks, to provide them with sufficient food and supplies for their journey, and to compensate them with new property, land, and goods necessary for their resettlement. But this decree was a sham. For one thing, massacres and deportations had already begun prior to its proclamation. For another, the Armenians were never informed of its existence, hence they could not even hypothetically insist on its observance. Above all, as is overwhelmingly borne out by the evidence, given both by numerous first-hand witnesses to the Ottoman atrocities and by survivors, the rights granted by the deportation decree had never been followed.

Take the provisions for adequate supplies for the journey and compensation for the loss of property. After the extermination of the male population of a particular town or village, an act normally preceding deportations, the Turks often extended a "grace period" to the rest of the populace, namely, women, children, and the old and the sick, so they could settle their affairs and prepare for their journey. But the ordinary term given was a bare week, and never more than a fortnight, which was utterly insufficient for all that had to be done. Moreover, the government often carried away its victims before the stated deadline, snatching them without warning from streets, places of employment, or even their beds. Last but not least, the local authorities prevented the deportees from selling their property or their stock under the official fiction that their expulsion was to be only temporary. Even in the rare cases in which Armenians managed to dispose of their property, their Muslim neighbors took advantage of their plight to buy their possessions at a fraction of their real value. Lepsius calculated that one billion German marks' worth of Armenian property had been confiscated by the Ottoman government.[8]

Nor did the deportees receive even a semblance of the protection promised by the deportation decree. On the contrary, from the moment they started on their march, indeed even before they had done so, they became public outcasts, never safe from the most atrocious outrages, constantly mobbed and plundered by the Muslim population as they straggled along, and their guards connived at this brutality. There were of course noteworthy exceptions in which Muslims, including Turks, helped the long-suffering Armenians, but these were very rare, isolated instances and were always rebuffed by the authorities.

Whenever the deportees arrived at a village or a town, they were exhibited like slaves in a public place, often before the Government Building itself. Female slave markets were established in the many ag-glomerations through which the Armenians were driven, and untold thousands of young Armenian women and girls were sold in this way. Even the clerics were quick to avail themselves of the bargains of the white slave market.[9]

Suffering on the deportation routes was intense. Travelers on the Levantine railway saw dogs feeding on the bodies of hundreds of men, women, and children on both sides of the track, with women searching the clothing of the corpses for hidden treasures. In some of the transfer stations, notably Aleppo, the hub where all convoys converged, thou-sands of Armenians would be piled up for weeks outdoors, starving, waiting to be taken away. Epidemics spread rapidly, chiefly spot typhus. In almost all these cases the dead were not buried for days, the reason being, as an Ottoman officer cheerfully explained to an inquisitive foreigner, that the epidemics might get rid of the Armenians once and for all.

Particularly horrific outrages befell the Armenians upon arriving in the mountainous areas of northern Mesopotamia, where they fell prey to gangs of Kurds and "chettis." The former had played a prominent role in the massacres of Armenians in 1895–1896 and were perfectly content to serve their suzerain in this fashion yet again; the latter were hardened criminals released from public prisons on the tacit understanding that they would take care of the Armenians. When these Kurds and chettis waylaid the convoys, the gendarmes fraternized with them and followed their lead. Indeed, the cruelty of the guards toward the deportees in-creased as the latter's physical suffering became more intense: women who lagged behind were bayoneted on the road or pushed over precipices or bridges; when crossing rivers, women and children were driven into the water, and were shot if it seemed likely that they would reach the far bank. The last survivors often straggled into Aleppo naked, every shred of their clothing torn from them on the way. According to eyewitnesses, there was hardly a young face to be found among them, and there was assuredly none surviving that was truly old—except insofar as it had been aged by suffering.

As the deportees settled into their new miserable existence, they were forced to work at hard labor, making roads, opening quarries, and the like, for which they were paid puny salaries that effectively reduced them to starvation. Work in the neighboring villages that could earn them some livelihood was strictly forbidden. Water was normally brought to the camps by trains; no springs were to be found within miles of the camps. The scenes at the arrival of the water trains, by no means a regular phenomenon, were heartbreaking. Thousands of people would rush toward the stopping place, earthenware jars and tin cans in hand, in a desperate bid for their share of this elixir of life. But when at long last the taps were opened, people would often be barred from filling their vessels. In desperation they would have to watch the precious water run onto the sun-baked ground.

II

REPRESSION IN THE HOLY LAND

The Armenian genocide was by far the worst manifestation of Ottoman imperialist frustration, but it was by no means the only one. As an adjunct to their Armenian massacre, for example, the Ottomans disposed of yet another Christian minority: the Assyrians. There was no obvious reason for this specific atrocity, for the tiny Assyrian community of between 100,000 and 150,000 people had never threatened the integrity of the Ottoman Empire the way the Armenians had. Yet the Assyrians were unfortunate enough both to reside on either side of the Ottoman-Iranian border, which made them natural suspects of "dual loyalty," and to be aware of their distinct religious and cultural identity, which made them victims of the xenophobic pan-Turanism of the Young Turks leadership. When the Ottomans captured northern Iran in the early months of 1915, they plundered and killed the Assyrian community there; when they were forced to withdraw several months later, they turned on their own Assyrians.

But whereas the Assyrians suffered for being in the wrong place at the wrong time, the nascent Jewish national revival in Palestine was a hair's breadth from extinction for precisely the same reason that brought about the destruction of the Armenian nation, namely, the unbridgeable gap between the ideal of national self-determination and imperialist mastery.

Ever since Jewish corporate existence in Palestine was dealt a mortal blow by the Roman Empire, exile and dispersion had become the hallmark of Jewish existence. Even in its ancestral homeland the Jewish community was relegated to a small minority under a long succession of foreign occupiers—Byzantines, Arabs, Seljuk Turks, Crusaders, Mamluks, and Ottoman Turks—who inflicted repression and dislocation upon Jewish life. At the time of the Muslim occupation of Palestine in the seventh century, Jews in Jerusalem alone numbered some 200,000; by the 1880s the Jewish community in the whole of Palestine had been reduced to about 24,000, or some 5 percent of the total population, mostly congregated in the holy towns of Jerusalem, Safad, Hebron, and Tiberias. In Jerusalem and Safad they remained a distinct majority.[1]

This forced marginalization notwithstanding, not only was the Jewish presence in Palestine never totally severed, but the Jews' longing for their ancestral homeland, or Zion, occupied a focal place in their collective memory for millennia and became an integral part of Jewish religious ritual. Moreover, Jews began returning to Palestine from the earliest days of dispersion, mostly on an individual basis, but also on a wide communal scale. The expulsion of the Jews from Spain in 1492, for example, brought in its wake a wave of new immigrants; an appreciable influx of Eastern European Hasidim occurred in the late eighteenth century, and of Yemenite Jews a hundred years later.

In the 1880s, however, an altogether different type of immigrant began arriving: the young nationalist who rejected diaspora life and sought to restore Jewish national existence in the historic homeland. Dozens of committees and societies for the settlement of the Land of Israel mushroomed in Russia and Eastern Europe, most notably Hibbat Zion ("Love of Zion"). By 1890 this group comprised some 14,000 members, about one-fifth of whom had already immigrated to Palestine.

A young and dynamic journalist by the name of Theodor Herzl (1860–1904) reinvigorated these humble national beginnings and transformed them into a full-fledged political movement that would come to be known as Zionism. In the influential book *Der Judenstaat* ("The Jewish State: An Attempt at a Modern Solution of the Jewish Question"), published in 1896, Herzl argued that the "Jewish Question" was neither social nor religious but rather national. Antisemitism had existed wherever Jews lived in appreciable numbers and would persist for as long as they continued their minority existence. No matter how hard they tried, Jews would never be allowed to assimilate fully into their respective societies and would always remain an alien minority living on the majority's sufferance. The only solution to this predicament, therefore, was for the Jews to cease their minority existence and become a majority in a state of their own.

Herzl was not the first to argue that the Jews constituted a distinct nation rather than a mere religious community; that exile condemned them to perennial misery and helplessness; and that the reestablishment of Jewish statehood in their ancestral homeland was the only solution to this millenarian predicament. Yet his unique blend of vision, practicality, and missionary zeal rendered Herzl the unquestioned leader of the Jewish national movement and allowed him to insert it, almost single-handedly, into world consciousness. In August 1897 he convened the First Zionist Congress in the Swiss town of Basel, with the participation of some two hundred delegates, a meeting that was to become a milestone in modern Jewish and Middle Eastern history. The congress defined the aim of Zionism as "the creation of a home for the Jewish people in Palestine to be secured by public law" and established institutions for the promotion of that goal. In one fell swoop Zionism was transformed from an embryonic and fragmented movement, beset by conflicting visions and a lack of leadership, into an effective political movement that was to strive tirelessly toward its objective.

To Sultan Abdul Hamid, Zionism was one of the many national movements that threatened his empire, and not the most dangerous one; compared with the nationalist surge in the Balkans or in Armenia, Zionism posed only a remote threat to Ottoman integrity. The sultan even envisaged some potential gains in a Jewish national enterprise: were the Zionists to gain access to the mythologized "world Jewish wealth," they might become a profitable source of income that could help the Ottoman Empire out of its dire financial straits.

These potential advantages notwithstanding, Abdul Hamid subscribed to the conventional view of the place and role of the Jews in the Ottoman order of things, namely, as a tolerated if inferior religious community *(millet)*. To surrender Islamic lands to these subordinate infidels, not to mention the territory where Islam's third holiest city resided, would be tantamount to blasphemy. Besides, though not overly alarmed by Zionism, the sultan had no intention of allowing yet another national group to put down roots in his empire, particularly if this meant a significant increase in the number of foreign subjects. "Why should we accept Jews whom the civilized European nations do not want in their countries and whom they had expelled," he wrote. "It is not expedient to do so, especially at a time when we are dealing with the Armenian subversion."[2]

In line with this stance, the sultan prohibited Jewish immigration to Palestine in the early 1880s, as well as the purchase of land for settlement purposes. These prohibitions, applicable specifically and uniquely to Jews, were constantly updated and revised to close remaining loopholes. And yet, between 1881–1882 and 1900, the Jewish community in Palestine, or the Yishuv, as it is known in Hebrew, had more than doubled, from approximately twenty-four thousand to about fifty thousand, with two-thirds of the rise resulting from immigration.

This discrepancy between policy guidelines and their implementation was due both to Zionist single-mindedness and to the mismanagement and corruption of the Ottoman authorities, who were no more astute at enforcing their own laws in Palestine than in any other part of the empire. But it also underscored Abdul Hamid's reluctance to close the door completely to the Zionist enterprise. When Herzl arrived in Istanbul in June 1896, he was denied an audience with the sultan, yet he was given a royal decoration and was urged to help improve the Ottomans' image in Europe, severely damaged by the Armenian massacres, as well as to obtain a loan of T£2,000,000.

In his meeting with the Zionist leader five years later, Abdul Hamid was in an affable mood. He allowed Herzl to take the lead in the conversation, disputed nothing of what he said, and even asked him to recommend an able financier who could create new resources for the Ottoman Empire. When Herzl offered to use his good offices to help resolve the Ottoman public debt in return for a public proclamation "particularly friendly to the Jews," Abdul Hamid concurred. He had a court jeweler who was a Jew, the sultan said. "He might say to him something favourable about the Jews and instruct him to put it in the papers." This bizarre suggestion was of course a far cry from what Herzl had in mind, and he politely turned it down. "It wouldn't get out into the world in a way that might be useful to us," he said. "I should like to put the active sympathies of Jewries to work for the Turkish Empire. Therefore the proclamation would have to have an imposing character." The sultan nodded in agreement. Herzl had carefully avoided any allusion to his ultimate objective—an Ottoman charter for a Jewish homeland in Palestine—and Abdul Hamid was happy to leave the matter shrouded in ambiguity.[3]

This arrangement was amenable to Herzl, who had managed to establish a *quid pro quo* between Jewish financial assistance and some (still undefined) measure of Ottoman reciprocation. Yet when he tried to translate this vague principle into concrete understandings with the sultan's lieutenants, making two additional visits to Istanbul to this end, he ran into a brick wall.

Despite Herzl's frustrations, however, the situation in Istanbul did not reduce the Zionist movement to despair. In March 1904, two years after Herzl's last abortive visit to Istanbul, two Zionist activists arrived in the Ottoman capital to try to obtain a limited charter for settlement in Palestine; but again, to no avail. Two further visits three years later by David Wolffsohn, who in 1904 succeeded Herzl as the leader of the Zionist movement following the latter's premature death, proved equally futile: the gap between the T£26 million the sultan requested and the T£2 million that Wolffsohn offered to raise was simply too wide to bridge. Still the Zionists decided to open an office in Istanbul, and at the end of August 1908 its first director, Victor Jacobson, the manager of the Anglo-Palestine Company, the Zionist bank, arrived in the Ottoman capital.

By now Abdul Hamid had been toppled by the Young Turks, and the Zionist movement was caught up in the general wave of euphoria attending this dramatic move—and not without reason. The initial attitude of the new leadership toward the Jewish national enterprise in Palestine was surprisingly positive: in a series of meetings with prominent Young Turks, including Grand Vizier Hussein Hilmi and Enver, then already a prominent member of the CUP, Jacobson heard positive if noncommittal responses to the idea of Jewish immigration to Palestine. Foreign Minister Tewfiq Ahmed Pasha was far more forthright in his support for the abolition of restrictions on Jewish immigration.[4] Even after the CUP's seizure of power in April 1909 and the subsequent repression of nationalist activities throughout the Ottoman Empire, the authorities did not close the door to Zionism. True, the official tone toward Jewish national aspirations hardened as the government toyed with several bills restricting and even prohibiting Jewish immigration to Palestine; yet at the same time the Zionists also heard sweeter tunes from Istanbul. Shortly after his appointment as minister of the interior in the summer of 1909, Talaat promised to abolish the "Red Slip," the temporary-residence permit issued since 1901 to visitors entering Palestine that had come to epitomize Ottoman restrictions on Jewish immigration, only to renege on his pledge several months later.

Four years later Talaat even propagated the fantastic idea of a "Muslim-Jewish Alliance." The Balkan wars had plunged the Ottoman Empire into financial ruin and Talaat, who became a key member of the CUP's ruling triumvirate following the military coup of January 1913, expected the Zionists to link the ailing empire with the (presumed) fabulous wealth of "world Jewry."[5] "Would the Jews come to our country to direct our affairs by forming an intimate alliance with us?" asked Esad Pasha, a member of the CUP's Central Committee who broached Talaat's proposition to Jacobson. Such an alliance, he claimed, would provide the Zionists with "a field of action" for realizing their aspirations, while at the same time reinvigorating Islam through the influx of Jewish genius, know-how, and capital investment.[6] As a token of goodwill, on September 20, 1914, the Young Turks abolished the Red Slip, to be followed four months later by the abolition of all restrictions on Jewish settlement in Palestine.

Though this decision was rather equivocal, and though many restrictions were still maintained in a somewhat less offensive form, immigration to Palestine during the year preceding the First World War was larger than any recorded in a single year: about 6,000 newcomers. By then, the Jewish population in Palestine had grown to some 85,000–100,000 people, twice its size at the turn of the century and four times its size in the early 1880s.[7]

This physical expansion reflected the broader development of the Yishuv into a cohesive and organized national community, with its own economic, political, and social institutions. The "old" agricultural settlements of the late nineteenth century were flourishing, while a string of new settlements was vigorously following suit. An influx of capital from the Diaspora allowed the development of the urban sector and laid the foundations of an industrial infrastructure; and while half of Palestine Jewry still lived in Jerusalem, the Jewish population in Jaffa and Haifa grew rapidly, and in 1909 Tel-Aviv was established as the first modern Hebrew city. The Hebrew language had been revived and was rapidly establishing itself as the national language of the community.

Against this backdrop, the First World War could not have come at a more inopportune moment for the Zionist movement in general, and for the Yishuv in particular. At the level of high politics, the war confronted the Zionists with the perennial predicament of weak international players thrown into the midst of a titanic clash—identification. To protect and preserve the Yishuv, without which the Zionist idea would be ren-

dered totally meaningless, they had to secure the goodwill and cooperation of the Ottoman Empire and its German war ally. At the same time,
they could ill afford to antagonize Russia, which was at war with Turkey
and was home to the largest Jewish community in the world. Add to this
the differences within the Zionist leadership about the ultimate winner
of the war, on the one hand, and the conflicting loyalties of many
Zionists as citizens of the respective belligerent states, on the other, to
make the problem of identification more than complex.

As a way out of their predicament, the Zionist movement adopted a
policy of strict neutrality. A special bureau was established in neutral
Copenhagen to maintain contact with Jewish communities in both warring camps; Zionist representatives were instructed to preserve existing
connections within their respective countries but to refrain from negotiations with any government at war with the Ottoman Empire. Although this decision was contested by a small minority of mainly British
Zionists, headed by the vibrant Dr. Chaim Weizmann, this was probably
the most effective way to save the Yishuv from a major calamity.

Indeed, the precariousness of the Yishuv's position during the war
cannot be overstated. In addition to the economic hardships occasioned
by the effective blockade of the Mediterranean, the authorities embarked
on systematic plundering of the Yishuv under the pretext of military
requisitioning—with devastating consequences. Food shortages were
further aggravated, as farmers refrained from sending their produce to
the markets for fear of "requisitioning"; prices sky-rocketed. To make
matters worse, in the spring of 1915 Palestine was hit by the worst locust
plague in nearly half a century, followed the next year by a poor summer
harvest resulting from a long and severe heat wave. Before long the
Yishuv was afflicted by famine, particularly in the towns. During the first
two years of the war, more than eight thousand Jerusalem Jews, about
one-fifth of the city's Jewish population, died of starvation and epidemics
that spread throughout the country like wildfire. By mid-1916 it was
estimated that more than two-thirds of Palestine Jewry was in need of
relief. By the end of the war, deaths in the Yishuv had exceeded births by
about fifteen thousand.[8]

An ominous indication of the Ottomans' determination to stamp out all
manifestations of Jewish nationalism came as early as October 1914,
when the newly appointed governor (*qaimaqam*) of Jaffa, Baha el-Din,
an avowed enemy of nationalism in general, and of Zionism in particu-

lar, took a series of draconian measures against the Jewish community under his jurisdiction. He prohibited Jewish immigration and settlement, made Zionist institutions illegal, outlawed the Zionist flag, made the use of Jewish National Funds stamps a capital offense, had Hebrew signposts removed, and forbade the use of Hebrew (and Yiddish) in letters. Authorities conducted house-to-house searches for hidden weapons and secessionist propaganda in Tel-Aviv; and while no evidence of either was found, the Jews were ordered to hand in all illegal weapons in their possession. As in the Armenian case, the Ottomans were not satisfied that all arms had actually been surrendered before the Zionists bought large quantities of weapons from their Arab neighbors and handed them in.

Things came to a head on December 17, when Baha el-Din ordered the deportation of all Jews who had not become Ottoman subjects. The Yishuv and the Zionist leadership were horrified. The overwhelming majority of new immigrants were non-Ottoman nationals, and their expulsion would spell the end of the Jewish national enterprise. "That one *kaimakam* is able to destroy the work of many years in a single day made me realize on what weak foundations all our efforts at settlement rest," wrote Arthur Ruppin, the head of the Palestine Zionist Office and perhaps the leading Zionist in the country.[9] At the Zionists' prodding, the German ambassador to Istanbul, Hans von Wangenheim, approached Talaat with the request that the deportations be halted; so did the American ambassador to Constantinople, Henry Morgenthau. The Porte gave in: the expulsions were suspended and foreign nationals were granted permission to stay in Palestine and encouraged to be Ottomanized; not least, Baha el-Din was removed from his post as *qaimaqam* of Jaffa.

This was no doubt a remarkable achievement. However, the gap between center and periphery in the Ottoman administration, which in the past had often allowed the Zionists to evade the government's restrictions, now worked to their detriment. While acquiescing in the order to stop the mass expulsions, Djemal Pasha, who was bent on compensating himself for the loss of power attending his removal to the Levant, sustained the pressure on the Yishuv in defiance of the Porte's instructions to the contrary. He thus appointed Baha el-Din as his adjutant and political adviser, which allowed the latter to intensify the persecution of the Jews. Hassan Bey, a ruthless official who had served as Jaffa's military commander under Baha, became the city's *qaimaqam*.

The restrictions imposed on the Jaffa and Tel-Aviv community were thus significantly exacerbated and expanded to encompass the entire country. The Porte's order to facilitate the Ottomanization of those Jews who desired it was effectively ignored as the local authorities conducted the process at a snail's pace. And while some twelve thousand to fifteen thousand people managed to become Ottoman subjects, many others were forced to leave. In January 1915 alone seven thousand Jews left the country; by the end of the year the number of Palestine Jews in Alexandria exceeded eleven thousand.

Zionist professions of loyalty fell on deaf ears. The Yishuv's leadership was progressively deported, including such staunch "Ottomanists" as David Ben-Gurion and Yitzhak Ben-Zvi, then young leaders of the small socialist party Poalei Zion, who advocated the establishment of a Jewish militia within the Ottoman army to fight the Entente. As Djemal told a Zionist official pleading the abolition of a deportation decree against one of his workers: "I have no trust in your loyalty; [had] you had no conspiratorial designs you would not have come to live here, in this desolate land, among the savage Arabs who hate you so intensely. We, the Young Turks, deem the Zionists to be deserving of hanging, but I am tired of hangings. [Hence], we will disperse you throughout the Turkish state and will not allow you to congregate in any one place."

He made good on his promise. In March 1917, as the British were knocking at the gates of Gaza, the *mutassarif* of Jerusalem, Izzat Bey, ordered the evacuation of Jaffa for "military reasons." Although this measure was intended for the city's entire population, it was effectively applied only to the Jewish community, for the Muslim inhabitants were allowed to remain in the neighboring orchards, from where they returned shortly afterward to the city. By mid-April the nine thousand–strong Jewish community of Jaffa and Tel-Aviv straggled aimlessly northward. As in Armenia, the authorities made no adequate provision for transport, food, or the protection of the deportees from the rapacious population en route. Numerous deportees were robbed of their last morsel, having already seen their property plundered by their Arab neighbors under the tolerant eyes of the Ottoman authorities; others succumbed to starvation and disease. Had it not been for the relief support offered by the Jewish agricultural settlements, which escaped the deportation decree, far more people would have perished.[10]

But this was not all. While Jaffa was being emptied of its Jewish population, Djemal informed the foreign consuls in Jerusalem of his intention to vacate the city without delay on grounds of military necessity. Since it was widely known by then that the British attack on Gaza had failed and that the situation in the south had stabilized, Djemal's announcement was interpreted as a sinister ploy to destroy the Jewish and Christian communities of Jerusalem, leaving the holy city as a purely Muslim site. As a result of German intervention, the Porte instructed Djemal to stop the deportations and to allow the deportees to return to their homes, but to little avail. Although he dropped his plan to deport the Jerusalem Jews, Djemal not only remained committed to keeping Jaffa a "Jewish-free" city but expressed his determination to prohibit Jewish settlement in the entire country after the war. Indeed, in October 1917 the Yishuv was thrown into its final, and perhaps most dangerous, wartime crisis. Its very existence hung in the balance.

The crisis was triggered by the accidental exposure of a Zionist intelligence ring, based in the agricultural settlement of Zichron Yaacov, some thirty kilometers south of Haifa. Code-named NILI—from the initials of its Hebrew password, Netzach Israel Lo Yeshaqer, "the eternal of Israel shall not lie down"—this group of young Zionists, disillusioned with Ottoman imperialism, provided the Entente Powers with indispensable intelligence on the strength and disposition of the Ottoman forces in the Levant, as well as on the region's geographical and socioeconomic conditions.

Djemal was beside himself with rage. It mattered not that NILI consisted of a handful of activists and that its activities were anathema to those Yishuv leaders who were aware of its existence; it confirmed his worst suspicions of Zionism as a treacherous and subversive movement bent on bringing down the Ottoman Empire. There was also an element of personal betrayal: he himself had appointed NILI's founder and leader, Aaron Aaronsohn, a brilliant, world-renowned agronomist, head the antilocust campaign. This not only gave Aaronsohn and his associates freedom of movement throughout the Levant, so vital for their intelligence work; it also put him in close contact with Dejmal, thus making the latter an unwitting accomplice.

Djemal's retribution was merciless. Hundreds of people, including most of the Yishuv's leaders, were arrested; many were tortured in an attempt to prove a collective anti-Ottoman conspiracy. The Jaffa deportees, congregating near the settlement of Petach Tikva in central Palestine, and throughout Galilee, were ordered to continue their journey and leave the country. Agricultural settlements were raided and their populations rounded up in search of spies, and the Muslim population was agitated to wreck havoc on the "treacherous" Jews. Local officials were openly comparing the impending fate of the Yishuv to that of the Armenians. In a meeting with Zionist leaders on November 5, 1917, Djemal threatened that if the Turks were forced to withdraw from Palestine, no Jew would live to welcome the British forces.[11]

Fortunately for the Jews, this proved a hollow threat. By this time Djemal was conducting a rearguard action for his political career. On November 5, the former German chief-of-staff, General Erich von Falkenhayn, arrived in Jerusalem to take command of the Yilderim Force, thus heralding Djemal's swan song as the commander of the Fourth Army and preventing him from embarking on a last-minute round of atrocities. At the same time, the Germans pressured the Ottoman government, Talaat in particular, into ordering the cessation of the anti-Zionist campaign and the release of all those who had been wrongfully detained. On December 9, 1917, British forces entered Jerusalem.

12

ISTANBUL AND THE ARABS

*W*ith the extinction of Armenian nationalism and the repression of Jewish nationalism, the Ottoman Empire confronted no indigenous threat to its integrity. In fact, it is extraordinary how little nationalist fervor there was among the Arabic-speaking Ottoman subjects during the First World War. Not only did the Ottoman Empire's entry into the war *not* trigger an Arab national revival, but the overwhelming majority of Arabic-speaking Ottoman subjects remained loyal to their suzerain to the bitter end. Between one hundred thousand and 300,000 of them even fought in the Ottoman army during the war.

According to conventional wisdom, articulated most forcefully in George Antonius's *The Arab Awakening* (1938) and accepted at face value by generations of Western and Arab scholars, the "Arab National Movement" originated in the mid-1850s in modest literary activity in Beirut, gained considerable momentum during the years of Hamidian despotism as increasing numbers of Arabs became disillusioned with Ottoman rule, and culminated in the "Great Arab Revolt" of 1916–1918, which ended centuries of Ottoman oppression of the Arabs.[1]

Reality, however, was quite different. This account mistakes a rather localized literary movement not only for a general cultural "awakening" but also for a popular national movement. In the words of the British historian Albert Hourani: "The Lebanese Christian literary movement was not a major factor. No strong line of descent can be traced from Nasif al-Yazji and Butrus al-Bustani to the nationalists of the next generation."[2] Moreover, this view grossly inflates the numerical strength and contemporary significance of the secret Arab societies. At the outbreak of the First World War, it has been estimated that there were a mere 350 activists operating in all of the secret Arab nationalist societies that mushroomed throughout the Ottoman Empire mainly after the Young Turks Revolution.[3] Their activities were scarcely noticed by the vast majority of the eight to ten million Arabic-speaking Ottoman subjects, who remained loyal to their imperial master. Even the highest-profile single activity of these societies, the joint Arab-Syrian Congress held in Paris in June 1913, with the participation of 23 representatives, left no perceptible impression on the Arab masses, and its participants even came under criticism from several Arab leaders (such as Aziz Ali al-Misri, one of the most prominent Arab nationalists of the time and the founding father of the al-Ahd secret society).

By comparison, the First Zionist Congress, convened in the Swiss town of Basel sixteen years earlier, included some 200 delegates representing thousands of nationalist activists. The Arab-Syrian Congress received letters and telegrams of support signed by 402 people; the Jewish Congress received well over 50,000 signed letters, telegrams, and petitions. In short, up to the outbreak of the First World War, Arab nationalism was, to use Ernest Dawn's words, nationalism without nationalists.[4]

But the most glaring flaw in this historiographical account is its presentation of Arab societies as being part of a unified national movement. In fact, such a unified national Arab Movement never existed before, during, or after the First World War. A multitude of small, disparate movements articulated not only the general cause of "Arab nationalism," as is universally believed, but rather several distinct varieties of proto-nationalism.

Some of these associations—such as the Society for Arab Union and the Arab Revolutionary Society—subscribed to the Arab imperial dream, namely, the creation of a vast Arab empire on the ruins of the Ottoman Empire. But they were the exception that proved the rule. Prior to the war, most Arab societies—such as al-Fatat, al-Qahtaniyya, al-Ahd, and the Literary Club—acquiesced in the continued domination of the Ottoman Empire and sought to enhance the political, economic, social, and cultural standing of the Arabic-speaking peoples within this imperial order. Yet other societies focused on promoting particularist regional interests within the empire. In Mount Lebanon, since 1861 an autonomous entity, several small associations, most notably the Society of Lebanese Revival, with branches in Cairo, Paris, New York, and San Paulo, were busy propagating the theory of a distinct Lebanese nation. In the neighboring velayet of Beirut, the Reform Society of Beirut was striving to establish virtual autonomy from Ottoman control, while in Baghdad and Mosul the National Scientific Club and the Green Flag secretly preached Iraqi independence. The Cairo-based Party for Administrative Decentralization, though ostensibly committed to the promotion of administrative reforms in all Ottoman provinces, was actually geared toward gaining Syrian independence under a Muslim prince.

Indeed, it was only the particularized societies that managed to make some modest inroads into their respective constituencies, and even these were essentially confined to Lebanon. To the decisive majority of Arabic-speaking Ottoman subjects, the message of most nationalist societies meant nothing. Beyond their unquestioning submission to the sultan-caliph as their temporal and religious ruler, their concerns were immediate and their affinities parochial: to clan, tribe, village, or town. As T. E. Lawrence (or "Lawrence of Arabia," as he is commonly known), the foremost contemporary champion of the pan-Arab cause, put it in a 1915 memorandum on the conditions in Syria:

> There is no national feeling. Between town and town, village and village, family and family, creed and creed, exist intimate jealousies, sedulously fostered by the Turks to render a spontaneous union impossible. The largest indigenous political entity in settled Syria is only the village under its sheikh, and in patriarchal Syria the tribe under its chief . . . All the constitution above them is the artificial bureaucracy of the Turk . . . By accident and time the Arabic language has gradually permeated the country, until it is now almost the only one in use; but this does not mean that Syria—any more than Egypt—is an Arabian country. On the sea coast there is little, if any, Arabic feeling or tradition; on the desert edge there is much.[5]

Thus only those societies that offered practical solutions to local needs were likely to have any appeal. But even then, they were normally outdone by the odd strong man, chieftain, or family who mustered the local material resources, and hence the loyalty of the population. Such local actors were more interested in the consolidation of their own power base, and, if possible, the establishment of their own kingdom, than in the national idea.

The sparsely inhabited North African plateau of Cyrenaica, for example, was under the effective control of the Sanusis, while Najd, at the heart of the Arabian Peninsula, came by and large under the sway of Abd al-Aziz Ibn Saud, who defeated the rival Rashid dynasty at the turn of the century and in 1913 put an end to Ottoman rule in the maritime province of Hasa, the easternmost part of the peninsula. He even attempted to establish a direct relationship with Britain, only to be told that this "would run counter to His Majesty's general policy of consolidating the power of the Porte in its Asiatic dominions," and that Britain would "be glad to see you reconciled to the Ottomans." Indeed, while the Foreign Office subsequently approved "an amicable exchange of views" with Ibn Saud, who, by virtue of his control of Hasa, was also a Persian Gulf coastal ruler, on July 29, 1913, Britain signed a treaty with the Porte in which it specifically recognized Ottoman sovereignty over Najd, including Hasa. This was anathema to Ibn Saud, yet he saw no choice but to recognize Ottoman sovereignty. In return he was made vali of Najd (including Hasa), from the Persian Gulf in the east to Yemen and Hazramawt in the west, which allowed him to retain his control over the province and to forestall the reinstatement of Ottoman garrisons there.[6]

Northeast of Najd, Sheikh Mubarak al-Sabah of Kuwait shielded himself from Ottoman reach by entering into a bilateral agreement with Britain (1899), giving the latter responsibility for Kuwait's defense and foreign affairs. Moreover, in July 1913 Britain and the Ottoman Empire signed "The Draft Convention on the Persian Gulf Area," which, though never ratified owing to the outbreak of the First World War, recognized the autonomy of the sheikh of Kuwait, acknowledged Britain's special status there, and eliminated Ottoman sovereignty over the sheikhdom in all but name. The territory of Kuwait proper was delineated by a semicircle to indicate the area within which the tribes were to be subordinated to Kuwait, and the Ottomans were not allowed to establish garrisons or undertake any military action in the sheikhdom without London's approval, or to exercise administrative measures independent of the sheikh of Kuwait.

Still further to the north, in Basra, a local strongman, Sayyid Talib al-Naqib, was the *de facto* ruler. With the support of Sheikh Mubarak, on the one hand, and the patronage of Abu al-Huda al-Sayyadi, Abdul Hamid's confidant, on the other, Talib defeated all his enemies, gained control over the local press, and levied an annual tax on the notables and distributed the extorted money, or rather part of it, among the poor. When Parliament was reopened by the Young Turks, he arranged the Basra seat for himself, and in February 1913 he launched his own party, the Reform Society of Basra, which demanded full administrative autonomy for the velayet of Basra and the use of Arabic as the official language. The society also charged the Young Turks with "selling Bulgaria and Bosnia-Herzegovina"; of acquiescing in the "Zionist plan" to buy Palestine; of planning to sell the lands of Iraq to foreigners; and of conspiring to make Sunday the day of worship, as in Europe. The enraged authorities tried to bring Talib to heel, even sending assassins to claim his life; eventually they relented and recognized some of Talib's demands for reforms in return for his help in mediating an agreement with Ibn Saud, who, for his part, showered Talib with lavish gifts for his mediation efforts.[7]

On the other side of the peninsula, in the province of Asir, north of Yemen, a new leader was rising: Sayyid Muhammad Ibn Ali, commonly known as al-Idrisi. His ancestors were Moroccan Arabs who had come to Mecca on a pilgrimage at the end of the eighteenth century and then established themselves as a ruling dynasty in the uplands of Asir. He revolted against the Ottomans, suffered defeat, rose again thanks to "infidel" Italian help, and in the end managed to achieve a stalemate that left him, as he had begun, the master of the hill country.

In the Hijaz, the birthplace of Islam, Hussein-Ibn-Ali of the Hashemite clan of the Quraish, Prophet Muhammad's tribe, was appointed in the spring of 1908 the new sharif of Mecca and its emir, protector of Islam's holiest shrines. Building on this key post, Hussein steadily extended his power, aided by his three eldest sons, Ali, Abdullah, and Faisal. While resisting any encroachment on his power by the central authorities, he conducted several successful expeditions against mutinous factions in the Arabian Peninsula, ostensibly on behalf of his Ottoman suzerain. In 1910 he reined in some tribes whom Ibn Saud tried to bring under his wing; in the following year he helped the central authorities to suppress al-Idrisi's uprising, only to discover that during his absence Medina had been made an independent *muhafaza*, bound directly to Istanbul rather than to the velayet of the Hijaz. In the following years, relations between Hussein and the Ottoman authorities deteriorated steadily, with the sharif resisting Istanbul's growing attempts at centralization and the Young Turks seeking his removal.

As war broke out and the Ottoman Empire threw in its lot with Germany, each of these potentates charted his own way. Ibn Rashid and Imam Yahya of Yemen chose to remain with their Ottoman suzerain. Sayyid Talib, in contrast, had no qualms about seeking "infidel" support against his Muslim ruler, cloaking his personal ambition in flashy nationalistic rhetoric.

On October 6, 1914, Talib called on the British ambassador to Istanbul, Sir Louis Mallet. He claimed that the Ottoman Empire was bent on war and asked to enter into negotiations regarding his position in case of an Anglo-Ottoman war. He then asked Mallet "to remind Lord Kitchener of a conversation with him in Cairo three years ago, and to say that the time has come."[8] What precisely had transpired in Cairo three years earlier remained shrouded in mystery; far less mysterious, however, was Talib's stark determination to become the ruler of Basra under British tutelage. On October 22, he let the British consul in Muhammarah know that Enver Pasha had invited him to Istanbul "to discuss matters of importance," and that he would head there peremptorily unless he received a definite offer from Britain within forty-eight hours.

This was a transparent attempt by a local potentate to blackmail the largest empire on Earth, and, indeed, the political resident in the Gulf, Sir Percy Cox, advised that the British call Talib's bluff. To his dismay, he was instructed by the government of India to enter into negotiations with the latter without delay: "We wish him to remain at Basra, and, in the event of war breaking out between Great Britain and Turkey, to cooperate with Ibn Saud and the Sheikhs of Muhammarah and Kuwait in our interests." Talib was to be handsomely rewarded for his cooperation: tax exemption for his date gardens; protection against Ottoman retaliation; and preservation of all his hereditary privileges, including the post of the Naqib. Were war with the Ottoman Empire to be averted, Talib could count on Britain's "support and liberal treatment." What was not on offer, however, was recognition of Talib as "Sheikh or Amir of Basra" under British tutelage; his eventual position would depend on his actual contribution to the British war effort.[9]

This was not good enough for Talib, and he stepped up the pressure. Using Sheikh Khazal of Muhammarah as a conduit yet again, he informed the British that he had been asked by the Porte to travel to Najd to prevent an imminent conflagration between Ibn Saud and Ibn Rashid and that he would leave within days; only a promise to make him the governor of Basra under British protection, with a fixed allowance of £2,000 a month, could prevent his departure.

This gamble failed miserably. The British would not fall for the same trick twice, and Talib was in no position to bargain: his power base in Basra was dwindling by the day as an Ottoman force, headed by the vali of Baghdad, was marching southward to arrest him on the order of Talaat Pasha. Had he accepted the generous British offer, his local standing would have been unassailable, and, over the long term, he might have even realized his dream of becoming the formal ruler of Basra, if not of Iraq. As things were, Talib found all doors slammed in his face: neither his past benefactor, Sheikh Mubarak of Kuwait, nor Ibn Saud, whom Talib had helped reach an agreement with the Porte just several months earlier, would have anything to do with him. In January 1915 he left for Bombay on board a British ship, not to see his native land again for five years.[10]

No less opportunistic, if far more prudent, than Talib were the rulers of the Gulf principalities and some prominent Arabian chiefs, such as Ibn Saud and Sharif Hussein. All of them were willing to turn their backs on the Ottoman Empire for the right price; and none did so for nationalistic reasons, though Hussein would skillfully sell his imperialist ambitions as all-Arab aspirations, both to contemporary British bureaucrats and to future historians.

The rest of Hussein's Arabian neighbors had no such luck; indeed, no such pretensions. Without much fanfare they concentrated on securing their personal rule and aggrandizing their possessions in an uncertain world; and who was better poised to help them achieve these goals than Britain, Mistress of India and Protector of Egypt? In mid-August 1914, upon hearing of the outbreak of war in Europe, Sheikh Mubarak offered Britain his loyalty and support and promised to convince Ibn Saud, whose family he had sheltered in Kuwait during their lean years, to follow suit.[11]

He made good on his promise. "According to what I hear this war is entirely the fault of the Germans, and they are inciting the Turks: May God abuse them both," he wrote to Ibn Saud,

and God has shown favour to the Arabs and Islam generally by bringing the Glorious English Government into existence . . . By following the wishes of the Glorious Government we shall find our happiness, and we have to be grateful to them, my son, *since our help is not necessary to them as theirs is to us.* Our comfort and welfare is from God then from them and may God never cause the others to reign over us who will injure us, namely, the Turks and the Germans who are inciting them.

Ibn Saud needed little incitement. There was no love lost between him and the Ottoman authorities who had supported his arch enemy, Ibn Rashid, and the only reason he had formally recognized their suzerainty three months prior to the outbreak of the war was that the British had rebuffed his repeated pleas for official patronage. Now that the opportunity to throw off the yoke of the hated Turk had suddenly availed itself, the desert ruler was eager to seize the moment. He cared little for the outcome of the war in Europe; all that interested him was that he would be one of its beneficiaries rather than one of its casualties. As he wrote back to Mubarak: "We hope that God will grant the victory to him to whom there will be profit therein to you and me."[12]

Profit indeed they made, and within days of the Ottoman entry into the war. Sheikh Mubarak was promised the continued hereditary possession of his date gardens between Fao and Qurna and their indefinite exemption from taxation; guarantees against all consequences of his expulsion of Ottoman forces from his territory of Umm Qasr, Safwan, and Bubiyan; and, last but not least, recognition of Kuwait as an independent principality under British protection. For his part Ibn Saud was promised British protection against Ottoman retaliation, recognition as the independent ruler of Najd and Hasa, and treaty relations with Britain. In return for these tangible gains, the two were asked to launch a joint attack on Basra, together with Sheikh Khazal of Muhammarah, who, likewise, was promised handsome rewards for his cooperation.[13]

This was music to Ibn Saud's ears. He quickly entered into negotiations with Britain over the long-coveted treaty, which was eventually concluded on December 26, 1915. Ibn Saud was recognized as the "Independent Ruler" of Najd, Hasa, Qatif, and Jubail and the "absolute Chief of their tribes, and after him his sons and descendants by inheritance"; he and his successors were also promised British aid in the event of "aggression by any Foreign Power." In return, Ibn Saud pledged to remain neutral in the Great War and to "refrain from all aggression on, or interference with the territories of Kuwait, Bahrain, and of the Sheikhs of Qatar and the Oman Coast, who are under the protection of the British Government."[14] For his allegiance, the newly won protégé received a monthly subsidy of £5,000: higher than the £2,000 allowance paid to Muhammad al-Idrisi of Asir to rebel against the pro-Ottoman ruler of Yemen, Imam Yahya, but a far cry from the £200,000 monthly subsidy paid to finance Sharif Hussein's revolt.

The secret societies were no less opportunistic than the local Arab chiefs, as vividly illustrated by the machinations of Aziz Ali al-Misri, the founder and leader of al-Ahd and the "grand old man" of Arab secret societies, who in the spring of 1914 moved to Egypt after being sentenced to death in Istanbul and saved by the personal intervention of Lord Kitchener, then the British consul-general and special agent in Egypt. In an interview with the historian Majid Khadduri in 1958, al-Misri claimed that he could have obtained the throne of Iraq or Yemen in the wake of the First World War, had he succumbed to British pleas to lead an expeditionary force in Iraq and in Yemen against the Ottomans; but he was neither interested in a throne nor believed in the possibility of a British victory.[15]

The truth of the matter is that it was al-Misri who offered his services to "infidel" Britain against his sultan-caliph, and it was the British who were lukewarm toward the idea. The first such overture was made within days of the outbreak of war, when al-Misri asked the British authorities in Egypt to support an Arab revolt in Iraq and Syria under his leadership. According to al-Misri, rebels would establish an Arab empire under British tutelage. On August 16, he met Captain R. E. M. Russell of military intelligence in Cairo and treated him to an excited exposition of his ideas. He envisioned the Arabs of Iraq, Najd, and Syria executing the revolt, most likely with the help of the Syrian Christians and Druzes; southern Arabia was admittedly too broken up by factionalism to be of immediate value. Were the British to provide the necessary military and financial support, they would be secured against an attack on India via Persia, and would be granted preferential economic status in the newly established Arab empire—which would comprise all the Arabic-speaking provinces of the Ottoman Empire, bounded in the north by the Alexandretta-Mosul-Persian frontier.

Russell poured cold water on al-Misri's enthusiasm. The Arab leader was asking Britain to risk a good deal, including its relationship with friendly powers, in return for extremely dubious gains. The moment was most inopportune to raise such a question, and al-Misri was well advised to stop pursuing the matter lest he lose the goodwill of the only great power that could make his dream come true.

Al-Misri remained undaunted. In a meeting at the end of October with Colonel Gilbert Clayton, the Cairo director of military intelligence, he reiterated his plan for an Arab revolt and censured Britain for failing to endorse it earlier. By now Turkey had already entered the war and Clayton was willing to give al-Misri's ideas a more sympathetic hearing. Yet he made it clear that so long as Britain had not officially declared war on the Ottoman Empire, any discussion of an anti-Ottoman uprising would be much too premature. As this reservation became purely academic within days, Foreign Secretary Grey instructed Cairo to give al-Misri all necessary help in preparing the revolt, including a subsidy of £2,000. This initiative was nevertheless thwarted by the India Office, under whose responsibility Mesopotamia fell. In early November 1914 the government of India promised its large Muslim population that "the holy places of Arabia, including the holy shrines of Mesopotamia and the port of Jeddah," would remain outside the Entente's theater of operations; and although this unequivocal pledge was quickly modified, the India Office, the government of India, and Sir Percy Cox, the political resident in the Persian Gulf and chief political officer in Mesopotamia, dismissed al-Misri's plan as ill-conceived and counterproductive. Consequently, Grey decided to call the whole thing off; a last-ditch attempt by al-Misri to resuscitate his imperial dream through a personal letter to Kitchener, who had meanwhile become the secretary of war, came to nought.[16]

With his grandiose dream in tatters, al-Misri turned his sights to Britain's war ally, France, to which he sang an altogether different tune. He no longer envisaged the substitution of an Arab empire for the Ottoman Empire. Instead, he suggested that France enter into peace negotiations with Turkey with a view toward bringing about the latter's peaceful departure from the war. By way of convincing his new interlocutors, he argued that Britain was bent on the occupation of Iraq, Arabia, and Palestine, if not the complete domination of the entire Muslim world, something that was clearly at odds with French imperial interests. He further claimed that Ottoman defeat was liable to exact an exorbitant human and material toll; even then, the Ottomans were likely to achieve victory in defeat by projecting themselves as champions of the Islamic cause, thereby creating immeasurable problems for the European powers in the East.

As in his dealings with the British, al-Misri portrayed himself as the answer to the (alleged) French predicament. Were he to be allowed to traverse the Arabic-speaking Ottoman provinces, he would be able to convince the entire population, which held him in great esteem, not to participate in the Ottoman war effort. This, in turn, would force the empire to sue for peace, provided that its territorial integrity was ensured. The French were not impressed.[17]

These ostensibly contradictory plans, of simultaneously establishing an Arab empire on Ottoman ruins and keeping the Ottoman Empire intact, underscored al-Misri's imperialist mindset and unbounded vanity. The future of the Middle East, as he saw it, was inextricably linked with the notion of an empire—be it Arab or Turco-Arab—in which he would play a key role. Having realized that this was not to be, he was prepared to sell his services to the highest bidder and to obstruct rebellious schemes by fellow Arabs. As he candidly told a senior British officer, he was working for himself and for himself alone.[18] Hence his contradictory negotiations with the British and the French; hence his flirtation with the Ottomans and the Germans following his arrival in Madrid in January 1918; and hence his abysmal performance as the first military commander of the "Arab Revolt," most notably his failure to capture Medina, which was largely rooted in his personal animosity toward Sharif Hussein, who among other things refused to grant him the title of emir.

This is not to say that there were no manifestations of sedition in the Arabic-speaking Ottoman provinces by the secret societies; but none of these amounted to anything owing to the societies' meager influence. At the height of Ottoman repression in the Levant in 1915, their security services held files on merely 513 suspected activists; and even if one discounts bureaucrats' propensity to inflate their activities, on the one hand, and allows for an additional number of activists who escaped the Ottoman net, on the other, these suspects were a drop in the ocean of general Arab subservience.[19]

It is scarcely surprising, then, that it was a local strongman, Sharif Hussein of Mecca, rather than a secret society who managed to dupe the British Empire into supporting his personal enterprise. It is true that Hussein's association with two of the secret societies, whose strength was greatly overrated by the British in Egypt, helped to underscore his false pretension to represent the "Arab Nation," but he would never have been able to stake this fantastic claim in the first place without a local power base, which, in his unique case, combined limited military muscle with impressive religious credentials.

Schemes to liberate the Arabic-speaking provinces, or part of them, were hatched by some secret societies well before the Great War spilled over to the Middle East. As early as August 1914 some Maronite activists asked the Entente's consuls-general in Beirut to arm a Lebanese uprising against the Ottomans, only to learn that none of the three powers would risk jeopardizing the integrity of the then-neutral Ottoman Empire.

Equally futile was a plan by some members of the Egyptian-based Syrian Decentralization Party and the Alliance Libanaise society of Cairo, two groups with mutually exclusive goals, with the former committed to the ideal of "Greater Syria" and the latter to Lebanese independence, to launch a joint revolt against the Ottoman Empire upon its entry into the war. The uprising was to begin in the Lebanese town of Zahla, and was reportedly promised military support by the French minister in Cairo, Albert Defrance, a staunch supporter of France's occupation of the Levant. But the revolt never got off the ground.

Other members of the Decentralization Party, including its president, Rafiq al-Azm, and the famous Muslim theoretician Rashid Rida, preferred to put their bets on Britain. Without informing their pro-French Christian co-members, they requested British support for the liberation of the Arabic-speaking territories of the Ottoman Empire, promising Britain preferential status in the liberated lands. This plan, too, came to nought. The party failed to foment sedition in the empire's Arab provinces, while London agreed to support the independence of the Arabian Peninsula in any peace treaty, but made no mention of the Levantine provinces of the Ottoman Empire. This was a nonstarter for the Decentralization Party, which was interested in Syrian, rather than Arabian, independence. In the summer of 1915 it dropped the project altogether and faded into obscurity.

The most significant seditious schemes on the part of the secret societies were those of the al-Fatat and al-Ahd, neither of which had desired the collapse of the Ottoman Empire prior to the outbreak of the war. Al-Fatat had initially hoped that the Ottoman Empire would stay clear of the war, and when this did not happen, the group expressed its readiness to side with the empire against "European imperialism" provided the Arabs were granted independence. At the same time, the society did not shy away from offering its services to those very "imperialists" whose aggressive designs it had so dutifully condemned. In a meeting with British officials in Cairo at the end of October 1914, a special emissary of al-Fatat claimed that most Syrian Muslims were prepared to throw in their lot with Britain provided they were assured that an independent Arab state would be established in the wake of the war and that France would be kept out of Syria. The British dismissed the idea out of hand.[20]

For its part al-Ahd had espoused the establishment of a joint Turco-Arab empire, along the lines of the Austro-Hungarian Dual Monarchy, but the outbreak of war changed this vision altogether. With the society's founder and leader, Aziz Ali al-Misri, out of touch with his fellow members owing to his exile in Egypt, actual leadership passed to a number of officers who substituted the idea of an Arab empire built on Ottoman ruins for the older notion of a dual Turco-Arab empire. The driving force in this group was Yasin al-Hashemi, the chief-of-staff of the 12th Army Corps, who at the end of 1914 or the beginning of 1915 joined al-Fatat, to be followed by other members of al-Ahd, thus ushering in a period of close collaboration between the two societies.

Before long a joint plan for an Arab revolt was put in place. It envisaged al-Hashemi leading the Arab troops of the 12th Army Corps, together with some tribes of the Syrian desert, in battle to liberate the Levant from Ottoman rule before expanding the revolt to the Arabian Peninsula. The idea was to establish a vast Arab empire, from the Mediterranean to the Iranian border, and from Asia Minor to the Indian Ocean, headed by a native of Arabia and tied to Britain in a defensive alliance.

Needless to say, this ambitious plan was well beyond the resources of the two societies. Al-Fatat, with a total of some forty activists, had virtually no roots within the military, while the al-Ahd's forty odd officers (or 80 percent of the society's total membership) constituted half of 1 percent of the estimated ten thousand Arab officers in the Ottoman army. This in turn casts serious doubt on their ability to sway the Arabic-speaking officers to their cause, particularly in light of the wide diversity within this group (and all the more so among Arab soldiers). In any event, by the summer of 1915 most Arab units in the Levant that were expected to start the revolt had been moved to other fronts, together with their officers.

Indeed, in the summer of 1915 Djemal Pasha embarked on a reign of terror aimed at eliminating any and all manifestations of sedition; the crackdown was to last for more than a year and would earn him the unflattering nickname of "Djemal the Butcher."[21] This about-face from his earlier attempts to win over the Arabs with a carrot-and-stick approach was largely rooted in Djemal's frustration over the abysmal failure of the campaign against the Suez Canal, for which he himself was responsible. Gone was the warm praise for the Arabs and their language— the language of the Holy Quran; in its place were beatings, arrests, torture, deportations, and executions, in accordance with Djemal's new conviction that "the Syrians and the Arabs only respect he who beats them." Gone were the lavish briberies showered on notables, propagandists, and journalists; in their place were widespread requisitions and heavy taxation on personal property, lands, livestock, and crops. By 1916, the entire Levant was ravaged by famine and epidemics as a result of Djemal's excesses, the worst locust plague in nearly half a century, and the Entente's naval blockade. Hundreds of thousands succumbed to their suffering; others narrowly survived. In this atmosphere of repression and deprivation, the notion of a revolt could not be more remote from the Arabic-speaking population of the Levant, which had not yet been infected by the nationalist virus and whose only concern was to survive the tremendous hardships of the war. The handful of activists, conceived as the spark that would ignite the bonfire of revolution, had been either imprisoned or executed, or, as in the case of the officers, were outside the Arabic-speaking provinces.

But even if al-Fatat and al-Ahd had never stood any realistic chance of setting the Levant ablaze, their imperialist dream took on a life of its own. Having failed to convince Ibn Saud to lead their revolt and become king of the future Arab empire, the societies turned their sights to Sharif Hussein of Mecca. They managed to impress upon him, and through him on the British, both their seriousness of purpose and their (nonexistent) potential prowess. No less important, the geographical expression of their imperial dream was largely adopted by the sharif in his negotiations with the British high commissioner in Egypt, Sir Arthur Henry McMahon. The imperialist vision of a few dozen political activists, voiced by a local potentate who represented little more than himself, would thus form the basis for the shaping of the post-Ottoman Middle East. It would also become a source of anti-Western grievances by Arab political elites and intellectuals for generations to come.

13

THE "GREAT ARAB REVOLT"

There is probably no more potent a rallying cry in the annals of the modern Middle East than the so-called Great Arab Revolt of the First World War. This uprising against the Ottoman Empire, headed by Sharif Hussein of Mecca and supported by Britain and France, began in June 1916 and ended two years later with the triumphant entry of Faisal, Hussein's third son, into Damascus under British auspices. In Arab historiography, accepted by generations of unquestioning Western scholars, the revolt signifies the culmination of an "Arab Awakening" that had long been in the making. Even those few critical observers who question the existence of such a national awakening prior to the war do not doubt the revolt's nationalist credentials, regarding it as an offspring of Sharif Hussein's (sudden) conversion from "Ottomanism" to "Arabism."[1]

These views, however, are far from the truth. Hussein's desert uprising failed to be the "Great Arab Revolt" for two main reasons. First, the sharif represented little more than himself, as most Arabic-speaking Ottoman subjects viewed the revolt with total indifference or even hostility. Second, Hussein was not a revolutionary in the service of national self-determination but rather an imperialist aspirant seeking to substitute his own empire for that of the Ottomans. If he had ever truly subscribed to the notion of "Ottomanism," which he had not, he discarded it not for the high ideals of "Arabism" but rather for the self-serving cause of "Hashemism."

Notwithstanding his attempts to sell himself to the British as the authorized spokesman of the "whole of the Arab Nation without exception," Hussein was painfully aware not only that he could not expect any help for his seditious plans beyond the Arabian Peninsula, but also that he could not even count on the support of his Arabian neighbors.[2] Far worse, even the unanimous support of his own constituents in the Hijaz was by no means guaranteed. Hussein had established himself as the regional strongman and reduced the Ottoman vali to virtual insignificance, yet his position was far from unassailable, not among the many local tribes and even less among the urban population. Medina (and to a lesser extent Taif) had had fairly regular interaction with the central Ottoman government, and its people were "accustomed to take the part of the Turk against the Arabs." Mecca and Jeddah were better disposed toward the sharif, but even there his authority was widely disputed, not least by the Dhawu-Zaid branch of the Hashemite clan (Hussein himself belonged to the Dhawu-Awn branch), which claimed the sharifate for itself. In October 1915, for example, it was reported that "the merchants of Jeddah instigated by the Turks have sent to the Porte a petition against the Sharif, that all troops thereupon had been transferred to Mecca and Taif and that the Sharif was in considerable danger of assassination." As late as December 1916, six months after the outbreak of the sharifian revolt, the residents of Mecca, Hussein's hometown, were "almost pro-Turks," and it would not be before the winter of 1917 that the pendulum would start swinging in the sharif's direction:

Many of the leading families dependent on Turkish pensions, doubted how long the Sharif could go on paying them, now that the Turks had gone; others feared that the Sharif's military power, exhausted in fighting the Turks, might soon be insufficient to protect them from tribal raids and forays; others again calculated the situation that might follow upon the death or murder of the Sharif, and the internal inter-family feuds that might disturb Mecca in consequence of rival claims to the Emirate. To these must be added an emotion common probably to all in varying degrees, namely, a half-conscious regret in assisting at what might be a fatal blow to the unity of Muslim power so long represented before the world by Turkey.[3]

On a wider level, the notion of the sharif of Mecca's seeking to wrest the caliphate from the Ottoman sultan, with whom their loyalty had rested for centuries, was anathema to most Arabs and Muslims. Even the grand qadi of the Sudan, Muhammad Mustafa al-Maraghi, himself no enemy of the sharif and his grandiose dreams, took the trouble of pointing out that

> universal acknowledgement of Muslims throughout the world of the Sultans of Turkey as Caliphs is a sufficient proof that they respect the latter's opinion, i.e., that it is not necessary for the Caliph to be a Quraishi . . . If the Muslims insist on the title [Quraish] they would be showing a dangerously poor knowledge of the true principles of the religion.[4]

Opposition to the sharif's seizure of the caliphate was particularly intense among Indian Muslims, who responded to the revolt with wholesale condemnation of the "detestable conduct of the Arab rebels," which put the safety and sanctity of the Holy Places of the Hijaz and Mesopotamia at peril, divided Islam at a time when unity was a vital necessity, and, above all, weakened the largest independent Muslim Empire on Earth. Similar furor was vented in Afghanistan, forcing the emir to suppress all news of the revolt and to prevent all discussion of it, in an attempt to maintain his country's traditional neutrality.[5]

Responses in the Arabic-speaking provinces were no less hostile. "Is the call of the Sharif of Mecca an appeal to the principle of nationality?", the Egyptian newspaper *al-Ahram* pondered rhetorically. "The correct answer is No! for the Turkish people as a whole have not tried to deprive other races of their birthright."[6] The prevailing theory among Egyptians from all walks of life was that the revolt was an Ottoman-sharifian conspiracy aimed at deceiving the British into making generous financial contributions to Hussein, as the Sanussi was believed to have done earlier in Libya. Another popular conspiracy theory claimed that the revolt was a fiction contrived by the Ottomans with a view toward reopening the naval routes between the Hijaz and Turkey. Some condemned the revolt as a British attempt to deceive the populace in order to discredit the Ottomans, while others were busy trying "to throw discredit on the Sharif by presenting him as a rebel against the Caliph, and the servile instrument of the English." Even when the reality of the revolt began to sink in, public opinion continued to swing between hostility and disinterest, and the *ulama* refused to recognize the sharif as caliph for as long as the Ottoman Empire remained intact. The Syrian-Lebanese émigré community was especially hostile to the idea of a revolt, despite its pro-British orientation, and it shuddered at the very thought that its rich and cultivated territories would be ruled by the "undisciplined riffraff" from the Hijaz.[7]

Native opinion in French-occupied North Africa was similarly hostile. Some condemned the revolt as an unlawful rising by an audacious subject against his lawful Muslim suzerain, others dismissed it as "one of the habitual Arab revolts." Among the educated classes it was widely believed that the sharif "may have been egged on by Great Britain with the secret intention of getting the Holy Places within her influence."

In the Persian Gulf principalities, where the general feeling was pro-Turkish, the revolt was received with indifference. Even the sheikhs of Kuwait and Muhammarah, who sent congratulations to the sharif, did so only in deference to British wishes, their real attitude being "one of expectancy, combined with some sympathy for the Turks, in that the Sharif has taken advantage of the difficulties in which the war has involved them." The powerful pro-British Arabian potentates, Ibn Saud and Muhammad al-Idrisi, were similarly inclined to defer to their patron and express sympathy with the revolt; but they lent it no material support and were bitterly resentful of Hussein's championship of the Arab cause lest this suggest some control on his part in the future. Ibn Saud, in particular, was "consumed with jealousy of Sharif Hussein, King of the Hijaz, and this jealousy has been . . . fanned to a white heat by the latter's assumption of the title of King of Arabia." Ibn Saud repeatedly demanded equality of treatment with Hussein and left no doubt that "not only will [he] never accept a position of vassalage to the Sherif but that he aspires to a status in Najd not inferior to that of King Hussein in Hijaz."[8]

Nor did the revolt win popular support in the Levant, let alone whip up nationalist sentiments there. In Syria the urban political leadership remained loyal to the Ottoman suzerain and frowned on the desert uprising, and the same was true in Palestine, where there was no corporate sense of national identity. As early as the autumn of 1912 a large number of Muslim bedouins entered Jaffa with the explicit aim of massacring Christian Arabs in revenge for Ottoman setbacks in the Balkan War; only the prompt personal intervention of the local Ottoman governor prevented bloodshed.[9] Now that the Ottomans had proclaimed a jihad against the Entente, enthusiasm in Palestine surged sharply, reaching a fever pitch in late 1914 and early 1915 as Djemal was preparing to attack the Suez Canal. Clerics made fiery speeches to ecstatic audiences. Parades and celebrations of all kinds took place across the country in anticipation of the triumphal march into Egypt. In Jaffa, for example, a camel, a dog, and a bull, decorated respectively with the flags of Russia, France, and England, were driven through the streets with the mob raining blows and flinging filth upon them. Not even the repressive measures Djemal Pasha took in the Levant from autumn 1915 onward could turn the local population against the sultan. Not before the summer of 1917, after the capture of Aqaba by the sharifian forces and the British advance from Egypt into Palestine had driven home the reality of allied successes, would mutterings of discontent begin to surface. But even these were due exclusively to the serious shortages of food, fodder, and wood caused by the Ottoman setbacks rather than to identification with the sharif. According to Colonel Richard Meinertzhagen, the director of the intelligence section of the Egyptian Expeditionary Force, on December 1, 1917, when British forces entered Ramleh, some twenty miles south of Jaffa,

> a large batch of Turkish prisoners were being marched through the village but they were not preceded by their British Guard. The Arabs, thinking that it was the return of the Turkish Army, turned out in force, yelling with delight and waving Turkish flags; it was not till the end of the column appeared and they saw the British soldiers with fixed bayonets that they realized their mistake[,] and great was their confusion. Their faces fell with a bump and they slunk disconsolate to their hovels.

As late as the end of August 1918, less than a month before the end of hostilities in the Middle East, a British report stated that

> the Muslim population of Judea took little or no interest in the Arab national movement. Even now the Effendi class, and particu-

larly the educated Muslim-Levantine population of Jaffa, evince a feeling somewhat akin to hostility toward the Arab movement very similar to the feeling so prevalent in Cairo and Alexandria. This Muslim-Effendi class which has no real political cohesion, and above all no power of organization, is either pro-Turk or pro-British.[10]

In Mesopotamia aloofness ran even deeper and wider. There was no anticipation of national liberation—not even in the British-occupied areas. The sharif's grandiosity was of little consequence to the overwhelmingly Shi'ite population, which abhorred his desire to incorporate their lands into his future empire: many individuals served in the Ottoman army, and numerous tribal chiefs collaborated with the central authorities. The British even had great difficulties persuading Mesopotamian prisoners of war, detained in India, to join the sharif's revolt: most of them remained loyal to their Ottoman sultan-caliph; others were concerned for their families' safety; still others were simply indifferent to the developments in the Hijaz. When in December 1916 two British ships brought 2,100 soldiers and 90 officers to the Hijaz, only 6 officers and 27 soldiers agreed to disembark; the rest were shipped to prisoner camps in Egypt.

Moreover, even those Mesopotamian prisoners of war who joined the sharif's army were greatly reluctant to fight their Ottoman co-religionists. Time and again they obstructed British plans for the capture of Medina, and proved highly resourceful in manufacturing colorful pretexts for nonparticipation in military operations, one such pretext being that their duty was to guard the sharif, not to fight; another—that their animals were too exhausted to participate in fighting. Mesopotamian officers incited Muslim soldiers sent by the French not to fight their Turkish Muslim brethren. Some of them went so far as to laud the Ottomans killed in combat as martyrs.

Nor did Mesopotamians feel any greater empathy toward the non-Arabian participants in the revolt, who were also shipped to Arabia by the British. Relations with Syrian officers were especially acrimonious, as both groups vied for greater power and influence in the sharifian armies. Indeed, disharmony among the revolt's constituent elements was a reflection of the wider attitude of the Arabic-speaking communities toward the sharifian venture: "The Syrian, from the height of his education and 'refinement[,]' looks down on the bedouin in his 'dirt and sand' as being

beyond real consideration, while the bedouin in turn despises the effemi-
nacy of the Syrian." Egyptians were particularly loathed by the Arabians.
On several occasions Hussein and his sons expressed their preference for
Sudanese over Egyptian troops, and the Egyptian forces sent to the Hijaz
were given a rough and humiliating treatment by the bedouins: they
were denied basic foodstuffs, were occasionally fired at, and their military preparations were often obstructed (a popular bedouin pastime, for
example, was to empty sandbags filled by the Egyptians and to steal the
sacks). "Most of the Egyptians are left to the mercy of the Arabs[,] who
are doubtful allies and putting up the rottenest fighting and making us
responsible for the result," Lieutenant-Colonel Pierce Joyce, who served
with the sharif's forces throughout much of the war, stated in his plea for
greater British control of the revolt.[11]

If anything, it was the glitter of British gold and the promise of ample
booty that rallied the Hijaz bedouins behind the sharif, not the lofty
ideals of freedom or national liberation. Many would disappear once
remunerated or forget everything about fighting once they fell upon a
caravan. "The plundering occupied all the energies of our Bedouins, and
Turkish counter-attacks came up unopposed from N. and S.," read a
report by T. E. Lawrence on a successful raid in the autumn of 1917.[12]

Lengthy negotiations between the sharif's sons and some of even the
smaller tribes on the terms of remuneration caused long delays in military operations; widespread desertions of tribes over the issue of material
gain remained a common occurrence up to the latest stages of the revolt.
"In this part of the world, gold is now so plentiful that the British
sovereign may almost be said to be the unit of coinage," observed Major
Herbert Garland, a military adviser to the sharifian army; and Lawrence
echoed this assertion. "The Sharif is feeding not only his fighting men
but their families, and this is the fattest time the tribes have ever known,"
he reported in November 1916. "Nothing else would have maintained a
nomad force for five months in the field." He knew what he was talking
about: nearly half a century later he would still be remembered by
bedouins as "the man with the gold."[13]

So did the sharif. By way of deceiving the British into believing that
his revolt was cost-effective, Hussein initially pitched his financial needs
at the "modest" sum of £50,000 in gold to pay his troops. Within a few
months, before fighting had even begun, this substantial sum had already
been spent, and the sharif came back for an additional £50,000 for

himself, as well as £10,000 for Abdullah (who had already received £3,000 in gold); and more was to come. In a meeting with a British delegation to the Hijaz on June 6, 1916, a day after the outbreak of the revolt, Zeid, the sharif's youngest son, raised his father's demands much further: he now needed a monthly subsidy of £130,000 "in order that the nations may be attracted to us and cherish good feelings towards us." Three weeks later this figure was adjusted to £125,000.

The Foreign Office found this demand "somewhat excessive," but since considerable British resources had already been committed to the sharifian cause, it relented and decided to approve the requested sum "for the present." By November 1916, Hussein had already received £773,000 worth of gold; within the first year of the revolt the sharif received about £2,000,000 worth of gold, with his monthly subsidy shooting from £125,000 to £200,000: forty times the size of Ibn Saud's subsidy and one hundred times that of Idrisi's.[14]

Nor were the sharif's sons blind to the shine of gold. "The King has promised £100,000 to Faisal whenever he shall definitely have broken the railway between Maan and Medina," Lawrence reported in October 1917, "and Faisal intends to make an effort very soon to earn this reward once [and] for all." The British advisers resorted to similar techniques in enticing the sharif's sons into action. "Sharif Faisal was justly pleased with your letter," Joyce reported in September 1917,

> only Lawrence and I did a dreadful thing and only gave him £10,000 instead of £50,000. The other £40,000 remains on the Humber to be given to him as occasion arises. We have been through so many of these critical moments when we have been told success or failure depends on a few thousands that we know the absolute necessity of a certain amount at short call and therefore dared to keep back the above amount.[15]

This is indicative of the underlying causes of the desert revolt. Just as the "Arab Nation" did not look to Hussein as their would-be savior, so the sharif was interested not in the "liberation" of his "Arab brethren" from the Ottoman yoke but rather in the establishment of his own kingdom.

The sharif's ruthless opportunism was vividly illustrated by his secret flirtation with the Ottoman authorities in tandem with his negotiations with Britain, which leaves little doubt as to his determination to secure for himself the best possible deal from either side, come what may. In a telegram to Enver Pasha in mid-March 1916, Hussein styled himself as the champion of the "Arab Nation," a habit that had by now become second nature. He argued that Arab participation in the war was vital for Ottoman success and stated three conditions for bringing about such an eventuality: general amnesty for all political prisoners arrested and tried in Syria; autonomy for Syria; and, last but not least, the making of the sharifate of Mecca hereditary in his family. "Were these demands to be met," Hussein promised, "the Arab nation will dutifully fulfil its obligations; and I undertake to gather the Arab tribes for Jihad, under the command of my sons, in the territories of Iraq and Palestine." Otherwise, he would content himself with wishing the empire the best of luck in its war.[16]

Since at the time the sharif had an understanding with Britain that he would launch a revolt, for which he had been promised far-reaching material and territorial gains, his overture to Enver was nothing but an unscrupulous act of double-dealing. Had his demands been accepted, Hussein would have had no further use for his British interlocutors: his Hijaz base would have been secured indefinitely, and he would have become the most prominent figure in the Arabic-speaking world. And all this without firing a single shot, let alone running the risks attending collusion with Britain.

Indeed, in March 1916 Hussein was apparently having second thoughts regarding his ability to deliver the promised revolt. Shortly before approaching Enver, he had written to the British high commissioner in Egypt, Sir Arthur Henry McMahon, with whom he had been corresponding since the summer of 1915 about the possibility of igniting an "Arab Revolt," to ask that Britain parallel the proclamation of the desert revolt with "an attack on some parts of the Syrian coast in order to encourage the people and destroy the hostile forces there."[17] He must have been aware of the absurdity of his proposition. Had Britain been capable of making this move on its own, which could have delivered the knock-out blow to the Ottoman Empire, it would not have needed the sharifian revolt in the first place: the foremost attraction of the revolt was its (false) promise of setting the Levant ablaze; and it was precisely this gnawing uncertainty about the British response to his escalating demands that made the Ottoman option so appealing to the sharif.

In the end, Hussein's mind was made up for him in Istanbul. Infuriated by this show of impertinence by his subject, Enver told Hussein that he had no business advising his suzerain on questions of grand strategy, and he instructed him peremptorily to send his tribesmen to the front, as he had promised, or face the consequences.[18] As if to underscore the seriousness of Enver's intentions, Hussein was informed of the imminent arrival of a three thousand–strong Ottoman force in the Hijaz on its way to the Yemen. This was the final straw for the sharif. Fearful of Ottoman retaliation, he opted for the spectacular, if somewhat precarious, gains offered by the British alliance: on June 5, 1916, without completing his war preparations or giving his British allies early notice, the sharif launched his revolt.

Hussein's discussion with Enver was not the Hashemites' last bid for a separate deal behind the back of their British ally; far more intricate negotiations with the Ottoman authorities were to take place during the revolt itself. Only this time it was the Ottomans who approached the Hashemites and not the other way around, and their primary interlocutor was Faisal, Hussein's third son, who, rather than Hussein, led the sharifian thrust into the Levant.

Ottoman attempts to detach the Hashemites from the Allied side were apparently made within months of the start of the revolt, and they gained momentum in the winter of 1917 following a string of military setbacks in Palestine, culminating in the loss of Jerusalem in December. As early as April 1917 the Allies received unconfirmed reports that the Ottomans were willing to offer Hussein a spiritual caliphate without temporal power. Then in December the sharif passed to the British three letters, written the previous month, from Djemal Pasha to Abdullah, to Faisal, and to Faisal's military commander, Jaafar al-Askari, a former Ottoman officer who deserted to the sharif after being captured by the British in February 1916. Invoking the Anglo-French-Russian agreement on the partition of the Ottoman Empire (the Sykes-Picot Agreement), whose substance the newly established Soviet government had just disclosed, Djemal sought to convince the three of their allies' perfidy. "There is only one standpoint from which your revolt can be justified in the interests of the Arabs," he wrote to Faisal,

> and that is the possibility of establishing an independent Arab Government, which would secure the independence, dignity and splendour of Islam under its influence. But what sort of an independence can you conceive in an Arab Government to be established, after Palestine has become an international country, as the

Allied Governments have openly and officially declared, with Syria completely under French domination and with Iraq and the whole of Mesopotamia forming part and parcel of British possessions?[19]

Why Hussein chose to pass Djemal's letters on to the British is not entirely clear. It was certainly not because he was shocked and disgusted at the invocation of the Sykes-Picot Agreement, the existence and general gist of which he had known about for several months.[20] Perhaps he wanted to demonstrate his loyalty so as to strengthen his hand in the postwar negotiations that he knew were bound to ensue; perhaps he was signaling that he had the option of making a separate peace with Turkey; or perhaps the sharif was using the British to bridle the burgeoning imperial aspirations of Faisal, which threatened his own dream of a grand Arab empire.

Indeed, as the revolt rolled northward, relations between father and son became increasingly strained. Placed in the autumn of 1917 under General Sir Edmund Allenby, the commander of the Egyptian Expeditionary Force, thus less susceptible to his father's influence; spellbound by the charismatic T. E. Lawrence and his dreams of creating a new Arab empire; and agitated by his Syrian and Iraqi officers, Faisal began toying with the idea of winning his own separate Syrian empire. He repeatedly complained that "his father and brothers are taking no interest in the Syrian movement," and he began to spread his personal influence among the Transjordanian and Syrian tribes.[21]

In these circumstances, it was quite natural for Faisal to pick up the gauntlet thrown by Djemal. In late December he sent a draft reply to his father for approval suggesting that Hussein mediate a separate Anglo-Ottoman peace, "provided the Turks would agree to evacuate certain places (to be specified by His Majesty's Government)." When his proposal was thrown back at him by his father and Reginald Wingate, the high commissioner in Egypt, Faisal established secret contacts not only with Djemal but also with Mustafa Kemal, the hero of Gallipoli and onetime commander of the Turkish 7th Army.[22] Neither the sharif nor Britain was informed.

In his celebrated account of the "Arab Revolt," *Seven Pillars of Wisdom,* T. E. Lawrence puts a romantic gloss on these contacts, portraying them as a clever ploy to widen the rift between the "nationalist" and the "Islamist" factions of the Ottoman leadership. In his view the trick worked brilliantly: "At first we were offered autonomy for Hijaz. Then

Syria was admitted to the benefit: then Mesopotamia. Faisal seemed still not content; so Djemal's deputy (while his master was in Constantinople) boldly added a Crown to the offered share of Hussein of Mecca. Lastly, they told us they saw logic in the claim of the prophet's family to the spiritual leadership of Islam!"[23]

The truth was less heroic. Faisal was engaged not in a brilliant feat of divisive diplomacy but rather in an unabashed exercise in duplicity; and none knew this better than Lawrence, who whole-heartedly endorsed this illicit adventure and kept most of its contours hidden from his own superiors. As he would tell one of his biographers years later, reluctantly admitting that the emir had hidden much of his double-dealing even from him, Faisal was "definitely 'selling us.'"[24] There was no rift to widen between Djemal and Kemal: the two were at the time aligned in opposition to the military strategy of Enver and his German advisers. Nor were the wholesale Ottoman concessions recounted by Lawrence actually made; had they been, Faisal might well have seized them, as he had occasionally intimated to his British advisers. Thus a letter to the German ambassador in Istanbul from Franz Papen, a latter-day German chancellor and then staff officer with the Ottoman forces in Syria, indicates that as late as May 24, 1918, the Turks still expected a "cheap" bargain with the Hashemites: "Djemal Pasha, my Army commander, like Tessim Bey, is convinced that an understanding could be reached even without a settlement of the caliphate question. It would be enough to provide the Sharif with an autonomous position in Mecca and Medina; the Syrian question would not be disturbed by such a settlement." No sweeping concessions had as yet been made.[25]

Djemal's optimism is not difficult to understand. On March 21, Germany had launched a major offensive in France, forcing Allenby to send some of his forces to Europe and to inform Faisal not to expect British military support east of the Jordan River. Then two British attacks in northwestern Transjordan were decisively beaten at the end of March and in late April respectively, leading to a sharp surge in Ottoman morale. "At the present day, the Ottoman government, the mightiest representative of Islam, [prevails] over the greatest enemies of the Muhammadan religion," Djemal wrote to Faisal. "I am persuaded that I am honouring the Prophet's name by inviting His most excellent and noble grandson to participate in the protection of Islam . . . I feel sure that we shall be able to fulfil the wishes of all Arabs." On June 10, without informing Lawrence, Faisal sent his conditions for peace to Turkey:

a. All Turkish forces in Medina and south of Amman to Amman must be withdrawn;

b. All Arab officers and men serving in the Turkish army in Anatolia and Rumelia must return to Syria and their enlistment in the Arab army;

c. Should the Arab and Turkish army fight side by side against the common enemy, the Arab army would be under its own commander;

d. Syria's future relationship with Turkey would be modeled on the relationship between Prussia, Austria, and Hungary; and

e. All supplies and foodstuffs in Syria should remain there and be placed under the control of the Arab army.[26]

Why did Faisal lump together Prussia and Austria-Hungary? The secret societies, with which he had maintained contacts in 1915–1916, had long toyed with the notion of Turco-Arab dualism on the lines of the Austro-Hungarian model, and Faisal was probably recycling their idea, with his own (irrelevant) addition of Prussia. It is clear, however, that in limiting his proposed arrangement to Syria, which he had doubtless earmarked for himself, Faisal was effectively accepting qualified Ottoman sovereignty in his own domain, and unqualified such rule in other Arabic-speaking territories, such as Mesopotamia. Indeed, as Djemal continued to push toward a rapprochement, in August 1918 Faisal scaled down his envisaged Ottoman-Arab political framework: now he was talking in terms of decentralization rather than full independence, something akin to Bavaria's existence as a separate kingdom within the German Empire. The Ottomans declined the proposal; the talks advanced no further.[27]

Even if one accepts Lawrence's handy quip that "all is fair in love, war and alliance," the Hashemites' negotiations with their Turkish masters, both prior to the revolt and in its course, were incredible for no other reason than that they underscored the falsehood of their own nationalist pretensions.[28] Had Enver met the sharif's demands in the spring of 1916, the revolt might have been averted altogether; had Faisal had his way with the Ottoman leadership two years later, the revolt might well have ended at that point. Either way, the Ottomans would have maintained their rule over most of their Arabic-speaking subjects in one form or another, though the Hashemites would have risen to dynastic prominence.

Similarly, when things seemed to be going his way, Hussein was not deterred from trying to extend the frontiers of his future empire well beyond the predominantly Arabic-speaking territories. As he told Lawrence in the summer of 1917: "If advisable we will pursue the Turks to Constantinople and Erzurum—so why talk about Beiruth, Aleppo and Hailo?"[29]

Whether these imperial ambitions were amenable to Hussein's future subjects was immaterial. Their capacity to grasp their real political and social needs was deemed too limited to allow them to control their own destiny. Faisal, for one, was disparaging of nearly all non-Hijazi Arabic-speaking communities. Yemenites in his view were the most docile and easy to hold and to rule among Arabs: "To imprison an officer his Sheikh had only to knot a thin string about his neck, and state his sentence, and the man would henceforward follow him about, with pretensions of innocence and appeals to be set at liberty." Egyptians were "weather cocks, with no political principle except disatisfaction, and intent only on pleasure and money getting"; Sudanese were "ignorant negroes, armed with broad bladed spears, and bows, and shields"; and Iraqis were "unimaginable masses of human beings, devoid of any national consciousness or sense of unity, imbued with religious traditions and absurdities, receptive to evil, prone to anarchy and always willing to rise against the government."[30]

In these circumstances only Hussein and his sons, scions of the Prophet, members of the noblest Arab family, could direct the region's new destinies. In January 1918, in a rare moment of truthfulness, momentarily shedding the false pretenses he had donned throughout his years of dealing with Britain, Hussein shared his views with David Hogarth, one-time director of the Cairo Arab Bureau:

He admits that Arabs as a whole have not asked him to be their King; but seeing how ignorant and disunited they are, how can this be expected of them until he is called? . . . Who else, he asks, in Arabia, Syria, or Iraq stands enough above his fellows to be King of the whole? . . . There is, in fact, no one.[31]

It was the imperialist ambitions of Minister of War Enver Pasha (above) and his partners in the collective leadership, Minister of the Interior Talaat Pasha and Minister of the Navy Djemal Pasha (following two pages), that brought the Ottoman Empire into the First World War, thus leading to the destruction of the empire and to the creation of the modern Middle East on its ruins.

Talaat Pasha

Djemal Pasha

The abortive Gallipoli campaign, and the surrender of the British expeditionary force in Kut al-Amara, south of Baghdad, after 143 days of siege, constituted the Ottoman Empire's finest moments in the war.

As the largest nationally aware community in Turkey-in-Asia, the Armenians were subjected to Ottoman persecution as early as the late nineteenth century, culminating in the genocidal policy of the First World War.

The proclamation of jihad by the Sheikh al-Islam struck a responsive chord among the Ottoman Empire's Arabic-speaking subjects, most of whom fought alongside their suzerain to the bitter end.

Hussein Ibn Ali, the sharif of Mecca, aligned himself with the Entente Powers against his Muslim suzerain with the intention of substituting his own empire for that of the Ottomans.

Hussein's imperial aspirations were anathema to his Arabian neighbors, notably Abd al-Aziz Ibn Saud (far right), who expelled Hussein and his family from the Hijaz after the war (to Ibn Saud's left are the sheikhs of Kuwait and Muhammara, respectively).

Even the capture of Aqaba, one of the high points of the "Arab Revolt," could scarcely conceal the fact that the vast majority of Arabs, from the Maghrib to Mesopotamia, viewed the desert uprising with indifference if not indignation.

Britain's eagerness to undo the Sykes-Picot Agreement allowed the Zionist leader Dr. Chaim Weizmann to extract an official British pledge to establish a Jewish homeland in Palestine.

Prime Minister Eleutherios Venizelos's attempt to exploit the Ottoman defeat to realize the "Great Idea" of a resurrected Greek empire collapsed ignominiously in the face of Turkish resistance, leading to the demise of the millenarian Greek presence in Anatolia.

Emir Faisal Ibn Hussein's appearance before the Paris Peace Conference was ostensibly designed to secure his father's coveted Arab empire. In reality, it was geared toward winning Faisal his own Syrian kingdom (Lawrence of Arabia stands behind Faisal, on the right).

Having lost his Syrian kingdom to the French, Faisal saw to it that an alternative kingdom—Iraq—was established for him. This was achieved in March 1921 at the Cairo Conference.

Disinherited from his desired Iraqi kingdom by his younger brother Faisal, Emir Abdullah Ibn Hussein, the moving spirit behind the "Arab Revolt," maneuvered the Cairo Conference into making him the effective ruler of Transjordan.

Mustafa Kemal (Atatürk), a celebrated war-hero-turned-national-leader, extricated Turkey from its imperial past and reestablished it as a modern nation-state.

The Lausanne Peace Conference drove the final nail into the coffin of the Allied war agreements, finalizing the creation of a new Middle East composed of independent states rather than a unified empire.

14

HUSSEIN'S IMPERIAL BID

The destruction of the Ottoman Empire was not a necessary, let alone an inevitable, consequence of the First World War. It was a disaster self-inflicted by a short-sighted leadership blinded by its imperial dream. Had the Ottomans heeded the Entente's repeated warnings to keep out of the war, Turkey-in-Asia would most likely have weathered the storm. But they did not. And no sooner had the Entente recovered from the Ottoman attack on Russia than the all-too-familiar Eastern Question crept back onto its agenda. What should the fate of the Muslim Empire be: partition? resuscitation?

The first indication of a possible departure from Britain's traditional support for the existence of the Ottoman Empire came as early as November 9, 1914, just over a week after the Ottoman attack on Russia, when Prime Minister Asquith prophesied that "it is the Ottoman Government and not we who have rung the death-knell of Ottoman Dominion, not only in Europe but in Asia."[1] This stark prognosis was accompanied by a series of concrete moves, carefully avoided until then, which were aimed at asserting Britain's authority over those Ottoman territories that had been under its effective control for quite some time. These included the annexation of Cyprus and the declaration of Kuwaiti independence under British protection. Most important, on December 18, 1914, Egypt was declared a British protectorate; Khedive Abbas Hilmi II was deposed and his uncle Hussein Kamil was appointed as the first sultan of Egypt. The supreme British representative in Egypt was upgraded from consul and general agent to high commissioner, and Sir Arthur Henry McMahon, a former secretary to the government of India, became the first to hold this powerful post. The British even considered annexing Egypt, but the idea was dropped owing to a lukewarm French reaction and reluctance to antagonize the local population.

These measures notwithstanding, Asquith had no wish for any imperial expansion at Ottoman expense. "Winston [Churchill] is very anxious that if, when the War ends, Russia has got Constantinople, and Italy Dalmatia, and France Syria, we should be able to appropriate some equivalent share of the spoils—Mesopotamia with or without Alexandretta, a sphere in Persia, and some German colonies etc.," the prime minister recorded in his diary on March 25, 1915.

> I believe that at the moment [Foreign Secretary Sir Edward] Grey and I are the only two men who doubt and distrust any such settlement. We both think that in the real interests of our own future the best thing would be if at the end of the War we could say that we had taken and gained nothing, and this not from a merely moral and sentimental point of view. Taking Mesopotamia, for instance, means spending millions on irrigation and development with no immediate or early return, keeping up quite a large army in an unfamiliar country, tackling every kind of tangled administrative question worse than any we have ever had in India, with a hornets' nest of Arab tribes, and even if that were all set right having a perpetual menace on our flank in Kurdistan.[2]

Given this fear of overextension on the part of the prime minister and his foreign secretary, it was scarcely surprising that the initiative for war spoils at Ottoman expense came from the Muslim Empire's immediate neighbor and rival. While sharing the British and French desire for Ottoman neutrality, Russia capitalized on the Turks' attack to indicate its expectation of a *quid pro quo* in Constantinople and the straits in exchange for acquiescing in the British protectorate over Egypt. And on March 6, 1916, the Russian ambassador in London, Count Benckendorff, communicated to Grey his government's official claim to these territories. In return, Russia promised to respect the special interests of

Britain and France in this area, and to view with sympathy the claims they entertained with regard to other parts of the Ottoman Empire.[3]

Neither Britain nor France was keen to comply with the Russian demand, lest "Russia's territorial gains open up the question of the partition of the whole of Turkey, thus whetting the appetite of many Powers." "The attribution of Constantinople, Thrace, the Straits and the coasts of the Sea of Marmara to Russia implies the partition of the Ottoman Empire," President Raymond Poincaré wrote to the French ambassador to St. Petersburg, Maurice Paléologue, on March 9, 1915. "We have no good reason to desire such a partition." Even such colonialist interest groups as the Comité de l'Asie Française preferred the continued existence of the Ottoman Empire, "one of the most favored areas for our economic activity and—more important still—for our culture."[4] Yet in their desire to keep the Triple Entente intact, the British and French felt obliged to submit to their ally, though neither of them "liked the thing."[5] London was the first to budge, and on March 12 conveyed its formal acceptance of the Russian claim to Istanbul "subject to the war being prosecuted to a successful conclusion, and to Great Britain and France realising their desiderata in the Ottoman Empire and elsewhere." The French followed suit a month later.[6]

Meanwhile the Italians, who had kept out of the war, seemed to have been infected by the still-flourishing Entente optimism about Gallipoli, and they indicated their readiness to join what they saw as the winning coalition. On April 26, 1915, a secret agreement was signed on Italy's entry into the war in return for generous territorial spoils from the Ottoman Empire. These included full sovereignty over the strategic Dodecanese Islands, off the Turkish coast, which Italy had occupied in 1912; all Ottoman rights and privileges in Libya; and, most important, recognition of Italy's right, in the event of the partition of Ottoman Asia, "to obtain a just share of the Mediterranean region adjacent to the province of Adalia, where Italy has already acquired rights and interests." The Entente was also to take Italy's interests into consideration "in the event of the territorial integrity of the Turkish Empire being maintained and of alterations being made in the zones of interest of the Powers." Content with these assurances, on August 21, 1915, Italy declared war on the Ottoman Empire.[7]

The Russian and Italian demands forced Britain and France to determine their own position regarding the Ottoman Empire, and on March 23, 1915, Paul Cambon, the French ambassador in London, proposed that

Britain and France begin discussions on the subject. Grey agreed but warned Cambon against excessive zeal since the British cabinet had not yet had the opportunity to consider British interests in the region. To this end, on April 8 Asquith appointed an interdepartmental committee to determine Britain's desiderata in Asiatic Turkey, while taking into account the interests and aspirations of its war allies and bearing in mind the distinct possibility that "those who are our Allies today . . . may be our competitors tomorrow."[8] The committee was headed by Sir Maurice de Bunsen, an unemployed senior diplomat who had seen service in Istanbul, and included representatives of the Foreign, India, and War offices, the Admiralty, and the Board of Trade. One of its members, though, was not a civil servant: Lieutenant-Colonel Sir Mark Sykes, MP, who had established a reputation as an expert on Turkey-in-Asia through travel and writing, served on the committee as Kitchener's personal representative.

Between April 12 and May 28, 1915, the de Bunsen Committee held thirteen meetings, during which it discussed four alternative schemes for the future of Turkey-in-Asia: confinement of Turkish sovereignty to Anatolia and the partitioning of the rest of the Ottoman Empire among the Allies; maintenance of a nominally independent Turkish Empire under effective European control exercised through great-power spheres of interest; preservation of Turkey-in-Asia as it existed before the war, but subject to certain territorial exceptions; and finally, maintenance of a somewhat reduced independent empire decentralized on federal lines.

That the committee was far less interested in falling upon the Ottoman carcass than in consolidating Britain's existing position was evidenced by its keen awareness of the delicate balance between the newly created opportunities for territorial aggrandizement and the hazards of imperial overextension: "Our Empire is wide enough already, and our task is to consolidate the possessions we already have, to make firm and lasting the position we already hold, and to pass on to those who come after an inheritance that stands four-square to the world." Indeed, though convinced that "the suggestion for the continuance of the Ottoman Empire, constituted as it is today, has nothing to recommend it beyond its deceptive appearance of simplicity," the committee viewed partition as the least desirable of the three other alternatives. Its clear preference was for the maintenance of an independent but decentralized empire comprising five major provinces: Anatolia, Armenia, Syria, Palestine, and Iraq-Jezirah; a second-best option was great-power indirect control of the empire through zones of interest.[9]

In other words, nearly a year after the outbreak of the First World War and several months after acquiescing in Russian and Italian territorial gains at Ottoman expense, British policymakers were still agreeable to the continued existence of Turkey-in-Asia. True, the envisaged postwar Turkey was to be smaller and more decentralized than its Ottoman predecessor, but this was considered the only viable way to resuscitate the clinically dead empire, which was the de Bunsen Committee's preferred solution.

This support for Ottoman survival, however, did not last long; and, paradoxically, the catalyst for Britain's change in position came not from among its war allies but rather from an Ottoman subject: Sharif Hussein of Mecca.

Hussein's first attempt to harness Britain to his imperial dream dates back to February 1914, when his second son and right-hand man, Abdullah, passed through Egypt on his way to Istanbul, where he sat for Mecca in the Parliament, and called on Lord Kitchener, then the British agent and consul-general, whose acquaintance he had reportedly made a year or two earlier. A new and assertive vali, Wahib Bey, had just taken over in the Hijaz with the explicit aim of tightening central control over the province, and Abdullah was anxious to rally British support behind his father in the impending confrontation with the Ottoman authorities. He claimed that the situation in the Hijaz was deteriorating owing to Wahib's arrival, and he asked that Britain use its good offices in Istanbul to prevent the dismissal of his father. He stated emphatically that any such move would trigger a general rising in the Hijaz against the Ottoman Empire and expressed the hope that in such circumstances "the British Government would not allow reinforcements to be sent by sea for the purpose of preventing the Arabs from exercising the rights which they have enjoyed from time immemorial in their own country round the holy places." In a follow-up meeting with Ronald Storrs, the Oriental Secretary at the agency, Abdullah was far more forthright: "Should the CUP force us to defend our country, and should you prevent them from shelling our shores and landing troops, and allow us to use Port Sudan for transport and communications, we would facilitate your trade and prefer you to all other Powers." In the meantime, could the sharif have a dozen or even half a dozen machine guns for "defense against attack from the Turks"?[10]

The evasive British response failed to discourage Abdullah. Two months later he again stopped in Egypt on his way back to Mecca and reiterated his seditious proposal. This time, however, he was not given an audience with Kitchener because of growing Ottoman sensitivities and had to content himself with a meeting with Storrs. Having treated his host to a lengthy discussion of pre-Islamic poetry, Abdullah laid the cards on the table. The Ottoman authorities would not listen to the voice of reason, he said; they were bent on pushing the Hijaz Railway on to Mecca, which would spell economic death for the camel-owning population of Arabia. Would Britain be prepared to give his father "an agreement similar to that existing between the Emir of Afghanistan and the government of India, in order to maintain the status quo in the Arabian peninsula and to do away with the danger of wanton Turkish aggression"?

After a brief consultation with Kitchener, Storrs returned to Abdullah. "The Arabs of the Hijaz should expect no encouragement from the British Government, [which] could never entertain the idea of supplying arms to be used against a Friendly Power [that is, the Ottoman government]," he said. Britain's sole interest in Arabia was the safety and comfort of the Indian pilgrims, and it "had in principle not the smallest wish to interfere in the government or the administration of the Holy Cities."[11]

The disappointed Hussein had thus to bide his time in anticipation of the right moment to outwit his Ottoman suzerain; but not for long. The outbreak of war in August 1914 and its extension to the Middle East some three months later generated unprecedented opportunities, which even the ambitious sharif could never have imagined before. As early as mid-October 1914 Abdullah received a message from Kitchener, now the secretary of state for war, inquiring with whom the sharif would side "should present armed German influence at Constantinople coerce Caliph against his will and Sublime Porte to acts of aggression and war against Great Britain." This was followed by yet another message from Kitchener in early November, shortly after the Ottoman entry into the war, offering Hussein a defensive alliance: "If the Emir and the Arabs in general assist Great Britain in this conflict that has been forced upon us by Turkey, Great Britain . . . recognizing and respecting the sacred and unique office of the Emir Hussein . . . will guarantee the independence, rights and privileges of the Sharifate against all external foreign aggression, in particular that of the Ottomans." And to clinch the deal Kitchener offered an added incentive:

Till now we have defended and befriended Islam in the person of the Turks; henceforward it shall be in that of the noble Arab . . . It may be that an Arab of true race will assume the Caliphate at Mecca or Medina and so good may come by the help of God out of all evil which is now occurring.[12]

This was no mean achievement for Hussein. Eight months earlier he had been refused a mere half-dozen machine guns from Britain; now all of a sudden he was being offered not only a defensive pact with the largest empire on earth but also the highest Islamic post worldwide: the caliphate. Yet the sharif preferred to chart his options carefully. The Ottoman Empire was now a full-fledged war ally of Germany, whose military prowess was held in great awe in the Near East, and Hussein, whose ambitions were aptly matched by his caution, would not take the plunge before ascertaining which way the current was flowing. He therefore reassured Kitchener of his benign neutrality and expressed regret for being unable to break with the Turks immediately owing to "his position in the world of Islam and the present political situation in the Hijaz," while promising to wait for "a reasonable pretext to do so."[13]

Not before the summer of 1915 would Hussein feel confident enough to make his move. Enver's catastrophic Transcaucasian setback, Djemal's abortive attack on the Suez Canal, and the beginning of the Gallipoli campaign all seem to have allowed Abdullah to convince his father that the moment was ripe for a serious exploration of the feasibility of an Anglo-sharifian alliance. He was aided in this by communications from the two Arab secret societies—al-Fatat and al-Ahd—which promised to stir a revolt by Arab officers and troops in Syria and urged Hussein to demand, in any negotiations with Britain, the establishment of a vast Arab empire stretching from Asia Minor to the Indian Ocean and from the Persian frontier to the Mediterranean Sea.

On July 12, 1915, shortly after a delegation of the secret societies had visited Arabia and sworn allegiance to the sharif, a personal envoy of Abdullah's arrived in the Sudan to explore the possibility of British military assistance to the sharif and his Arab supporters. Two days later Abdullah sent a letter on his father's behalf to Storrs, which was to inaugurate a long, drawn-out, and controversial correspondence between the sharif of Mecca and British High Commissioner McMahon, the echoes of which would reverberate in Middle Eastern politics and historiography for many years to come.[14]

The letter reflected the sea change in Hussein's worldview since the beginning of the Great War. The vast Arab empire envisioned by the secret societies coalesced with Kitchener's allusion to the caliphate to whet the sharif's appetite. He no longer spoke for himself and his family, or even for the whole of the Hijaz; styling himself as the champion of "the whole of the Arab nation without any exception," he presented a long list of conditions for an Anglo-Arab alliance, including first and foremost British recognition of

> the independence of the Arab country,[15] bounded on the north by Mersina and Adana up to the 37° of latitude, on which degree fall Birijik, Urfa, Mardin, Midiat, Jezirat (Ibn Umar), Amadia, up to the border of Persia; on the east by borders of Persia up to the Gulf of Basra; on the south by the Indian Ocean, with the exception of the position of Aden to remain as it is; on the west by the Red Sea, the Mediterranean Sea up to Mersina. England to approve of the proclamation of an Arab Khalifate of Islam.[16]

When it reached Cairo on August 18, the sharif's letter took the British completely by surprise. The de Bunsen Committee had just defined the preservation of a decentralized and largely intact Ottoman Empire as the most desirable postwar option, and despite their concessions to Russia and Italy, British decisionmakers were greatly reluctant to entertain the prospect of partitioning the Ottoman Empire, not least at the suggestion of a junior subject of that very empire.

But even if such an undesirable development were to ensue, the idea of a unified Arab state was inconceivable to British officialdom. Even the tight-knit group in Cairo and its Khartum extension, which more than any other part of British bureaucracy would champion the sharif's cause, largely subscribed to this view.

"Arab unity and brotherhood has been discussed for a long time," reported Aubrey Herbert, MP, himself a one-time intelligence officer in Cairo, following a visit to the Egyptian capital at the end of October 1915. "Till recently it seemed as remote as the accomplishment of the Young Turkish organization appeared ten years ago. The character of the people and the geography of the country are insuperable obstacles to any real unity for years and perhaps generations to come." This was also the view of T. E. Lawrence, then a lieutenant at the Intelligence Department in Cairo. In a memorandum entitled the "Politics of Mecca," he claimed that "the Arabs are even less stable than the Turks. If properly handled they would remain in a state of political mosaic, a tissue of small jealous principalities, incapable of cohesion, and yet always ready to combine against an outside force."[17]

For his part McMahon believed that "the idea of an Arabian unity under one ruler recognized as supreme by other Arab chiefs is as yet inconceivable to [the] Arab mind." David Hogarth, Lawrence's mentor and the director of the Arab Bureau, established in Cairo early in 1916, was no less scathing than his protégé over the prospects of Arab unification. "When we look back over the history of the early Caliphates, and we must so do, since the present hopes and pretensions of the Arabs, and the popular belief in their coming Renaissance[,] rest equally on ancient history," he wrote in April 1917, "we find the period of genuine Arab Empire extraordinarily short. Arabs governed Arabs, through Arabs[,] on an imperial scale much less than a century. It is just the Omayyad Caliphate—the Damascus period and no more." In his view, "the brevity of purely Arab Empire was determined less by the force of non-Arab elements than by the inability of Arabs themselves to develop any system of imperial administration more adequate than the Patriarchal."[18]

Even Reginald Wingate, the governor-general of the Sudan and sirdar of the Egyptian army, who felt "increasingly drawn to an attempted solution on Pan-Arabian lines . . . which might wean Sunni Islam from the aggressive Pan-Islamism of the Ottoman school," envisaged not a unified Arab empire but rather "a federation of semi-independent Arab states . . . linked together by racial and religious bonds, owing spiritual allegiance to a single Arab Primate, and looking to Great Britain as its Patron and Protector."[19]

Indeed, the idea that Ottoman collapse would give rise to an Arab caliphate of sorts with its center in the Muslim Holy Places was deeply embedded in the minds of Kitchener and his Cairo disciples. Given their keen awareness of the colorful mosaic that was the Arabic-speaking communities and their perception of the caliphate in purely religious terms, they viewed this institution as a magic formula that could bring together the disparate elements of the Arabic-speaking peoples, under British tutelage, without creating a unified empire that would endanger Britain's own imperial interests. Brushing aside the warning that the caliphate "must, if it is to be more than a mere empty claim, have [the] substance of an extensive temporal empire," they were prepared to guarantee that in any postwar agreement "the Arabian Peninsula and its Muslim Holy Places should remain in the hands of a Sovereign Muslim State"; and if this state was to be headed by a spiritual caliph, all the better, though it was up to the Muslims to settle this issue among themselves without interference from the European powers. Yet this caliph was to wield no temporal powers whatsoever, and the promised sovereignty was interpreted "in a generic sense" owing to skepticism regarding the feasibility of Arab unity. In short, Sharif Hussein was to be given hereditary rule over the Hijaz—not even the entire Arabian Peninsula—and if he managed to "conciliate his powerful neighbors of Najd, Yemen, and Asir, and to impress upon them that he has no idea of pretending to any temporal rights within their territories, his chances of a general—though hardly yet of a universal—recognition as Caliph will be very good."[20]

Given this restrictive vision, it was scarcely surprising that Cairo responded to Hussein's demands with indignant disbelief, and none more so than Ronald Storrs. "While it is clear that the [sharif] endeavours to reconcile local Arabian interests, it may be regarded as certain that he has received no sort of mandate from other potentates," he thought to himself while translating Hussein's letter. "He knows he is demanding[,] possibly as a basis of negotiation, far more than he has the right, the hope or power to expect. Like his co-religionists elsewhere, he will probably modify his tone upon the fall of Constantinople." Under the circumstances, there was little that could be done to encourage the sharif apart from sending him some foodstuffs and money:

> The question of the Arabian Caliphate has already been left to the decision of Islam; the British government having been especially precise upon that point. That of the limits and boundaries could be reserved for subsequent discussion: the chief point for immediate decision being the expulsion of the Turks and the Germans and the maintenance of tranquillity in Arabia.[21]

McMahon took his cue from Storrs. Hand-picked for this post by Kitchener, who wished to reserve the Egyptian vacancy for himself for the postwar era, this lackluster middle-aged civil servant of a legendary slowness of mind never forgot who had buttered his bread; he showed little interest in state affairs, leaving the daily running of the country to his aides and keeping Kitchener constantly informed. His reply to the sharif's letter, dated August 30, was thus a near-verbatim replication of

Storrs' ideas: reaffirmation of Kitchener's support for "the independence of Arabia and its inhabitants, together with our approval of the Arab Caliphate when it should be proclaimed," coupled with rejection of the sharif's territorial demands: "With regard to the questions of limits and boundaries, it would appear to be premature to consume our time in discussing such details in the heat of war, and while, in many portions of them, the Turk is up to now in effective occupation; especially as we have learned, with surprise and regret, that some of the Arabs in those very parts, far from assisting us, are neglecting this supreme opportunity and are lending their arms to the German and the Turk, to the new despoiler and the old oppressor." Ending on a generous note, McMahon offered to send Hussein "whatever quantities of grain and other charitable gifts may be owed by Egypt to the Holy Land of Arabia."[22]

Hussein was enraged. He cared not for such gestures, though the supply of grain would doubtless have relieved the acute food shortages caused by the war. Nor would he settle for a local fiefdom in the Hijaz or even for the government of the whole Arabian Peninsula; his mind had been set on a far more ambitious objective—the establishment of his own empire on the ruins of that of the Ottomans—and as far as he was concerned McMahon had totally evaded this issue.

The spiritual caliphate offered by McMahon meant nothing to the sharif. He viewed the traditional position of caliph as both the temporal and the religious headship of the Muslim community, and if anything, he was interested in the temporal power bestowed by this supreme post. He had used the sharifate of Mecca as a springboard for political aggrandizement, not for religious piety. And just as he had sought British "infidel" support to obtain that revered Muslim post and to defy the wishes of his lawful Muslim suzerain, the Ottoman sultan-caliph, he now used a Christian power to sponsor his quest for the caliphate and the political power that accompanied it. From a religious point of view this was sheer blasphemy, and it would have made no sense for Hussein to risk his spiritual standing unless the caliphate was a code word for the vast Arab empire demanded in his first letter.

Indeed, in his reply to McMahon, dated September 9, Hussein merely paid lip service to the notion of the caliphate. "God have mercy on its soul and comfort the Muslims for their loss," he said, focusing instead on his real task of securing the territories he had set his sights upon. "For our aim, O respected Minister," he argued, "is to ensure that the conditions which are essential to our future shall be secured on a foundation of reality, and not on highly decorated phrases and titles." And the sharif left no doubt as to what this "foundation of reality" meant:

> [T]he limits and boundaries demanded are not those of one individual whose claim might well await the conclusion of the war, but are those of our people who have decided that those frontiers are as a minimum vitally necessary to their new life, and whose resolution is final on this point.

And again:

> I am confident that your Excellency will not doubt that it is not I personally who am demanding of these limits which include only our race, but that they are all proposals of the people, who, in short, believe that they are necessary for economic life.

Yet for all his feigned concern for the future of the Arab race and the finality of his territorial demands, Hussein left the door open to further bargaining: "Whatever the illustrious Government of Great Britain finds comfortable to its policy on this subject, communicate it to us and specify to us the course we should follow."[23]

To the sharif's great relief, McMahon took no notice of this alluded retreat from his earlier demands. In his second letter, dated October 24, the high commissioner suddenly changed his position. Dropping the question of the caliphate altogether, he not only agreed to discuss the boundaries of the envisaged Arab empire but also effectively delineated its territorial extent:

> The two districts of Mersina and Alexandretta and portions of Syria lying to the west of the districts of Damascus, Homs, Hama and Aleppo cannot be said to be purely Arab, and should be excluded from the limits demanded. With the above modification, and without prejudice to our existing treaties with Arab chiefs, we accept those limits.
>
> As for those regions lying within those frontiers wherein Great Britain is free to act without detriment to the interests of her ally, France, I am empowered in the name of the Government of Great Britain to give the following assurances and make the following reply to your letter:

(1) Subject to the above modifications, Great Britain is prepared to recognize and support the independence of the Arabs in all the regions within the limits demanded by the Sharif of Mecca.

(2) Great Britain will guarantee the Holy Places against all external aggression and will recognize their inviolability.

(3) When the situation admits, Great Britain will give to the Arabs her advice and will assist them to establish what may appear to be the most suitable forms of government . . .

(4) On the other hand, it is understood that the Arabs have decided to seek the advice and guidance of Great Britain only, and that such European advisers and officials as may be required for the formation of a sound form of administration will be British.

(5) With regard to the *vilayets* of Baghdad and Basra, the Arabs will recognize that the established position and interests of Great Britain necessitate special administrative arrangements in order to secure these territories from foreign aggression, to promote the welfare of the local populations and to safeguard our mutual economic interests.[24]

In one critical respect McMahon was not telling the whole truth: he had not been empowered "in the name of the Government of Great Britain" to make these promises. Quite the reverse—he had been strictly instructed by Grey to avoid any specific pledges beyond the Arabian Peninsula and its Holy Places unless this was absolutely imperative: "The simplest plan would be to give an assurance of Arab independence saying that we will proceed at once to discuss boundaries if they will send representatives for that purpose."[25]

For Hussein, nevertheless, McMahon's letter was a great relief. Of course it fell short of his maximum demands and was wrapped in a thick layer of qualifications and ambiguities, yet it accepted his claim for an Arab empire, as opposed to the notional caliphate, and a very substantial one indeed. The sharif thus lost no time in seizing the opportunity handed to him just as he began to question the feasibility of his grandiose dream. He therefore agreed, in his letter of November 5, not to include the two velayets of Mersina and Adana in the Arab Kingdom, but insisted that "the two *vilayets* of Aleppo and Beirut and their sea coasts are purely Arab *vilayets.*" Similarly, he argued that the Iraqi velayets were "parts of the pure Arab Kingdom, and were in fact the seat of its Government in the time of Ali Ibn-Abu-Talib, and in the time of all the Caliphs who succeeded him." Yet he expressed readiness to accept a temporary arrangement that would "leave under the British administration for a short time those [Mesopotamian] districts now occupied by the British troops without the rights of either party being prejudiced thereby (especially those of the Arab nation; which interests are to it economic and vital), and against a suitable sum paid as compensation to the Arab Kingdom for the period of occupation . . . at the same time respecting your agreements with the Sheikhs of those districts." This said, Hussein ended the letter on a pious note. "Had it not been for the determination which I see in the Arabs for the attainment of their objects, I would have preferred to seclude myself on one of the heights of a mountain," he wrote. "But they, the Arabs, have insisted that I should guide the movement to this end."[26]

McMahon tried to set the record straight. In a letter on December 14, he complimented Hussein for recognizing Britain's agreements with the Arab chiefs, but rejected his ideas on the future of both Syria and Mesopotamia. In the former case he argued that because the velayets of Aleppo and Beirut involved the interests of Britain's ally, France, "the question will require careful consideration and a further communication on the subject will be addressed to you in due course." With regard to the Mesopotamian provinces, including the velayet of Baghdad, he claimed that the adequate safeguarding of British interests "calls for a much fuller and more detailed consideration than the present situation and the urgency of these negotiations permit." He reassured Hussein that Britain would not conclude "any peace in terms of which the freedom of the Arab peoples from German and Turkish domination does not form an essential condition," yet he reminded him of the need for reciprocity in their relationship:

> It is most essential that you should spare no effort to attach all the Arab peoples to our united cause and urge them to afford no assistance to our enemies. It is on the success of these efforts and on the more active measures which the Arabs may hereafter take in support of our cause, when the time for action comes, that the permanence and strength of our agreement must depend.[27]

Hussein stayed his course. "I do not find it necessary to draw your attention to the fact that our plan is of greater security to the interests and protection of the rights of Great Britain than it is to us, and will necessarily be so whatever may happen," he reprimanded McMahon. "Consequently, it is impossible to allow any derogation that gives France, or any other Power, a span of land in those regions." Were such an adverse development to occur, the Arabs might be forced "to undertake new measures which may exercise Great Britain, certainly not less than her present troubles." As a show of goodwill, he was prepared to defer his claim to "the northern parts and their coasts" so as not to rock the Anglo-French war alliance; but let there be no doubt of his determination to retain them in the future.[28]

Ignoring this patronizing snub from a junior would-be ally who had yet to prove his ability to deliver on his promises, McMahon preferred to dwell on the positive points in the sharif's reply. "As regards the northern parts," he wrote to Hussein in a letter of January 25, the last one to deal with the territorial issue,

> we note with satisfaction your desire to avoid anything which might possibly injure the alliance of Great Britain and France. It is, as you know, our fixed determination that nothing shall be permitted to interfere in the slightest degree with our united prosecution of this war to a victorious conclusion. Moreover, when the victory has been won, the friendship of Great Britain and France will become yet more firm and enduring, cemented by the blood of Englishmen and Frenchmen who have died side by side fighting for the cause of right and liberty.[29]

The question that begs answer at this juncture is what caused the about-face in McMahon's position, from bemused indignation to qualified acquiescence in the main thrust of the sharif's demands. Part of the explanation doubtless lies in the conviction of McMahon, and his superiors in London, that the assurances to Hussein were part of an ongoing bargaining process rather than its end result; hence they were far from final and subject to future revision in accordance with the vicissitudes of the negotiations, which in turn were expected to be influenced by wider developments such as the course of the Great War and the state of the Anglo-French alliance. As things were, the Hussein-McMahon correspondence never culminated in an official agreement as had those concluded with Britain's other Arabian allies, such as Sheikh Mubarak of Kuwait (1899), Abd al-Aziz Ibn Saud of Najd (1915), or Muhammad al-Idrisi of Asir (1915). In fact, it did not even result in an informal

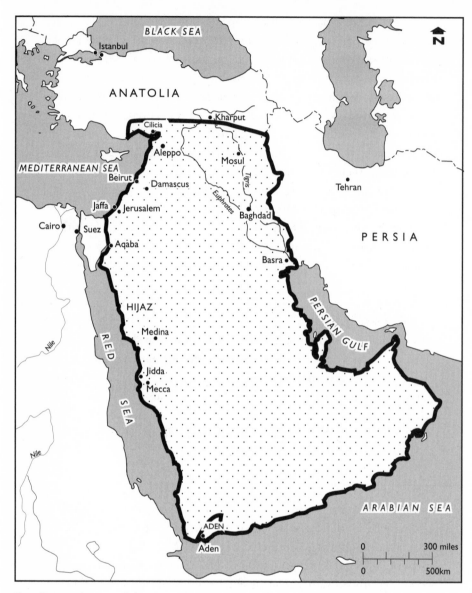

Sharif Hussein's imperial dream

agreement beyond the general understanding that the sharif would rise against the Ottomans and would be generously rewarded in territorial, economic, and military terms. Paradoxically, this inconclusive accord was to assume an air of finality, which Britain had never intended, and to sow the seeds of future grievances and recriminations.

An interrelated reason that McMahon was driven to make territorial promises, despite his superior's instruction to the contrary, was his belief that such pledges were sufficiently equivocal and convoluted so as to make them amenable to the sharif while leaving "as free a hand as possible to His Majesty's Government in the future." As he wrote to Grey in explanation of his letter of October 24:

> I have been definite enough in stating that Great Britain will recognize the principle of Arab independence in purely Arab territory, this being the main point on which [the] agreement depends, but have been equally definite in excluding Mersina, Alexandretta and those districts on the northern coast of Syria, which cannot be said to be Arab, and where I understand that French interests have been recognized. I am not aware of the extent of French claims in Syria, nor of how far His Majesty's Government have agreed to recognize them. Hence, while recognizing the towns of Damascus, Hama, Homs and Aleppo as being within the circle of Arab countries, I have endeavoured to provide for possible French pretensions to those places by a general modification to the effect [that] His Majesty's Government can only give assurances in regard to those territories "in which she can act without detriment to the interests of her ally France."[30]

But above all, McMahon's volte-face was a reflection of a wider change in attitude that took place in Cairo during the summer of 1915. It was Cairo officialdom, notably Storrs, Wingate, and Gilbert Clayton, the director of military intelligence, who, together with their former master-turned-secretary-of-war Lord Kitchener, had conceived of separating the Arabic-speaking subjects of the Ottoman Empire from their suzerain as a means of winning the war in the East. And who was a better candidate for such a venture than the sharif of Mecca, whose unique combination of "the strongest religious with weakest material power" was deemed sufficiently attractive for weaning the Arabs away from the Ottoman Empire without endangering Britain's imperial interests through the creation of a new powerful empire?[31]

Given this mindset, Cairo used every shred of evidence of the sharif's prominence in order to win over the skeptical minds in London and India to its grand design; and its trump card was found, wholly inadvertently, in September 1915, in the form of an obscure twenty-four-year old Arab officer, Lieutenant Muhammad Sharif al-Faruqi, who deserted to the Allied lines in Gallipoli. A native of the town of Mosul, in northern Mesopotamia, Faruqi was a member of al-Ahd Arab secret society who, together with his fellow members, all of them military officers, joined forces with the al-Fatat secret society after the outbreak of the war. In his debriefing by the Cairo Intelligence Department, he painted a grandiose picture of the two secret societies: they had a branch in "every important town or station," commanded the loyalty of "the natives, sedentary and nomads, and all sects including the Nuseiria," and their treasury had accumulated the impressive sum of £T100,000 from membership subscriptions. Ninety percent of the Arab officers in the Turkish army and some of the Kurdish officers were al-Ahd members, and they had already stirred up a number of local revolts. So formidable was the societies' power throughout the Ottoman dominions that the Turks and the Germans had not only forgone any attempts to suppress them but had actually offered to fulfill their demands. Both societies, however, "would sooner have a promise of half from England than of the whole from Turkey and Germany."

The overriding goal of both societies, in Faruqi's account, was to establish an Arab empire comprising Arabia, Mesopotamia, and the Levant, though they realized that the attainment of this objective in its entirety "is probably outside the region of practical realities at present, and he at any rate appreciates the fact that England is bound by obligations to her Allies in this war." To this end, both societies had pledged their allegiance to Sharif Hussein, who, in their understanding, had been promised British military support and been sanctioned to establish an Arab empire, the precise limits of which had yet to be determined. In the view of the societies, the empire's northern border should run along the Mersina-Diarbekir line.[32]

Faruqi's account of the prowess of the secret societies owed more to fiction than to fact. The combined strength of both societies was about one hundred activists, half of whom were military officers.[33] This in turn meant that their political influence in Mesopotamia and the Levant was negligible; their financial resources, a far cry from Faruqi's fantastic figures; and their military power of no real consequence: the fifty-odd al-Ahd officers in the Turkish army constituted about one half of 1 percent of the Arab officer corps rather than the fantastic 90 percent noted by Faruqi. Nor is there any evidence of German or Ottoman courtship of these societies; to the contrary, as narrated by Faruqi himself, from mid-1915 onward the Ottomans adopted harsh measures to suppress all traces of anti-Ottoman activity, real or imaginary, which virtually incapacitated the secret societies operating in the Levant.

But British officials in Cairo would not be troubled by any twinge of self-doubt. Having long advocated the merits of an Anglo-sharifian alliance, they had no intention of questioning the authenticity of the "ultimate proof" that had unexpectedly fallen into their hands; it just fitted too neatly with their preconceptions. Did Faruqi not reveal that the sharif had won the allegiance of the "Young Arab Party"? And did he not say that this party commanded the loyalty of the Arabic-speaking masses? Hence, as Clayton put it in his official report on Faruqi's debriefing: "That the attitude of the Shariff is that of the majority of the Arab peoples there can be little doubt."[34]

If anything, Clayton's memorandum epitomized the self-delusion in which Cairo officialdom immersed itself. Taking the claims of the deserter at face value, the intelligence director cautioned that Britain was rapidly approaching the eleventh hour in its relations with the sharif, who, as the leader of the "Young Arab Party," represented the general Arab will. Hussein's second letter complaining about McMahon's evasion of the boundaries question had just arrived in Cairo, and Clayton urged his superiors to move toward appeasing the sharif:

A favourable reply to the Arab proposals, even though it did not satisfy their aspirations entirely, would probably put the seal on their friendship. The influential leaders appear open to reason and ready to accept a considerably less ambitious scheme than that which they have formulated, which the mere enlightened allow to be beyond their hopes at present. The Committee would at once begin to work actively and their operations, begun in the Hijaz where the sharif is a great power, would soon extend to Syria and Palestine where the Turkish forces are much reduced, and to Baghdad and Mosul where the Committee's influence is perhaps greatest.

On the other hand [he continued in an alarmist tone] to reject the Arab proposals entirely, or even to seek to evade the issues, will be to throw the Young Arab party definitely into the arms of the enemy. Their machinery will at once be employed against us throughout the Arab countries, and the various Arab chiefs, who are almost to a man members of or connected with the Young Arab party, will be undoubtedly won over. Moreover, the religious element will come into play and the "Jehad," so far a failure, may become a very grim reality, the effects of which would certainly be far-reaching and at the present crisis might well be disastrous.[35]

In no time this doomsday scenario was relayed to London through several channels simultaneously. "A powerful organization with considerable influence in the army and among Arab Chiefs, viz: the Young Arab Committee appears to have made up its mind that the moment for action has arrived," General Sir John Maxwell, the commander of the British forces in Egypt, telegraphed to Lord Kitchener on October 12, a day after Clayton had written his memorandum:

The Turks and Germans are already in negotiation with them and spending money to win their support. The Arab party, however, is strongly inclined towards England but what they ask is a definite statement of sympathy and support even if their complete programme cannot be accepted.

[The] Sharif [of] Mecca, who is in communication with the Arab party, also seems uneasy and is pressing for a declaration of policy on the part of England. If their overtures are rejected or a reply is delayed any longer the Arab party will go over to the enemy and work with them, which would mean stirring up religious feeling at once and might well result in a genuine Jehad. On the other hand the active assistance which the Arabs would render in return for our support would be of the greatest value in Arabia, Mesopotamia, Syria and Palestine.

Four days later he was even more alarmed:

We are up against a big question of the future of Islam, and if we can make the French realise this fact they may be more inclined to agree to settlement. I feel certain that time is of the greatest importance, and that, unless we make [a] definite and agreeable proposal to the Sharif at once, we may have a united Islam against us.[36]

Like Clayton and Maxwell, McMahon erroneously construed Faruqi's account as vindicating the sharif's claim to represent the general Arab will; and like the two, he believed that Britain's moment of truth had come. "From further conversation with Faruqi it appears evident that [the] Arab party are at [a] parting of the ways," he wrote to Grey on October 18,

and unless we can give them immediate assurance . . . to satisfy them they will throw themselves into the hands of Germany who he says has furnished them fulfilment of all their demands. In the one case they seem ready to work actively with us which will greatly influence the course of [the] Mesopotamia and Syrian campaigns while in the other Arabs will throw in their lot against us and we may have all Islam in the East united against the Allies.[37]

Even the more stoical Storrs, hitherto dismissive of the sharif's wider pretensions, seemed to have been infected with his peers' alarm. In a letter to Kitchener's military secretary, Lieutenant-Colonel Oswald Fitzgerald, on October 12, he urged that Maxwell's message be given "all possible prominence," as time was running out:

I gather from the Sharif, as does Clayton from Faruqi that they feel, rightly or wrongly, that their time has come to choose between us and Germany. The latter promises all things, but is mistrusted: the Arabs have more confidence in, and would accept much less from, us.[38]

These messages were received with mixed feelings in London. Wholeheartedly endorsing his disciples' prognosis, Kitchener informed Maxwell that "the government are most desirous of dealing with the Arab question in a manner satisfactory to the Arabs" and ordered him to do his best "to prevent any alienation of the Arabs' traditional loyalty towards Britain."[39] The Foreign Office, however, took a more cautious approach. "We are told that not only the Arabs in Arabia, but also the

Arab officers and men in the Turkish army are ready to work against the CUP and the Turks, if we will accept their pretensions, while if we cannot come to terms they will definitely side with the Germans and Turks against us," George Clerk, the head of the newly established war department at the Foreign Office, commented on Maxwell's telegrams. "The advantages of the one are as obvious as the dangers of the other, and I would venture to suggest that no time should be lost in getting officers from Egypt and the Dardanelles, with broad knowledge and experience, and a representative of the French military authorities, to come to London to discuss the position and work out plans."[40]

But before any such discussion could take place, Britain had to determine whether it was prepared "to accept in principle the idea of Arabia— even an exaggerated Arabia such as the Sharif proposes—for the Arabs." In Clerk's opinion, the best solution would be "an independent Arabia, looking to Great Britain as its founder and protector, and provided with territory rich and wide enough to furnish adequate resources." Yet he saw three major obstacles to the creation of such a state: French claims and ambitions in the Levant, British interests in Mesopotamia, and last but not least, the identity of the future ruler of the Arab empire: "Ibn Saud can rule Najd, Sharif Hussein can govern the Hijaz, the Idrisi or Imam Yahya may be master of the Yemen, but no one is indicated as Emir of Damascus or Caliph of Baghdad."

Since the question of who was to rule could be clarified only when discussions with the Arabs were more advanced, Clerk recommended informing the sharif that "H.M.G. agree in principle to the establishment of an independent Arabia and that we are ready to discuss the boundaries of such a State, and the measures to be taken to call [it] into being, with qualified Arabian representatives without delay."[41] Grey telegraphed a message in this spirit to McMahon on October 20, but the high commissioner chose to ignore his superior's wishes. On October 24, anxious to seal a deal without delay, he sent the most fateful letter in the entire correspondence, recognizing, albeit reservedly, the sharif's territorial demands. "In view of the urgency of the matter I seized a suitable opportunity which occurred today of sending a reply to the Sharif of Mecca," he reported to Grey two days later.[42]

The importance of McMahon's letter cannot be overstated. It signified a break with the established British position, based on the quite accurate reading of the diversity and fragmentation of the Arabic-speaking peoples, that a unified Arab empire was a chimera. On the basis of no more than the account of an obscure member of two small secret societies, Cairo had committed His Majesty's government to creating a vast empire for the sake of a local potentate, whom they had hitherto deemed to represent none other than himself, and who, in the view of significant segments of British officialdom, did not command the loyalty and empathy of most of his would-be diverse subjects. "I am not in a position to estimate the value of information as to Arab feeling collected in Egypt," India Secretary Austen Chamberlin commented on McMahon's pledges,

> but I learn from my sources of information that the Sharif is a nonentity—powerless to carry out his proposals—that unity or possibility of unity are entirely lacking in the Arabs; and the hopes of the suggested Arab revolt in the Army and elsewhere seem to me to be groundless and its efficacy doubtful. It must be remembered that friendly chieftains like Ibn Saud and the Idrisi are said to be anti-Sharif, while pro-Sharif chiefs like Ibn Rashid and the Imam are also pro-Turkish.[43]

It is clear from the vague formulation of McMahon's territorial promises that he saw the concessions not as a final commitment but rather as a basis for future negotiation. It may also be the case that Cairo remained skeptical of the viability of the empire whose formation it now advocated, viewing the idea as a mere tactical ploy to get the sharif to join forces with the Entente. Nevertheless, in their short-sighted frenzy these officials failed to comprehend that once the genie of the Arab empire was set free, it could not be bottled again. Had Britain adhered to its original position of recognizing Hussein as the ruler of the Hijaz, with or without the title of the caliphate—a solution that corresponded to the delicate balance of power and loyalties in the Arabian Peninsula—the sharif's imperial ambitions might have died peacefully. As things were, the promise of an empire was to excite the imagination of generations of pan-Arabists and to create a lasting source of friction and acrimony, both among the Arabs themselves and between the Arabs and the West.

15

DIVIDING THE BEAR'S SKIN

*M*cMahon's promises to Hussein forced the British government to consider partitioning the Ottoman Empire, a Pandora's box that it had hitherto avoided opening at all costs. Although these pledges were conditioned on the satisfaction of French desiderata in the region, their very articulation contradicted the letter and spirit of the wartime alliance, spelled out in the Declaration of London of September 4, 1914, which committed the Entente Powers to coordinating their peace terms. Hence, on October 21, 1915, a day after authorizing McMahon to give a favorable if noncommittal reply to Hussein, Foreign Secretary Grey informed the French ambassador to London, Paul Cambon, of the correspondence with the sharif and suggested that the two allies discuss their respective interests in Ottoman Asia. Cambon agreed and designated François Georges-Picot, the former consul-general in Beirut and now first secretary at the French Embassy in London, to represent France.

A diehard colonialist and staunch advocate of French annexation of "la Syrie intégrale," Picot had been posted to the London Embassy in August 1915 and immediately set upon converting Cambon to the colonialist cause. This he achieved within a few months, as demonstrated by his selection as negotiator in the Anglo-French talks. Grey had scarcely made his proposal to Cambon when Picot arrived in Paris, where he obtained approval for his colonialist vision from the new prime minister and foreign minister, Aristide Briand.

Armed with this highest authorization, Picot returned to London, where on November 23 he confronted a seven-member interdepartmental committee headed by Sir Arthur Nicolson, the permanent undersecretary at the Foreign Office. Undaunted by this overwhelming numerical superiority, Picot rebuffed Nicolson's suggestion that, in the sphere of influence that might be allotted to them, the French make promises similar to those made by Britain with regard to Arab independence. He in turn tabled France's demand for the whole of Syria and Palestine (with the possible exception of Jerusalem and Bethlehem), from Cilicia in the north to the Egyptian-Ottoman frontier in the south, and from the Mediterranean in the west to Kirkuk in the east. He claimed that "Syria was very near the heart of the French and that now, after the expenditure of so many lives, France would never consent to offer independence to the Arabs, though at the beginning of the war she might have done so." "It was unthinkable," he said, "that the French people would acquiesce in the placing of the Christians of the Lebanon under a Mohammedan ruler." Besides, since there was no suitable person in Syria "to be a ruling prince . . . discord must arise immediately, necessitating military action." The furthest Picot was prepared to go in the direction of the Arabs was to offer them independence in the Mosul area; in his view, if the British did the same in Baghdad, Basra, and the rest of Arabia, the Arabs might be satisfied, but he seriously doubted whether they could all be appeased.

When Nicolson expounded on the merits of an Arab revolt, which in his view could lead to the defection of the one hundred thousand Arabs serving in the Ottoman army, Picot remained unimpressed. He asked for proof of the strength of the Arab nationalist movement, claiming that it had little or no following and that its strength had been grossly inflated by the Cairo office. He then dismissed out of hand Nicolson's stark warning that failure to rally the Arabs behind the Entente could result in a Muslim backlash that would cause "great embarrassment to the Authorities in Tunis, Algeria, Morocco, Tripoli, and Egypt." According to Picot, not only was there no risk of such trouble, but France's North African subjects "had demonstrated their loyalty by their heroic defense of our territory." To rub salt in Nicolson's wounds, Picot conceded that public opinion in Egypt was largely hostile to the Entente, adding sarcastically that although France was not directly threatened by this restiveness, it "would willingly take account of the different situation of our Allies and would be happy to come to their aid."[1]

In the second round of negotiations, held in London on December 21, the British faced a far more lenient Picot. In a burst of magnanimity he stated that in view of the Entente's recent setbacks in the East, and by way of subverting Ottoman efforts to sustain the active loyalty of their Arab subjects, France was prepared to make the painful concession of accepting a zone of influence in the Syrian interior that would in turn form part of an independent Arab State, rather than the direct rule to which it was rightly entitled. It was now Picot's turn to be unpleasantly surprised. His interlocutors not only failed to reward this "selfless" gesture, but also hardened their position regarding the southern delimitation of the region that was to come under direct French rule. Particularly galling to the Frenchman was the demand that Lebanon, including Beirut, be made "a nominal part" of the new Arab State under the administration of a French-appointed governor.[2]

As far as the French could ascertain, responsibility for this negative twist lay mainly with Sir Mark Sykes, who joined the British team for the second round of talks and immediately established himself as *primus inter pares*. The French were not the only ones to have formed this judgment. So impressed was Nicolson with Sykes's performance that he asked him to meet privately with Picot in an attempt to break the deadlock in the talks. The mercurial Sykes agreed unflinchingly, though he had no previous experience in diplomatic negotiations. During the following week he held a series of "almost daily" meetings with Picot at the French Embassy. Despite their initial wariness, the two got along famously, establishing a close friendship that was to last until Sykes's premature death in February 1919 at the age of thirty-nine. The main obstacles between the two parties were quickly removed. Sykes dropped the demand to make Lebanon part of the proposed Arab State and agreed to the inclusion of Mosul within the French sphere of influence, while Picot accepted the inclusion of Haifa and Acre within the British zone as the Mediterranean termini for a British trans-Asian railway. But they remained hopelessly polarized over the question of Palestine, with both insistent on receiving all of it and neither prepared to budge. Eventually they reached a compromise whereby half of the country was to be placed under international administration and the other half included within the new Arab State.

On January 3, 1916, Sykes and Picot initialed a draft agreement on the partition of the Ottoman Empire in which Britain and France undertook "to recognize and protect an independent Arab State or a Confederation of Arab States . . . under the suzerainty of an Arab chief." Occupying vast territory, from Aleppo to Rawandaz and from the Egyptian-Ottoman border to Kuwait, the new state was divided into two spheres of indirect influence in which Britain and France respectively were to have "priority of right of enterprise and local loans," as well as the exclusive right to "supply advisers or foreign functionaries at the request of the Arab State or Confederation of Arab States."[3]

In those parts of the Ottoman Empire excluded from the Arab State, Britain and France were "allowed to establish such direct or indirect administration or control as they desire and as they may think fit to arrange with the Arab State or Confederation of Arab States." The area of direct French control, the "Blue Zone," extended from Cilicia to the Iranian frontier in the east and to Acre in the south, including the Syrian coastal strip, Lebanon, and northern Galilee. The area of direct British control, the "Red Zone," encompassed southern Mesopotamia including Baghdad, the northeastern Arabian coast, including Kuwait, and the ports of Haifa and Acre in Palestine.

Palestine itself, as noted, was split into two: the southern part, or the Negev, was to be included in the Arab State (and to fall within the British sphere of indirect influence); its northern part, except for northern Galilee, included in the zone of direct French rule, was to be placed under "an international administration, the form of which is to be decided upon after consultation with Russia, and subsequently in consultation with the other Allies, and the representatives of the Sharif of Mecca."

Most members of Nicolson's committee were unimpressed by the proposed agreement. "I must confess that it seems to me that we are rather in the position of the hunters who divided up the skin of the bear before they had killed it," argued Brigadier-General George Macdonough, the director of military intelligence in the War Office and Sykes's close friend. "I personally cannot foresee the situation in which we may find ourselves at the end of the war, and I therefore think that any discussion at the present time of how we are going to cut up the Turkish Empire is chiefly of academic interest." In his view, the only thing that mattered was harnessing the Arabs to the Allied war effort as quickly as possible, and to this end the sharif had to be informed about "the approximate limits of the country which we and the French propose to let him rule over."[4]

For their part, Sir Thomas Holderness and Sir Arthur Hirtzel of the India Office feared the detrimental economic and strategic consequences attending the inclusion of Mosul in the zone of indirect French influence. But the most scathing criticism of the agreement came from Captain Reginald Hall, the director of naval intelligence in the Admiralty. Sharing Macdonough's skepticism of the prudence of "dividing the bear's skin while the bear is still alive," Hall viewed the agreement as tilted in France's favor and worth signing only "on general grounds of policy if it would lessen any risk of a break in the relations between France and England or increase their friendly cooperation."[5]

Notwithstanding these criticisms, the draft agreement was approved on February 4, 1916, by an interdepartmental conference at the Foreign Office with only slight amendments; the French cabinet followed suit four days later.[6] It now remained for the two governments to secure Russia's consent for the deal, as required by the Declaration of London, and at the end of February Sykes and Picot set out for St. Petersburg, where they presented the draft agreement to Sazonov.

Though taken by complete surprise, the foreign minister proved well disposed to the Anglo-French agreement. In informal discussions with his guests and their respective ambassadors, he raised no objection to the establishment of an Arab State, or to the internationalization of part of Palestine—provided that the religious freedoms and privileges of Orthodox Christianity in the Holy Land were secured—or to large-scale Jewish immigration and settlement in Palestine (a subject totally ignored by the Sykes-Picot Agreement). His only concern was the extension of the French zone of indirect influence to the Iranian border, and he proposed an exchange in which France would surrender this territory to Russia in return for a share in Ottoman Armenia. In the end a compromise agreement was reached in an exchange of notes between Sazonov and Paléologue on April 26, 1916, giving Russia a 60,000-square-mile band of territory between the Black Sea and the Mosul area, including the provinces of Erzerum, Trebizond, Van, and Bitlis in Ottoman Armenia, and substantial parts of northern Kurdistan. The following month Britain gave its formal approval to the modified Sykes-Picot Agreement in an exchange of notes between Grey and the French and the Russian ambassadors to London, Cambon and Benckendorff.[7]

In the historiography of the modern Middle East, the Sykes-Picot Agreement has gained lasting notoriety as the source of evil, the epitome of the

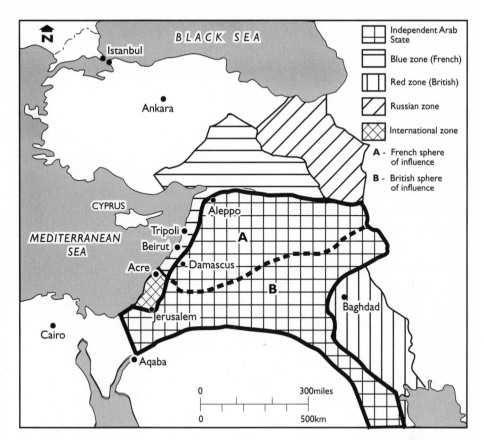

The Sykes-Picot Agreement

(alleged) Western disruption of the natural development of the Middle East through its arbitrary partition into wholly artificial entities. "What the Sykes-Picot Agreement did was, first, to cut up the Arab Rectangle in such a manner as to place artificial obstacles in the way of unity," argued George Antonius. "That may have been the deliberate intention of its authors—an unconscious echo perhaps of Palmerston's hostility to the idea of a stable Arab state planting itself across the overland route to India; but it was none the less retrograde and in conflict with the natural forces at work." "But more serious even than those errors of judgment was the breach of faith," Antonius lamented:

> The Agreement had been negotiated and concluded without the knowledge of the Sharif Hussein, and it contained provisions which were in direct conflict with the terms of Sir Henry McMahon's

compact with him. Worse still, the fact of its conclusion was dis-honestly concealed from him because it was realised that, were he to have been apprised of it, he would have unhesitatingly denounced his alliance with Great Britain. He only heard of the existence of the Agreement some eighteen months later.

In short, the Sykes-Picot Agreement is "not only the product of greed at its worst, that is to say, of greed allied to suspicion and so leading to stupidity: it also stands out as a startling piece of double-dealing."[8]

Given worldwide currency by T. E. Lawrence's autobiographical ac-count *Seven Pillars of Wisdom* and the vast industry of Lawrence lore, including Lowell Thomas's 1919 show *The Last Crusade,* played to full houses in New York and London, and David Lean's 1960s feature film *Lawrence of Arabia,* this view has become the conventional wisdom regarding the Sykes-Picot Agreement.[9] Its rebuttal by the British histo-rian Elie Kedourie has been virtually ignored by Arab and Western scholars alike.[10] In the Middle East itself this indictment has become the standard grievance against the West to this very day, indoctrinated into the local populations through a regular diet of school and university textbooks, media commentaries, and speeches from political leaders.

Yet for all its pervasiveness, this interpretation is totally misconceived. If Anglo-Hashemite negotiations involved "a startling piece of double-dealing," as indeed they did, it was on the part of Hussein and his sons rather than their British interlocutors. By providing for the estab-lishment of a large independent Arab State or Confederation, the Sykes-Picot Agreement acted as a catalyst for Arab unification rather than fragmentation. There was no fundamental contradiction between the territorial provisions of the Sykes-Picot Agreement and those of the Hussein-McMahon correspondence, which never culminated in an ac-cepted agreement; indeed, in the spring of 1917 Hussein was acquainted with the broad lines of the Anglo-French agreement and gave it his consent.

Not only did the Hashemites initiate negotiations with the Cairo Office on the false pretense that they were representing "the whole of the Arab nation without any exception" and sustain this assertion throughout the talks; not only did they inflate their military strength and make false promises (for example, to detach the Arab forces in the Ottoman army from their imperial master) that they knew they could never keep; not only did they encourage the unwarranted British fears of the Arabs' joining the enemy camp, but they also secretly double-dealt with the Ottomans behind the backs of the British both before the declaration of the revolt and in the late stages of the war.

That the sharif managed to mislead his British interlocutors was vividly demonstrated by the Cairo leadership's frenzied attempts to convince their skeptical superiors in London of the veracity of his pretensions and, more important, by the magnitude of the territorial concessions and financial subsidies heaped on him. Had Cairo officialdom recognized the sharif's meager political and military power base—that he did not command total loyalty even in his Meccan hometown—they would undoubtedly have shunned his grandiose demands, as indeed was their initial inclination. As things were, they succumbed to Hussein's offer, but even then, not without making their territorial and financial largesse contingent on his harnessing the entire "Arab Nation" to the Entente's cause and its subsequent liberation of the Arabic-speaking Ottoman provinces. In McMahon's words: "It is most essential that you should spare no effort to attach *all the Arab peoples* to our united cause and urge them to afford no assistance to our enemies. It is on the success of these efforts and on the more active measures which the Arabs may hereafter take in support of our cause, when the time for action comes, that the permanence and strength of our agreement must depend."[11]

Needless to say, the Hashemites never came close to fulfilling this fundamental condition on which the entire deal was predicated, for the overwhelming majority of Arabs remained loyal to their Ottoman suzerain to the very end. Nevertheless, this failure to deliver on their part of the bargain did not prevent the Hashemites from enjoying the deal's many benefits while censuring the British for foul play.

In contrast, there was nothing perfidious about the Anglo-French talks. England and France were war allies in a mortal struggle over their destiny, and it was only natural for them to coordinate their strategies, especially since this was officially required by the 1914 Declaration of London. If anything, it was France that could ostensibly harbor a grievance against Britain for breaching the terms of their wartime alliance by making unauthorized promises to a minor third party that had not even decided to ally itself with the Entente. It was precisely to nip this grievance in the bud that the British initiated the talks with the French: not as a means to renege on their tentative understanding with Hussein, but rather to give it the widest possible international recognition. In the words of Albert Hourani: "It seems clear now that the intention of the British government, when it made the Sykes-Picot agreement, was to reconcile the interests of France with the pledges given to the Sharif Hussein."[12]

This objective was clearly reflected in the two rounds of talks between Nicolson's committee and Picot, in which the British tried to convince the skeptical Frenchman of the merits of both an Arab revolt and the establishment of an independent Arab State, or rather an empire. They even went so far as to demand that Lebanon be included in this prospective empire, which is more than McMahon promised the sharif. In other words, far from seeking to prevent the unification of the "Arab Nation," Britain was instrumental in developing the notion of Arab unity by "buying" Hussein's imperial dream and then "selling" it to their wartime allies.

From the beginning of the war British policymakers were amenable to some form of Arab independence in the Arabian Peninsula. "We had already stipulated that, when Turkey disappeared from Constantinople and the Straits, there must, in the interests of Islam, be an independent Moslem political unit somewhere else," Grey cabled the British ambassador in France on March 23, 1915, following a conversation with Ambassador Cambon. "Its centre would naturally be the Moslem Holy Places, and it would include Arabia. But we must settle what else should be included." In line with this view, the de Bunsen report insisted that "in all circumstances Arabia and the Moslem holy places should remain under independent Moslem rule."[13]

It is true that the British were extremely skeptical of the idea of a large unified pan-Arab empire, both because they were keenly aware of the diversity and fragmentation of the Arabic-speaking Ottoman provinces, and because they were not yet resigned to the destruction of the Ottoman Empire. Once convinced by the sharif to drop these articles of faith, however, they preached this gospel to their French allies with the enthusiasm typical of new converts.

Indeed, the main stumbling block in the Anglo-French negotiations was the French opposition to the idea of Arab independence. As late as December 28, 1915, less than a week before Sykes and Picot submitted their draft agreement to Nicolson, President Poincaré voiced his concern over the proposed creation of an Arab State. In Whitehall there were no such qualms. "I never regarded this treaty as entailing any obligation on us, except to fulfil a promise to give the Arabs independence," wrote Grey in his memoirs. That the final agreement contained a joint undertaking "to recognize and protect an independent Arab State or a Confederation of Arab States" was therefore a clear victory for Britain's championship of Arab independence and unity, prompted by the sharif's demands, over France's opposition to the idea.[14]

The Sykes-Picot Agreement thus constituted the first ever great-power recognition of the Arabs' right to self-determination, well before U.S. President Woodrow Wilson turned this principle into the driving force of international politics. As such, it was scarcely the divisive instrument it is commonly taken for but rather an agent of unification aimed at forging a large number of disparate and diverse communities into a single nation, a daunting task indeed. To be sure, the attribution of spheres of privileged economic treatment within the Arab State to the two great powers reflected their paternalistic perception of independence; but this notion of independence was fully in line with the spirit and custom of the day. Hussein himself envisaged his kingdom not as a modern-day nation-state but as an empire in which he would reign supreme over a large and variegated number of subjects. He not only was amenable to British economic prerogatives in his kingdom but viewed them as indispensable; in his first letter to McMahon he had already proposed that "England shall have the preference in all economic enterprises in the Arab countries whenever conditions of enterprises are otherwise equal" and that England would act as a protector of the newly established Arab State.[15] Hussein then readily concurred with McMahon's demand "that the Arabs have decided to seek the advice and guidance of Great Britain only, and that such European advisers and officials as may be required for the formation of a sound form of administration will be British."[16]

This in turn meant that the Anglo-French "priority of right of enterprise and local loans" stipulated by the Sykes-Picot Agreement and the two countries' exclusive right "to supply advisers or foreign functionaries at the request of the Arab State" were fully commensurate with the idea of Arab independence as envisioned by the Hussein-McMahon correspondence, the only difference being that France, too, and not only Britain, was to enjoy these prerogatives. But even this possibility, as will be shown, was not imposed on Hussein out of the blue but was cleared by Sykes with the person who had greatly helped sway Cairo in the sharif's direction: the Lieutenant Muhammad Faruqi.

It is true that upon learning of the newly signed Sykes-Picot Agreement in May 1916, Cairo officials asked London to withhold *temporarily* its existence from Hussein, or for that matter from other Arab allies, but this had nothing to do with their fear of a "direct conflict" between its provisions and the terms of the Hussein-McMahon correspondence. To the contrary, they saw no principal contradiction between the two documents. Clayton, for example, praised the agreement as "the best possible," and Hogarth called it "remarkable." Both believed, as did McMahon, that "there is nothing in [the] arrangement agreed between France and Russia and ourselves . . . that conflicts with any agreements made by ourselves or assurances given to Shareef and other Arab parties." Even T. E. Lawrence, in stark contrast to his later claims, conceded, in a letter to the *London Times* on September 11, 1919, that "I can see no inconsistencies or incompatibilities in these four documents, and I know nobody who does."[17]

That the Anglo-French negotiations and their resultant agreement were not made public, therefore, reflected the simple fact that belligerents are normally not in the habit of divulging their political and military strategies to their enemies. In this particular case, the revelation of Allied-Hashemite designs on the largest Muslim empire on earth would not only have allowed the Central Powers to devise an effective counterstrategy, but would also have compromised the position of Hussein, whose revolt was anathema to most Arabs and Muslims. The Sykes-Picot Agreement was not the only agreement to be kept secret: the sharif's negotiations with the British in general, and the precise contents of the Hussein-McMahon correspondence in particular, were hidden under a thick veil of secrecy.

The suggestion that Hussein would have renounced his alliance with Britain had he been aware of the Sykes-Picot Agreement does not hold water. For all his lofty pretensions, the sharif was not an Arab nationalist but an aspiring imperialist bent on empire-building rather than on nation-building. His decision to launch the revolt was motivated exclusively by considerations of personal gain; and having negotiated simultaneously with the British and the Ottomans, with neither of them aware of this double-dealing, he decided to sell his loyalty to the highest bidder. Had the Ottoman government met Hussein's demands in the summer of 1916, the revolt might have been averted altogether. Similarly, the sharif was fully prepared to settle for less with the British. His initial demand for the lion's share of Turkey-in-Asia was clearly an opening shot in what was expected to be a prolonged and tiresome bargaining process—not his final position. In his second letter to McMahon he was already backing down from his maximum demands: "Whatever the illustrious Government of Great Britain finds comfortable to its policy on this subject, communicate it to us and specify to us the course we should follow."[18] As things were, McMahon's sudden about-face and his (equivocal) acceptance of many of Hussein's demands kept the latter's imperial dream alive. But there is little doubt that had McMahon held his ground, the sharif would have nevertheless revolted if for no other reason than that a lesser British reward would have still been infinitely more than that offered by the Ottomans. Indeed, the actual timing of the revolt was purely dictated by Hussein's ulterior motives, namely, his fear of imminent Ottoman reprisals. Had it been up to his British allies, the outbreak of the revolt would have been postponed to allow more adequate preparation.

But whatever Hussein's motivations in launching the revolt, the fact of the matter is that he was introduced to the existence of the Sykes-Picot Agreement and its main provisions well before it was published in November 1917 as part of Bolshevik Russia's renunciation of the engagements of the *ancien régime*. Details of the agreement were revealed to Syrian circles in Cairo as early as October 1916 by Emile Edde, a Lebanese notable who had been informed of this deal during a visit to Paris. It is inconceivable that what was common knowledge in the expatriate Syrian community in Cairo would have evaded Fuad al-Khatib, the sharif's dexterous secretary and himself a Lebanese.[19] Indeed, in a memorandum dated April 3, 1917, Clayton surmised that while Hussein had never been officially informed of the terms of the Sykes-Picot Agreement, "it appears extremely probable that he is now to some extent aware of those terms."[20]

Moreover, in April 1917 Sykes and Picot held several meetings in Cairo with "three delegates representative of Moslem Syrian feeling," informed them of the main provisions of the agreement (though without divulging its precise geographical delimitation), and, according to Sykes, gained their acceptance of the following points:

1. . . . [T]hat Great Britain and France should be prepared to contemplate the establishment of an Arab State or confederation in an area approximating to Areas A and B [as stipulated by the Sykes-Picot Agreement].

2. That for defence and protection such a state or confederation would be obliged to rely upon France and Great Britain.

3. In return France and Great Britain should have a monopoly of exploitation, finance and political advisers in that state or confederation.

4. . . . [T]hat for a new and weak state such as the Arab must be, Palestine presented too many international problems to assume responsibility for, but that in the event of the Jews being recognised as a millet or "nation" in Palestine, they insisted that equal recognition must be accorded the actual population.

5. . . . [T]hat as regards Baghdad there could be no doubt that H.M.G. would reserve for itself the right to maintain a permanent military occupation, and insist that the local government would have to be of a kind sufficient to maintain law and order so that British commerce should not suffer; at the same time I did not know what form of Government H.M.G. would establish there.[21]

The contents of these meetings were quickly relayed to the sharif by his Cairo representative, Lieutenant Faruqi, but this was largely unnecessary, for Sykes set out to the Hijaz to brief Hussein in person. On May 2, he met Faisal at Wejh and explained to him the gist of the accord, to which Faisal reportedly agreed "after much argument and seemed satisfied." From there Sykes continued to Jeddah, where three days later he explained to Hussein "the principle of the agreement as regards an Arab Confederation or State." "I am satisfied with my interviews with Sherif Feisal and King of the Hijaz, both of whom now stand at the same point as was reached at our last joint meeting in Cairo with the three Syrian delegates," he reported to Wingate, now the high commissioner in Egypt, asking him to pass the message on to Picot. A report of the meetings in the *Arab Bulletin* was more laconic but still quite explicit: "[Sykes] reports the results of both interviews to be satisfactory, inasmuch as the Hejaz leaders have been brought to understand that they have to deal with an indivisible Entente; that, under whatever overlord, an enlightened progressive régime must be established in Syria; and that certain districts of the latter, which present peculiar difficulties, must remain under special tutelage in any event."[22]

A fortnight later, on May 19–20, Sykes held two further meetings with Hussein, this time with the participation of Picot, on the one hand, and Faisal and Fuad al-Khatib, on the other. After much haggling, the sharif declared that "he would be content if the French Government pursued the same policy towards Arab aspirations on Moslem Syrian Littoral as [the] British did in Baghdad" and that he would be "ready to cooperate with France in Syria to the fullest extent and England in Mesopotamia."[23]

Whether the sharif was given a thorough explanation of "the outline and detail of the agreement," as claimed by Sykes, or merely "a hasty perusal and explanation (with little opportunity given him to think it over or criticise) of the Sykes-Picot agreement," as argued by al-Khatib, is immaterial.[24] Either way Hussein was informed of the existence of the agreement and introduced to its main provisions, as vividly illustrated by his vehement opposition to the French presence in Syria and his insistence on the inclusion of the Syrian littoral in his future empire. His later claims that he had heard nothing of the Sykes-Picot Agreement until after its disclosure by the Bolsheviks could not be further from the truth.

Since both the Hussein-McMahon correspondence and the Sykes-Picot Agreement acknowledge the Arabs' right to self-determination and provide for the establishment of a large Arab State, or rather an empire, their (alleged) incompatibility becomes a matter of degree rather than of substance; that is, the (alleged) discrepancy is in their territorial delineation of the prospective Arab empire.

Recall that the Hussein-McMahon correspondence never culminated in an official and legally binding agreement, or indeed, in any agreement whatsoever. It was a process of intricate bargaining in which both parties pitched for the highest possible prize: Hussein for the largest empire he could secure for himself and his family; McMahon for harnessing the entire "Arab Nation" to the Allied cause. Neither of them accepted the other's offers as final and both tried to improve on them until the territorial haggling was dropped without agreement, leaving each party to put the best possible gloss on his alleged gains and commitments. The sharif interpreted the correspondence as giving him the coveted empire over most of Turkey-in-Asia (though when pressed on occasion he begrudgingly conceded that McMahon did not promise the rule of this prospective empire to him or his family).[25] But since his interlocutors kept beating around the bush and never told him in a forthright manner to drop these false claims, the sharif (and his sons) continued to articulate them with impunity, unwittingly creating a lasting legacy of acrimony in Anglo-Arab relations.

For their part the British took McMahon's tentative promises for what they actually were: a general statement of intent that had to be subjected to detailed scrutiny during the postwar negotiations. As noted, on October 20, 1915, Grey instructed McMahon to avoid concrete territorial pledges to Hussein unless these were absolutely necessary, only to be ignored by the latter, who believed that his promises were equivocal enough to leave "as free a hand as possible to His Majesty's Government in the future" and sufficiently definite to exclude those areas that involved British and French interests. It was precisely this equivocation that was to give rise to the longstanding accusation of British perfidy.

Broadly speaking, McMahon's exclusion of certain territories from the area of the prospective Arab empire rested on four interconnected grounds, the first of which was Britain's existing treaties with other Arab chiefs, such as the sheikhs of Kuwait and Muhammarah, al-Idrisi, and Ibn Saud. These in turn excluded much of the Arabian Peninsula from the territory of the prospective Arab empire, something that Hussein could never bring himself to accept. He repeatedly pleaded with Britain to goad these potentates into recognizing his supreme authority, albeit to no avail; none of them was willing to come under the Hashemite wing, and Ibn Saud eventually kicked the Hashemites out of the Hijaz.

Second, the British had to consider Anglo-Indian interests, which focused by and large on securing the British position in Mesopotamia. In his message to McMahon cited above, Grey instructed the high commissioner to extend the proposed sphere of British control in the velayet of Basra northward to Baghdad. McMahon presented this to the sharif as follows: "With regard to the *vilayets* of Baghdad and Basra, the Arabs will recognise that the established position and interests of Great Britain necessitate special administrative arrangements in order to secure these territories from foreign aggression, to promote the welfare of the local populations and to safeguard our mutual economic interests." When Hussein contested this provision, McMahon reiterated the importance of a "friendly and stable administration in the vilayet of Baghdad" for British interests and suggested they leave the issue for the time being, since "the adequate safeguarding of these interests calls for a much fuller and more detailed consideration than the present situation and the urgency of these negotiations permit."[26]

In other words, Hussein was not only *not* promised the whole of Mesopotamia, the future of which remained open-ended, but he was also informed of the extent of British interest in this area. To be sure, McMahon did not use the strong terms suggested by Grey, but even his more equivocal phrasing left little doubt about the exclusion of southern Mesopotamia up to Baghdad from the prospective Arab empire—hence the sharif's objection. In this respect the Sykes-Picot Agreement did little more than delineate those areas of British interests that McMahon intimated to Hussein.

Third, the British excluded areas that were not purely Arab, defined by McMahon as "the two districts of Mersina and Alexandretta and portions of Syria lying to the west of the districts of Damascus, Homs, Hama and Aleppo [which] cannot be said to be purely Arab."[27] This vague geographical expression was to become the central bone of Anglo-Arab contention with regard to the compatibility of the Sykes-Picot Agreement with the Hussein-McMahon correspondence in general, and the exclusion of Palestine from the area of the prospective Arab empire in particular. According to a standard British interpretation, first articulated in 1920, Palestine was indeed excluded from the territory of such an empire owing to its position west of the Ottoman district, or velayet, of Damascus, which at the time included the area that was to become the Emirate of Transjordan.[28]

The weakness of this contention, as Hussein's third son, Faisal, pointed out at a meeting in London in March 1921, in what was to become the standard pan-Arab claim, was that

> if His Majesty's Government relied upon the strict interpretation of the word "vilayet," as applied to Damascus, they must also interpret the word to mean the same with regard to Homs and Hama. There was not, and never had been, a vilayet of Homs and Hama . . . [Hence] as the Arabic stood, it would clearly be interpreted by any Arab, and had been so interpreted by King Hussein, to refer to the four towns and their immediate surroundings. Palestine did not lie to the west of the four towns, and was therefore in his opinion, included in the area for which His Majesty's Government had given pledges to his father.[29]

Declassified documents in the British archives confirm that contemporary officialdom in Cairo and London did indeed interpret McMahon's four "districts" as meaning "towns": but *not* in the expansive geographical sense claimed by Arab partisans. Quite the reverse, in fact. *They viewed the four towns as synonymous with the entire territory of the prospective Arab empire in Syria; ipso facto* this excluded Palestine from the territory of this empire. Indeed, even Faisal, in the London meeting cited above, while contesting the British interpretation of McMahon's promises, said that "he was quite prepared to accept . . . that it had been the original intention of His Majesty's Government to exclude Palestine."[30]

"It was my intention to exclude Palestine from independent Arabia, and I hoped that I had so worded the letter as to make this sufficiently clear for all practical purposes," McMahon wrote to Sir John Shuckburgh of the Colonial Office on March 12, 1922:

> My reasons for restricting myself to specific mention of Damascus, Hama, Homs and Aleppo in that connection in my letter were: (1) that these were places to which the Arabs attached vital importance and (2) that there was no place I could think of at the time of sufficient importance for purposes of definition further South of the above.
>
> It was as fully my intention to exclude Palestine as it was to exclude the more Northern coastal tracts of Syria.
>
> I did not make use of the Jordan to define the limits of the Southern area, because I thought it might possib[ly] be considered desirable at some later stage of negotiations to endeavour to find some more suitable frontier line east of the Jordan and between that river and the Hedjaz Railway.[31]

If this was a gallant attempt by McMahon to put a shiny gloss on his promise of seven years earlier so as to help his government at a time when the Palestine question was gaining international momentum, then British officialdom miserably failed to appreciate it: they never used McMahon's letter to support their case, which had by then become largely associated with the untenable claim that Palestine lay west of the velayet of Damascus. Nor did they ever allow this letter to be published. Indeed, even the Arab members of the joint Anglo-Arab committee, set up in February 1939 to consider the Hussein-McMahon correspondence, did not question the veracity of McMahon's emphatic denial when this was made public in a letter to the *London Times* on July 23, 1937; they only challenged its relevance: "That which Sir Henry said he intended to mean is of no consequence whatever, for it was not he who was giving the pledge but His Majesty's Government, whose instrument he was."[32] As a legalistic sophistry this contention may have some merit; as a description of a specific political reality it has none at all. McMahon was an instrument of His Majesty's Government all right, but not the passive messenger he was taken for. Not only did he not convey his government's pledge to the sharif but, clearly overstepping his instructions, he committed this government to something that ran *counter* to its wishes. Hence, McMahon was as qualified as the next man to know what he actually meant by these promises; all the more so since his retroactive explanation reflected the received wisdom in Cairo and London at the time of the correspondence, which equated the four towns with the entire territory of the Arab empire in Syria—nothing more, nothing less.

In his memorandum on Syria of early 1915, T. E. Lawrence identified Damascus, Aleppo, Homs, and Hama as "the four ancient cities in which Syria takes pride . . . They are Arab and know themselves such." Conversely, the other two "great Syrian towns" of Beirut and Jerusalem were not "purely Arab"—the former was "as representative of Syria as Soho of the Home Counties," while the latter was as far from "questions of Arabs and their nationality . . . as bimetallism from the life of Texas."[33] Hence these two areas, or the velayet of Beirut and the sanjak of Jerusalem, as they were administratively arranged at the time, could safely be detached from the purely Arab interior.

This prognosis was by no means at variance with the general view in Cairo. In his report of October 11, 1915, on his conversation with Faruqi, which set in motion the process culminating in McMahon's promises to the sharif a fortnight later, Clayton claimed that the Arabs "would almost certainly press for the inclusion of Damascus, Aleppo, Hama and Homs in the Arab Confederation." He then cited Faruqi as saying: "Our scheme embraces all the Arab countries including Syria and Mesopotamia, but if we cannot have all, we want as much as we can get."[34] That is to say, in Britain's eyes the four towns were the epitome of "purely Arab" Syria, which could make or break the negotiations; apart from them, everything was subject to compromise, not least Palestine, which not even Faruqi considered to be part of "purely Arab" Syria. In a conversation with Sykes on November 20, 1915, Faruqi defined Syria "as bounded by [the] Euphrates as far south as Deir Zor and from there to Deraa and along the Hedjaz Railway to Maan," namely, east of the river Jordan.[35] Moreover, in the de Bunsen Committee's map delineating the Ottoman Devolution Scheme, Palestine appears as a vast, distinct state south of Syria, stretching from the Mediterranean to the Mesopotamian desert.

The same view regarding the four towns was expressed by the general commanding officer in Egypt, Lieutenant-General Sir John Maxwell, in his urgent cable to Kitchener on October 16, requesting permission to make territorial pledges to Hussein. Describing the extent of Arab demands in Syria, Maxwell claimed that "the Arab party will, I think, insist on Homs Aleppo Hama, and Damascus being in their sphere."[36] And McMahon reiterated the same message in defense of his decision to overstep his bounds and promise these towns to Hussein: "Arabs attach very great importance to inclusion of Damascus Hama, Homs and Aleppo in Arab boundaries and have, in fact, repeatedly expressed the determination to fight for those territories if necessary."[37]

Aubrey Herbert succinctly summed up the consensus in Cairo regarding the extent of Arab demands in Syria. "While the Arabs would accept modifications in the frontiers which they were asking," he wrote following a visit to the city in October 1915, "Homs, Hama, Damascus and Aleppo were essential to them." In his view, this state of affairs made it imperative "to reconcile the French to making the large concessions involved"; and to achieve this goal Aubrey suggested adopting "a policy of British disinterestedness in Palestine, in favour of France."[38] In other words, Palestine not only fell outside the bounds of the Arab empire, but also was the *quid pro quo* that could be given to France in return for granting the four towns to the Arabs.

The perception of the four towns as the essence of Arab demands also dominated British deliberations on the Sykes-Picot Agreement. In passing the draft agreement to Grey, Nicolson emphasized that "the four towns of Homs, Hama, Aleppo, and Damascus will be included in the Arab State or Confederation, though in the area where the French will have priority of enterprise."[39] Similarly, when in a meeting of the War Committee on March 23, 1916, Asquith wondered whether the Arabs would be content with the area awarded to their prospective empire by the Sykes-Picot Agreement, Grey reassured him that "the four cities, Homs, Damascus, Hama and Aleppo had been assigned to them, which would satisfy them." Arthur James Balfour, then the first lord of the

Admiralty, added emphatically that "they were all in truly Arab Country."[40]

How did British officialdom come to equate these particular towns with the embodiment of "Arabism" in Syria, when Homs and Hama had never played any meaningful role in Arab or Muslim history and Aleppo was not even purely Arab? It has been suggested that the answer lies in Edward Gibbon's *The Decline and Fall of the Roman Empire,* which cited the four towns as the only Muslim sites to have withstood the Crusaders' onslaught, and that it was Ronald Storrs who introduced this "literary reminiscence" into the Hussein-McMahon correspondence.[41] But this "Tale of Four Towns" was already well etched on the minds of many educated Englishmen who served in Cairo and London during the war, as evidenced by Lawrence's 1915 memorandum. Similarly, a memorandum submitted to Prime Minister David Lloyd George in February 1919 by the former ambassador to Istanbul, Sir Louis Mallet, and the historian Arnold Toynbee, then a member of the Turkish section of the British delegation to the peace talks in Paris headed by Mallet, argued that during the period of the crusades, "Aleppo, Hama, Homs, and Damascus were never included in the boundaries of the Latin principalities."[42]

While this memorandum was designed to undermine the French claim to a long historical association with the Syrian hinterland, the obverse of its argument was that the territories beyond these four towns were part of the crusading kingdoms and as such were not historically "purely Arab."[43] No territory fitted this characterization better than the Holy Land, home to the crusading Kingdom of Jerusalem and the object of inter-Christian competition during the nineteenth century. Indeed, it was the keen British awareness of the importance attached to Palestine by its two war allies, France and Russia, that accounted for the last, and probably the most important, reason McMahon was hesitant in his correspondence with the sharif: French interests in the Levant. In his letter of October 24, 1915, McMahon excluded from the area of the Arab empire all those regions in which Great Britain was not "free to act without detriment to the interests of her ally, France."[44] He did not go beyond this general formulation because he had no definite idea "of the extent of French claims in Syria, nor of how far His Majesty's Government have agreed to recognize them"; but he claimed to have "endeavoured to provide for possible French pretensions to those places" by his general reservation.[45]

It was a matter of common knowledge at the time, however, that the

French had a keen interest in and a deep emotional attachment to Syria, "in which latter term they included Palestine and the Christian Holy Places."[46] This was naturally not amenable to British policymakers, who wished to retain Palestine within their own sphere of influence. But none of them had the slightest illusion that they could award the Holy Land to a *potential* junior partner behind the backs of their war allies without raising the furor not only of France but of Russia as well—hence the de Bunsen Committee's conclusion that "Palestine must be recognised as a country whose destiny must be the subject of special negotiations, in which both belligerents and neutrals are alike interested."[47]

Significantly enough, awareness of the extent of French interests was not limited to the British but was also shared by many Arabs. In his conversation with Sykes, Faruqi claimed that the "Arabs would agree to convention with France granting her monopoly of all concessionary enterprise in Syria and Palestine" and "would agree to all French Educational establishments having special recognition in this area."[48] Moreover, in his reply to McMahon's promises, Hussein agreed to exclude the two velayets of Mersina and Adana from the Arab kingdom, but insisted that "the two *vilayets* of Aleppo and Beirut and their sea coasts are purely Arab *vilayets.*"[49]

As noted, Palestine at the time did not exist as a unified political or administrative entity, but rather was divided into two separate units: the northern part, extending nearly to Jaffa, belonged to the velayet of Beirut, and the southern part was defined as the independent sanjak of Jerusalem. In his letter of October 24, McMahon avoided a specific definition both of the areas that "cannot be said to be purely Arab" and of those in which Britain was not "free to act without detriment to the interests of her ally, France." Had Hussein let this ambiguity stand, he could have later disowned any precise idea of its territorial delimitation. In choosing to interpret McMahon's vague reservation as including the velayet of Beirut, however, the sharif explicitly acknowledged its application to the northern half of Palestine, and implicitly—to the entire country. As McMahon quickly endorsed Hussein's terminology, specifically emphasizing in his reply to the sharif that French interests were involved in the velayet of Beirut, there could be no doubt in the minds of both negotiators that Palestine was excluded from the area of the prospective Arab empire.[50]

It is true that Hussein did not accept this reservation, but he could scarcely claim ignorance of its existence, having been the first to associate it explicitly with Palestine. Hence, the exclusion of the northern part of Palestine from the area of the Arab empire by the Sykes-Picot Agreement could not have come as a surprise to the sharif; the southern part of Palestine, or much of the sanjak of Jerusalem, was in any event awarded by this agreement to the independent Arab empire.

Part Three

UNITE
AND
RULE

16

THE BALFOUR DECLARATION

*I*n one important respect the historiographical debate about the Sykes-Picot Agreement has been a tempest in a teacup. Whatever its merits and flaws, the agreement did little to shape the form of the post–First World War Middle East, as even a glance at a map would reveal. The vast Arab empire it envisaged never materialized, its designated territory being divided among the present-day states of Iraq, Saudi Arabia, Syria, Transjordan (later Jordan), and Israel. Conversely, Turkey emerged from the war a significantly larger country than the truncated state it was intended to be. In brief, the new imperial system devised by the Sykes-Picot Agreement in which the Arabs, or rather the Hashemites, would substitute for the Turks, that is, the Ottomans, as the Middle East's imperial masters gave way to a wholly different international order based on the newly articulated ideal of the nation-state. This, to be sure, stemmed neither from an orderly and rational decisionmaking process nor from great-power sympathy for the national ideal. Rather, it was a reflection of the overall balance of forces and opportunities in the wake of the Great War, in which global and local imperialists scrambled for the best possible cut, and nationalist movements, for their place under the sun.

Dissatisfaction with the provisions of the Sykes-Picot Agreement was felt by its makers even before it was concluded. "The French government (which cannot ignore the powerful sentiments impelling French opinion to claim Palestine)," Prime Minister Briand telegraphed Ambassador Paléologue on March 25, 1916, "does not rule out the possibility of resuming constructive talks with the English at the opportune moment, and relies on Russian support for the French position." Hence the Franco-Russian exchange of notes on April 26, 1916, which made St. Petersburg a party to the Sykes-Picot Agreement, was accompanied by a secret Russian pledge to support the French objectives in Palestine in future negotiations with Britain.[1]

But whereas France had only the will to renege on the agreement, Britain possessed both the will and the muscle. During the war Britain sent more than 1,400,000 troops to the Middle East, as opposed to France's meager military contribution to this theater of war, and it was not going to allow its war ally to reap what were seen as grossly disproportionate gains. "I wonder if you have any rights to make claims under [the Sykes-Picot] agreement, after having refused to take part in the effort that made its execution possible," Prime Minister David Lloyd George reprimanded his French counterpart, Georges Clemenceau, during the Paris Peace Conference. Acting Foreign Secretary Lord George Nathaniel Curzon took this argument a step further. "When the Sykes-Picot agreement was concluded it was on the hypothesis that France and England would make approximately equal efforts in the matter of men and money in conquering Turkey," he told an Anglo-French meeting on December 23, 1919. "Unfortunately it had turned out that the war in this theatre had had to be fought almost entirely by Great Britain, who had expended some £750,000,000 on all the Turkish operations . . . If the French Government would reimburse His Majesty's Government one half of this sum they might have any boundary they liked here or elsewhere."[2]

This was of course a bogus claim. The Sykes-Picot Agreement had never been preconditioned on an equal division of labor between Britain and France in the Middle East, nor for that matter between Britain and Russia, which was also a signatory to the agreement. On the contrary, in their eagerness to gain international approval for their tentative understandings with Sharif Hussein, which is what the Sykes-Picot Agreement meant to them, British policymakers were prepared to pander to French (and Russian) imperial sensitivities; and it was precisely these conjunctural "concessions," notably the internationalization of Palestine and the severance of Mosul from Mesopotamia, that made the agreement less than popular in Whitehall and sowed the seeds of its undoing, not least with regard to Palestine.

As early as November 9, 1914, a week after the Ottoman entry into the war and some eighteen months before the conclusion of the Sykes-Picot Agreement, Herbert Samuel, the first Jew to serve as a British cabinet minister, went to see Foreign Secretary Grey. Now that Turkey had thrown itself into the European War, he argued, "it was probable that her empire would be broken up."

This would most likely raise the question of the future control of Palestine, and given that great-power jealousies would make it difficult to allot the country to any one of them, "perhaps the opportunity might arise for the fulfilment of the ancient aspiration of the Jewish people and the restoration there of a Jewish State." "British influence ought to play a considerable part in the formation of such a state," he argued, appealing to the practical, rather than the purely altruistic, sentiments of his interlocutor, "because the geographical situation of Palestine, and especially its proximity to Egypt, would render its goodwill to England a matter of importance to the British Empire."[3]

Grey's response was sufficiently encouraging for Samuel to commit his ideas to paper and to send a memorandum on the subject to the prime minister and a number of cabinet members. Several months later, on March 9, 1915, he presented a revised version of the memorandum to a cabinet meeting—to no avail. Notwithstanding enthusiastic support from some colleagues, notably Chancellor of the Exchequer Lloyd George and First Sea Lord Admiral John Fisher, Prime Minister Asquith would have nothing to do with Samuel's initiative. For one thing, he was "not attracted by this proposed addition to our responsibilities"; for another, he abhorred the idea that Britain "should take Palestine, into which the scattered Jews [could] in time swarm back from all quarters of the globe, and in due course obtain Home Rule. (What an attractive community!)."[4]

This by no means closed the lid on the Palestine question. To the contrary, no sooner had Sykes and Picot submitted their draft agreement to Nicolson's interdepartmental committee in January 1916 than the linkage between Zionism and Palestine was reestablished. In his criticism of the proposed agreement, Reginald Hall not only claimed that it gave

France far more than it actually deserved but also warned that "opposition must be expected from the *Jewish interest* throughout the world to any scheme recognising Arab independence and foreshadowing Arab predominance in the southern Near East." "Jewish opposition may be partly placated by the status proposed for the *Brown area* (i.e., northern Palestine)," he claimed, "but it may not be wholly or, indeed, very largely, placated."[5]

By that time the Foreign Office had been largely convinced of the "international power of the Jews." This was of course a stereotypical myth that had little to do with reality, but to Whitehall officialdom it seemed real enough. They knew that Jews in the West were deeply disturbed by the brutal oppression of their brethren in Russia; and while in Britain and France Jewish response could readily be kept under control, the far more self-assured and vociferous American Jewry was a different issue altogether. American Jews were, moreover, believed to wield considerable influence over both public opinion and the administration, whose political and financial goodwill the Entente Powers were anxious to buy (for example, Supreme Court Justice Louis Brandeis, the leader of the American Zionists, was known to be a close friend of President Woodrow Wilson's).

On the face of it, the road to the heart of American Jewry was clear and simple: the cessation of the persecution of Russian Jews. But this was more easily said than done, for it was evident that the Russians would not relent in their repression and that Britain and France would not pressure them to do so. The only way to square this vicious circle, so the Foreign Office came to believe, was to sponsor Jewish restoration in Palestine.[6] This would placate "World Jewry" without alienating the Russians; and, no less important, it would spell the end of France's designs on Palestine, as the restored Jewish commonwealth would most likely seek British (or American) patronage. As Hugh O'Beirne of the Foreign Office put it on March 8, 1916: "It is clear that the Palestine scheme has in it the most far-reaching political possibilities and we should, if I may be allowed to say so, be losing a great opportunity if we did not do our utmost to overcome any difficulties that may be raised by France and Russia."[7]

Later that month, Grey instructed Nicolson to "tell M. Cambon that it has been suggested that Jewish feeling which is now hostile and favours a German protectorate over Palestine might be entirely changed if an American protectorate was favoured with the object of restoring Jews to

Palestine. There would have to be international control of Christian Holy Places." The ambassadors in Paris and St. Petersburg were similarly instructed to inform their respective governments that "the scheme might be made far more attractive to the majority of Jews if it held out to them the prospect that when in the course of time the Jewish colonists in Palestine grow strong enough to cope with the Arab population they may be allowed to take the management of the internal affairs of Palestine (with the exception of Jerusalem and the Holy places) into their own hands."[8]

This initiative did not travel very far. The French dismissed the idea out of hand, whereas the Russians, though favorable to large-scale Jewish immigration and settlement in Palestine, connived with the French to outmaneuver the British in the postwar negotiations over Palestine.[9] Foreign Secretary Grey, failing in health and regularly replaced by the marquess of Crewe, and Prime Minister Asquith, increasingly resigned to the looming end of his leadership, lacked the vigor necessary to pursue the "Palestine scheme." It was only after Lloyd George succeeded Asquith in December 1916 that this scheme got off the ground.

The new prime minister was a sworn "Easterner" who had long advocated a greater military effort against Turkey, which he considered a "decadent Empire" whose "misrule" had reduced "the most flourishing civilisations in the world . . . [to] a wilderness of decay and ruin." He was also a fierce critic of the Sykes-Picot Agreement, deeming it "a foolish document" and failing to understand how "a man of Sir Mark Sykes' fine intelligence should ever have appended his signature to such an arrangement."[10] Indeed, for a brief while it appeared as if Lloyd George's fear of France's presence in the Levant outweighed his anti-Turkish sentiments. Shortly after coming to power he held secret talks with Enver Pasha on Turkey's departure from the war, in blatant violation of the September 1914 Declaration of London, which prohibited the war allies from opting for a separate peace. Appealing to Enver's personal greed, Lloyd George offered him and his associates generous financial rewards for leaving the war. He capitalized on his interlocutor's imperialist ambitions, promising to preserve the Ottoman Empire, if in a reduced form that would accommodate British interests, but not those of its war allies, France, Russia, and Italy. Within this framework, Arabia would be fully independent; Mesopotamia and Palestine would become *de facto* British protectorates; and Armenia and Syria would enjoy local autonomy within the Ottoman Empire.[11] When this initiative came to nought, Lloyd George embarked on a vigorous campaign to deal the Ottoman Empire a mortal blow while in the process nipping the Sykes-Picot Agreement in the bud. As the "Committee on the Terms of Peace," set up by the Imperial War Cabinet in April 1917, and headed by Lord Curzon, put it,

> It is desirable that His Majesty's Government should secure such a modification of the agreement with France of May 1916 as would give Britain definite and exclusive control over Palestine and would take the frontier of the British sphere of control to the River Leontes [that is, the Litani] and north of the Hauran.[12]

Since the British could not openly revoke a formal, written agreement with their two principal allies at a time when the end of the war was not yet in sight, the Zionist scheme was taken off the shelf yet again. As Lloyd George saw it, "the Jews might be able to render us more assistance than the Arabs."[13] Apart from offering a subtle means of easing the French out of Palestine, Zionism was still believed to hold the key to the goodwill and support of "World Jewry," whose importance in British eyes did not subside following America's entry into the war, in April 1917, and even increased in tandem with Russia's slide into anarchy, for it was hoped that Jewish influence within revolutionary circles would counteract the growing call in Russia to leave the war.

An additional factor made the Zionist card all the more appealing to Lloyd George: genuine sympathy for the idea of the Jews' restoration in their ancestral homeland. In March 1916 Asquith had been scathing about Lloyd George's support for Samuel's Palestine memorandum: "[He] does not care a damn for the Jews or their past or their future, but thinks it will be an outrage to let the Holy Places pass into the possession or under the protectorate of 'agnostic, atheistic France.'"[14] This observation could not be further from the truth. Lloyd George wished to see the French out of Palestine all right, but he also cared for the Zionist ideal of the Jews' return to Palestine. As a Welshman whose upbringing was steeped in the Bible, Lloyd George subscribed to the special creed of so-called "Gentile Zionism," whose roots dated to the religious evangelical revival in eighteenth-century Britain and whose adherents believed in the imminence of Jewish restoration and England's duty to help it along.

Nor was Lloyd George alone in his sympathy for Jewish national aspirations. Approval of Zionism as a worthy national movement, rather than as merely a handy tool, was gaining wide currency in the higher reaches of the British political and administrative establishment. For some, such as Foreign Secretary Arthur James Balfour, this sympathy was a matter of conviction largely divorced from ulterior motives; for others, such as Foreign Office mandarins Lord Cecil, the Marquess Crewe, and Sir Ronald Graham, it is difficult to say where political considerations ended and moral sympathy began. In any case, the British desire to undo the Sykes-Picot Agreement created a unique opportunity that the Zionist leader Dr. Chaim Weizmann was quick to exploit.

A Russian Jewish chemist who in 1904 had settled in Britain, where he obtained a position at Manchester University, Weizmann was a secondary figure in the Zionist movement at the outbreak of the war. But his personal charm, burning ambition, immense energy, and, above all, his ability to sense a great opportunity and to seize it, catapulted him within a few years to the movement's leadership.

A firm believer in the eventual victory of the Entente, Weizmann considered the policy of neutrality adopted by the Zionist movement at the beginning of the war a cardinal mistake. Alignment, not neutrality, should be the Zionist policy, especially since the Entente Powers championed "the cause of smaller nationalities."[15] In line with this view, he managed to establish a toehold in Whitehall and to expand it into a firm foothold once the circumstances were ripe.

The most valuable contact made by Weizmann was probably C. P. Scott, the proprietor-editor of the *Manchester Guardian,* whom he converted to Zionism shortly after the outbreak of the war. It was Scott who introduced Weizmann to a number of influential politicians, notably Lloyd George, with whom Weizmann conferred on several occasions between November 1914 and early 1917. None of these conversations involved concrete negotiations over the future of Palestine, nor did Weizmann intend them to do so. Rather, he sought to sow the Zionist seed within the British establishment so as to reap the fruit of international support for the Jewish national cause in the postwar settlement.

Before long, however, Weizmann raised his sights much higher. In mid-April 1917, shortly after his election as president of the British Zionist Federation, he heard from Scott, who had it from a fellow French journalist, of the existence of the secret Sykes-Picot Agreement and of its main provisions. This threatened to cut the ground from underneath Weizmann's feet, for his entire strategy was predicated on the assumption that the association of Zionist purposes with Britain, and vice versa, would win the Jews their ancestral homeland in Palestine, and he went on the offensive. In June 1917 Weizmann and his followers began to press for an official statement by the British government that would express "sympathy with, and support of, Zionist aims" and would "publicly recognise the justice of Jewish claims in Palestine." The following month, after discussions with the Foreign Office, the Zionists presented Balfour with the following proposal for the official statement: "His Majesty's Government accepts the principle that Palestine should be reconstituted as the national home of the Jewish people." Three and a half months later, on October 31, having discussed the matter twice and having ascertained the views of U.S. President Woodrow Wilson and of ten "representative [British] Jewish leaders," both Zionist and anti-Zionist, the War Cabinet approved the text of the official statement and authorized Balfour to publish it. Issued two days later in the form of a letter from Balfour to Lord Rothschild, the government's statement, or the Balfour Declaration, as it came to be known, stated that

> His Majesty's Government views with favour the establishment in Palestine of a national home for the Jewish people, and will use its best endeavours to facilitate the achievement of this object, it being clearly understood that nothing shall be done which may prejudice the civil and religious rights of existing non-Jewish communities in Palestine, or the rights and political status enjoyed by Jews in any other country.[16]

At the postwar peace conference, convened in Paris in January 1919, the Zionists sought to turn this formal British pledge into an international commitment to their national venture. To this end they asked the conference to recognize "the historic title of the Jewish people to Palestine and the right of the Jews to reconstitute in Palestine their National Home," to vest the country's "sovereign possession" in the League of Nations, and to appoint Britain as "Mandatory of the League," tasked with creating "such political, administrative and economic conditions as will secure the establishment there of the Jewish National Home and ultimately render possible the creation of an autonomous Commonwealth, it being clearly understood that nothing shall be done which may prejudice the civil and religious rights of existing non-Jewish communities in Palestine or the rights and political status enjoyed by Jews in any other country."[17]

The northern boundary of the Jewish national home was to start at a point on the Mediterranean south of Sidon and to follow the watersheds of the foothills of the Lebanon Mountains past Mount Hermon to the vicinity of the Hijaz Railway. In the east, the frontier was to run close to and west of the Hijaz Railway terminating in the Gulf of Aqaba, while in the south it was to be agreed upon with the Egyptian government; in the west, Palestine was to be bounded by the Mediterranean.[18]

Far more expansive than the Sykes-Picot scheme, this Zionist vision was not very different from local perceptions of Palestine's boundaries, and far more restrictive than the views held by some British officials. Recall, for example, that Muhammad Faruqi, who was instrumental in extracting McMahon's fateful promises to Hussein, considered the Hijaz Railway Palestine's eastern frontier, while the 1915 de Bunsen Committee went much further and defined Palestine as the much larger area stretching from the Mediterranean to Mesopotamia and comprising today's states of Israel and Jordan. As for Balfour, his perception of Palestine's eastern frontier was almost identical to that of the Zionists. "Palestine should extend into the lands lying east of the Jordan," he wrote in a special memorandum on August 11, 1919. "It should not, however, be allowed to include the Hedjaz Railway, which is too distinctly bound up with exclusively Arab interests." As far as the country's northern frontier was concerned, he deemed it "eminently desirable" that Palestine "should obtain the command of the water-power which naturally belongs to it, whether by extending its borders to the north, or by treaty with the mandatory of Syria, to whom the southward flowing waters of [Hermon] could not in any event be of much value." The delineation of these frontiers, in Balfour's opinion, should be determined not by considerations of Egyptian defense, as suggested by the military, but rather by the need "to make a Zionist policy possible by giving the fullest scope to economic development in Palestine."[19] Indeed, Lloyd George's vision of Palestine "from Dan to Beersheba," which constituted the British position during the postwar peace negotiations, was highly reminiscent of the Zionist demands as far as the country's northern and eastern frontiers were concerned, though far more restrictive with respect to the southern border (that is, the exclusion of the Negev from Palestine's territory).

Although this biblical definition was adopted by the Supreme Powers Conference, which reconvened in London on February 12, 1920, with the salient absence of the United States, its precise meaning was to constitute an Anglo-French bone of contention. The British wanted the

Sykes-Picot line to be pushed several dozen miles northward "so as to include the Litani bend, the headwaters of the Jordan, and the streams flowing south from Mount Hermon in Palestine." The French, however, would not relinquish the areas assigned to them by the Sykes-Picot Agreement, "the rich Kaza of Safed and, east of the Jordan, the waters of the Yarmuk valley and the Jebel Druze area."[20] In the end a compromise was devised whereby the frontier was extended north of the Sykes-Picot line to include upper Galilee in Palestine, but not the headwaters of the Jordan River on the Golan Heights or the Litani River and its immediately adjoining territory. This agreement, which was more amenable to the French than to the British position, received its final form in 1923.

An equally spirited debate revolved around the British suggestion that Balfour's promise of a Jewish national home in Palestine be written into the Palestine Mandate. The French government was keenly aware "that the whole world was sympathetic to the aspiration of the Jews to establish a national home in Palestine, and they would be prepared to do their utmost to satisfy their legitimate desires," argued the secretary-general of the French Ministry of Foreign Affairs, Philippe Berthelot. It was essential, however, that there should be no misunderstanding on the issue; and to the best of his recollection, the Balfour Declaration had never been officially accepted by the Allied Powers.

Curzon was taken aback. "M. Berthelot was possibly not fully acquainted with the history of the question," he said. The terms of the declaration had been communicated in February 1918 to Foreign Minister Pichon and approved by him, as they had been by the president of the United States, and also by Italy, Greece, China, Serbia, and Siam. Curzon thought, therefore, that "he was quite justified in saying that Mr. Balfour's declaration had been accepted by a large number of the Allied Powers." Berthelot would not budge. "As he had already pointed out, the French Government had never taken official cognisance of Mr. Balfour's declaration, and M. Pichon's connection with that declaration was, he submitted, somewhat vague." Hence, France was categorically opposed to "any reference in an official instrument, such as the Turkish treaty, to an unofficial declaration made by one Power, which had never been formally accepted by the Allies generally."[21]

At this point the Italian prime minister, Francesco Nitti, intervened. He thought that "it was useless to go into past history. It appeared to him that in principle the Powers were generally in agreement as to the desirability of instituting a national home for the Jews." However, the discussion had revealed a gap between the British and the French positions regarding the rights of the non-Jewish communities in Palestine, and had, moreover, raised the entire issue of the position of Roman Catholics in the East. Hence, without questioning Britain's ability to safeguard the rights and privileges of the non-Jewish communities in Palestine, he suggested the establishment of an international commission that would propose new regulations for the Holy Places, in lieu of the existing ones, as well as methods for the adjudication of interfaith disputes.

This proposal prompted the French to take action. Prime Minister Alexandre Millerand, who in January 1920 succeeded Clemenceau, urged his allies "not to ask the French delegation to state that they agreed to surrender long-existing rights and privileges." Berthelot, in contrast, preferred to look on the bright side. Since France stood to lose Palestine to Britain anyway, it might as well use the Italian initiative as a springboard for maintaining a firm foothold there as the custodian of Christianity's holiest sites.

Lloyd George, however, would hear nothing of the sort. "He quite understood the political difficulties that confronted M. Millerand," but

> the present trouble. . . was a practical one. It was most undesirable to have two mandatories in Palestine; one of the mandatories would incur all the trouble and expenses and cost, and yet would have no power at all in regard to religious bodies. The other mandatory would, it was suggested, have full authority in regard to religious matters . . . To have two mandatory Powers in Palestine would make it quite impossible for Great Britain to administer the country, and it might even easily raise difficulties in regard to her relations with France.[22]

This view prevailed, and the French backed down. In the Turkish Peace Treaty, drawn up by the London Conference (February 12–April 10, 1920), finalized by the San Remo Conference (April 18–26, 1920), and signed by the Turkish government at the French town of Sèvres on August 10, 1920, the Mandatory for Palestine was tasked with

> putting into effect the declaration originally made on November 2, 1917, by the British Government, and adopted by the other Allied Powers, in favour of the establishment in Palestine of a national

home for the Jewish people, it being clearly understood that nothing shall be done which may prejudice the civil and religious rights of existing non-Jewish communities in Palestine, or the rights and political status enjoyed by Jews in any other country.[23]

This was an outstanding success for the Zionists. Though they failed to achieve their territorial goals owing to Britain's compromise with France over Palestine's northern frontier, and the effective separation of Transjordan from Palestine that followed in 1921, the verbatim incorporation of the Balfour Declaration into the Turkish Peace Treaty and, two years later, into the League of Nations' Mandate for Palestine, gave Zionism the international recognition that its founding fathers, first and foremost Theodor Herzl, had been so eager to obtain.

17

THE UNDOING OF THE
SYKES-PICOT AGREEMENT

$\mathcal{P}$alestine was by no means the only area in which the British sought to undo the Sykes-Picot Agreement. The desire to exclude France from the Levant burned strong in Lloyd George and some of his key ministers, notably Curzon and Secretary of War Alfred Milner, and was shared by many within the British establishment, both in London and in Cairo. In a letter to Sykes on November 28, 1917, Gilbert Clayton, now the chief political officer of the Egyptian Expeditionary Force, advocated "a definite [French] pronouncement disclaiming any idea of annexation in Syria (including blue area) and emphasising their intention of assuring [the] liberty of *all* Syrians and helping them along the path towards independence and Government by [the] people."[1] To Lawrence, Clayton wrote that the Sykes-Picot Agreement "is in fact dead and, if we wait quietly, this fact will soon be realized"; to Picot he said that the agreement was no longer applicable since it was "completely out of date."[2]

The British high commissioner in Egypt, Reginald Wingate, shared this prognosis. When on December 6, 1917, Djemal Pasha revealed the terms of the Sykes-Picot Agreement, which the newly established Soviet government had just disclosed, Wingate asked London to refute Djemal's assertions so as to reassure the Hashemites. When the following summer Hussein inquired about the truth of Djemal's revelations, the high commissioner made no attempt to remind him that he had personally been informed of the Sykes-Picot Agreement by its two makers well before its publication by the Bolsheviks and had given his consent to France's control of the Syrian littoral along the lines of the British rule in Baghdad. Instead Wingate chose, without clearing the matter with London, to inform Hussein that Djemal was inaccurately recycling "a record of old conversations and of a provisional understanding (not a formal treaty)" that the Bolsheviks had found in the Russian foreign office.[3] Hussein was to exploit this assertion in his efforts to secure British acceptance of his imperial dream.

T. E. Lawrence, who has done more than anybody else to glorify Sharif Hussein's revolt, viewed the French presence in the Levant as the nemesis of the Hashemite imperial order he sought to establish. "I want to pull them all together, & to roll up Syria by way of the Hijaz in the name of the Sharif. You know how big his repute is in Syria," he wrote to his mentor, David Hogarth, on March 22, 1915. "This could be done by Idrisi only," he continued, ignoring the intense hostility between Idrisi and Hussein. "If Idrisi is anything like as good as we hope we can rush right up to Damascus, & biff the French out of all hope of Syria. It's a big game, and at last one worth playing."[4]

Three years later Lawrence was still playing his "big game," only now with the added weight of his newly acquired aura as the legendary desert warrior "Lawrence of Arabia." In his evidence to the cabinet's Eastern Committee on October 29, 1918, buttressed by a memorandum submitted to the committee a week later, he launched a spirited attack on the French ambitions in the Levant and made the case for Hashemite domination of the Middle East. He warned that France was out to "build up a colonial empire in the east" and that it was pursuing this objective under the wing of the Egyptian Expeditionary Force, headed by General Sir Edmund Allenby, which had just captured Palestine and Syria (this was of course the precise opposite of the truth, as Faisal enjoyed Allenby's protection while the French were being systematically obstructed by the general). As an immediate countermeasure, Lawrence suggested that Faisal should have "complete liberty to choose any foreign advisers he wants of any nationality he pleases," instead of the French advisers he was required to take by the Sykes-Picot Agreement.[5]

Lawrence's plan for a permanent arrangement was straightforward: the Hashemites would take over most of the Middle East. Hussein would be the king of Arabia, assisted and ultimately succeeded by his eldest son, Ali. Abdullah would become the ruler of Irak (that is, lower Mesopotamia), with Zeid reigning over the Jesireh (upper Mesopotamia) and Faisal over Syria. As for Beirut and Lebanon, Faisal might reluctantly agree to leave them "to French tutelage, provided that there was no question of French annexation." In Palestine, "the Arabs hope that the British will keep what they have conquered. They will not approve Jewish Independence for Palestine but will support as far as they can Jewish infiltration, if it is behind a British, as opposed to an international façade."[6]

Even Sir Mark Sykes seemed to be edging away from the agreement bearing his name—not out of rabid Francophobia, for he was a firm believer in the value of the Entente, but rather because he was genuinely convinced that the agreement had largely been made moot by international developments, such as Russia's departure from the war and, no less important, the advent of the concept of national self-determination on the international scene. "For the time at which it was made the agreement was conceived on liberal lines," Sykes wrote to Wingate, "but the world has moved so far since then that the Agreement can only be considered a reactionary measure."[7] In line with this view, Sykes sought to water down the "annexationist" provisions of the agreement. In his "Memorandum on the Asia-Minor Agreement," written in August 1917, he suggested that in the "blue" and "red" zones along the Syrian-Lebanese coast and in Lower Mesopotamia, excluded from the territory of the prospective Arab empire and placed under direct French and British control, the two powers should "both agree not to annex but to administer the country in consonance with the ascertained wishes of the people." The Hijaz was to be recognized as a "sovereign independent state," while Palestine was to be administered by Britain, as the "appointed trustee of the Powers," with France acting as "patron or protector of the various Catholic institutions outside the Holy Places," an international board governing Jerusalem and Bethlehem, and Haifa serving as "an Arab port for Area B."[8]

A year later, in July 1918, Sykes convinced Picot to introduce certain amendments to their 1916 agreement, so as to allay Arab fears of Anglo-French annexation of the territories included in the red and blue zones. They quickly drafted two working papers—"Declaration to the King of Hijaz" and an "Exchange of Views"—which stated that "with regard to such areas as are now occupied by the Allied forces it is the intention and desire of the two Governments that those areas should be permanently delivered from the oppression under which they formerly suffered, and that their future Government should be based upon the principle of the consent of the governed." The papers also promised that "on the part of neither Government has there ever been any intention of annexing these areas nor of disposing of them, nor allowing them to be disposed of by any other party, in any way other than is desired by the populations thereof." Yet they emphasized that "in view of the condition of these areas arising from mis-government, devastation, and massacre, it is the opinion of the two Powers, that a period of tutelage must supervene before the inhabitants of these areas are capable of complete self government, and in a position to maintain their independence."[9]

Although these proposals were not adopted by the British and the French governments, their spirit was largely incorporated into the joint Anglo-French Declaration of November 7, 1918, stating their aims at the end of the war:

> The object aimed at by France and Great Britain in prosecuting in the East the war let loose by German ambition is the complete and definite emancipation of the peoples so long oppressed by the Turks, and the establishment of National Governments and administrations deriving their authority from the initiative and free choice of the indigenous populations.
>
> In order to carry out these intentions France and Great Britain are at one in encouraging and assisting the establishment of indigenous Governments and administrations in Syria and Mesopotamia, now liberated by the Allies, and in territories the liberation of which they are engaged in securing, and in recognizing these as soon as they are actually established. Far from wishing to impose on the populations of these regions any particular institutions, they are only concerned to ensure by their support and by adequate assistance the regular working of Governments and administrations freely chosen by the populations themselves.[10]

The declaration was a compromise between the British desire to overturn the Sykes-Picot Agreement altogether and the French desire to keep it in place. By promising "the complete and definite emancipation of the peoples so long oppressed by the Turks," it precluded a possible Anglo-

French annexation of the territories included in the blue and red zones; by reserving the great-power right "to ensure by their support and by adequate assistance the regular working of Governments and administrations," it preserved the zones of indirect influence provided by the Sykes-Picot Agreement. Indeed, the declaration's equivocal language, which was at once precise and abstract, allowed both parties to have their cake and eat it too. To Britain it signified the demise of the Sykes-Picot Agreement; to France—its survival.

Before long the two war allies were locked in an acrimonious debate, with French anger at Whitehall's general desire to undo the Sykes-Picot Agreement matched only by French ire at the behavior of British officialdom on the spot. The Egyptian Expeditionary Force, now in complete control of the Levant, did little to conceal its contempt for the meager French presence. Allenby himself set the tone by openly encouraging Arab communal leaders in the French zone to bypass Picot, who arrived in Beirut as France's chief political adviser. French banks were refused licenses in Beirut; the circulation of French currency was prohibited; and instruction in the French language was not permitted even within the area of direct French occupation.[11]

No less galling for the French was British support for Hashemite activities in Syria, especially in the Syrian littoral designated by the Sykes-Picot Agreement as an area of direct French control. While ostensibly restricting his activities to the maintenance of the military status quo so as not to prejudice a future political settlement, Allenby made several significant political decisions that favored the Hashemites. No measures were adopted to annul the declarations that Hussein was the king of Syria and the Hijaz, thus effectively legitimizing his bid for the Levant; the sharifian flag was allowed to fly on government buildings; and when Faisal proclaimed an independent Arab government, he was congratulated by Balfour and Sykes on "the successful establishment of a humane and ordered Government in Damascus which commands the enthusiastic support of its citizens." For his part Allenby made it eminently clear that he regarded Faisal "as supreme authority in Syria on all Arab matters whether administrative or military," giving him a free hand to intimidate political opponents and to conduct a virulent anti-French propaganda campaign. On October 13, 1918, Allenby gave Faisal his "personal assurance that whatever arrangement may be made now for districts in the coastal area, they are of a military nature and without prejudice to the final settlement which will be decided upon by the Allies at the Peace Conference." He also promised that the Hashemites would participate in this decisionmaking process. In French eyes all this amounted to back-stabbing by a comrade in arms.[12]

A special source of French resentment was the British refusal to withdraw Allenby's occupying force from the Levant before the peace conference, which convened in Paris in January 1919, had reached its decision. Requests to increase the number of French troops in Syria were refused time and again; Britain remained firmly in control, leaving the French with a frustrating sense of impotence.[13] The hapless Picot felt that France's standing in the Levant was being progressively undermined, yet there was little he could do apart from filing repeated protests against the anti-French bias of the British military administration, which were then forwarded to London.

This situation was becoming too much even for Prime Minister Clemenceau, one of the least imperialistically minded of French politicians. During a visit to London in December 1918, he acquiesced in Lloyd George's request that Britain be given control over Palestine (designated by the Sykes-Picot Agreement as an international zone) and Mosul (included in the French sphere). The armistice with Germany had been signed the previous month and Clemenceau, whose attention was fixed on ensuring France's security vis-à-vis Germany in general, and its position on the Rhine in particular, was prepared to sacrifice French interests overseas in return for British (and American) support for France's border claims. To his dismay, Lloyd George later seemed to have "forgotten" their London deal, which drove Clemenceau to lock horns with the British premier in negotiations during the Paris Peace Conference. Even after the two leaders had agreed on the withdrawal of British forces from Cilicia and Syria, beginning on November 1, 1919, and their replacement by French forces "west of the Sykes-Picot line" and by an Arab force "at Damascus, Homs, Hama, and Aleppo," Clemenceau would not forgive Lloyd George for what he perceived as an attempted double-crossing. "As regards our conversation of December 1918, I cannot admit that I consented without an equivalent to the extension of the British mandate to Mosul and to Palestine," he wrote to the British prime minister on November 9. "It would have been unprecedented that such concessions should have been made without any precise definition on paper, all the advantage being on the one side."[14]

This squabbling was conducted under the watchful eye of U.S. President Woodrow Wilson. From the moment he sent the United States to war on the Entente's side, Wilson took the moral high ground. He disavowed any ulterior motives for his decision, presenting it as a selfless move to make the world "safe for democracy"; he kept his distance from his European partners and their imperialist schemes, choosing to be designated an "associate" rather than a full-fledged ally; and he never declared or waged war on the Ottoman Empire. On January 8, 1918, in an address to a joint session of Congress, Wilson proclaimed his famous Fourteen Points, which were to form the basis for the postwar settlement and the conduct of international politics generally. Of these, three were of direct relevance to the Entente: Point One, renouncing secret diplomacy and secret agreements; Point Fourteen, calling for the formation of a general association of nations to guarantee the independence and territorial integrity of all states; and Point Twelve, specifically addressing the future of the Ottoman Empire: "The Turkish portions of the present Ottoman Empire should be assured a secure sovereignty, but the other nationalities which are now under Turkish rule should be assured an undoubted security of life and an absolutely unmolested opportunity of autonomous development."

Yet for all his high rhetoric, Woodrow Wilson was as much a power broker as his European partners. He was ostensibly opposed to their secret agreements, yet having joined the war, he did his utmost to keep them secret, going so far as to try—unsuccessfully—to prevent the publication of these treaties in the United States after the Bolsheviks had published their contents.[15] More important, as a prominent member of the Council of Four, whose deliberations were held in the strictest secrecy, Wilson became a party to precisely the same secret diplomacy he had so loudly derided.

Even Wilson's celebrated Point Twelve was regressive in comparison with the much-maligned Sykes-Picot Agreement. The latter provided for "an independent Arab State or a Confederation of Arab States," and the November 1918 Declaration went still further to promise "complete and definite emancipation of the peoples so long oppressed by the Turks, and the establishment of National Governments and administrations deriving their authority from the initiative and free choice of the indigenous populations." In contrast, not only did Point Twelve not envisage the full independence of the former Ottoman nationalities (only their "autonomous development"); it did not even preclude possible great-power annexation of these territories so long as their inhabitants were ensured "an undoubted security of life and an absolutely unmolested opportunity of autonomous development."

All this, to be sure, did not prevent Wilson from seeking to overturn the secret wartime agreements, and his primary tool for achieving this goal was the mandatory system associated with the nascent League of Nations. Interestingly enough, the first concrete plan in this vein came from a member of the British Empire peace delegation: Lieutenant-General Jan Christian Smuts, South Africa's minister of defense and its representative in the Imperial War Cabinet. On December 16, 1918, he suggested that the territories of the Austro-Hungarian, Russian, and Ottoman empires be placed under the mandatory control of a single power, accountable to the League of Nations. Annexation was forbidden, and the mandatory power was to oversee the mandated territory from tutelage to eventual independence.

After much haggling, the territories of the defunct Austro-Hungarian and Russian empires were excluded from the mandates system and given immediate independence; conversely, it was decided that "the well-being and development" of those German and Ottoman territories "inhabited by peoples not yet able to stand by themselves under the strenuous conditions of the modern world" formed "a sacred trust of civilisation and that securities for the performance of this trust should be embodied in the constitution of the League of Nations." More specifically, it was agreed that "Armenia, Syria, Mesopotamia, Palestine and Arabia must be completely severed from the Turkish Empire," and that certain communities in these territories "have reached a stage of development where their existence as independent nations can be provisionally recognised subject to the rendering of administrative advice and assistance by a mandatory power until such time as they are able to stand alone."[16]

While Wilson was unquestionably the moving spirit behind the installment of the mandates system, it was by no means anathema to the British and the French. Like the U.S. president, Lloyd George viewed the mandates as a useful means to undo the wartime territorial arrangements, notably the Sykes-Picot Agreement, and to legitimize Britain's control of further territories, primarily Mosul and Palestine. Moreover, an American-guaranteed mandates system could shield Britain's Middle Eastern interests both from Russia, whose perceived threat to British India had waned following the Bolshevik takeover but had not disappeared altogether, and from a resurgent Germany. For its part, France was similarly interested and recast its sights on "Greater Syria" as a future mandate, including territories promised to the prospective Arab empire by the Sykes-Picot Agreement. As it was put to the peace conference, "there was no Government in the world which had such a position as France in the regions claimed."[17]

But this is where the common sentiments between the American president and his European partners ended. Wilson did not view the mandates as a means for territorial and strategic aggrandizement; Lloyd George and Clemenceau did, hence their insistence on an immediate distribution of the Ottoman spoils. Since a settlement at any given time would be made by the same powers and perhaps even by the same people, Lloyd George argued, they had better resolve the mandates issue once and for all. Besides, it was impossible for His Majesty's government to sustain the 1,084,000 British and imperial troops then in the Ottoman Empire while waiting for a settlement that seemed very far away. Britain must have relief, and a permanent designation of mandates seemed the best and quickest way to achieve this end.

This raised immediate problems for Wilson. He was the chief architect of the mandates system all right, but he could scarcely guarantee America's active participation in this system, not least because such a move rested with the Senate, which was dominated by a hostile Republican party led by Wilson's archenemy, Henry Cabot Lodge. Thus the American president not only opposed the British proposal for an immediate assignment of mandates but also seemed bent on preventing the two European powers from obtaining what they viewed as a just reward for their exorbitant human and material sacrifices during the war. Lloyd George in particular was contemptuous of Wilson and his attempt to determine the future of the Middle East without having sent a single soldier to fight there, indeed, without even declaring war on the Ottoman Empire. "Our people are fed up with Wilson," he declared in April 1919. "They are tired of playing second fiddle, considering what we have done in the war." Even when the mortally ill American president was confined to his bed, Lloyd George remained vindictive: "The only faculty that remained unimpaired to the end—which was delayed for four years—was his abnormal stubbornness."[18]

Nothing underscored the gap between these two positions more starkly than Wilson's insistence, incorporated into Article 22 of the League of Nations' Covenant, that the wishes of the former Ottoman subjects "must be a principal consideration in the selection of the mandatory power"; and by way of implementing this principle the president suggested that an inter-Allied commission go to Syria to gauge opinion there and to tell the conference "the facts as they found them." This was totally unacceptable to Lloyd George and Clemenceau, both of whom dreaded the very notion of predicating their presence in the Middle East upon local "consent." Since neither of them found it in himself to dismiss the plan out of hand, they felt obliged to play along; but they spared no effort to bring about its quick demise.

When it was announced on March 25 that a commission of inquiry comprising British, French, American, and Italian members would be sent to Syria, Wilson promptly appointed its two American members: Henry Churchill King, the president of Oberlin College and a firm believer in Anglo-Saxon superiority over the French, and Charles R. Crane, a Chicago valve manufacturer and influential contributor to the Democratic party who was to become an ardent Arabophile. The foremost reason for their selection for this sensitive mission was that "the President felt these two men were particularly qualified to go to Syria because they knew nothing about it."[19]

To Wilson's exasperation, the British and the French were in no hurry to appoint their own delegates, instead trying to convince him that the idea of a commission was both dangerous and unnecessary. Even when Lloyd George made a sudden volte-face on April 22 and expressed support for the immediate departure of the commission, Clemenceau remained defiant. As far as he was concerned, any inquiry into the Syrian situation would *ipso facto* be tilted in Britain's favor owing to its physical occupation of the Levant. "I am ready to send my representatives to Syria as soon as the relief of the occupation troops [has] begun," he told Wilson and Lloyd George on May 21. "But I find it useless to send a commission to Syria to make an inquiry under the dictatorship of General Allenby." The next day, following yet another acrimonious exchange with his French counterpart, Lloyd George decided not to put further strain on Anglo-French relations and announced that Britain would not participate in the commission.[20] The irritated Wilson decided to go it alone, only to discard his brainchild a few months later. By the time the King-Crane Commission reported back in July 1919, the Treaty of Versailles had already been signed and the president had left for America. Subsequently, the commission's report had no impact whatsoever on the future of the modern Middle East; indeed, Wilson did not even bother to send it to the deliberations over the Turkish Peace Treaty, which continued after the Paris Peace Conference, and its findings were not made public until 1922.

It was thus left to the two great European powers (with a little help from Italy) to complete the destruction of the Ottoman Empire and to build a new regional order on its ruins. The Turkish Peace Treaty, signed at Sèvres on August 10, 1920, constituted a death sentence for the Ottoman Empire, forcing the surrender of the lion's share of its territory. The Hijaz and Armenia were recognized as "free and independent" states; Syria and Mesopotamia were "provisionally recognized as independent States subject to the rendering of administrative advice and assistance by a Mandatory until such time as they are able to stand alone."[21] Kurdistan was granted local autonomy and given the opportunity to convince the Council of the League of Nations, within one year from the time the Sèvres Treaty was to go into effect, that the majority of Kurds wanted independence from Turkey. Should the council accept this claim, Turkey was to execute the league's recommendation and to renounce all rights and title over the area.[22]

Other Ottoman concessions included the renunciation of all rights and title in or over Egypt (taking effect as of November 5, 1914) and recognition of the British protectorate over the country; renunciation of all rights and title in or over Cyprus and recognition of the November 5, 1914, British annexation of the island; recognition of the French protectorate over Morocco (taking effect as of March 30, 1912) and Tunis (dating back to May 12, 1881), with all its attendant consequences; renunciation of all rights and privileges left to the sultan in Libya; renunciation in favor of Italy of all rights and title over the Dodecanese Islands (later ceded to Greece); the surrender of Eastern Thrace to Greece, together with most of the Aegean Islands; and the placement of the western Anatolian town and district of Smyrna under Greek administration for a period of five years, after which the population would be allowed to request permanent incorporation into Greece.

The "Sick Man" of Europe had finally breathed his last breath, but the scramble for his territorial bequest, while officially settled, was far from over.

18

LOSING SYRIA

$\mathcal{N}$o sooner had Hussein misled Britain into approving his imperial dream than he embarked on a sustained effort to obtain the widest possible international endorsement for his plans. He repeatedly threatened to abdicate if his demands were not met; castigated the Sykes-Picot Agreement as an act of betrayal by a perfidious ally, as if he had not already accepted its main provisions in the spring of 1917; and, above all, disseminated a wholly fictitious version of McMahon's promises.[1]

In a memorandum entitled "Translation of the Agreement Come to with the British Government regarding the (Arab) Rising and Its Foundation," sent to High Commissioner Wingate on August 28, 1918, Hussein claimed that the British government had agreed

> to the formation of an independent Arab Government in every
> meaning of the word "independence," internally and externally; the
> boundaries of the said Government being, on the east, the Persian
> Gulf; on the west, the Red Sea, the Egyptian frontier, and the
> Mediterranean; on the north, the northern boundaries of the
> vilayets of Aleppo and Mosul up to the river Euphrates and its
> junction with the Tigris as far as their mouths in the Persian Gulf,

but with the exception of the Aden colony, which is excluded from these boundaries.

This claim could not be further from the truth, as officials from the Foreign Office were keenly aware. They pointed out that the alleged agreement produced by Hussein "does not correspond to any document which has been assented to, or even seen by, His Majesty's Government," and that "the version of these commitments set out in the King's memorandum in no way corresponds to the actual facts, but is simply a repetition, in more concise form, of the demands originally made by the King when he opened negotiations in July 1915." Yet even at this late stage of the war these officials could not bring themselves to admit that they had been outwitted by a local potentate. "It is not suggested that, in presenting this memorandum, the King is acting in bad faith," they noted with the paternalistic tone of an imperial power absolving the acts of a local client as manifestations of "native" immaturity. "Oriental diplomacy is seldom precise unless compelled to be so, and the method by which the negotiations were conducted in 1915–8 left something to be desired in this respect. It is more probable that the King genuinely believes his memorandum to represent the sense of what was tacitly, if not explicitly, agreed to by His Majesty's Government."[2]

Whether Hussein genuinely believed in the authenticity of his memorandum—and his behavior throughout the war was scarcely indicative of the "oriental" naïveté attributed to him by British officialdom—he was adamant about the Entente's complying with this alleged agreement. In a meeting at 10 Downing Street on September 19, 1919, in which he was informed of Britain's intention to withdraw its forces from Syria and Lebanon, Hussein's third son, Faisal, objected to French occupation of any of the evacuated areas, invoking the alleged Anglo-Hashemite Treaty, which supposedly gave "as the boundaries for the Arab Provinces the Persian Gulf and the Red Sea, and did not exclude any province at all right up to the Taurus Mountains. As regards the west coast, it included everything." Lloyd George was taken aback. He protested that this was the first time he had heard of any definite treaty with King Hussein, other than the Hussein-McMahon correspondence. But Faisal would not budge. "The whole correspondence would be submitted to the Prime Minister officially," he promised, admitting that he had never seen the full agreement, and had only seen certain articles of it about ten days before leaving for Britain; but this was merely because the agreement "had been entered into by his Father alone, and His Majesty had never shown it to anyone . . . [and] had never wanted to make the agreement public."[3]

When they met again four days later, the British were far more definitive. "The first thing the Foreign Office did when they saw the translation of the excerpts of the alleged Treaty was to ask Sir Henry McMahon, who had been High Commissioner in Egypt when the negotiations were first conducted with the Sheriff of Mecca, if the Treaty was in any way authentic," Curzon told Faisal. "Sir Henry wrote in reply, 'I have read alleged Treaty with amazement; it bears no resemblance to the original document.'" This statement led him to look exhaustively into the entire Anglo-Sharifian correspondence of 1915–1916, Curzon continued, and his unequivocal conclusion was that "there had been a serious mistake. The document in question represented what the Arabs had been pressing, and not what H.M. Government had accepted." He then brushed aside Faisal's request to defer discussion of the matter until he had received further clarifications from his father. "It was no use to ask King Hussein for copies of the agreement, as it did not exist," he said. "The 'understanding' between H.M. Government and the King arose from a series of letters, copies of which H.M. Government would gladly produce for His Highness's perusal."[4]

In private Faisal was far less certain of the veracity of his father's claims. "Inform me of date of Treaty which you sent to us on July 17 because it arrived without indispensable date," he cabled Hussein, "it being the latest official document which contains the signature of Sir H. McMahon: or is there any other? They feign ignorance of its existence." Hussein's assurance that he was "by help of God one of those who say but the truth" and that his agreement with Britain was expressed in McMahon's letter of March 10, 1916, deposited in the high commissioner's office, did little to allay Faisal's doubts. "To which decision before the revolt do you refer?" he queried. "They pretend here that there was no convention. They showed me a document signed by [Mc]-Mahon and dated October 24 1920 [sic] which stipulates separation of Iraq and Syrian coast." A few days later Faisal was more forthright: "Great Britain is no doubt acting as usual with regard to keeping her word: but non-existence of any registration in Foreign Office led to these arguments." Hussein was incensed by this apparent lack of trust. "Our communications are with High Commissioner and naturally they are not registered in London Foreign Office," he coldly wrote to his son. "This is [the] long and short of [the] matter. Please hurry up decision."[5]

Whatever his private thoughts and beliefs, Faisal had never shrunk from misleading his British interlocutors, and nowhere was this practice more visible than in his efforts to secure his own share of the spoils. As shown, he had no qualms about negotiating during the war with Djemal Pasha behind Britain's back, keeping in the dark even his close friend and confidant, the legendary Lawrence of Arabia, to whom he owed an immeasurable debt of gratitude. This discourtesy, nevertheless, did not prevent Lawrence, who got wind of it through his own sources, from backing other deceptive claims by Faisal. At a meeting with Allenby in Damascus on October 3, 1918, a few days after the city's capture by the Egyptian Expeditionary Force, Faisal feigned total ignorance of the Sykes-Picot Agreement, of which he had been aware for at least a year and a half. In his account, he knew nothing of the intention to give France a significant foothold in the Levant, hence he "declined to have a French Liaison Officer or to recognise French guidance in any way." Rather, he "understood from the Advisor that Sir Edmund Allenby had sent him [presumably Lawrence] that the Arabs were to have the whole of Syria including the Lebanon but excluding Palestine; a Country without a Port was no good to him."

Allenby turned to Lawrence: "But did you not tell him that the French were to have the Protectorate over Syria?"

"No Sir, I know nothing about it."

"But you knew definitely that he, Faisal, was to have nothing to do with the Lebanon."

"No Sir, I did not," Lawrence unflinchingly repeated.

This was an extraordinary claim, especially when coming from a person who in his own published account had "betrayed the treaty's existence to Feisal" well before its public disclosure by the Bolsheviks in the autumn of 1917. Yet Allenby seemed surprisingly unperturbed. "You would like Faisal," he wrote to his wife. "He is a keen slim highly strung man. He has beautiful hands, like a woman's; and his fingers are always moving nervously, when he talks. But he is strong in will and straight in principle."[6]

Why Allenby failed to pay closer attention to the underlying causes of Faisal's nervousness is not entirely clear. Perhaps he shared the belief that "oriental diplomacy is seldom precise"; perhaps he subscribed to the heroic image of Faisal contrived by Lawrence, whom Allenby held in great esteem and affection; or perhaps he viewed Faisal as a useful tool in undermining France's position in the Levant. Be that as it may, Allenby was not alone in allowing Faisal to get away with his economical use of the truth.

In Paris, having listened to Faisal's idealized account of the Hashemite revolt given to the Council of Ten, the supreme decisionmaking body of the peace conference, Lloyd George lent the emir a helping hand, asking how many troops the Hijaz had put into the field. Faisal seized the opportunity to inflate the Hashemite contribution to the Allied war effort. "It was impossible to give an exact figure, but, including the Hedjaz Army, the Arabs had put about 100,000 men into the field. There was, in addition, a considerable number of Irregulars who were not on his registers. He thought he could assert that every man of fighting age in possession of a rifle between Mecca and Aleppo had joined the Arab standards."

This was a hollow pretense, as Lloyd George knew full well. "What the Arabs were apt to overlook is the fact that their contribution in the conquest of Palestine and Syria was almost insignificant compared with that of the British Empire," he wrote in his memoirs of the Paris Peace Conference. "The Arabs only claimed that their army mustered in all a force of 100,000 light cavalry. Eastern arithmetic is proverbially romantic."[7] The fact that despite these views Lloyd George helped Faisal mislead the peace conference spoke volumes about the intensity of his desire to elbow France out of the Levant: if Britain were not to assume the mandate for this area, it would rather have it ruled by its most prominent local client than by its European war ally.

This preference did not escape Faisal. On the face of it, he acted as his father's representative to the peace conference, voicing the latter's demand for a pan-Arab empire; in actual fact he was a free agent seeking to carve his own Syrian empire. It was this desire that had almost led him to drop his British allies for a deal with Djemal Pasha; and it was for this goal that he was prepared to "put off the breach between his father and himself as long as possible": open defiance of Hussein at that particular stage would have cost Faisal the headship of the Hijazi delegation to the peace conference, with its attendant access to great-power high politics.[8]

Yet this did not deter Faisal. In his testimony to the Council of Ten, he claimed that there were few nations in the world as homogenous as the

Arabs and that "personally he was afraid of partition. His principle was Arab unity. It was for this that the Arabs had fought." At the same time, he made the contradictory admission that "Syria claimed her unity and her independence" and that "the object of all Arab hopes and fears" was a confederation of independent states—not a unitary empire.[9]

In a memorandum submitted to the peace conference on January 1, 1919, a month before his oral evidence, Faisal went much further in revealing his real agenda. While paying the customary lip service to the ideal of eventual Arab unity, he candidly admitted that "the various provinces of Arab Asia—Syria, Irak, Jezireh, Hejaz, Nejd, Yemen—are very different economically and socially, and it is impossible to constrain them into one frame of government." Defining himself as a predominantly Syrian patriot—"an old member of the Syrian Committee" (that is, al-Fatat) and leader of "the Syrian revolt"—Faisal dwelt at considerable length on the divisions among the Arabic-speaking territories before proposing his own solution: great-power support for a Mesopotamian government, appointed rather than elected "until time makes the broader basis possible"; complete independence for the Hijaz, Najd, and Yemen, something that was anathema to his father and Abdullah, who wished to see these areas under Hashemite rule; and "the effective superposition of a great trustee" for Palestine. As for Syria, he believed that this "agricultural and industrial area thickly peopled with sedentary classes" was "sufficiently advanced politically to manage her own internal affairs," if given adequate foreign and technical assistance.[10]

Apart from reflecting his lack of belief in the ideal of pan-Arab unity, whose institutionalization in regional and international consciousness was largely of his family's making, Faisal's memorandum revealed his imperialist mindset. As he put it on one occasion, since Syria was "merchandise which has no owner," it was only natural for Britain, France, and himself to "try to appropriate it before the others."[11] The hopes and wishes of the governed, needless to say, counted for nothing, not least since there was tough opposition in the Levant to Hashemite domination in general, and to Faisal's personal rule in particular.

During the war the traditional urban elites collaborated with the Ottomans, conveniently switching allegiance only when confronted by the stark facts on the ground; but they were far from enthusiastic about their prospective domination by Hijazis, whom they considered an inferior and uncivilized lot, and whom they viewed not as liberators but as alien invaders; and they resented the prominent role played by the small nationalist societies, especially al-Fatat, in Faisal's administration. As for the vast majority of Syrians, Faisal's lofty protestations of Arab unity meant little. Lacking any sense of common Syrian identity, their loyalties were predominantly parochial—to family, clan, local potentate, religious, ethnic, social, or linguistic group. There was no real political interaction between the two provincial capitals of Damascus and Aleppo, both of which had been administered separately by the Ottomans, and the immediate concern of their residents was to recover from the dislocations of war, to get food and work. The two cities were flooded with rural refugees who had fled their famine-stricken districts; Aleppo, in addition, was swamped with Armenians fleeing Ottoman oppression. These wretched people now competed with natives in an already depressed labor market. Tensions ran so high as to trigger a massacre of Armenians in early 1919.

Nor did Faisal enjoy the support of the non-Muslim communities. His rule was feared by the Christians, mainly but not exclusively in Lebanon, where his popularity was generally very low. A British officer in Beirut, for example, estimated that a mere 15 percent would prefer a Hashemite government. Similarly, the patriarch of Antioch, accompanied by the archbishop of Beirut and the bishop of Baalbek, took the trouble of pleading with the British delegation to the Paris Peace Conference that Lebanon "should not be placed in any way under an Arab and Moslem Government." For their part the leading chiefs of Jabel Druze saw the French as a lesser evil than Faisal, and neither the emir's personal pleas nor those of the British did much to boost his popularity. Moreover, the excesses of Faisal's government, rife with nepotism and corruption, did little to endear the Hashemites to their would-be Syrian subjects.[12]

Under the circumstances it was only natural for Faisal to leave nothing to chance. Having heard of the Entente's intention to send an Inter-Allied Commission of Inquiry to the Middle East, he quickly assembled a General Syrian Congress that would "make clear the wishes of the Syrian people to the American Commission of Enquiry."[13] Yet the Congress, which convened for the first time on June 3, 1919, was anything but representative. No real elections were ever held, and its delegates came by and large from the ranks of the small circle of nationalists who fought alongside Faisal during the war and who controlled his administration in its wake. One only has to note that 35 of the Congress's 120 seats were held by al-Fatat members, who even after the war numbered a mere 200, or that only 2 of the 16 delegates who allegedly represented the predominantly Christian Lebanon were Maronites, to appreciate the oligarchic and nonrepresentative nature of this assembly.[14]

But the Syrian Congress, which told the Commission of Enquiry of the (alleged) Syrian desire for an independent constitutional monarchy ruled by Faisal, "without protectorate or trusteeship," or failing this, for an American mandate for no longer than twenty years (with Britain as a second choice), was not the only means used by Faisal to manipulate public opinion: extensive propaganda, orchestrated demonstrations, and intimidation of opponents were all employed by the emir, under the watchful eye if not the tacit connivance of the British military authorities. "Feisal has taken the whole of the political campaign into his own hands and has already sent instructions to all parts of the country," Clayton reported to Curzon shortly before the commission's arrival in Syria. "The people have been told to ask for complete independence for Syria, and, at the same time, to express a hope that it will be granted to other Arab countries. By this compromise Feisal has reconciled the 'Ittihad-es-Suri,' which thinks only of Syria, with the pan-Arab empire enthusiasts represented in the 'Istiklal-el-Arabi.'"[15]

Even the American Commission of Enquiry did not fail to notice these machinations. According to a confidential appendix to the commission's report ("for the use of Americans only"), "there were evidences of considerable pressure exerted by the Government to secure the union of all elements upon one program . . . government agents tried hard to persuade, cajole, or threaten all, Christians and Moslems alike, into subscribing . . . Evidence was presented that the Emir had tried immediately before the arrival of the Commission in Damascus to secure the support of certain councils for a request for a British mandate."[16]

The fact that the two chief commissioners, Charles King and Henry Crane, preferred the recommendations of the Syrian Congress to the suggestion of some of their advisers that Syria be placed under a joint Anglo-French mandate, Lebanon under a French mandate, and Palestine under a British mandate, was clearly a victory for Faisal—but only a Pyrrhic one.[17] Had he sought accommodation with France, however tactically, his position in the Levant might have been salvaged. As things turned out, in choosing to give the French the cold shoulder and to concentrate instead on manipulating the conclusions of a commission, whose report had no influence whatsoever on the policymaking process, Faisal effectively signed away his imperial Syrian dream.

On April 13, 1919, the emir met Clemenceau in Paris. He promised "to use his efforts with the people to secure a French mandate for Syria" and was assured of France's recognition of "the right of Syria to independence in the form of a federation of autonomous local communities corresponding to the traditions and wishes of their populations." Yet in a letter to the prime minister a week later, as he was about to depart for Syria, Faisal made no mention of their understanding of the previous week: only the noncommittal promise that "on my arrival in Syria, I will do my best to assure my people of your kindly feelings towards us and will work to increase the friendly bonds between the French and the Arabs." This was unacceptable to Clemenceau. Their understanding went no further.[18]

Why Faisal "had never any intention of carrying out this arrangement," as he candidly admitted shortly after returning to Damascus, is not difficult to understand. For one thing, he believed that "France, to all appearances, relies solely on England and America for her future existence," hence the key to his coveted Syrian empire lay elsewhere. For another, he feared that the French would use the League of Nations' mandate to colonize the Levant along the lines of the North African model, whereas such a risk under a British mandate was virtually nonexistent. Above all, Faisal's maneuvering bore the hallmarks of Lawrence, the emir's closest confidant and adviser during the Paris Peace Conference. The legendary Englishman, who joined Faisal for his meeting with Clemenceau, denied on several occasions the existence of any agreement between the two; yet in Faisal's own account, he not only entered into a "verbal agreement" with Clemenceau, but did it on Lawrence's advice.[19] This leads to the conclusion that the meeting was a tactical ploy to lure the French into a false sense of security at a time when the great powers were haggling over the dispatch of the Inter-Allied Commission of Enquiry to the Middle East.

Both Lawrence and Faisal were bent on keeping France out of the Levant, and both viewed the commission as a handy tool to achieve this goal. The fact that the commission turned out to be a purely American rather than an inter-Allied body did little to dampen their optimism, not least because they saw President Wilson as the real power broker in the peace conference. In January 1919 Lawrence told the American delegation to the conference of his hope that "the United States would administer Syria." Faisal reiterated the same hope a month later in a conversation with Captain William Yale, the American representative in the Middle East and an expert with the Commission of Enquiry.[20]

So blinded was Faisal by this hope that he would not read the writing on the wall. He failed to grasp the depth of American reluctance to undertake new and unprecedented international commitments, and he failed to detect the lukewarm American attitude toward Hashemite domination of the entire Middle East (the intelligence report presented to President Wilson, for example, suggested that in Arabia King Hussein "be not aided to establish an artificial and unwelcome dominion over tribes unwilling to accept his rule," and that Syria, Palestine, and Mesopotamia be kept as separate entities under great-power mandates). Even when told by Colonel Edward Mandell House, Woodrow Wilson's close friend and confidant, that "he was very doubtful whether the United States would accept the mandate," Faisal did not lose hope. It was only after the president had left Paris for the United States at the end of June 1919 that the emir despaired of the idea.[21]

Equally misconceived was Faisal's expectation that the commission ("the best thing he had ever heard of in his life," to use his own words) would decide the fate of the region, a misapprehension that was largely fueled by none other than the commander-in-chief of the Egyptian Expeditionary Force, General Edmund Allenby. Allenby not only allowed Faisal to establish a *de facto* state apparatus under the nose of the British occupation force, whose task was to ensure the preservation of the existing status quo until the peace conference decided the fate of the region, but he also shared Faisal's exaggerated view of the commission and, moreover, failed to convey to him the unwavering British determination to decline the Syrian mandate. "Unless you can at once enable me to reassure Feisal and tell him that the Commission is coming out and will decide the future of the country," Allenby cabled Balfour on May 30, 1919, "it is certain he will raise the Arabs against the French and ourselves." Balfour corrected Allenby. "You appear to think that the Commission will decide the future of the various ex-Turkish territories," he wrote. "This is not correct. They will have no power to decide, but after examining all the facts of the case will tender their advice to the Council of the Principal Allied Powers, who will have to take the final decision." Yet he authorized the general to inform Faisal that "the British Government will give the fullest weight to the advice which the Council of the Principal Allied and Associated Powers will receive from the American

Commissioners." But when Allenby passed on this message, Faisal gave it his own interpretation. "I have noted Great Britain's expression of unwillingness to take mandate for Syria," he wrote to Allenby. "Its intention to give the fullest weight to advice of Peace Commission[,] however[,] is cheerfully understood by us all. The Syrians will be unanimous in expressing to Commission their wish to have Britain and no other."[22]

All these high expectations were cruelly shattered in mid-September 1919, when Faisal was told of Britain's intention to withdraw its forces from Syria and Lebanon. The fundamental assumption under which he had long labored—that British support for his Syrian ambitions would be forthcoming no matter what—collapsed overnight, as Faisal realized to his horror that he had been left out in the cold. His plea that the British decision "should be cancelled, or at least its execution suspended," fell on deaf ears. Lloyd George wryly informed him that "it does not seem to me that the proposal you now make is practicable. His Majesty's Government have made up their mind that it is impossible for them to continue the occupation of Syria by British troops." Curzon went further than that. He reminded Faisal that "the Arabs owe their freedom in a large measure to the supreme sacrifices made by the French people in the late war," and he urged him "to go to Paris without delay, unaccompanied by any Englishman, and with no evidence of British inspiration or backing, to see Clemenceau personally; to put before him his own position with clearness, cogency, and moderation; to realise that this was in all probability the last opportunity of coming to a friendly agreement with the French."[23]

The disillusioned Faisal saw no alternative but to act on Curzon's advice. But even in this dark moment he did not despair of pitting the British against the French. "I came to Paris, as you advised, and have been here about fifteen days," he wrote to Lloyd George on November 6, to complain about what he described as unabashed French recalcitrance. To underscore his claim, Faisal narrated a conversation with General Henri Gouraud, the newly appointed commander of the French forces in the Levant, in which the latter (allegedly) "admitted that the Arabs were right and that they cannot accept the division of their country" yet expressed his determination "to carry out all orders he might receive," including the use of force should the need arise. In Faisal's view, the conversation epitomized the impossibility of finding a peaceful solution to the Syrian question without the application of international pressure on France. "I beg, therefore, for your assistance before the Supreme Council, as you have kindly given it before in your approval of assembling a special mixed commission," he pleaded with Lloyd George. "Without that we can never put an end to the present disagreement."[24]

This was not how Clemenceau viewed the situation. Slighted by Faisal's disavowal of their agreement of April 1919, he wanted nothing to do with the emir, for whom he had a lasting aversion. Being the realist that he was, however, Clemenceau realized that Faisal was there to stay, at least for the time being. The main problem with the emir, in the French perception, was his inflated sense of self-importance and his failure to grasp the realities on the ground. As Clemenceau put it to Lloyd George: "The essential difficulty lies not in the excessive ambitions of France, but in the absolute designs of the Emir, who does not seem yet really to understand the necessity for the Arabs to accept a French mandate and a British mandate with a view to organising and developing the Arab States . . . I would not despair of convincing him."[25]

Convince him indeed he did, and by the time Faisal left for Beirut on board a French warship in January 1920, the two had already clinched a new agreement, not dissimilar to their failed understanding of April 1919. According to the new agreement, Syria would become a *de facto* French mandate: France would recognize and uphold the independence and territorial integrity of Syria, within borders to be determined by the peace conference, in return for which France would gain economic, political, and diplomatic preeminence in the country, including control over its foreign policy and the exclusive right to provide the advisers, instructors, and technical personnel required for the running of the state's civilian and military affairs. Faisal would recognize the independence and territorial integrity of Lebanon, under French mandate, and allow the separate organization of the Druzes of the Hawran within the Syrian State. No French troops would be deployed on Syrian soil or enter the country unless explicitly asked to do so by the head of the Syrian State in agreement with the French high commissioner (residing in Aleppo). "You will find no authorized French statesman after me who would offer you a similar agreement," Clemenceau assured the hesitant Emir.[26]

It is not clear how seriously Faisal took this assurance. On the one hand, he attempted to convince al-Fatat, the mainstay of his personal rule, of the many virtues of the agreement. On the other hand, he made no bones about his displeasure with the deal he had just struck. "I am still the same man you thought I was, good or bad," the emir told a national-ist gathering in Damascus shortly after returning from Paris. "I have one goal, to see my country independent. And by my country I do not limit myself to a single area, for every Arab country is my country." In private Faisal was even more forthright. According to the British political officer in Beirut, Colonel Waters Taylor, Faisal complained that "this agreement was largely distasteful to him, and would be unpopular with his people[,] but the attitude of British authorities gave him no choice and . . . he had been [handed over] by feet and hands to [the] French." And yet again to a Transjordanian dignitary: "The agreement I signed with the French is merely temporary. They are fools to believe me. You can rest assured that I will never allow a Christian Government to control a single inch of Palestine or Syria."[27]

But whatever Faisal's real intentions, they were becoming increasingly irrelevant. Never exceedingly popular among his would-be Syrian sub-jects, Faisal ran the territory under his control through the small group of (mainly Iraqi) nationalists who had fought with him during the war. But his weak and indecisive character, and his prolonged absence from Syria (he spent some nine and a half months of his twenty-two months in power in Europe), made him a captive of this group rather than its master. This in turn afflicted Faisal's fledgling popularity with the local elites, who resented their domination by this small "foreign" oligarchy, driving him further into his comrades' embrace.

As the emir was negotiating in vain with the French, his standing in Syria was weakening by the day. "In spite of my best efforts to calm the excitement in order to facilitate you I am unable to resist swelling current through which blood will be shed and I shall not in any way hold myself responsible in case of [protest?] under heavy [burden?] which I beg should be taken away from me and from the nation in general," Faisal's younger brother, Zeid, who filled in for him in his absence, cautioned in late October 1919.[28] At the same time Zeid asked his father to relieve him of his job and to allow him to return to Mecca. His request was not granted, and by December 1919 Zeid had been forced to plead for Druze protection against his Damascene subjects.

On October 21, the Egyptian Expeditionary Force's chief political adviser, Colonel Richard Meinertzhagen, informed Curzon of indica-tions that "the whole movement is Pan-Islamic but is Pro-Turk and Anti-Sherifian." A fortnight later Meinertzhagen was far more alarmed. "Turkish influence is gradually creeping back, and signs are not wanting of a rejuvenated popularity of Turkish rule with all its forgotten disadvantages," he reported. "Yasin [al-Hashemi] Pasha [Faisal's chief-of-staff], the leading spirit in Syria, is now known to be in correspondence with Mustapha Kemal . . . There is little doubt that at the present moment Yasin's influence has replaced for the bad the more moderate and reasonable influence of Faisal." A similarly stark prognosis was provided by the political officer in Damascus, Major J. N. Clayton, who reported "signs that a considerable section of the people, while disliking the idea of a French mandate as much as ever, are nevertheless becoming resigned to it, and the ardent Nationalist and pro-English party are rather despairing. Some of the notables are already approaching the French with a view to securing their future should the latter come to the country." This was coupled with the significant intensification of anti-sharifian sentiments: "King Hussein's name carries no weight whatever, and there is no question in Syria of accepting him as Caliph." As for Zeid and Faisal, their position "is undoubtedly unenviable, since they are mistrusted and disliked by many of the people, and can hope for no active support from us."[29]

By February 1920, Clayton was sounding the loudest alarm bells: "Feisal is doing all he can to keep country quiet but is rapidly losing power and control in face of extremist party." Indeed, in a letter to Allenby, now lord and high commissioner for Egypt, Faisal warned of the growing difficulties confronting his regime and pleaded for a significant British gesture, such as a policy statement regarding Palestine and Mesopotamia, that would enable him to show some achievement to his constituents. In these circumstances, the chances of Faisal's "selling" his deal with Clemenceau to his followers were deemed very slight indeed:

> His three alternatives are to throw in his lot with the extremists, to allow himself to be reinstated in Damascus by French bayonets, or to abandon his position in favour of an extremist leader. Feisal's nature does not lend itself to the policy of the extremists[,] which is a moderate form of Bolshevism, and it is unthinkable that Feisal should allow himself to be reinstated by French troops, though doubtless this latter course is the one which will be urged on him by the French.[30]

What this assessment failed to take into account was the tenacity of Faisal's imperial dream. It may well be that his nature did not "lend itself to the policy of the extremists," but this was not to stand in the way of his quest for empire. Having failed to sway his associates in his direction, he decided to throw in his lot with them. When on March 7, 1920, the Syrian Congress decided, against Faisal's advice, to proclaim Syria's independence "within its natural boundaries, including Palestine," in political and economic union with Iraq, and named the emir its constitutional monarch, Faisal graciously accepted. The following day he was crowned at the Damascus City Hall as King Faisal I, and France and Britain were asked to vacate the western (Lebanon) and the southern (Palestine) parts of Syria. Shortly afterwards, the "General Iraqi Congress," yet another self-styled organization, proclaimed the "complete independence of Iraq" under the kingship of Faisal's older brother Abdullah. At the same time messages were passed to the great powers, including a personal letter from Faisal to Woodrow Wilson, explaining the circumstances of the proclamation of Syria's independence and expressing the new state's benevolence toward those powers.[31]

Despite an attempt by Faisal's close associate Nuri al-Said to sweeten the pill by presenting the developments in Damascus as "a protest against the inordinate delay in arriving at a settlement with the Turks," the Anglo-French reaction to the proclamation of Syrian (and Iraqi) independence was sharp and unequivocal.[32] "You should inform Amir Feisal at once that H.M. Government cannot recognize right of Damascus Congress, of whose composition or authority they know nothing, to settle future of Syria, Palestine, Mosul, or Mesopotamia," Curzon instructed Allenby on March 13. "H.M. Government cannot recognize the right of a self-constituted body at Damascus to regulate these matters, and H.M. Government, together with the French Government, are compelled to say that they regard these proceedings as null and void."[33]

Allenby was not convinced. Having shielded Faisal for a year and a half behind the comfortable wall of British power, he now made an emotional plea on the emir's behalf. "If Powers persist in their attitude of declaring null and void the action of Feisal and Syrian Congress, I feel certain that war must ensue," he warned. "If hostilities arise, the Arabs will regard both French and English as their enemies and we shall be dragged by the French into a war which is against our own interests and for which we are ill-prepared." The only way to avert this catastrophic development, in Allenby's view, was to recognize Faisal's sovereignty over "an Arab nation or Confederation embracing Syria, Palestine, and Mesopotamia, the Administration of Syria being secured to [the] French and that of Palestine and Mesopotamia to [the] British. This arrangement would I think be accepted by Feisal, and Arabs would be our friends and I cannot see how we could be losers by it."[34]

Like a parent explaining a complex problem to a small child, Curzon corrected the field marshal. No, Britain was not contemplating war with Faisal or a military campaign in Syria; but neither would it allow a "self-constituted body without representative character or authority" like the Syrian Congress to confront the peace conference with a *fait accompli*. Hence, "while we have no objection to Feisal being declared King of Syria by a properly constituted Syrian authority, and while we would willingly recognise him as such ourselves, we could not regard decision of Congress as superseding duties and decisions of Peace Conference now sitting in London, or as entitling Feisal to force our hands." Besides, what precisely did Allenby have in mind: was he suggesting that the machinery that had been applied to every other mandated territory should be dispensed with in the Middle East? And how did he propose to reconcile the recognition of Faisal as the king of a Syrian-Palestinian-Mesopotamian empire with the Balfour Declaration on the one hand, and with Mesopotamian resentment of the Hashemites on the other? "When we consulted representative people in all parts of that country [that is, Mesopotamia] in 1918–1919 as to a Shereefian ruler with Abdullah in our minds, they pronounced by a large majority against either [Abdullah or Faisal]," Curzon argued. "How then is it proposed now to make either Abdullah or Feisal their King, and what reason is there to suppose that they want him [Faisal]?"[35]

Allenby stuck to his guns. Disputing Curzon's diminution of the Syrian Congress, he proposed that Faisal be recognized by the peace conference as "representative of Arab peoples of Syria and Palestine" and that these two peoples be allowed "to unite under one suzerainty" and to confederate with Mesopotamia, provided that the Anglo-French special claims in Mesopotamia, Syria, and Lebanon were recognized and that those of the Zionists in Palestine were admitted.

Curzon did not fall for this attempt to push Faisal through the back door as king of a vast Arab empire. He had nothing against recognizing Faisal as representative of the "Arab peoples of Syria and Palestine," provided that he came to the peace conference "with corresponding recognition of special positions of France in Syria and Lebanon and British in Palestine, the latter including obligation to provide a national home for Zionists in that country." Yet he would hear nothing of the vast empire envisaged by Allenby: "We do not know what Faisal has to do with Mesopotamia. Arab interest in Mesopotamia is primarily that of Arab inhabitants, and our willingness to give full scope to their desires follows from our engagements with King Hussein and our declaration of November 1918. But it has no connection with Feisal or a Damascus Congress." This said, Curzon left the door open to a possible compromise. "Points of divergence appear to be by no means insuperable," he concluded his cable to Allenby, "and, if Feisal comes to Peace Conference on above understanding, we do not think it ought to be difficult to arrive at a satisfactory settlement." At a meeting with the French ambassador to London, Paul Cambon, Curzon elaborated on this theme. "Should Feisal or one of his brothers attend the Peace Conference," he suggested, "the French and British Governments will be prepared to recognise Feisal as King of Syria on certain conditions," namely: (1) "that his election is validated by a constitutional procedure, demonstrating that he is the chosen representative of the peoples of Syria, and not merely of an unauthorised body, possessing no legal position or power"; and (2) "that he will be prepared to make separate arrangements (as we understand him to be willing to do) with the French Government about Syria and the Lebanon, and with the British Government about Palestine." Having consulted his superiors, Cambon gave his qualified approval to the compromise.[36]

Had Faisal accepted these proposals, his imperial dream might still have materialized, if on a smaller scale than he wished. But by now he had become the captive of his own creation, and the Syrian Congress was in no mood for compromise.[37] Faisal thus rebuffed the Anglo-French rejection of the congress's legitimacy, declining repeated requests to appear before the peace conference unless his independence was recognized by the two great powers. Yet when informed of the readiness of the San Remo Conference to recognize him provisionally as the head of an independent Syrian State provided that he came to Europe without further delay to state his case, Faisal revoked the claim for the vast Arab empire, allegedly promised to his father by McMahon, and refused to come to Europe unless he received "a positive declaration to my agitated people stating that Conference does in no way allow Palestine to be separated from Syria." To Millerand, Faisal forthrightly stated that "the 'assistance' given by France has given rise to so many dangers that he

cannot recognize San Remo decisions." "Syria is already in effect independent," he wrote to the French premier, and he "wishes only recognition of this fact."[38]

It was only in early July 1920, amid escalating violence between French
and Hashemite forces throughout Syria, that Faisal sent Nuri al-Said to
the French high commissioner in Beirut, General Henri Gouraud, with
the request that France recognize Syria's independence under his kingship. This was far too late. Both Britain and France had despaired of ever
reaching an agreement with Faisal. As early as mid-May Curzon had
offered Faisal one more chance to attend the next meeting of the peace
conference, scheduled for the end of June, where he and his representatives would be treated "with every consideration"; should he fail to
appear, the invitation would not be renewed and the emir must be
prepared to face the following consequences:

1. That he would no longer be recognised as representing the
Hedjaz at the Peace Conference of the Powers.
2. That all financial assistance both from the French Government
and from His Majesty's Government would cease forthwith.
3. That the French Government would be at liberty to occupy the
Homs-Aleppo Railway for the objects specified by them.

When Faisal failed to respond to this initiative, the French felt no com-
pelling reason to pander to him any longer. On July 14, Gouraud issued
an ultimatum warning that unless Faisal unequivocally and unreservedly
recognized the French mandate for Syria by midnight of July 20 and
took concrete measures to ensure France's effective control of the country, French forces would occupy Syria.[39]

After a desperate plea to Allenby convinced Faisal that he was totally
on his own to confront the French threat, and a bitter struggle with the
nationalists fielding his administration forced him to disband the Syrian
Congress for a two-month period, Faisal decided to give in. In the late
afternoon hours of July 20, about six hours before the expiration of
Gouraud's ultimatum, he handed his acceptance to the French liaison
officer in Damascus. This was promptly cabled to Gouraud. But it failed
to reach him until 8:00 A.M. the next morning, eight hours after the
ultimatum's expiration.

The reasons for this tragic delay were to become a source of lasting
controversy in the historiography of Faisal's state. Explanations abound,

from a deliberate procrastination on the part of the French aimed at providing them with a pretext to occupy Syria; to obstructionism by the head of the Damascus post office, a member of al-Fatat opposed to the surrender to the French; to human errors in the chain of communication. Be that as it may, in the early morning hours of July 21, French forces began their advance eastward. Three days later, after rejection of a French demand for an unconditional surrender, French and Arab forces clashed at Khan Maisalun, west of Damascus. Within a few hours all was over. Faisal's army collapsed like a house of cards, and the next day the king fled Damascus for the small town of Kiswa, from where he made a final plea for his throne. But the French would hear nothing of it, and on July 28, 1920, Faisal left Syria for good. His dream of a Syrian empire lay in ruins. Now the ambitious ruler would have to find a suitable alternative.

19

A Kingdom for Faisal

Once ejected from Damascus, Faisal reluctantly began to cast his glance eastward. Mesopotamia, that vast stretch of land from Russia to the Persian Gulf, had never figured prominently in his imperial plan. Torn by ethnic, social, and religious schisms, with the dominant Arab population hopelessly polarized between the Shi'ite and the Sunni communities, each further split into rival clans—and with the Kurdish population of the north implacably opposed to Arab domination yet deeply fragmented along tribal lines—Mesopotamia held little appeal for foreign occupiers. As early as the 1830s, Ibrahim Pasha, the debonair warlord who had brought the Ottoman Empire to its knees, advised his father, Muhammad Ali, to shun control of Mesopotamia altogether: "Upon my word, Baghdad is as unimportant as the district of Sennar [in the Sudan]. It is not worth the expenses involved in retaining it." Faisal himself, in a memorandum written in March 1932, a year before his untimely death, candidly opined that as yet there was no such thing as an Iraqi people.[1]

Yet in the eventful summer of 1920, with Faisal's imperial Syrian dream in tatters, all these problems suddenly seemed marginal compared with the desire for a consolation prize, however unsatisfactory it might be. Come what may, a kingdom had to be found—or rather founded—for the emir.

Ironically, it was the archenemies of Hashemite ambitions in Mesopotamia—the civil commissioner in Baghdad, Sir Percy Cox, and even more so his successor to that post, Arnold Talbot Wilson—who gave the idea of a unified Mesopotamia, or Iraq, as it increasingly came to be called, its main intellectual and political firepower.

For centuries Mesopotamia had been divided into the three separate provinces of Basra, Baghdad, and Mosul, and their postwar amalgamation into a new kingdom was by no means a forgone conclusion. Whether because of the lack of an overarching Mesopotamian corporate identity, or the award of Mosul to France by the Sykes-Picot Agreement, or sibling rivalry among the Hashemite emirs, or the desire of the government of India for the control and possession of the velayet of Basra, the notion of several Mesopotamian kingdoms, as opposed to a unified state, reigned supreme. Even Lawrence of Arabia, the foremost champion of the Hashemite cause, had not suggested the unification of Mesopotamia on behalf of his desert friends but rather its partition into two kingdoms: Irak (lower Mesopotamia), with Abdullah as its head, and the Jesireh (upper Mesopotamia), with Zeid as its ruler.

Cox, in contrast, while not averse in principle to British annexation of the velayet of Basra and the exercise of a veiled protectorate over the velayet of Baghdad, as decided by the War Cabinet on March 29, 1917, deemed it "essential in the interests of the country that the administration of both vilayets should be uniform." "To attempt to run the two *vilayets, which are from every point of view inseparable,* on conflicting lines and inconsistent principles would, I am sure, result in great prejudice to all interests concerned," he wrote to the Foreign Office on April 7, 1917.[2]

Wilson went significantly further in articulating the notion of a unified Mesopotamia. He had always conceived of the country, including the velayet of Mosul, for whose inclusion in Mesopotamia he fought tooth and nail, as "an indivisible whole" lacking almost entirely any "political, racial or other connexion . . . [with] the rest of Arabia." "There is no community of feeling whatever between Syria and Mesopotamia[,] and the people of this country are as little likely as those of Nejd to accept a Government inaugurated in Syria and dominated by Syrian politicians," he wrote to his superior, India Secretary Edwin Montague, on March 21, 1920, dismissing the suggestion that Faisal, who had just been declared the king of Syria, would also be recognized as Mesopotamia's suzerain. The "fact that Abdullah appears to have been declared King of Mesopotamia simultaneously with declaration of Faisal as King of Syria, &c., seems to indicate that even in Syria it is recognised that Mesopotamia is entitled to its own Government."[3]

As a veteran of Arab affairs (with a decade of service in the Persian Gulf to his credit), Wilson was painfully aware of Mesopotamia's internal schisms and had serious misgivings regarding the country's ripeness for immediate independence. He doubted whether its predominantly tribal society, accounting for three-quarters of the population and lacking a "previous tradition of obedience to any Government except that of Constantinople, and with an almost instinctive hostility to Arab 'Effendis' in positions of authority," could instantaneously be transformed into a full-fledged civil society; whether the almost two million Shi'ites would be prepared to accept domination by their Sunni brethren, whom they outnumbered more than three to one, given that "no form of Arab Government has yet been envisaged . . . which would not involve a practical monopoly of power by Sunnis"; and whether "the warlike Kurds in Mesopotamia, who number nearly half a million," would ever accept an Arab ruler.[4]

Yet the young and abrasive Wilson (he was thirty-four years old upon becoming the acting civil commissioner) was also the quintessential civil servant, schooled in the imperialist tradition of the "white man's burden." As such he believed not only that Mesopotamia would be able to overcome its many weaknesses if lent a helping hand by a benign patron, but also that a British protectorate was an object of desire for most Iraqi politicians. "With the experience of my Political Officers behind me, I can confidently declare that the country as a whole neither expects nor desires any such sweeping scheme of independence as is adumbrated, if not clearly denoted, in the Anglo-French Declaration," he responded to the famous statement of November 1918. "The Arabs are content with our occupation; the non-Muhammadan element clings to it as the tardy fulfilment of the hopes of many generations." This assessment was shared by Wilson's Oriental Secretary, the renowned writer on Arab affairs Gertrude Bell. "In Mesopotamia they want us and no one else, because they know we'll govern in accordance with the custom of the country," she wrote to her father on December 27, 1918. Two months later she reported on a conversation with Abd al-Rahman al-Qailani, the naqib of Baghdad and probably the most distinguished political figure in Mesopotamia. "The English have conquered this country, they have expended their wealth and they have watered the soil with their blood . . . Shall they not enjoy what they have won?" he posed the rhetorical question. "Other conquerors have overwhelmed the country. As it fell to them, so it has fallen to the English . . . I recognize your victory. You are the governors and I am the governed."[5]

This conviction led Wilson to suggest, by way of discrediting Lawrence's proposal to split Mesopotamia between Abdullah and Zeid, that a plebiscite be held "in a manner consonant with educated opinion and not inconsistent with the maintenance of public order" before the cabinet made up its mind. The results seemed to vindicate Wilson's predictions that the velayets of Baghdad and Basra should be united with Mosul to create a new Iraqi State and that most Iraqis desired the continuation of British tutelage, with or without a titular Arab emir. On February 14, 1919, he was instructed by the cabinet to telegraph an outline of a constitution for the Arab state or group of states, and on April 6 he presented his scheme to the Inter-Departmental Committee on Eastern Affairs, headed by Acting Foreign Secretary Curzon. His blueprint provided for the rule of Iraq by a British high commissioner, the newly established country being divided into the provinces of Basra, Baghdad, Euphrates, and Mosul (if Kurdistan were to be included in Iraq, it would form a fifth province). Each of the provinces was to be administered by a provincial council, with "considerable powers but not at present to be made responsible for legislation," and headed by an Arab governor assisted by "a specially chosen British official of ability and character as Municipal Commissioner and Adviser to the Governor, in which dual capacity he could control finance, and mitigate inevitable inefficiency in early stages." On May 9, 1919, the government approved the scheme and instructed Wilson to press ahead with its implementation.[6]

Wilson had advocated, and the government accepted, the principle of "unite and rule." Mesopotamia was neither to be divided into several kingdoms to accommodate the imperialist ambitions of Sharif Hussein and his sons (or, for that matter, of the government of India), nor to be incorporated into a wider Hashemite kingdom, were such to be established. Rather, its disparate elements were to be assembled into a unified whole, its diverse communities integrated into a coherent people. This new entity was to include the province of Mosul, in addition to those of Basra and Baghdad, "since there is no suitable physical boundary for

Mesopotamia in the plains between Mosul and the Persian Gulf; since the inhabitants object to the partition of their country; and since the oil-bearing regions of Mosul are essential to the revenues on which the future development of the whole country will depend."[7]

"Iraq for the Iraqis" was thus to be the guiding principle in the reconfiguration of Mesopotamia, but not immediately. The infant state had to learn to walk before it could realistically expect to start running; and who was better qualified to instruct it in the art of government than the largest empire on Earth? As Lloyd George put it in the House of Commons on March 25, 1920: "It is not proposed that we should govern this country as if it were an essential part of the British Empire, making its laws. That is not our point of view. Our point of view is that they should govern themselves and that we should be responsible as the mandatory for advising, for counselling, for assisting, but that the government must be Arab. That is a condition of the League of Nations, and we mean to respect it." Three months later, on June 3, he told the House that under the terms of the League of Nations' mandate, Britain was obliged to create in Mesopotamia "an independent nation, subject to the rendering of administrative advice and assistance by a mandatory until such time as she is able to stand alone."[8]

This paternalistic worldview failed to take into account the fact that Mesopotamia's predominantly tribal society would not necessarily be more receptive to the "civilizing message" of the newly arrived Western imperialism than it had been to that articulated during centuries of Ottoman imperialism. No less important, this view grossly underestimated the intensity of the Hashemite imperial dream and its destabilizing potential both in London and in Mesopotamia itself.

Not that British decisionmakers were averse to Hashemite rule in Mesopotamia. On the contrary, on March 23, 1920, to mention one example, the cabinet decided that it "would have no objection to the candidature of a member of King Hussein's family, if acceptable to the inhabitants." Yet this decision did not preclude the possibility of a non-Hashemite ruler if the Mesopotamians so desired, something that was totally unacceptable to Hussein and his sons; and it envisaged an orderly and prolonged transition to statehood under the League of Nations' mandatory system, to which the Hashemites were violently opposed, given their self-perception as the rightful representatives of the Arabic-speaking populations of the defunct Ottoman Empire.[9]

Nor was the assessment of Faisal and his nationalist Iraqi officers regarding Mesopotamia's capacity for self-rule more upbeat than that of Wilson. At a meeting with Gertrude Bell in Damascus in October 1919, Yasin al-Hashemi, the leader of al-Ahd al-Iraqi, established the previous year by Iraqi officers in Faisal's administration who seceded from the veteran al-Ahd, admitted that "the country was not ready for representative institutions" and that "it was obvious that Mesopotamia could not for the next 10 years be left without foreign guidance." A similarly candid admission was made by Jaafar al-Askari, another prominent member of al-Ahd al-Iraqi, in a conversation with a member of the India Office. Not least, when officially offered the Iraqi throne, in a conversation with Lawrence on April 15, 1921, Faisal deemed "the people of Irak as not fitted yet for responsible Government." According to Lawrence, the emir believed that "if he is left at the mercy of local people in all things there will be a disaster. He will require British help sometimes against his own people, and he hopes his opinion on permanent garrison will be taken eventually."[10]

Yet whatever they were prepared to concede in private, the Hashemites and their supporters would not admit in public. Hussein, who had had no compunction about collaborating with the great Christian powers against his Muslim Ottoman suzerain, and who was still the recipient of a handsome British subsidy, now incited tribal leaders to reject the rule of Christian Britain. He dispensed large sums of money by way of enhancing Hashemite standing and prestige among Mesopotamian Shi'ites, and by March 1920 the prominent Shi'ite divine Imam Muhammad Taqi al-Shirazi had been convinced to issue a religious ruling (fatwa) decrying service in the British administration as anathema to Islamic law.

In early 1919, when the King-Crane Commission seemed likely to visit Iraq, al-Ahd al-Iraqi sent letters to nationalist activists, tribal chiefs, and religious divines in Iraq, instructing them what to tell the commissioners. In their own evidence to the commission in June 1919, Yasin al-Hashemi and his fellow officers made the case for an independent Iraqi kingdom under the rule of Abdullah or Zeid. A similar message was relayed the same month in a personal letter from Faisal to the chief political officer of the Egyptian Expeditionary Force, Gilbert Clayton, claiming the existence of "a general feeling that the time had come for a change if the promises of the Anglo-French declaration were to be fulfilled." Faisal admitted that his Baghdadi officers were "well aware that it was not possible for Mesopotamia to stand alone for a considerable time," yet he argued that they "felt strongly the need of despatch in the constitution of a National Government, and perceived clearly that the longer it took to change the system the greater would be the difficulty in making the change." The letter was written in such eloquent English that Major Hubert Young, a former officer with Faisal's army and now a member of the Foreign Office, concluded that it must have been drafted by Lawrence.[11]

But Lawrence also had more direct channels to voice his views. In a personal letter to Curzon on September 27, 1919, he urged the foreign secretary to ask the cabinet "for an assurance that our pledges with regard to the Arab character of the Government of Mesopotamia hold good, and that to relieve the local situation now (pending the Peace Conference decision) Sir P. Z. Cox again take charge there, and his present deputy be employed outside the province." In a parallel memorandum to the Foreign Office, Lawrence warned: "I regard the situation in Mesopotamia as disquieting, and if we do not mend our ways, will expect revolt there about March next."[12]

This stark prognosis was fully shared by Acting Civil Commissioner Wilson, but on wholly different grounds. For Lawrence, Hashemite rule was the answer to the Mesopotamian predicament, or more accurately, to Hashemite sibling rivalry; for Wilson, it was the source of all evil. As early as June 1919 he suggested that since "the Arab Army is still financed entirely from His Majesty's Treasury, pressure should be brought to bear upon Sharif Faisal to restrict his activities and those of his staff to Syria"; three months later he warned that the "time has come to tell Feisal to leave Mesopotamia alone, otherwise his subsidy and that of his father will be discontinued."[13]

By the spring of 1920 Wilson was predicting imminent doom. "It is my duty solemnly to express to [the] Government my conviction that the policy which they are apparently about to adopt is likely before long to prove fatal to the retention of Mesopotamia," he wrote to India Secretary Montagu on March 25. A week later he warned Sir Arthur Hirtzel, the assistant undersecretary of state for India, that "I anticipate trouble on the Euphrates during the summer[,] particularly in the Shamiyah Division round Najaf[,] which has been apparently selected by the Syrian Party as the most promising ground for their propaganda."[14] Wilson delivered similar warnings to the newly appointed commander-in-chief of the British forces in Mesopotamia, Lieutenant-General Sir Aylmer Haldane.

On June 9, 1920, Wilson warned Montagu that "our army is now, alike in numbers, composition and fighting efficiency, incapable of defending the population of frontier divisions of Mosul and Dulaim against aggression, and of maintaining, or, in case of need, restoring internal order over any considerable area." "The history of this country for the past few thousand years and the practical experience of the past three," he continued, "alike convince me that we cannot give effect to mandate without risk of disaster, unless we are prepared to maintain for the next two years at least as many troops in the country as we may have, and in a state considerably more efficient than they are now." Either the British government was prepared to proceed with the slow development of Mesopotamia into a self-governing democratic country, which would demand the expenditure of men and money for years to come, or it "would do better to face the alternative . . . formidable, and, from [a] local point of view, terrible as it is, and evacuate Mesopotamia."[15]

Wilson's pleas were unavailing. In early February the cabinet's Finance Committee had decided "that the cost of such a garrison for Mesopotamia was prohibitive and that it must be curtailed," leaving it to the War Office to determine by which method the necessary reduction should be secured. Shortly before his departure for Baghdad, Haldane had been personally lectured by Winston Churchill, the secretary of state for war, on "the necessity for making drastic reductions in the garrison of Mesopotamia," and the lackluster general, who at the time of his appointment was on the verge of retirement, had no intention whatsoever of making waves. As late as mid-June 1920 Haldane rejected Wilson's desperate pleas for reinforcements, subscribing instead to the buoyant assessment of Gertrude Bell, with whom he had established a close personal relationship, that "the bottom seems to have dropped out of the agitation, and most of the leaders seem only too anxious to let bygones be bygones." Even Cox, considered by Whitehall to be the foremost authority on Mesopotamia, failed to read the writing on the wall. As late as July 24, a month after the tribes of the Middle Euphrates had risen in revolt, he still downplayed this event as "a local affair, engineered from outside by agitators at Nejaf who want no mandate."[16]

The only Whitehall mandarins who seemed disturbed by Britain's military posture in Mesopotamia were Churchill and his top military adviser, Chief of the Imperial General Staff Field-Marshal Sir Henry Wilson. But even they were preoccupied not with the Mesopotamian situation *per se*, but rather with the wider question of the sufficiency of Britain's military resources for the pursuit of its imperial policy. Their warning of an impending disaster "should the Cabinet decide to continue the attempt to maintain simultaneously our existing commitments at Constantinople, Palestine, Mesopotamia, and Persia" was not made with a view to a popular uprising in any or all of these theaters. Henry Wilson, for one, "did not think that it would be possible to continue holding the area which we at present occupied with the number of troops at our disposal. It was not that he expected an actual attack but he foresaw the country getting very unsettled, the railways would be cut and everyone would have to move about under escort."

Under these circumstances cabinet members decided that "they do not accept Wilson's view that true alternative lies between extension of control . . . and withdrawal to Basra. They are irrevocably committed to policy of creating an effective Arab State[,] not a camouflaged British protectorate[,] and they regard practical alternatives as being either to get to work at once on lines they have already indicated or completely to evacuate Mesopotamia."[17]

Whether greater responsiveness to Wilson's warnings would have saved the day is difficult to say. While there is little doubt that Britain's much-reduced military presence in Mesopotamia, together with occasional setbacks (notably the occupation of the desert town of Dair al-Zur at the end of 1919 by tribal forces led by officers attached to Faisal's administration), damaged its prestige and deterrent posture and created a widespread belief in the imminence of a British withdrawal from Mesopotamia, the multiplicity of causes behind the uprising would have made it exceedingly difficult, if not virtually impossible, for the British to avert this eruption altogether. Even had a firmer policy both by London and by Wilson himself, whose actual conduct had not always corresponded to his own alarming predictions, decisively curbed the destabilizing impact of Hashemite anti-British agitation in Mesopotamia, chances are myriad factors would have made a revolt almost inevitable. These ranged from frustration over the economic dislocation occasioned by the war (especially price increases and shortages of certain necessities), to opposition to British taxation and irrigation policies by peasants and landowners alike, to personal ambitions of local leaders, to religious incitement against "infidel" rule, to intensifying nationalist agitation, and to the general insubordination of the tribal population in the Middle Euphrates, between Baghdad and Basra, where the revolt ensued and was largely fought.

Yet for all its multitudinous causes, the 1920 uprising quickly acquired a life of its own. It was not a national revolt in the full sense of the word, that is, a concerted, premeditated nationwide effort to bring about the establishment of an independent Iraqi state, but rather a string of spontaneous localized insurrections aimed at several targets and conducted in a decentralized fashion. Yet the Hashemites and their British partisans wasted no time in depicting it as such in their effort to gain control over the country.

"The Arabs rebelled against the Turks during the war not because the Turk Government was notably bad, but because they wanted independence," wrote Lawrence in the *London Times* of July 22, "forgetting" that the overwhelming majority of Arabs remained loyal to their Ottoman suzerain to the end of the war and frowned on the Hashemite revolt, which in itself was motivated by imperialist, rather than nationalist, aspirations. "Whether they are fit for independence or not remains to be tried," he argued, making a thinly veiled hint to the person who, in his view, should be king: "Feisal's Government in Syria has been completely independent for two years, and has maintained public security and public services in its area." And yet again: "My little experience in helping to set up Feisal showed me that the art of government wants more character than brains."[18]

In an interview published in the *Daily News* on August 25, Lawrence painted an almost saintly picture of Faisal. "It is a fantastic mistake to suppose that he is a personally ambitious man," he claimed. "Remember that Feisul [*sic*], though an inspired leader at a time of crisis, is a mild and kindly man . . . He is inspired by one ambition—and that is to produce somewhere an independent Arab Government."[19]

This was of course an extraordinary claim, especially when coming from a person who not only was fully aware of the magnitude of Faisal's imperial aspirations, but who also had done so much to fuel them. Indeed, at a time when Lawrence pretended that "we don't even know whether he would be willing to accept the position," Faisal had already told Abd al-Malik al-Khatib, his father's agent in Egypt, that "if the British Government wished him to go, he was ready, either as a ruler or as Regent for Abdullah," and that "whichever of the two were selected, he should go at once in order to stop the troubles now occurring in that country."[20]

Faisal's eagerness to secure the Mesopotamian throne is not difficult to understand. As he left Syria, never to return, the future looked bleak. To be sure, Lawrence was rallying public opinion behind his cause, his London partisans were lobbying the government on his behalf, and the press was rife with reports that he was being offered Mesopotamia as compensation for his lost Syrian kingdom. Yet Faisal had no illusions regarding the obstacles that lay ahead. In the first place, he had to override Abdullah, who, during his brother's short-lived reign in Damascus, had established himself as the frontline contender to the Mesopotamian throne. In this endeavor Faisal could expect little support from his father, who had always favored Abdullah over him and who considered Faisal's quest for a Syrian kingdom anathema to his own dream of a pan-Arab empire. "If you had remained simply a representative of Your Father and had not inaugurated a separate kingdom, the French would not have been able to take against you the action they did, as King Hussein is one of the Treaty Allies recognised by the important powers and they would therefore have been afraid to attack him," al-Khatib reprimanded Faisal, before telling Major Garland, the acting director of the Arab Bureau, that "Abdullah would be the more suitable person." "If Feisal were to go he would be surrounded by the same avaricious, place-seeking clique of officers and officials who lived on him at Damascus," al-Khatib claimed. "Abdullah had no such clique. He once had, but fortunately Providence gathered them all in at Tarabah (i.e., Abdullah's defeat by Ibn Saud in 1919)."[21]

An even higher hurdle on Faisal's road to Baghdad was France's vehement opposition to his leadership of Iraq. The dust had scarcely settled on Maisalun when the French press began castigating the emir, and French politicians and diplomats began trying to block his road to Baghdad. Although the British did not take this anti-Faisal propaganda at face value, they were sufficiently attuned to French sensitivities to give Faisal the cold shoulder. When it transpired, within days of his ignominious eviction, that the French would not allow Faisal to stay in the desert town of Deraa, where he had sought refuge, the general view in London was that the emir should join his father in the Hijaz, where he might be given compensation of sorts, and, more important, where he would be in no position to further complicate Anglo-French relations.

Faisal, however, would not follow the script written for him by Britain. Keenly aware that his return to the Hijaz would almost certainly mean the demise of his imperial dream, he informed the high commissioner for Palestine, Sir Herbert Samuel, of his wish to go from Haifa, where he had arrived after his defeat, either to Switzerland or to Italy, "as he is 'ill' and wants rest." He assured Samuel that "he does not wish to complicate matters between [the] British and French, nor does he wish to take any further steps against [the] French." Though taken by surprise, the Foreign Office did not demur. "You should inform Feisal that His Majesty's Government appreciate his desire to create no complications between England and France," the office instructed Samuel. "They are fully aware that he has made every effort to sustain a difficult position with due regard to the interests of the Allied Powers, and they trust that they may in the future have an opportunity of showing to him that his loyal attitude to the British Government has not been forgotten."[22]

Encouraged by this response, Faisal pitched higher. Italy and Switzerland were no longer seen as a safe haven for the "ill" emir, but rather as transit stops en route to London. "Sir, I beg to submit the enclosed note on the Arab question," Faisal wrote to Lloyd George on September 11, from the scenic Lake Como in northern Italy, where he had settled for a comfortable stay. "May I add that my father, the King of the Hedjaz, has again entrusted me with the mission of representing him in the Arab question in general, including that of presiding over the delegation appointed by him to offer his thanks to King George for the presents graciously sent by His Majesty," he stated, getting down to the real purpose of his letter: "I am forwarding my note through General Haddad Pasha, in whom my father and myself have implicit trust. I hope that you will soon inform him of your desire to see me personally in England, as I have verbal communications to make you, especially in view of the present situation."

Just what Faisal meant by these "verbal communications" was clarified in an accompanying letter from the emir. "In spite of the distress and preoccupation events in Syria for several months past have caused me, I have been following affairs in Mesopotamia carefully and, believe me, have felt much grief at the change in the former cordial relations between the Arabs there and the British," Faisal stated, laying the groundwork for his proposed *quid pro quo:*

> I believe the present evils are not incurable, resulting as they do from misunderstandings between the two peoples. Both have the same objects. Those of Great Britain were declared to my father, King Hussein, and my father's were stated to you. Both approved the other's. How then can their policies not agree? If the pledges given to the Arabs through King Hussein are fulfilled, I am confident things will settle down. My great hope, and that of every Arab, is that this will soon be done.[23]

This was a proposition the prime minister could hardly ignore. Like the legendary phoenix rising from its ashes, Faisal had engineered a remarkable political comeback less than two months after the collapse of his imperial dream. He was no longer a stateless fugitive begging for a handout, but rather the foremost official representative of the Arab cause—an ally, however junior, among allies. It would be infinitely more difficult for the British government to prevent Faisal's coming to London now that he was yet again his father's representative to the peace talks than it had been prior to this development.

Why Hussein agreed to reinstate his son in the driver's seat, given his greater affinity for Abdullah and his distrust of Faisal's intentions, is not entirely clear. Perhaps he believed that owing to his intimate contacts in London Faisal was better suited for the job; or perhaps he figured that a bird in the hand was worth two in the bush, namely, that it was better to have a satisfied Faisal in his service than a disgruntled emir conniving against him in the European chancelleries. Indeed, Faisal was not deterred from using his potential obstructionist capacity to goad the British into acquiescing in his demands. During his stay in London, Haddad Pasha warned whoever was prepared to listen "that Faisal is now desperate and that if he cannot obtain any satisfaction he will be compelled to return to Arabia and assemble a Moslem conference at Mecca before which he and his father will lay their case in justification of their revolt against the Caliph."

Haddad's warning fell on receptive ears. "It is not easy to see what result such action might have," a Foreign Office memorandum stated, "but there have been indications of communication between Faisal (or at any rate some of his entourage) and Mustapha Kemal, and there seems little doubt that this organization which is the mainspring of that gentleman's activities would not be slow to turn it to their advantage. There must also be considered the effect in India of any public announcement in Mecca to the effect that King Hussein and Faisal—the allies and proteges of Great Britain—had been left in the lurch."[24]

Meanwhile, Faisal was stepping up the pressure. "I have received twelve telegrams from my father, in which he insists on my going to England," he wrote to Haddad on October 6. "I have been trying to calm him down by saying that the reasons for my not proceeding at once is that the date for the reception of the delegation of which I am the head by His Majesty the King has not yet been fixed, besides giving other trifling reasons. I am afraid if I tell him the British Government is hesitating to receive me he will be offended. I am now between two fires.

On one side I have to urge my case, and on the other I have to quiet my father." And by way of impressing upon the British the urgency of the matter, Faisal enclosed the latest message he had received from his father. "I have wired Mr. Lloyd George . . . saying you are my representative," Hussein wrote:

> I want you to proceed to London to head the delegation. Your interview with our allies in war will be [the] basis of our action. If you think there is anything derogatory to your dignity, please return at once to your country, because my only object is to prove my loyalty and continue my friendship to Great Britain. At the same time I want to show we are a nation that adheres to its rights, as do Western nations.[25]

By now the Foreign Office was sufficiently alarmed to grant Faisal's request. "We had deferred the visit as long as possible, out of regard for the French, and because we did not wish in the smallest degree to offend their susceptibilities," Foreign Secretary Curzon told Ambassador Cambon on November 11, "but his father, King Hussein, had some time ago definitely appointed Feisal as head of a mission to make certain return presents to our King, and was exceedingly vexed at our apparent reluctance to receive him in this honorific capacity. We could find no excuse for further postponement, and the King had agreed to receive the Emir early in December."[26] On December 4, 1920, Faisal had an audience with King George V.

Faisal's arrival in London brought to a head the Mesopotamian question, with which the government had been grappling for the past two years. By now the rebellion had been largely suppressed and Sir Percy Cox had returned as high commissioner to Baghdad, where he quickly established a Council of State, or a provisional government, headed by Abd al-Rahman al-Qailani, the naqib of Baghdad. But the identity of the ruler of the state-to-be remained as obscure as ever. Cox himself had maintained in late July 1920, at the height of the revolt, that "Mesopotamia itself contains no eligible candidate. In the case of any aspirant from outside . . . two or three have been mentioned, such as Abdullah, son of the Sheriff, and Ibn Saud. The objections which could be forwarded in either instance seem to me at present insuperable."[27]

This view mimicked Wilson's longstanding claim that "far from making the Arabs on this side our friends, recognition of Faisal as King of Mesopotamia can only be regarded in this country as a betrayal of its interests and we shall alienate the best elements here." Yet by the time Cox was parroting his old ideas, Wilson was already singing an altogether different refrain. "Will His Majesty's Government consider possibility of offering him Amirate of Mesopotamia?" he cabled Montagu on July 31, a week after Faisal had been expelled from Damascus:

> Objections entertained on this side to creation of Amirate have hitherto been primarily that no suitable person could be found. We have always regarded Faisal as booked for Syria. Nothing that I have heard during the last few months has led me to modify my views of unsuitability of Abdullah[,] and our experience of last few weeks in Baghdad makes it fairly clear that no local candidate will be successful in obtaining sufficient support here to enable him to make good. Faisal alone of all Arabian potentates has any idea of practical difficulties of running a civilized government on Arab lines. He can scarcely fail to realize that foreign assistance is vital to the continued existence of an Arab State. He realizes danger of relying on an Arab army.[28]

Wilson's suggestion was instantly incorporated into draft instructions, prepared on August 5 by the cabinet's Finance Committee for Cox's personal guidance upon his appointment as high commissioner for Mesopotamia, only to be dropped a week later owing to uncompromising French opposition. The revised instructions thus reflected the cabinet's desire to have its cake and eat it too: to keep the Hashemites in the picture, if out of sight, without antagonizing the French. Faisal's name was extricated, and Cox was instructed "that the precise form of the Government to be created, in which the sovereignty of the Arab State will be vested (subject to such limitations for the time being as may be prescribed in the Mandate) will be a matter for the free choice of the peoples of Mesopotamia, whose wishes you will endeavour to ascertain by whatever means you think fit. Similarly the choice of a ruler (if they decide in favour of a monarchy) will be left to them."[29]

On December 26, Cox cabled from Baghdad for further instructions. He had always understood it to be his government's view that Britain should not impose a ruler but should leave the choice to the will of the people, which was precisely what he and members of his staff had been telling their Mesopotamian counterparts. It had become increasingly evident, however, that the "majority would prefer to have the question decided for them, or at any rate that we should give them a lead; also that a great majority are in favour of an outsider rather than an inhabitant of Irak, and among outsiders a Sherif for choice." As a result, the British might have to take an alternative approach. "If the policy of His Majesty's Government makes it desirable to expedite a decision, I think it can be done without waiting for the elections, and if so, the sooner the better," he argued. "I should, of course, like to be consulted further before any other steps were taken, but if, for example, the way is not clear for Faisal, I think, *primâ facie,* that the best way to give him an opening would be to inspire a Reuter to the effect that the French had now withdrawn their opposition to Faisal's candidature, and that, if the people of Irak wanted him, His Majesty's Government were prepared to accept him. He would then be able formally to offer himself."[30]

This was an offer the cabinet could not accept. Although Faisal's stay in London got the pendulum swinging in his direction yet again, it did not end the British vacillation altogether. To the contrary, none of the emir's three official meetings at the Foreign Office, including a conversation with Curzon on January 13, 1921, addressed the future status of Mesopotamia (or for that matter the future of Syria or Transjordan), for his hosts avoided these thorny issues, focusing instead on the ratification of the Treaty of Versailles by King Hussein. The French were pressuring British decisionmakers, who were loath to strain Anglo-French relations any further. On January 4, Curzon informed the cabinet of a recent conversation between Hardinge and Georges Leygues, the French prime minister, in the course of which the latter "had raised strong objections to the candidature of Shereef Feisal which, in his view, would arouse a storm of indignation in France." After some discussion the cabinet agreed "to postpone any decision on the question pending the making of further enquiries by the Secretary of State for Foreign Affairs into various aspects of the matter."[31]

Three days later Curzon made his move. Colonel Kinahan Cornwallis, the former head of the Cairo Arab Bureau now attached to the Foreign Office, was instructed to approach Faisal, "speaking to him not officially but as a personal friend," and to indicate to him that Britain would view with favor his ascendance to the Mesopotamian throne, provided that he induced his father to ratify the Treaty of Versailles. Cornwallis was to reassure Faisal that French opposition to his candidacy could be overcome if the Mesopotamians were to elect him as their ruler. At the same time, he was to tell the emir that Britain could not endorse any candidate who was not "prepared loyally to accept and to act up to the terms of the Mandate as agreed upon by the Great Powers and laid before the Council of the League of Nations," and "who is likely to give us trouble with the French." Moreover, since the British government could neither impose a ruler on Mesopotamia nor even suggest who should rule—it could only "consider carefully the merits and the claims of any candidates whom the Mesopotamian Congress may be disposed to recommend"—it was up to Faisal to seize the initiative: to secure his father's support for his candidacy and then put himself forward, but "not with the knowledge or approval of the British government," because the whole point was that he should be acting on his own.[32]

This was not good enough for Faisal. He had not taken all the trouble of coming to London only to return empty-handed to the Hijaz. Had he remotely believed that his father preferred him to Abdullah with regard to Mesopotamia, he would have not traveled to London in the first place. Putting himself forward as yet another candidate was absolutely out of the question; either the British were prepared to endorse him officially, and to inform his father and the French to that effect, or they should look elsewhere for candidates. Besides, in his conversation with Abd al-Malik al-Khatib, shortly before going to Europe, Faisal had been warned that "if he were to go to Mesopotamia people would say that he was 'crown hunting,'" and the emir took full notice of this warning.[33]

When he met Cornwallis on January 8, 1921, Faisal played hard to get. "As regards your proposal about myself, I am deeply grateful but I must reject it definitely," he said, feigning self-effacement before reiterating al-Khatib's advice almost verbatim. "My father, who really wants Abdullah to go to Mesopotamia[,] would never approve, and he and all the people would believe that I am working for myself and not for my nation, in agreement with the British. I will never put myself forward as a candidate. My honour is my dearest possession and I will never allow myself to be accused of self-interest." There was, however, a way out. Were Abdullah to be moved out of the way and Mesopotamian public opinion swayed in Faisal's direction, he would be willing to step into the fold. As he put it: "I would only go to Mesopotamia if H.M.G. rejected Abdullah and asked me to undertake the task and if the people said they wanted me. In such a case both my father and Abdullah would agree for they could not go against the wishes of the people."[34]

Curzon failed to see through Faisal's disingenuousness. He was inclined to see Faisal ascend the Mesopotamian throne and even favored him over Abdullah—a sea change from his previous position that "we do not know what Feisal has to do with Mesopotamia." Yet he refused to see Faisal's transparent plea to get his elder brother out of the way for what it was, instead interpreting the emir's feigned deference to Abdullah as an honorable act of selflessness. "His Majesty's Government are not opposed in principle to Feisal's candidature, provided it is acceptable locally, but they see serious objection to any procedure involving intervention or what may be regarded as intervention by British Government pending spontaneous expression of wishes of Mesopotamian State," Curzon wrote to Cox on January 9, rejecting his suggestion that the British manipulate Mesopotamian public opinion on Faisal's behalf and proposing the alternative course of action offered by Cornwallis to Faisal. The high commissioner concurred.[35]

Although Faisal failed to win the immediate endorsement of the British government, his meeting with Cornwallis helped establish him as the clear front-runner in the race for the Mesopotamian throne. "Feisal behaved like a real gentleman & with a fine sense of honour & loyalty," on January 9 Curzon informed Churchill, who was about to replace Lord Milner as the secretary of state for the colonies. Two days earlier Lloyd George had accepted Churchill's demand that Mesopotamia and Palestine be administered by a new department, to be established at the Colonial Office, and the energetic minister was eager to put his policy in place before taking up his new post. He had no strong views about Mesopotamia apart from his long-held belief in the imperative need to reduce Britain's expenses there; and the best way to achieve that goal, in his opinion, was "to set up an Arab Government, through whose agency the peaceful development of the country may be assured without undue demands upon Great Britain. It is to this policy that we must devote our efforts."[36]

This concern inevitably raised the question of the country's future ruler. On January 8 Churchill discussed the issue with T. E. Lawrence, who also agreed to join the Colonial Office as an adviser on Arabian affairs, before writing to Lloyd George: "A little more time & consideration are needed before definitely launching Feisal. I must feel my way & feel sure of my way." Four days later he telegraphed to Cox:

Do you think that Feisal is the right man and the best man? Failing him, do you prefer Abdullah to any local man? Have you put forward Feisal because you consider taking a long view he is the best man or as a desperate expedient in the hopes of reducing the garrisons quickly? If you are really convinced that Feisal is necessary, can you make sure he is chosen locally? Once I know your true mind on these points [a] decision can be taken here immediately.

Yet Churchill did not wait for Cox's reply. "I have a strong feeling that Feisal is the best man, and I do not think there is much to be gained by putting forward an inferior man in the hopes that he will be rejected and smooth away certain difficulties in the selection of the best candidate," he wrote to Curzon on January 12, rejecting the latter's suggestion to encourage Abdullah to run for the headship of Mesopotamia before Faisal. "I observe that Mr. Cornwallis has no doubts that Feisal is the right man and that he would like to undertake the task. All that you say about his honourable scruples impress[es] me the more with his qualifications. We must certainly see that we get 'turtle' and not 'mock turtle.'"

Lawrence was accordingly instructed to ascertain Faisal's views, and on January 17 he reported back to Edward Marsh, Churchill's private secretary. The emir was well disposed to British sensibilities, he stated, and would agree to make no reference to the French-occupied area of Syria in his talks with the British government and to abandon his father's claims to Palestine. "This leaves four questions," Lawrence said:

(a) Mesopotamia: for which he claims a watching brief in respect of the McMahon papers.

(b) Trans-Jordan: where he hopes to have a recognized Arab State with British advice.

(c) Nejd: where he wants the Hussein-Ibn Saud question regulated.

(d) Yemen: on which he has a suggestion to make.

Lawrence continued:

The advantage of his taking this new ground of discussion is that all question of pledges & promises, fulfilled or broken, are set aside.

You begin a new discussion on the actual positions today & the best way of doing something constructive with them. It's so much more useful than splitting hairs. Feisal can help very much towards a rapid settlement of these countries, if he wants to: and if we can only get them working like a team they will be a surprising big thing in two or three years.

"I think all he asks in a.b.c.d. can be made useful to ourselves," Lawrence concluded, stressing Churchill's deepest sentiment. "They tend towards cheapness & speed of settlement." Churchill was duly impressed.[37]

By the time Churchill had assumed his new post on February 15, 1921, the die had been cast. The previous day the cabinet had authorized the incoming secretary of state for the colonies "to visit Egypt in the early part of March next for the purpose of consulting with the British authorities in Palestine and Arabia," and Churchill, who planned to leave for Cairo on March 3, began preparations in earnest.[38]

At Churchill's instructions Lawrence held yet another conversation with Faisal on February 16. He informed him of the impending conference, expressing the upbeat assessment that "present signs justified his being reasonably hopeful of a settlement satisfactory to all parties," especially with regard to "the Mesopotamian, and Trans-Jordan questions." He also told Faisal that he had just accepted an appointment at the Colonial Office, which would necessarily change the nature of their relationship. But he reassured the emir that "the appointment had not changed [his] opinions and hoped he would take it as an indication that H.M. Government were not wholly adverse to our past policy." Faisal remained conspicuously unperturbed: "He would like to lose all his friends in the same way."[39]

Faisal knew what he was talking about. With Lawrence acting as Churchill's adviser on Arabian affairs and Hubert Young as the head of the political and administrative branch of the newly established Middle Eastern Department at the Colonial Office, charged with the administration of Mesopotamia, Palestine, and Aden, the formulation of Britain's Middle East policy was effectively in the hands of the emir's partisans.

Indeed, when on February 18 Churchill drafted an outline of his proposed agenda for the Cairo Conference, it was Lawrence and Young who were to beef up this skeletal proposal and frame it in such a way that would *ipso facto* ensure Faisal's appointment to the Mesopotamian throne. On the first item on the agenda—the election of a ruler and his relationship with the British government under the mandate—they engineered the following collective departmental view: "We consider that Feisal should be the ruler, and the first step is to ascertain from Sir P. Cox that he can ensure the Council of State selecting him . . . As soon as the Council have notified their choice Feisal should be invited to proceed forthwith to Mesopotamia."

Lawrence and Young also orchestrated a departmental consensus favorable to Faisal's request for a qualified acceptance of the mandate: "Before putting Feisal's name before the Council of State we should obtain his provisional acceptance of the draft mandate, on the understanding that as soon as the Organic Law has been brought into operation, we shall be prepared to consider any proposals the Mesopotamian Government may wish to make for re-adjusting their relations with H.M.G."[40]

These and other recommendations contained in the draft agenda, all of which received Churchill's warm endorsement, were discussed at an interdepartmental conference on February 26. In addition to Lawrence and Young, Colonels Cornwallis and Joyce, two staunch Hashemite partisans, as well as Sir Arnold Wilson (knighted in 1920), a more recent convert to Faisal's cause, attended the meeting. Hence, not only was there no objection to Faisal's ascendancy to the Mesopotamian throne, but the Foreign Office representative reassured his counterparts "that the difficulty of getting the French to agree was not insuperable and that if they were faced with a fait accompli no trouble was likely to ensue."[41]

When it opened on the glorious Saturday morning of March 12, the Cairo Conference had little difficulty reaffirming the collective recommendations of the Middle Eastern Department. In his review of the candidates for the Mesopotamian throne, Cox identified Faisal as by far the leading contender. Ibn Saud seemed to him out of the question, if only for religious reasons, Sheikh Khaz'al of Muhammarah (a Persian subject), for the lack of a meaningful following, and Prince Burhan al-Din (a son of Sultan Abdul Hamid), for the fact that a Turkish ruler was no longer deemed desirable. As for the naqib of Baghdad and Sayyid Talib, the Basra strongman turned minister of the interior in the provisional government, Cox believed that neither had a chance, since "local opinion would never agree on a local candidate." This in turn left a Hashemite ruler as the only viable alternative, and "this solution would,

[Cox] thought, be welcomed by the majority of Mesopotamians, provided that it was not too obvious that he was being nominated by His Majesty's Government."[42]

Lawrence followed suit. He supported the candidature of Amir Faisal not only because he was a personal friend, but also because he believed that, "in order to counteract the claims of rival candidates and to pull together the scattered elements of a backward and half civilised country, it was essential that the first ruler should be an active and inspiring personality. Amir Abdullah was lazy, and by no means dominating."[43]

Churchill pointed to another advantage of the sharifian solution, namely, that it gave Britain an important lever in its relations with the Arab countries: "If Faisal knew that not only his father's subsidy and the protection of the Holy Places from Wahhabi attack, but also the position of his brother in Trans-Jordan was dependent upon his own good behaviour, he would be much easier to deal with. The same argument applied *mutatis mutandis* to King Hussein and Amir Abdullah." There was, however, a potential fly in the ointment, on which Churchill wished to hear the views of his experts: "The French Government had tried to convince him that by adopting a Sherifian policy he would risk being destroyed, like Frankenstein, by a monster of his own creation."[44]

Lawrence demurred. He thought that "[p]erhaps the French point of view was unduly coloured by their own experiences in Syria. He did not himself anticipate that a Sherifian policy would have this effect on British interests." Gertrude Bell agreed: "The only pan-Arab propaganda which was at all likely to make headway was the Sherifian propaganda. It was much better to turn this to our own use than to leave it as a potential enemy."[45]

Churchill needed no more encouragement. "I think we shall reach unanimous conclusion among all authorities that Feisal offers hope of best and cheapest solutions," he cabled Lloyd George on March 14. "I have no doubt personally Feisal offers far away best chance of saving our money. Please therefore endeavour to telegraph to me as soon as you possibly can that I am free to make plans on basis of formula."[46]

A week later, after an angry exchange with Lloyd George, who seemed lukewarm to the Cairo recommendations, Churchill received the green light. "Cabinet devoted exhaustive consideration to your proposals this morning," Lloyd George informed Churchill on March 22. "They were much impressed by collective force of your recommendations . . . and it was thought that order of events should be as follows:

Sir P. Cox should return with as little delay as possible to Mesopotamia, and should set going the machinery which may result in acceptance of Feisal's candidature and invitation to him to accept position of ruler of Irak. In the meantime, no announcement or communication to the French should be made. Feisal, however, will be told privately that there is no longer any need for him to remain in England, and that he should return without delay to Mecca to consult his father, who appears from our latest reports to be in a more than usually unamiable frame of mind. Feisal also will be told that if, with his father's and brother's consent, he becomes a candidate for Mesopotamia and is accepted by people of that country, we shall welcome their choice, subject, of course, to the double condition that he is prepared to accept terms of mandate as laid before League of Nations, and that he will not utilise his position to intrigue against or attack the French . . .

If above conditions are fulfilled, Feisal would then from Mecca make known at the right moment his desire to offer himself as candidate, and should make his appeal to the Mesopotamian people. At this stage we could, if necessary, communicate with the French, who, whatever their suspicions or annoyance, would have no ground for protest against a course of action in strict accordance with our previous declarations.[47]

This was music to Faisal's ears. Six months earlier he had been a spent ruler who would not even be seen by his British partisans in Egypt. Now he not only became His Majesty's Government's official candidate for the Mesopotamian throne, but had done so very much on his own terms. He therefore had little difficulty accepting the Cairo program, but not before extracting a promise from Lawrence that within a year from his arrival in Mesopotamia the League of Nations' mandate would be replaced by a mutually negotiated treaty. "Feisal expressed his appreciation of general policy outlined, and promised to do all he could to make his part of it work," Lawrence telegraphed to Churchill on April 15, after meeting with the emir.[48]

What remained to be done for Faisal was to convince his father to accept the Cairo program; then he had to bide his time while his supporters in Mesopotamia and Sir Percy Cox prepared the way to the throne for him. The first task proved easy enough, as Faisal found his father in a surprisingly friendly mood. The second task, however, turned out to be more complicated, for the local candidates would not bow out of the race with the ease predicted by Cox. While "friendly advice" from the high commissioner sufficed to get the sheikh of Muhammarah out of the way, and recognition of his title as the sultan of Najd accompanied by a lavish gift of £20,000 achieved the same result with Ibn Saud, the naqib, though "tottering on the brink of [the] grave,"[49] and Sayyid Talib proved more resilient.

Having returned in February 1920 after a four-year exile, Talib was determined to secure for himself the top Mesopotamian spot, even if this meant partitioning the country into two separate states, the first comprising the velayets of Mosul and Baghdad and the second—that of Basra. He managed to gain ground in Baghdad by pretending to champion the cause of the naqib, with whom he had come to a secret agreement; and he assiduously courted key British officials, notably H. St. John Philby, his adviser at the Interior Ministry, and Gertrude Bell, who exerted immense influence on Cox. "What's needed in this administration is experience," Talib told a British acquaintance of his. "I've got it. A doctor before he learns his trade will kill at least two hundred people. I've killed my two hundred—no one knows it better than yourself."[50]

For a brief while Talib managed to secure Wilson's support for his claim to the leadership of Mesopotamia, and at the height of the uprising Montagu even suggested that he be appointed governor of Basra in tandem with the appointment of Faisal as "king" at Baghdad. However, given Bell's relentless opposition to his appointment and Cox's mistrust and dislike of him, Talib never stood a real chance. At the Cairo Conference he was derided as "a man of bad character and untrustworthy"; and when Cox returned to Mesopotamia with the instruction to engineer Faisal's election, he seemed bent on elbowing Talib out of the way at the first available opportunity.

He didn't have to wait long. Driven by a mixture of overconfidence with the perceived grassroots support for his candidacy and anxiety over the growing British partisanship of the Hashemite cause, Talib overplayed his hand. At a dinner party in his home on April 14, attended *inter alia* by the French and Persian consuls, he complained of undue influence "in favour of one of the candidates to the throne of Iraq," and threatened that there would be another armed uprising "should there be indications that the declared policy of the British Government was not being carried out." This was precisely the kind of "incriminating evidence" Cox had been waiting for. On April 16 Talib was arrested and sent by boat to the southern port town of Fao. A few days later he was on his way to exile on the island of Ceylon, never to return to the country he dreamed of ruling.[51]

With Talib's departure from the political scene the scales were irrevocably tilted in Faisal's favor. There were still some murmurings that he was too "English," and a growing opposition in the velayet of Basra to inclusion in an Iraqi State for fear of being drawn "into the vortex of Baghdad politics and religious troubles," but in Baghdad and Kadhimain it was generally believed that Hashemites would sweep the board. Nationwide, the dominant sentiment was one of keen anticipation for a British-backed candidate. Even the naqib, while not withdrawing his own candidacy, relented in his opposition to a Hashemite solution "to the extent of saying that the country will be best to follow the wishes of H.M.G. whatever they may be."[52]

In the circumstances, Faisal decided to make his move. Notwithstanding the unexpected cordiality meted out to him by his father, the emir was anxious to proceed to his destination before the political mood changed either in the Hijaz or in Mesopotamia, and he did not shrink from making his displeasure with the slow pace of events known in London. "I anticipated that things would happen much more quickly," Bell wrote to her father on May 22. "But they haven't happened. They are, I may say, just beginning now, for the telegrams from Mecca . . . are making an appreciable effect." Two days later Lawrence sent an urgent telegram to Faisal. "I am very sorry for the delay which has been due to the time it takes to get telegraphic replies from Mesopotamia," he said, seeking to appease his friend. "In two days time we hope to be able to give you definite dates for yourself."[53] This they did, and on June 12 Faisal and his retinue sailed for Basra on board the British vessel the *Northbrook,* arriving at their destination twelve days later.

The following month, on July 11, the Council of State passed a unanimous resolution declaring Faisal the king of Iraq "provided that His Highness' Government shall be a constitutional representative and democratic Government limited by law." Five days later, at the instruction of Cox, who deemed the resolution insufficient for giving Faisal enough public clout, the council authorized a plebiscite, which Faisal won by a landslide 96 percent. On August 23, 1921, Faisal was crowned king of Iraq.[54]

20

AND ONE FOR ABDULLAH

*F*aisal's ascendance to the Mesopotamian throne left one major component of the Hashemite equation unresolved: his elder brother Abdullah. Until the eventful summer of 1920, Abdullah had been the front-runner in the race for the would-be Mesopotamian kingdom. Though the brightest and most politically astute of Hussein's sons and the main instigator of the Hashemite revolt, he found himself marginalized by his younger brother, who, largely as a result of Lawrence's exertions on his behalf, managed at first to secure for himself the most desired imperial prize: Syria.

To make matters worse, in May 1919 Abdullah suffered a crushing defeat at the hands of Khalid Ibn Mansur Ibn Luway, the ruler of the key town of Khurma, on the northeastern border of the Hijaz, aided by Ibn Saud's Wahhabi fighters. Most of Abdullah's 4,000–5,000 troops, including many of his close associates, were slaughtered in a lightning night attack, with the emir himself escaping by the skin of his teeth. Partial redemption from this ignominy came in March 1920 when the self-styled Iraqi Congress proclaimed Abdullah the king of Iraq. Despite his stoic response to the proclamation, owing to its categorical rejection by the British and the French, the emir had no intention of allowing this prize to slip from his fingers. Having convinced his father to substitute him for Faisal as the head of the Hijaz delegation to the peace talks, he traveled to Cairo, from where he intended to proceed to Paris, only to be peremptorily told by Allenby that the Allies considered Faisal the head of the delegation and that he had better return to the Hijaz.

Against this backdrop, it was scarcely surprising that Abdullah viewed Faisal's expulsion from Damascus with grave misgivings. Keenly aware of his brother's many connections in the British corridors of power, Abdullah had little doubt that it was only a matter of time before Faisal would disinherit him from his spoils by substituting Iraq for his lost Syrian kingdom. In a desperate bid to forestall this eventuality, Abdullah complained to Major Batten, the acting British consul in Jeddah, of the wholehearted British embrace of Faisal to the total neglect of himself, despite his weighty contribution to the Allied cause during the war and in its aftermath. He also let it be known in no uncertain terms that he had no intention whatsoever of letting Faisal take his place in Mesopotamia.[1]

But Abdullah did not stop there. At the end of September 1920 he led several hundred tribesmen out of Mecca and into the small oasis town of Maan, at the northern tip of the Hijaz, arriving there in mid-November. Ostensibly, Abdullah was responding to appeals by Syrian nationalists, camped in Transjordan since the collapse of Faisal's kingdom, to help them drive the French out of Syria on behalf of his deposed brother. In reality he was establishing himself as a key player in the scramble for the defunct Ottoman Empire.

Abdullah's move pushed to the fore the status of the sparsely populated and desolate territory east of the Jordan River, or Transjordan, as it came to be widely known. Recall that the 1915 de Bunsen Committee viewed Transjordan as an integral part of a vast Palestine stretching from the Mediterranean to Mesopotamia. The Sykes-Picot Agreement, in contrast, earmarked this territory as part of the prospective independent Arab empire falling within the British sphere of influence. This definition was overturned yet again by the San Remo Conference of April 1920, which placed Transjordan within the Palestine Mandate granted to Britain, which is precisely how this territory was viewed at the time by most British policymakers.

This state of affairs notwithstanding, it was not long before Transjordan's fortunes took a separate path from those of Palestine. Whether because of the country's unimposing geographic attributes and its socioeconomic underdevelopment compared with Palestine, or because of their reluctance to open it to Jewish immigration and settlement as required by the Palestine Mandate, the British withdrew their forces from Transjordan upon the Ottoman surrender, leaving Faisal to administer the area as an effective province of his Syrian kingdom. But the collapse of this kingdom created a dangerous power vacuum that the British were anxious to fill lest Transjordan slide into anarchy or, alternatively, fall under French influence and control.

To Sir Herbert Samuel, the first British high commissioner for Palestine, the solution to this problem was simple and straightforward. "Am deeply convinced that we shall be making grave error of policy if we do not include Trans-Jordania in Palestine," he telegraphed to Curzon on August 7, 1920. "It will certainly result in anarchy or French control across the border. Either would be disastrous and involve larger garrison here and greater expense." At the very minimum Samuel recommended keeping the comparatively fertile territory west of the Hijaz Railway line under indirect British control, while leaving the barren and sparsely populated area east of this line under the control of the king of the Hijaz. "Very small number of troops required as occupation greatly desired by tribes," he reassured Curzon, reporting on numerous appeals for British intervention by leading Transjordanian sheikhs.[2]

This position was vehemently opposed by members of the Foreign Office. They supported Transjordan's military occupation all right, but only as a means to prevent the French from going there, not with a view to its incorporation into Palestine.[3] In their opinion, despite the economic interconnectedness of the two territories, Palestine had been specifically excluded from the prospective Arab empire by Sir Henry McMahon, "lying as it does to the west of the 'district of Damascus,'" whereas Transjordan fell within the bounds of this empire and hence deserved an independent existence.[4]

Curzon found both options wanting. He ruled out military occupation both because of the War Office's opposition to such a move and because he wished to avoid any appearance of exploiting the situation to Britain's advantage. He also rejected Transjordan's immediate annexation to Mandatory Palestine, if only to prevent widespread Jewish settlement there. Instead, he steered a middle course that would keep all of Britain's options open, namely, Transjordan's separate administration through several self-governing municipal and district bodies assisted by a handful of competent British advisers.

But what about the country's final status? Here Curzon spoke from both sides of his mouth. To Samuel he promised that the British advisers in Transjordan would spare no effort to encourage trade with Palestine so as to facilitate the eventual fusion of the two territories: "The inclusion of Trans-Jordanian districts in the administration of Palestine will be more easily effected when the people have had a better opportunity of expressing a definite and final desire to accept not only the advantages but also the obligations of British rule." At the same time he wrote to Robert Vansittart, the head of the political section of the British Peace Delegation in Paris who was then engaged in the delimitation of the boundaries of Syria and Palestine, that "His Majesty's Government are already treating 'Trans-Jordania' as separate from the Damascus State, while at the same time avoiding any definite connection between it and Palestine, thus leaving the way open for the establishment there, should it become advisable, of some form of independent Arab Government, perhaps by arrangement with King Hussein or other Arab chiefs concerned."[5]

The problem with this last option, as Curzon and his advisers were painfully aware, was that since the Mandate constituted the sole legal basis of Britain's position in Transjordan, any British claim to this territory had to be based "upon the assumption that Trans-Jordan forms part of the area covered by the Palestine Mandate. In default of this assumption Trans-Jordan would be left, under article 132 of the Treaty of Sèvres, to the disposal of the principal Allied Powers."[6]

By way of reconciling the need to apply the Palestine Mandate to Transjordan with the "recognition and support of the independence of the Arabs" promised in the Hussein-McMahon correspondence, the newly established Middle East Department suggested setting up in Transjordan "a political system somewhat different from that in force on the other side of the river" without creating a separate new judiciary. "If it is accepted that Trans-Jordan is to be legally included in Palestine," ran the departmental recommendation, "we consider that the terms 'Palestine' and 'Eastern Palestine' should be brought into use for the territories lying respectively to the west and east of the River Jordan."[7]

This plan for an autonomous Transjordanian province within Mandatory Palestine, which formed the basis of the British deliberations in Cairo, was thwarted by Abdullah. As the Cairo Conference convened, its participants learned that the emir had moved from Maan to the northern town of Amman, thus positioning himself in close proximity to the

French. Coming as it did in the wake of assurances from Faisal and Hussein that Abdullah would not move northward, this was an unpleasant surprise for the British, who failed to realize that Abdullah had made his move precisely because of these familial reassurances—not in spite of them. Having little trust in Faisal, Abdullah followed warily his brother's talks in London; and upon hearing that "trouble in Trans-Jordan will ruin our negotiations in London, which otherwise will go well," he apparently determined that inaction on his part would condemn him to oblivion.[8]

These apprehensions were fully justified. Faisal had already managed to elbow Abdullah out of Mesopotamia, and now he sought to exclude him from Transjordan as well. In a letter to his father on March 1, Faisal suggested that Zeid be appointed king of "Southern Syria" as a means to deflect the French objection to Syrian unification. To Zeid himself he portrayed the establishment of a Transjordanian kingdom, together with an Iraqi one, as a crucial step on the road "to Damascus and beyond." In making these suggestions, Faisal was echoing the standard perception of Abdullah in Whitehall, which his intimate friend Lawrence had done so much to establish, as the least worthy of Hussein's sons. Hence, when the British began seriously to entertain the possibility of Hashemite rule over Transjordan, Abdullah lagged far behind his two brothers. To Curzon, Zeid appeared the natural "Emir of the area between Palestine and the Hijaz south of [the] Sykes-Picot line," while Young suggested that they "inform Feisal that if he finds it impossible to stay in Damascus under a French Mandate we are willing to accept him as ruler of Trans-Jordan and to enter [into] the necessary economic treaty with him to ensure his being able to support an administration in that country."[9]

It was only after Abdullah had established himself in Maan, spreading Hashemite and anti-French propaganda throughout the country, and showing no inclination to return to the Hijaz, that the British reluctantly began to consider him Transjordan's potential ruler. "Still holding to our view that in present circumstances a *Sherifian* policy is the only practicable one for us," Lawrence and Young opined shortly before the Cairo Conference, "we are prepared to allow Abdullah to consolidate his position in this region, provided he is ready to act in general accordance with the advice of our political officers." In their view, it might even be possible at some future point to hint to the French that if they wished to set Abdullah up in Damascus, "such a solution will have our cordial approval and will be particularly agreeable to us as an unmistakable sign of Franco-British solidarity in Arabian policy." "We see no menace to French interests in this," they reasoned. "On the contrary; Abdullah, like Feisal, will be much less dangerous as a settled ruler than as a freelancer."[10]

This was indeed the logic that drove the Cairo Conference begrudgingly to endorse Abdullah as Transjordan's ruler—not as the best possible option, but as the least of all evils. None of the participants was particularly enthusiastic about this appointment, yet all conceded that Abdullah's move to Amman had given him a decisive say in Transjordan's future. Moreover, in Churchill's view, the British needed to harmonize their policy in Transjordan and Mesopotamia. "To support the Sherif in Iraq and not in Trans-Jordania would be courting trouble," he argued. "If we were to curb the activities of Abdullah, while allowing him to remain in Trans-Jordania, we must obtain the goodwill of the Sherifian family and place them as a whole under an obligation to His Majesty's Government in one sphere or another."[11]

On March 18, Churchill telegraphed to Lloyd George recommending the immediate military occupation of Transjordan so as to secure a stable government that would prevent bedouin raids into Palestine, stop anti-French activities, and reopen the Hijaz Railway to pilgrimage to Mecca. This in turn depended on the attainment of a satisfactory arrangement with Abdullah whereby "either he will become governor in our name under High Commissioner of Palestine or . . . someone agreeable to him will undertake this task with his approval and support." "As we cannot contemplate hostilities with Abdullah in any circumstances, there is no alternative to this policy," Churchill argued. "We must therefore proceed in co-operation and accord with him. On the other hand, Abdullah with best will in the world will not be able to restrain his people from disturbing the French and even making war upon them unless he is fortified and restrained at once by presence of a British force, which must be strong enough to provide for its own safety."[12]

Four days later Lloyd George informed Churchill of "considerable misgivings" within the cabinet regarding his proposals for Transjordan. For one thing, "it was felt that almost simultaneous installation of the two brothers in regions contiguous to French sphere of influence would be regarded with great suspicion by [the French] and would be interpreted as a menace to their position in Syria, deliberately plotted by ourselves." For another, "it was urged by our military advisers that this occupation would involve a military commitment, the extension and duration of which it was impossible to forecast." Above all, it was doubt-ful whether Abdullah "would accept such a position as that suggested, in a territory too small for a Kingdom." True, Abdullah's presence in Am-man, combined with the government's desire to fulfill its earlier promises to Hussein regarding Arab independence, "undoubtedly [favors] an Arab rather than a Palestinian solution." British policymakers felt, however, that "the price to be paid for these advantages seems to be high and the results doubtful." The cabinet thus advised Churchill to keep an open mind in his forthcoming meeting with Abdullah and not to exclude any alternative plan. "It might, for instance, be possible, while preserving Arab character of the area and administration, to treat it as an Arab province or adjunct of Palestine."[13]

As this was precisely what his own Middle East Department had proposed, Churchill had no difficulty concurring. "We do not expect or particularly desire, indeed, Abdullah himself to undertake Governship. He will, as Cabinet rightly apprehend, almost certainly think it too small," he wrote to Lloyd George:

> But that his influence should be upon our side and that [? person] elected for local Governship shall be one in whose nomination he has cordially concurred is the vital point. Abdullah has power to do a great deal of harm, particularly against French in Transjordania, and if he became actively hostile we should have no means of coping with him. The actual solution which we have always had in mind and for which I shall work is that which you described as follows: "while preserving Arab character of area and administration to treat it as an Arab province or adjunct of Palestine."[14]

This was a far cry from what Abdullah had hoped to achieve. He had gone to great lengths to make himself an imperial ruler and a key player in regional affairs, not a subordinate provincial governor. If a certain territory had to be incorporated into another as a province, then it should be Palestine into Transjordan, under his headship, and not the other way around. This was the ambition that he was to nurture for most of his life, and this is precisely what he told Churchill at their first meeting in Jerusalem, on March 28, 1921.

The colonial secretary opened the conversation by stating his inten-tion to abide by McMahon's promises regarding Arab independence, using the Hashemite family as a medium. There were, however, certain territories that were to be excluded from this arrangement owing to the decisions of the Allies and to British promises to third parties, namely, "Syria and Palestine west of the Jordan." Turning to Transjordan, Churchill explained that

> His Majesty's Government were responsible for this area under a mandate given them by the Allied Powers in the peace settlement with Turkey. They recognised its Arab character, but felt it was too small to stand alone. Economically and geographically it should go with Palestine, and he proposed that it be constituted as an Arab province under an Arab Governor responsible to the High Commissioner for Palestine.

Abdullah demurred. While conceding that "the peace settlement and their promises to third parties did not leave Great Britain free to act in Syria and in Western Palestine," he suggested that the British establish a unified Transjordanian-Palestinian kingdom:

> If His Majesty's Government could agree that there should be an Arab Emir over Palestine and Trans-Jordania in the same relation with the High Commissioner for Palestine as that of the Emir Feisal with the High Commissioner for Mesopotamia, he was convinced that the present difficulties between Arabs and Jews would be most easily overcome.

Churchill's explanation that there was a fundamental difference between the status of Mesopotamia, which had been provisionally recognized as an independent state, and Palestine, which had been entrusted to the administration of a mandatory, failed to impress Abdullah. He argued that "His Majesty's Government proposed to have his brother Feisal in Mesopotamia with a High Commissioner or a mandate, or whatever term they might like to employ. He felt strongly that a similar régime should be adopted for Palestine and Trans-Jordania."[15]

This proposition was indicative not only of Abdullah's own ambitions, but also of the sibling rivalry between the two Hashemite emirs. If Faisal were to receive the largest (remaining) imperial prize, Iraq, then Abdullah should have his cake, too, and not mere crumbs. Indeed, while pretending to accept the plan for Faisal's enthronement in Iraq, Abdullah showed no enthusiasm for the idea. He declined Churchill's request to write to Mesopotamia in favor of his brother's candidacy on the pretext that he "had no contacts" in the country, and, moreover, he lost no opportunity to besmirch his brother, however subtly. Thus, for example, he told Churchill that it was Faisal who had engineered his proclamation as king of Mesopotamia in March 1920, while "he himself had not only had no part in this arrangement, but had pointed out to his brother that he was unwise in taking a step which could only embarrass His Majesty's Government."[16]

Viewed in this light, Abdullah's suggestion that if Transjordan and Palestine were not to be unified the former should be cut off from the latter altogether and combined with Mesopotamia, was a mere tactical ploy to discredit Churchill's idea. So was his transparent claim that "though he might have been prepared to suggest a name for an Emir of Palestine and Trans-Jordania, he could not advise on an Arab Governor for Trans-Jordania alone under the authority of the High Commissioner for Palestine."[17]

But in Churchill Abdullah had found his match. The colonial secretary stuck to the position that, His Majesty's Government being the mandatory, the Arab governor of Transjordan would have to recognize British control over his administration, and would be expected to refrain from any anti-French activities and to accept British policy in Palestine west of the Jordan. On the other hand, "Trans-Jordania would not be included in the present administrative system of Palestine, and therefore the Zionist clauses of the mandate would not apply." "He wished the Emir to understand that he was taking a great responsibility as the new Minister in charge of the Middle East in advising his colleagues to join hands with the Sherifian family," Churchill informed Abdullah, trying to impress upon him the significance of their meeting.

> He had been advised by certain other people that this was a very dangerous policy. He had been told that His Majesty's Government would be better advised to split up the Arabs into distinct and separate Local Governments. This had been the policy of Rome and of Turkey in the past and appeared to be to some extent the policy of other Powers at the present time. He wished to impress upon the Emir that a very grave choice had to be made within the next few days by His Majesty's Government, namely, whether they should divide or unite the Arab peoples with whom they had to deal.

Abdullah was impressed. He still considered his own suggestion for a unified Palestinian-Transjordanian kingdom the best solution, but he was quite prepared to consider the matter in the light of the new proposals that had been made, though it was impossible for him to give any final commitment without first consulting his father and brother.

Churchill readily accepted Abdullah's position, and by way of strengthening the emir's hand offered him the ultimate incentive. "The French authorities in Syria were not at the moment pursuing a Sherifian policy and it was not for His Majesty's Government to press them to do so," he said.

> At the same time it appeared to him that if an example was set in the British sphere and at the same time His Majesty's Government could point to the admirable results achieved there by themselves, the French might possibly come round to the British way of thinking. It was obvious that to this end absolute order should be preserved on the frontier between Syria and Trans-Jordania; the Arab attitude must be as correct as possible, and every personal effort must be made by the Emir himself to improve his relations with the French.[18]

This was just what Abdullah wanted to hear. In contrast to his vehement opposition to Transjordan's westward expansion, Churchill had effectively signaled Britain's possible acquiescence in Hashemite domination of Syria, this time under Abdullah's, rather than Faisal's, leadership. True, this was a long shot that might or might not pay off, but Abdullah felt that it was infinitely better to have a bird in the hand than two in the bush. And being the political realist that he was, the emir was fully aware that he had pressed his luck to its utmost limits, and that there was absolutely no chance of his extracting further British concessions at that particular historical juncture. Hence, in his second meeting with Churchill Abdullah went out of his way to reassure his interlocutor of his determination to prevent any anti-French activities in Transjordan; and when in their third meeting the colonial secretary suggested that "the Emir himself should remain in Trans-Jordania for a period of six months to prepare the way for the appointment, with his consent, at the end of that time of an Arab Governor under the High Commissioner," Abdullah readily accepted, his only request being "that he might be regarded as a British officer and trusted accordingly." This the relieved Churchill was ready to grant: he warmly thanked Abdullah for his goodwill and assured him that he would be given free rein to complete the very difficult task that he had undertaken.[19]

"The Emir Abdullah has promised to work with us and for us to do his best to restrain the people from anti-French action and to form, with our assistance, a local administration which can later on be handed over to a native Governor of less consequence than himself," Churchill wrote to Samuel on board the ship carrying him home, explaining the procedure to be adopted with regard to Transjordan during the next six months. "His position will be informal, and no question either of governorship or sovereignty is raised. He must be given a very free hand, as he has a most difficult task to perform. Not only has he been checked in mid-career in his campaign against the French, but he has been asked to execute a complete *volte-face* and to take active steps to nullify the effects of his previous policy."[20]

Churchill could not have been more mistaken. Far from being checked in mid-career, let alone forced to execute a complete about face, Abdullah had resurrected his imperial dream. Prior to his venture to Transjordan, he had largely been a spent force. Deprecated by the British, ridiculed in Arabia, and disfavored by his father following the Khurma defeat, Abdullah would most likely have been passed over in the division of the remaining Ottoman spoils. Now he had not only managed to establish himself as a key Hashemite player, but also secured effective control, however legally constrained, over a territory of his own. To British officialdom Abdullah's appointment was a temporary measure to prevent Transjordan's slide into anarchy and to ease its development into an autonomous province of Palestine—"under the British mandate for Palestine and under the general control of the High Commissioner for Palestine"—ruled most likely by an Arab governor other than Abdullah but amenable to him. To Abdullah, his new position was a golden opportunity to transform Transjordan into a springboard for the realization of his imperial dream: a vast kingdom comprising Syria and Palestine under his leadership.

In the end, neither of the two visions came to fruition. Contrary to initial British expectations, Abdullah's six-month stint turned out to be a lifetime enterprise, with Transjordan becoming an independent kingdom rather than an autonomous province of Palestine. Contrary to Abdullah's hopes, the vast empire he coveted never transpired, his maximum gains being the capture of a sizeable part of Western Palestine in 1948 and its incorporation into his kingdom. Yet Abdullah's dogged imperial quest, from the early 1920s until his assassination in 1951, was to have a decisive impact on the shaping of the modern Middle East.

21

From Empire to Nation

*T*he final nail in the coffin of the secret wartime agreements on the partition of the Ottoman Empire was driven in by none other than the intended target of those very agreements. The empire was to be stripped not only of its vast Arabic-speaking provinces, but also of most of the Turkish homeland itself: Istanbul and the straits were to go to Russia, together with most of Turkish Armenia, while the rest of Asia Minor, apart from a tiny Turkish state in eastern and north-central Anatolia, was to be split between France and Italy.

This planned division of spoils never occurred, partly because Russia departed from the war following the 1917 Bolshevik Revolution and repudiated the secret wartime agreements, and partly because the peace conference failed to reach a quick decision on the future of the defunct Ottoman Empire owing to Anglo-French-Italian differences and American indecision. But the foremost factor contributing to the failure of these plans was the surge of a new and vibrant brand of Turkish nationalism, ready to disown the Ottoman imperial legacy but never to accept the partition and subjugation of the Turkish homeland. The person who was almost single-handedly responsible for this historic turning point in Turkish history was the dashing war hero General Mustafa Kemal, later known as Kemal Atatürk.

The son of a humble timber merchant, Kemal was born in Salonika in 1881, only to lose his father at the tender age of seven. Against his mother's wishes, he embarked on a military career at the remarkably young age of twelve, when he entered a military school in his hometown. Two years later he was already at the military academy in Monastir, and in 1899 he moved to the War College in Istanbul, graduating six years later with the rank of staff-captain.[1]

Despite his active participation in the anti-Hamidian clandestine movement, the 1908 revolution did not bring political prominence for Kemal, whose relations with the CUP leadership vacillated between coolness and hostility. Instead, the young officer focused his boundless energy on his career, proving his mettle in the Libyan and the Balkan wars and playing a pivotal role in the Ottoman victory in Gallipoli, which spared the empire a humiliating retreat from the war.

From Gallipoli Kemal, now a general and a national hero, went on to excel in the Russian campaigns, and he was eventually given command of the Seventh Army of the Yilderim Army Group, the empire's elite force. The expulsion of this group from Palestine and southern Syria by General Allenby, which helped drive the Ottoman Empire out of the war, did little to affect Kemal's professional standing. On October 31, 1918, a day after the signing of an armistice agreement on board His Britannic Majesty's Ship *Agamemnon* at Port Mudros, Lemnos, the thirty-eight-year-old veteran general was made commander of the Yilderim Army Group, only to be summoned to Istanbul shortly thereafter, following the group's dissolution.

Kemal found the capital in the throes of defeat and the regime bent on self-preservation. Fearful of following in the footsteps of the unfortunate German and Austro-Hungarian emperors and losing his newly gained throne (which he had ascended in July 1918), Sultan Mehmed Vehideddin, a younger brother of Abdul Hamid, went out of his way to buy the Allies' benevolence: he dissolved Parliament in order to prevent anti-Entente criticism or the possible resurgence of the CUP; imprisoned members of the Unionist government, together with scores of suspected political activists; initiated court martial proceedings *in absentia* against Enver and Djemal, who had fled the country; and progressively disarmed and demobilized the Turkish army throughout the country, resigning himself to the idea that Asia Minor would be occupied by foreign powers—Istanbul by a joint Allied administration, the Dardanelles and the Anatolian Railway by Britain, Cilicia and Adana by France, and Antalya by Italy. On November 13, 1918, an Allied armada made a triumphal entry into the Bosphorus, anchoring off the Golden Horn. Four months later, emulating Mehmed the Conqueror, the city's Ottoman occupier of 1453, General Franchet d'Espérey entered Constantinople at the head of a French contingent, riding without reins on a white horse. The Turks watched these scenes with quiet rage and a sense of helplessness.

But not Kemal. He had reconciled himself to Turkey's loss of the Arabic-speaking provinces—and even, for that matter, to its demise as an imperial power—but not to the subjugation or partition of the Turkish homeland itself. "As they have come, so they shall go" was his stoic response to the entry of the Allied fleet into the Bosphorus. Yet he was painfully aware that this was easier said than done: the Allies would not leave of their own free will, and the war-weary Turks were not in the mood to push them out. As he later put it: "The idea that it was impossible to fight even one of these Powers had taken root in the mind of nearly everybody. Consequently, to think of doing so and thus bring on another war after the Ottoman Empire, all-powerful Germany and Austria-Hungary together had been defeated and crushed would have been looked upon as sheer madness."[2]

Nor was Kemal impressed by the two apparent options facing Turkey at the time: either to preserve the Ottoman Empire under British or American protection, or "to deliver the country by allowing each district to act in its own way and according to its own capability." In his opinion, both solutions were equally misconceived—the former because the foundations of the Ottoman Empire had been irrevocably shattered, making its preservation, even under great-power protection, a chimera; the latter because total decentralization of the defunct empire would mean the complete suffocation of Turkish national existence. This in turn left the Turks no choice but to make a clean break with their Ottoman imperial legacy and "to create a New Turkish State, the sovereignty and independence of which would be unreservedly recognised by the whole world." This sovereignty would reside with the nation itself, rather than with the person of the sultan-caliph, and would be vested in an elected government: "To labour for the maintenance of the Ottoman dynasty and its sovereign would have been to inflict the greatest injustice upon the Turkish nation . . . As for the Caliphate, it could only have been a laughing-stock in the eyes of the really civilised and cultured people of the world."[3]

The significance of Kemal's shift from desiring an empire to envisioning a republic cannot be overstated. Notwithstanding the widespread lip service paid to Woodrow Wilson's precept of national self-determination, imperialism was still the catchphrase of the day, and neither the great powers nor their Middle Eastern interlocutors sought to predicate the region's future political system on the national principle. There was of course the occasional half-hearted Allied recognition of national aspirations, notably those of Armenians and Jews, but on the whole, the postwar arrangements reflected an imperial rather than a nationalist mindset. The partition of the Fertile Crescent into two Arab kingdoms rather than into several nation-states in accordance with the existing realities of local patriotism, to note a salient example, was an uneasy compromise between the Hashemite and the French imperial ambitions. Similarly, the envisioned disposal of the purely Turkish parts of the Ottoman Empire was a direct corollary of great-power greed, fear, and distrust. By way of forestalling Italian entrenchment in Asia Minor, President Wilson in May 1919 teamed up with prime ministers Lloyd George and Clemenceau to give his blessing to Greek occupation of the western coast of Asia Minor; by way of preventing British domination of Istanbul and the straits, the French resisted Curzon's attempts to sever the city from the future Turkish state, together with its remaining European possessions. Nowhere were the aspirations of the Turkish population itself taken into account.

More important, as Kemal knew full well, his advocacy of Turkish national-statism and sovereignty flew in the face of the millenarian Islamic political culture. "We never disclosed the views we had," he revealed in his historic speech of October 1927, narrating the course of the revolution he had kindled. "If we had done so we would have been looked upon as dreamers and illusionists . . . The only practical and safe road to success lay in making each step perfectly understood at the right time."[4]

This combination of vision and pragmatism, of absolute commitment to an ultimate grand design coupled with contemporaneous flexibility, stood at the core of Kemal's extraordinary success. Thus, when offered the inspector-generalship of the Anatolian Ninth Army (a month later renumbered the Third Army), charged with demobilizing the remaining Ottoman forces and dispersing the numerous armed militias roaming that part of the country, Kemal quickly seized the moment. On May 19, 1919, he landed in the Black Sea port town of Samsun.

Why the authorities chose to invest such extensive powers in Kemal is not entirely clear. Some historians have suggested that "he was sent because his superiors in the Ministry of War, and possibly the grand vezir and sultan, fully expected him to organize resistance," but this is belied by the simple fact that, from the moment he set foot in Samsun, Kemal was at loggerheads with his superiors, which in turn led to his recall less than a month after beginning his mission.[5]

A more plausible explanation is that in their eagerness to kill two birds with one stone—to keep Turkey's most celebrated war hero as far from the capital as possible while having him do their dirty work—the Turkish government apparently played into Kemal's hands. The Allies were threatening that unless the lawlessness in Anatolia was brought to an immediate halt they would be forced to intervene themselves, and Kemal seemed the obvious person to avert this dire development.

True, in his appearance before the peace conference on June 17, 1919, and in a memorandum submitted to the conference a few days later, Grand Vizier Damad Ferid Pasha, a kindly, cultivated, but incompetent elderly gentleman whose main asset was being the sultan's brother-in-law, defiantly claimed that the Turkish people "will not accept the dismemberment of the Empire or its division under different mandates."[6] But this was nothing more than a desperate attempt to flaunt the sultan's patriotic credentials in the face of mounting public outrage following the Greek landing in the west Anatolian town of Smyrna on May 15, 1919.

The landing was the high point of Prime Minister Eleutherios Venizelos's relentless pursuit of the Megali Idea, "The Great Idea" of a resurrected Greek empire with Constantinople as its capital, uniting all Greeks under the flag of Hellas. Linking twentieth-century Greece with its illustrious imperial past, Venizelos based his claim to substantial parts of Western Asia Minor not on the mere existence of a sizeable Greek minority there, but also on (alleged) Greek cultural superiority, which made the Greeks far more "suitable" than Turkey to rule these areas. The Greeks, he argued, represented "an old and advanced civilization," whereas

> the Turks were good workers, honest in their relations, and a good people as subjects. But as rulers they were insupportable and a disgrace to civilization, as was proved by their having exterminated over a million Armenians and 300,000 Greeks during the last four years.[7]

Keenly aware of the wide gap between his grandiose dreams and the realities of Greek power, Venizelos made the most of the limited resources at his disposal. He used his considerable personal charm and eloquence to make the Allies feel indebted to him for bringing Greece into the war (Lloyd George described him as "the greatest statesman Greece has thrown up since the days of Pericles"), then capitalized on their anxiety over his domestic standing by linking his stability as a leader to his ability to deliver the territories he had promised to the Greek people. He also exploited the differences among the Allies: when Italy deployed military forces in Anatolia in April 1920 to seize what it considered to be its just share of the Ottoman spoils, Venizelos quickly secured Anglo-American-French blessings for a Greek landing in Smyrna to prevent the city's occupation by Italian forces. So anxious was Wilson to see Greek forces land in Asia Minor that he told Venizelos that "men did not keep in good condition on board ship."[8]

To ordinary Turks the Greek invasion was anathema; to the sultan it was a personal affront by a former minor subject people. Kemal, in contrast, saw it as a lightning strike galvanizing the defeatist masses into a reinvigorated national effort. As news of the invasion spread across the country, his calls for rebuffing the foreign occupation of the Turkish homeland struck increasingly responsive chords: organized resistance groups were springing up throughout Anatolia, and weapons and ammunition were being seized from military dumps, unearthed from old army caches, or smuggled in from the Russian Caucasus.

On June 3, 1919, Kemal telegraphed a number of key military and civil figures, urging them to forestall the government's intended surrender of Turkish districts to, and acceptance of foreign mandate over, the newly established Armenian State. In yet another circular telegram, sent on June 21, he went further, warning that Turkey's territorial integrity and national independence were in "imminent jeopardy" and that "the Government is unequal to the task for which it has assumed responsibility; the consequence being that our nation is not considered at all." Since only the nation's will and resilience could save the day, a (secret) national conference had to be convened immediately to establish that national will and the ways and means for its implementation.[9]

This was too much for the authorities, and on July 8 Kemal was peremptorily informed of the cancellation of his commission. His immediate response was to resign his post and, as a full-time rebel, to press ahead with his plans: between July 23 and August 7, 1919, a congress of delegates from the eastern provinces assembled in Erzerum, followed a month later by a more comprehensive gathering at Sivas, with delegates from all over the country. The two conferences established the primary instrument of political struggle (the Association for the Defense of the

Rights of Anatolia and Rumelia, successor to the Association for the Defense of the Rights of Eastern Anatolia, founded in March 1919), with Kemal at its head, and drafted a manifesto containing the principles and objectives guiding the resistance movement, which would later become known as the National Pact. The manifesto rejected foreign restrictions "inimical to our development," demanded the preservation of Turkey's territorial integrity and independence, and claimed the right to use armed resistance in pursuit of these goals.[10]

Interestingly enough, despite his insistence that "the will of the Turkish Nation to be master of her own destiny could only spring from Anatolia," and that in the event of the government's failure to preserve the country's territorial integrity and independence "a provisional Government shall be formed for the purpose of safeguarding these aims," Kemal went out of his way to avoid challenging the sultan's authority, directing his ire instead at Grand Vizier Damad Ferid and his ministers. This reflected Kemal's political caution and realism. Since a millenarian tradition predicating political and social life on the principle of religion could not be eradicated overnight, the revolutionary movement would have to take one step at a time. So long as the Turks considered the sultan-caliph to be their supreme religious and temporal ruler, there was no point in launching a frontal assault on this cherished institution; it would be infinitely better to pretend to defer to the sultan while effectively pulling the rug out from under him. As Kemal himself put it: "History is teeming with examples showing what fate awaits people whose battle-cry is 'Onward!' and let us trust that the nation that is accustomed to be downtrodden will follow us!"[11]

For a while this strategy worked. Confronted with mounting public restiveness, and with the control of most of Anatolia by Kemal's followers, on October 1, 1919, the sultan substituted Ali Reza Pasha for Damad Ferid as grand vizier. Reza's sympathy for their cause was quickly translated into concrete gains for the nationalists, most notably the holding of free elections for the Ottoman Parliament in December 1919, in which they won a handsome majority. On January 28, 1920, the reassembled Parliament embraced the National Pact, based on the Erzerum and Sivas declarations. For its part the government went so far as to restore Kemal's decorations and rank on the pretext that he had not been dismissed from the army but had, rather, resigned.

No sooner had the nationalists made their gains, than they were confronted with a new formidable challenge. For quite some time the Allies had been alarmed by Kemal's rising power, by the surge of pro-Kemalist sentiments across the Levant, and by reported contacts between the Turkish nationalists and the Hashemites, which threatened the Entente's plans not only for Asia Minor but also for the entire Middle Eastern settlement. These fears were further exacerbated by the Allies' general inability to ascertain Kemal's objectives, the true nature of his revolutionary movement, and its actual strength.[12] Hence, when thousands of Armenians were massacred by Kemal's forces during the occupation of the Cilician town of Marash, the Allies moved into action. On March 16, 1920, Istanbul was seized by British and French troops: key ministries and services (for example, mail, telegraphs and telephones, the police) were taken over to ensure the normal continuation of life and the maintenance of law and order, and scores of political activists and nationalist sympathizers were arrested and deported. A week later the buoyant British high commissioner in Istanbul, Admiral Sir J. de Robeck, reported to Curzon that "occupation of Constantinople has so far constituted success exceeding expectations." "I do not wish to exaggerate this success prematurely," he wrote, feigning modesty, "but without being a knockout blow it has been [a] severe blow for the nationalist movement."[13]

This was a gross miscalculation. Far from ebbing the tide of the nationalist resistance movement, the occupation of Istanbul helped confirm its success. On April 23, 1920, eleven days after the sultan had dissolved Parliament, a Grand National Assembly opened in the small Anatolian town of Ankara (since December 1919 the base of the nationalist movement), with Kemal elected as its president. Assuming both legislative and executive powers, the Grand National Assembly was progressively transformed into Turkey's effective government, and Ankara into the country's *de facto* capital.

This process gained momentum with the announcement of the Entente's harsh peace terms in May 1920, and reached its peak three months later following the signing of the Treaty of Sèvres, which not only signaled the end of the Ottoman Empire but also truncated the Turkish homeland of Anatolia and Rumelia in the most humiliating fashion. Particularly galling to the Turks were the territorial concessions to the Greeks and the Armenians, two despised former subject peoples, and to a lesser extent, to the Kurds. A tidal wave of revulsion swept the nation, discrediting Damad Ferid Pasha (who had been reinstated as grand vizier on April 5) and his cabinet, leading to the collapse of the antinationalist campaign launched by the sultan following the Allied occupation of Istanbul, and rallying the nation behind Kemal and his followers, who were seen as heroic patriots struggling to liberate their homeland from the clutches of foreign occupiers.

This perception was fully justified. Slowly but surely, through skillful exploitation of dissension among the Allies, Kemal was reasserting Turkish sovereignty in Asia Minor. By the end of May 1920 the French had been expelled from much of Cilicia and forced into a provisional armistice agreement with Kemal, to the considerable dismay of their British allies. Even more exasperating for the British was the overt affinity between the Italian forces and the nationalists. "At Constantinople the independent attitude of the Italians was so notorious that it was a matter of common belief that the Alliance no longer existed," Curzon told his fellow ministers. "Everywhere the Italians were reported as assuring the Turks that they were behind them in resisting the Turkish Peace Treaty, while in Anatolia we were credibly informed that Italian agents were in close touch with the partisans of Mustafa Kemal."[14]

The tensions among the Allies came to a head in June 1920, when Kemal sought to capitalize on Turkish anger over the draconian peace terms by attempting to march on Istanbul and the straits. With the French and the Italians seeking to evade a joint action against the nationalists, Lord Hardinge of the Foreign Office suggested the formation of a Turkish government, "composed of the present Government and representatives of Mustapha Kemal on the understanding that there shall be a revision of the Treaty of which the principal point shall be the complete evacuation of Asia Minor." "I know . . . the objections to this policy, which have been explained to me by the S. of State," he said, defending his far-reaching compromise proposal, "but my conviction is that if there is not revision now, one will be forced on us in a few months' time."[15]

Lloyd George dismissed the idea out of hand. If Britain's major war allies failed to honor their commitments, then "the greatest statesman Greece has thrown up since the days of Pericles" would contain the nationalist threat to Istanbul. Venizelos did not have to be asked twice. On June 23, the Greek army ventured out of its positions in the Smyrna area, and in a brilliant gambit drove the nationalists from the straits and occupied the town of Bursa; a simultaneous offensive in Thrace made impressive gains against tough resistance by regular Turkish forces. On July 26, King Alexander of Greece made a triumphant entry into the "liberated" city of Adrianople.

This setback forced Kemal to cast his glance elsewhere. In August 1920 the Ankara government reached an agreement with Soviet Russia on the establishment of diplomatic relations, and seven months later signed a bilateral Treaty of Friendship with Moscow. Within this framework, the Soviets accepted the National Pact in its totality, including its delimitation of Turkey's frontiers, repudiated all treaties concluded between the Ottoman Empire and Tsarist Russia (including the Capitulations, which had been restored by the Treaty of Sèvres), and promised to extend military aid to Nationalist Turkey in its struggle against "imperialists."

Having secured his northern front, Kemal could concentrate his efforts on the Armenian problem. In the Treaty of Sèvres Turkey had recognized the independence of Armenia, created on the ruins of the Russian Empire, and pledged to abide by President Wilson's decision regarding their joint border. But in late October 1920, as Wilson was about to announce the award of large tracts of Turkish territory to Armenia, Kemal's forces invaded the country, defeated the Armenian army, and advanced as far as Alexandropol. The following month Russian forces invaded northern Armenia and declared the formation of a Soviet government there. In the ensuing Treaty of Gümrü (also known as Leninakan), concluded on December 3, 1920, Armenia surrendered all its territorial gains to Turkey, including the strategic fortresses of Kars and Ardahan, and repudiated all claims on Turkish territories.

By now the groundwork had been laid for the final showdown with the Greeks. The death of King Alexander in October 1920 and his succession by his exiled father, Constantine I, who had been forced off the throne in 1917 by Venizelos, was a major boon for Kemal. Venizelos, who left Greece immediately after his disastrous defeat in the national elections that he himself had called following Alexander's demise, had successfully harnessed Allied goodwill and support to his imperial designs. By contrast Constantine, who had refused to bring Greece into the Great War and was consequently seen as a German stooge, could scarcely expect any such support, especially in view of the Italian and French unhappiness with the Treaty of Sèvres. Indeed, when in January 1921 one of Kemal's ablest commanders, Colonel Ismet, defeated a fresh Greek offensive near the small village of Inönü, the Allies not only failed to offer their help but began edging toward a rapprochement with the nationalists.

The Ankara government thus made its international debut at the Allied Powers Third Conference of London, held between February 18 and March 18, 1921, on a par with the official Turkish and Greek governments. Yet the gap between the Greek imperial dream and Turkish national objectives was too wide to bridge by diplomatic niceties: the former insisted on nothing less than full implementation of the Sèvres Treaty, the latter on its destruction. On March 17 the Kemalist delegate, Bekir Sami Bey, departed for Ankara with the Entente's proposed modifications to the Treaty of Sèvres, having indicated his dissatisfaction with their scope. The following day the Greek delegation informed Lloyd George that their army would attack within a week. The prime minister begrudgingly concurred, but not without striking a note of caution. "He wished to make it quite clear to the Greek delegation that if the Greek army thought it necessary to take steps to provide for its safety in view of the increase of Mustapha Kemal's forces, the conference could not take the responsibility for forbidding them," he told Prime Minister Dimitrios Gounaris and Foreign Minister Nikolaos Kalogeropoulos. "He would add, on his own account, however, that presumably the Greek Ministry had taken into consideration the fact that if the Greek army sustained a reverse it would make the Angora [that is, Ankara] Government impossible to deal with."[16]

This foreboding proved prophetic. In a replay of the January setback, the new Greek offensive, launched on March 23, was defeated yet again by Ismet, in the same site as its precursor: Inönü. In a desperate bid to reverse their declining fortunes, the Greeks renewed the offensive in July 1921, having doubled their forces in Anatolia to some two hundred thousand and taken the morale-boosting step of appointing King Constantine the commander-in-chief of the army. After some initial Greek successes, the decisive battle was joined in late August on the Sakarya River, west of Ankara. The Turkish forces under the personal command of Mustafa Kemal won an astounding victory; the elimination of Greece's Anatolian presence had become a question of time.

On October 20, the Ankara government signed a bilateral peace agreement with France (known as the Franklin-Bouillon Agreement after the French negotiator, the Turcophile senator Henri Franklin-Bouillon), which provided, *inter alia,* for the French evacuation of Cilicia and the redrawing of the Turco-Syrian border along a line far more favorable to Turkey than that laid down by the Treaty of Sèvres. This was a significant achievement for Kemal: with friendly relations and a measure of military cooperation with Soviet Russia established by the March 1921 Treaty, and with Italy ending its occupation of Antalya four months later, the withdrawal of France's eighty thousand troops from Cilicia freed the nationalists to concentrate on the Greeks without fear of great-power attack.

Moreover, the vast quantities of weapons and war *matériel* left by the French in Cilicia proved vital for the rebuilding and reorganization of Kemal's army. Only Britain, which viewed "the Latins" and the deal they had struck with nationalist Turkey as nothing short of perfidy, remained behind the Greeks. "The Italians sold arms to Mustapha Kemal to fight the Greeks, and were paid out of money supplied by Moscow. The French Government negotiated a secret treaty with Kemal behind the backs of the British Ministry," the embittered Lloyd George recorded in his memoirs.[17]

The final push came in the early morning hours of August 26, 1922, and was inaugurated by Kemal's famous battle order: "Soldiers, your final goal is the Mediterranean—Forward!" The Greek army was literally driven to the sea; last-ditch attempts to arrange a truce that would keep a modicum of Greek rule in Smyrna were contemptuously rebuffed by Kemal. On September 9, Turkish forces entered Smyrna, which, except for the Muslim quarter, was burned to the ground under the eyes of the Allied fleets. Bursa fell on September 10, and the following day the nationalist forces reached the straits. On September 18, Kemal triumphantly announced that the Greek army in Anatolia had been completely destroyed.

With Anatolia cleared of foreign powers, Kemal prepared for the high point of his struggle: the capture of Istanbul and the straits and the expulsion of the Greeks from Eastern Thrace. This was no mean task, not least since the straits, earmarked for neutralization by the Treaty of Sèvres, were still occupied by an inter-Allied force; and while the French and the Italians quickly withdrew their contingents in the face of the nationalist threat, the British stood their ground, thus raising the ominous specter of an Anglo-Turkish confrontation.

On September 7, at the height of the Turkish offensive, Lloyd George still could not bring himself to concede that the Greek army "had suffered a complete *débâcle.*" "We should stand by the European part of the Paris agreement," he warned his ministers. "In no circumstances could we allow the Gallipoli Peninsula to be held by the Turks. It was the most important strategic position in the world, and the closing of the Straits had prolonged the war by two years."[18] Yet while Lloyd George was prepared to resort to arms in order to stop Kemal, others were far less trigger-happy. These included not only France and Italy, which anxiously sought a peaceful settlement with the nationalists, but also most of the British Dominions, notably Canada and Australia, which declined

Whitehall's request to dispatch troops to the Turkish front. Several members of the British cabinet were also opposed to the resumption of hostilities, and the Allied commander-in-chief at Istanbul, Lieutenant-General Sir Charles Harington, toiled tirelessly to prevent an Anglo-Turkish conflagration, going so far as to forgo delivering an official ultimatum to Kemal.

Even Churchill, who was ready to fight for the straits, had little sympathy for the Greeks, having urged a rapprochement with Kemal as early as the spring of 1921. On September 15 he made his views clear to the cabinet:

> However fatigued it might be, he thought that the Empire would put up some force to preserve Gallipoli, with the graves of so many of its soldiers, and they might even be willing to do this without the co-operation of France. As regards Thrace, however, there would be a grave danger if the British government were isolated and depicted as the sole enemy of Islam. Our safety in this matter was to keep as close as possible with France. He thought we ought to obtain as much as we could for Greece, but we ought not to be placed in the position of being the sole and isolated champion of Greek claims.[19]

In these circumstances, the cabinet relented. On October 11, 1922, an armistice agreement was signed at the Marmara small port town of Mudanya, providing for the restoration to Turkey of Istanbul, the straits, and Eastern Thrace, in return for Turkish acquiescence in continued British occupation of the straits zones until the conclusion of a final peace treaty. On October 14, the Greeks accepted the agreement; the following day a special commission from the Grand National Assembly triumphantly sailed from Mudanya to Istanbul.

The importance of the Mudanya Agreement cannot be overstated: it undid years of great-power secret negotiations culminating in the Treaty of Sèvres and brought Turkey back from the dead into the family of nations. Now this achievement had only to be institutionalized in a permanent, legally binding international agreement that would eliminate the Ottoman legacy once and for all. That this was also the Allies' view was evidenced by their invitation, a fortnight after the conclusion of the armistice agreement, to both the Istanbul and the Ankara governments to attend a peace conference in the Swiss town of Lausanne.

This was totally unacceptable to Kemal. Having just liberated Turkey from foreign occupation, with his forces in full control of the country, he had no intention of sharing power with the *ancien régime* that he had resolved to destroy. Consequently, on November 1, 1922, the Grand National Assembly passed new legislation separating the sultanate from the caliphate. The former, representing temporal power, was abolished; the latter was retained as a purely spiritual post, to be filled by the Grand National Assembly. Three days later Grand Vizier Ahmed Tewfiq Pasha and his cabinet resigned, and on November 16, Sultan Vahideddin fled the country aboard a British warship to luxurious exile in San Remo. Prince Abdul Mejid II, the sultan's cousin and the son of Abdul Aziz, accepted the residual title of caliph.

The peace conference convened in Lausanne on November 21, with the participation of Turkey, Britain, France, Italy, Russia, Japan, Greece, Yugoslavia, Bulgaria, and Romania. The United States did not participate, but sent unofficial observers.

On the face of it, the conditions for a quick resolution of the Turkish problem could not have been better. On November 15, the violently anti-Turkish Lloyd George lost the premiership to the sixty-four-year-old Andrew Bonar Law, who had made no bones about his conviction that Britain could no longer act alone "as the policeman of the world," and that responsibility for the settlement in Asia had to be borne by its wartime Allies as well.[20] In view of the proven predilection of France and Italy to strike separate deals with Kemal, and Britain's reluctance to confront the nationalists on the battlefield in the twilight of Lloyd George's government, Bonar Law's view could well imply Britain's readiness for a rapid settlement.

Contrary to all indications, the negotiations turned out to be long and arduous, rife with confrontations between the chief British and Turkish negotiators: Lord Curzon and General Ismet Pasha. Having retained his influential position in the new cabinet owing to a last-minute collusion with Bonar Law, Curzon was bent on making Lausanne the climax of his career, if not the steppingstone to the premiership, by reasserting British influence and prestige in the Middle East at Turkey's expense. In Ismet, however, he found his match. Though far less versed in the machinations of great-power politics and the articulation of ideas than in the art of war, Ismet fought tooth and nail for Turkish sovereignty. Between February 4 and April 23, 1923, the conference was suspended because of sharp disagreements on the thorny issue of the Capitulations.[21]

In the end the Treaty of Lausanne was signed on July 24, 1923, recognizing Turkish sovereignty and territorial integrity within the boundaries of the National Pact, apart from Mosul. Asia Minor was regained in its entirety (including Smyrna), together with Eastern Thrace up to the Maritza River. The boundary with Syria was to follow the line laid down in the Franklin-Bouillon Agreement. The border with Iraq was to be delineated within nine months in an Anglo-Turkish agreement, with Mosul remaining for the interim period under British control. No mention was made of Kurdistan or Armenia, thus implying the demise of the promise of statehood for these two nations entailed in the Treaty of Sèvres and the effective incorporation of their territories into Turkey and the Soviet Union. Turkey also regained the islands of Imbros and Tenedos, but acquiesced in the British annexation of Cyprus and the Greek and Italian acquisition of several islands. Finally, a vivid illustration of Turkey's extrication from its imperial past was afforded by its renunciation of all rights and titles over Egypt and the Sudan, on the one hand, and by its release from all undertakings and obligations in regard to the Ottoman loans guaranteed on the Egyptian tribute, on the other.

The Lausanne Treaty also undid some of the most humiliating constraints imposed on Turkey's sovereignty by the Treaty of Sèvres, most notably the size of the Turkish army and the Capitulations.[22] The major remaining limitation on Turkish sovereignty was the partial demilitarization of the straits and the internationalization of their control. Yet Turkey was permitted to garrison 12,000 troops in Istanbul and to move forces across the specified neutral zones. Furthermore, an international commission under the auspices of the League of Nations and headed by Turkey was established to oversee the passage of military vessels and aircraft through the straits.

Last but not least, the Lausanne treaty was accompanied by a Turco-Greek agreement on the compulsory exchange of populations. This harsh agreement, which led to the exodus of some 1.3 million Greeks from Anatolia and Thrace, and about 500,000 Turks from Greece, was yet another indication of Kemal's determination to retreat from empire and to forge a new and homogenous Turkish nation, come what may.

In this respect the Treaty of Lausanne was a shining victory for Kemal. It is true that certain territories which he considered to be Turkish, notably Mosul and Hatay (Alexandretta), remained outside Turkey: the former forever; the latter for nearly two decades. Yet the treaty reaffirmed the rise of a new Turkish nation-state from the ashes of the Ottoman

Empire, unencumbered by the debilitating load of its imperial predecessor.

As the last contingent of Allied troops left Istanbul in early October 1923, to the ecstatic cheers of the crowd, the Grand National Assembly pressed ahead with the final stage of Turkey's transformation into a nation-state: on October 16, Ankara was made the new state capital, and two weeks later a Western-style constitution was promulgated, declaring Turkey a republic and entrusting sovereignty to the people and their representative—the Grand National Assembly.[23] Kemal was elected the republic's first president; Ismet, its first prime minister.

Only one link remained with the imperial past: the caliph. On March 3, 1924, the Grand National Assembly abolished the caliphate, delivering the final blow to what had been at its peak the most powerful empire on Earth. The Ottoman Empire was no more.

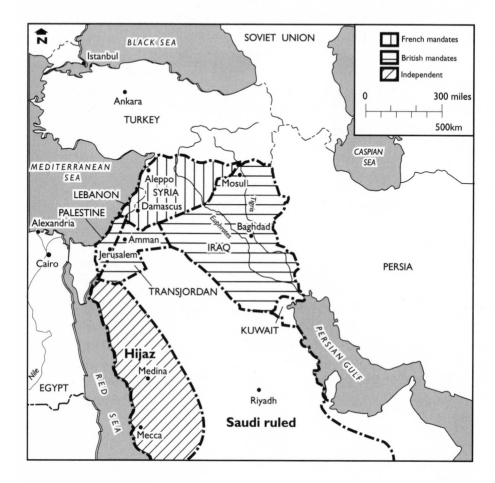

The post–World War I Middle East

EPILOGUE

$\mathcal{W}$hile Mustafa Kemal (Atatürk) was busy extricating Turkey from its imperial past and reestablishing it as a modern nation-state, other regional rulers remained spell-bound by the imperial dream. Colonel Reza Khan, for example, the commander of the Cossack brigade in the Persian army, who in February 1921 seized power in a military coup and four years later deposed the ruling shah, preferred to establish his own royal dynasty rather than transform his country into a republic. Like Atatürk, Reza was a reforming modernizer; unlike the Turkish leader, however, not only would he not discard Persia's imperial past, but he went to great lengths to link his family to this millenarian legacy, as vividly illustrated by the adoption of both the surname Pahlavi, of ancient Persian origins, and the name Iran, or "the land of the Aryans," as the country's official title.

This imperial mindset was passed on to Reza's son and heir, Shah Muhammad Reza Pahlavi (ruled 1941–1979), as evidenced by the celebration of his fifty-second birthday in October 1970. Perhaps the biggest birthday extravaganza in modern times, the party was scheduled to coincide with the 2,500th anniversary of the founding of the first Persian empire in the sixth century B.C. by the Achaemenids. As his soldiers, dressed as warriors from different imperial epochs in Iran's history, marched across the ruins of Persepolis Palace, the shah vowed his allegiance to the imperial legacy of Cyrus the Great, the Achaemenid monarch who had subdued proud Babylon, in front of his worldwide assembly of guests:

> To you Cyrus, Great King, King of Kings, from Myself, Shahanshah of Iran, and from my people, hail! . . . We are here at this moment when Iran renews its pledge to History to bear witness to the immense gratitude of an entire people to you, immortal Hero of History, founder of the world's oldest empire, great liberator of all time, worthy son of mankind.[1]

While the shah's imperial vision was translated into an extensive military buildup, transforming Iran by the mid-1970s into the preeminent power in the Persian Gulf and a close ally of the United States, its effects remained by and large localized as a result of Iran's peripheral location.[2] Not so the imperial ambitions of the Hashemites, which, by virtue of the overwhelming demographic preponderance of the Arab peoples in the post–World War I Middle East, have exerted a decisive impact on the general course of regional development.

Although the Hashemites were generously rewarded by the Entente Powers for their desert revolt—in the form of vast territories several times the size of the British Isles—they were never satisfied with their gains. Their complaint that they were "robbed" of the fruits of victory promised to them during the war was soon "nationalized" to become the standard grievance that Arab intellectuals and politicians alike leveled at the Western powers, Britain in particular.

The desire to redress this alleged grievance has produced an imperialist theory of pan-Arabism, which has dominated Middle Eastern political discourse for most of the twentieth century. To be sure, this doctrine had already been articulated before the First World War, most notably by the Syrian political exiles Abd al-Rahman al-Kawakibi (1854–1902) and Najib Azuri (1873–1916), as well as by some of the secret Arab societies operating in the Ottoman Empire. But it was only after the Hashemites had gained access to the great-power decisionmaking process as representatives of the "Arab Nation," and, moreover, had been given control over the newly established Arab states in the wake of the war, that the pan-Arab ideal began to be inculcated in the Arab masses, transcending in the process the Hashemite imperial dream, which was virtually focused on the Fertile Crescent, to the total exclusion of Egypt and North Africa.[3]

Giving the notion of the territorial nation-state short shrift as a temporary aberration destined to wither away before long, pan-Arabism views the Arabs as "a single nation bound by the common ties of language, religion and history" occupying the vast stretch of land "from the Zagros Mountains in the east to the Atlantic Ocean in the west, and from the Mediterranean shores and the Anatolian hills in the north to the Indian Ocean, the sources of the Nile, and the Great Desert in the south."[4] In the words of Nuri al-Said, King Faisal I's comrade in arms, longtime "strong man" of Iraq, and a prominent champion of pan-Arabism:

> All Arabs and particularly those of the Near and Middle East have deep down in their hearts the feeling that they are "members one of another." Their "nationalism" springs from the Muslim feeling of brotherhood enjoined on them by the Prophet Muhammad in his last public speech. It differs therefore from a great deal of European nationalism and patriotism. Although Arabs are naturally attached to their native land their nationalism is not confined by boundaries. It is an aspiration to restore the great tolerant civilisation of the early Caliphate.[5]

This equating of the "Arab Country" (al-Bilad al-Arabiyya), or the "Arab Fatherland" (al-Watan al-Arabi), with the early Arab-Islamic Empire is not difficult to understand, given that it was only after the First World War that the millenarian predication of the imperial regional order on the principle of religion was effectively broken. Indeed, the early exponents of pan-Arabism, such as Kawakibi, viewed it as inextricably linked with Islam, the religion that the Arabs had given to the world and had practiced for longer than anyone else. Similarly, the Hashemite claim to represent the "whole of the Arab Nation without exception," and Britain's willingness to acquiesce in this pretense, were both based on Sharif Hussein's high religious credentials.

It is true that great efforts were subsequently made to dilute the role of religion in pan-Arab identity, not least by Abu Khaldun Sati al-Husri, perhaps the most prolific and articulate exponent of this doctrine, for whom an Arab was defined as any Arabic-speaking member of the "Arab

Country," regardless of his religion.[6] For all its professed secularism, however, pan-Arabism has not only had to claim allegiance to the religious beliefs and traditions to which most Arabs remain attached to this very day, but has effectively been Muslim in its ethos, worldview, and territorial vision. Hence Nuri al-al-Said's perception of pan-Arabism as the "aspiration to restore the great tolerant civilisation of the early Caliphate," reiterated in a somewhat different form by the secretary-general of the Arab League, Abd al-Rahman Azzam, at a secret meeting with Zionist officials in September 1947: "We succeeded in expelling the Crusaders, but lost Spain and Persia, and may lose Palestine"; hence the interconnectedness between the Arab and the Islamic circles in Nasser's nationalist thinking, the provisions in the Syrian and Iraqi constitutions that the head of state be a Muslim, despite both countries' avowedly secularist Ba'th leaderships, and Hafiz Asad's and Saddam Hussein's repeated brandishing of their religious credentials.[7]

An important strand in the anti-Western indictment has been the charge that Europeans unwittingly exported their own ideas to the Middle East, notably those of nationalism and statehood, which are at variance with older and deeply ingrained regional traditions, attitudes, and concepts: "A rash, a malady, an infection spreading from western Europe through the Balkans, the Ottoman empire, India, the far east and Africa, eating up the fabric of settled society to leave it weakened and defenceless before ignorant and unscrupulous adventurers, for further horror and atrocity: such are the terms to describe what the west has done to the rest of the world, not wilfully, not knowingly, but mostly out of excellent intentions and by example of its prestige and prosperity."[8]

This lamentation is evocative of the wider tendency to view nationalism as the scourge of international relations, the primary source of interstate conflict and war, a tendency that has gained considerable currency following the end of the Cold War and the bloody wars of dissolution in the former Yugoslavia and several former Soviet Asiatic republics. "From the very beginning the principle of nationalism was almost indissolubly linked, both in theory and practice, with the idea of war," writes the British military historian Michael Howard. "It is hard to think of any nation-state, with the possible exception of Norway, that came into existence before the middle of the twentieth century which was not created, and had its boundaries defined, by wars, by internal violence, or by a combination of the two."[9]

This historical diagnosis raises the question of cause and effect. For if nationalism is the desire of a specific group of people—sharing such attributes as common descent, language, culture, tradition, and history—for self-determination in a definite, well-demarcated, and bounded territory that they consider to be their historical or ancestral homeland, then there is nothing inherently violent about it as far as its international ramifications are concerned. Nationalism and interstate violence go hand in hand only when one nation tries to seize foreign territory or impose its domination over another, in which case it transgresses the line between a nationalist and an imperialist policy, or when one's quest for national self-determination is hindered by another party. And since most of the globe was under the sway of a handful of empires during the past few centuries, every community becoming sufficiently aware of its distinct national identity so as to demand its own place under the sun, be it in Europe, America, Asia, or Africa, has had to contest this right by force of arms: *not because* of its inherent predilection for violence but because the respective imperial master would not voluntarily concede this right.

In other words, imperialism, rather than nationalism, has constituted the foremost generator of violence in modern world history. For it is the desire to dominate foreign creeds, nations, or communities, and to occupy territories well beyond the "ancestral homeland," that contains the inevitable seeds of violence—not the wish to be allowed to follow an independent path of development. In each of imperialism's three phases—empire-building, administration, and disintegration—force was the midwife of the historical process as the imperial power vied to assert its authority and maintain its control over perennially hostile populations. True, violence was not the only means of subjugation, as many incentives were offered for those prepared to be integrated within the imperial order, but it was always there, like a huge sword of Damocles, and was occasionally used with great ferocity as the ultimate penalty for nonsubservience.

"Royal authority is a noble and enjoyable position," wrote the great medieval Muslim philosopher Ibn Khaldun. "It comprises all good things of the world, the pleasure of the body, and the joys of the soul. Therefore . . . it rarely is handed over (voluntarily), but it may be taken away."[10] This observation applies to the imperialist mindset. Though most empires have justified their position in terms of a civilizing mission of sorts, no empire would willfully shed its colonies, let alone its imperial status, well after they had outlived their usefulness, or had even become an albatross. Hence the disintegration of multinational, multireligious, and multilinguistic empires has rarely been a peaceful process. On rare occasions, the collapse of the Soviet Union being a salient example, violence has followed the actual demise of the imperial power. In most instances, however, such as the collapse of the British, the French, and the Portuguese empires, among others, violence has been endemic to the process of decolonization as the occupied peoples fight their way to national liberation. The Ottoman Empire clearly belonged to the latter category. A far cry from the tranquil domain it is often taken for, Turkey-in-Europe was the most violent part of the Continent between the Napoleonic upheavals and the First World War. The Greek war of independence of the 1820s; the Danubian nationalist uprisings of 1848 and the attendant Crimean War; the Balkan explosion of the 1870s; and the Greco-Ottoman War of 1897 were all painful reminders of the costs of breaking free from an imperial master. Conversely, the Balkan wars of 1912–1913, in which the Ottoman Empire was on the receiving side as its former subject peoples fought to carve a new empire for themselves at the expense of their past imperial master, underscored the violence attending the imperial dream.

Nor was violence confined to Ottoman Europe. Turkey's Afro-Asiatic provinces, though far less infected with the nationalist virus than their European counterparts, were rife with mayhem and destruction, as the Muslim Empire successfully secured its position in the face of powerful centrifugal forces. The Wahhabi raids in Mesopotamia and the Levant in the early nineteenth century; Muhammad Ali's Levantine campaigns of the 1830s; the Lebanese civil strife of the 1840s and its culmination in the 1860 massacres in Mount Lebanon and Damascus; a string of Kurdish uprisings; and the national awakening of the Armenians in the 1890s, which was sunk in rivers of blood—a taste of the horrors that lay ahead in the Armenian genocide of the First World War.

Violence, then, has not been imported into the Middle East as a by-product of European nationalism, or, for that matter, of European imperialism; it was an integral part of the region's political culture well before the area's occupation by the European powers, indeed well before the rise of modern European nationalism in the late eighteenth century: not because of its inextricable linkage with the political legacy of Islam, as is often suggested, but as the inevitable outcome of the Middle East's millenarian imperial tradition. In this respect Europe has had little to teach the Middle East.

From the ancient great empires of the Mediterranean and the Fertile Crescent (for example, Egypt, Greece, Rome, Carthage, Persia, Assyria, Babylon, and so on), through the early Muslim empires, to the Ottoman Empire, the story of the Middle East has been the story of the rise and fall of universal empires and, no less important, of imperial dreams. Politics during this lengthy period has been characterized by a constant struggle for regional mastery in which the dominant power has sought to subdue, and preferably to eliminate, all potential challengers, so as to bring the entire region under its domination. Such imperialist ambitions, however, have often remained largely unsatisfied, for the determined pursuit of absolutism has been matched by the equally formidable forces of fragmentation and degeneration. This wide gap between delusions of grandeur and the stark realities of weakness, between the imperial dream and the centrifugal forces of parochialism and local patriotism, gained rapid momentum during the last phases of the Ottoman Empire—culminating not only in its disastrous decision to enter the war on the losing side, but also in the creation of an imperial dream that would survive the Ottoman demise to haunt Middle Eastern politics for generations to come.

Indeed, contrary to the conventional wisdom, European interaction with the main claimant to the Ottoman bequest, that is, the Hashemites as the self-styled representatives of the "Arab Nation," constituted a dialogue not between imperialism and nationalism, but rather between like-minded, if unmatched, imperialists. The desert uprising against the Ottomans, on which the Hashemite claim for pan-Arab leadership hinged, was not the "Great Arab Revolt" it is assumed to be by Arab and Western historiographies; rather, it was Hussein's expedient bid for an empire. The sharif and his sons were no champions of national liberation seeking to unshackle the "Arab Nation" from the chains of Ottoman captivity; they were imperialist aspirants eager to exploit a unique window of opportunity to substitute their own empire for that of the Ottomans.

For all the rhetoric of Arab independence in which Hussein couched his contacts with the British, his behavior throughout the revolt showed far less interest in Arab liberation than in cutting the best possible deal for himself and his family. He had demonstrated no nationalist sentiments prior to the war, when he had been considered a loyal Ottoman *apparatchik* both by his immediate Arabian neighbors and by the Arab secret societies operating in the Levant and Mesopotamia; and neither he nor his sons changed in this respect during the revolt. They did not regard themselves as part of a wider "Arab Nation" bound together by a shared language, religion, history, or culture; rather, they held themselves superior to those ignorant creatures whom they were "destined" to rule and educate: it was the "white man's burden" Hijaz style. In the words of David Hogarth, the one-time director of the Cairo Arab Bureau, who in January 1918 held extensive interviews with the sharif: "It is obvious that the King regards Arab Unity as synonymous with his own Kingship."[11]

What the Hashemites demanded of Britain, then, was not self-determination for the Arabic-speaking subjects of the Ottoman Empire, but the formation of a successor empire, headed by themselves and comprising such diverse ethnic, national, and religious groups as Turks, Armenians, Kurds, Assyrians, and Jews—in addition, of course, to the Arabs, who were to form the majority group. This in turn presented a dilemma for British decisionmakers. On the one hand, as quintessential imperialists, they had no compunction about substituting a Hashemite empire for that of the Ottomans, especially if the new empire was to fall under British tutelage. Their only recurring doubt, raised mainly but not exclusively by the India Office and government, related to the Hashemites' ability to muster the popular support necessary for championing this endeavour. This doubt was allayed, however, by effective propaganda by the Hashemites and their numerous partisans both in London and in the Middle East, not least the legendary Lawrence of Arabia.

On the other hand, the British were keenly aware of the diversity and fragmentation of the Arabic-speaking communities of the Ottoman Empire, with whom they had interacted for quite some time. Even Lawrence, who had done more than any other person to impose Hashemite rule over much of the modern Middle East, acknowledged, in a lengthy memorandum on the conditions in Syria written in 1915 for the Cairo Bureau, the existence of a string of geographical, cultural, racial, linguistic, and religious divergencies and "no national feeling" at all. He praised "the suggestion—thrown in the teeth of geography and economics—of putting the littoral under one government, and the interior under another."[12] Years later Lawrence would still subscribe to this skepticism. "Arab unity is a madman's notion—for this century or next, probably," he told Robert Graves, one of his biographers. "English-speaking unity is a fair parallel. I am sure I never dreamed of uniting even the Hijaz and Syria. My conception was of a number of small states."[13]

This tension between Britain's instinctive imperialist support for pan-Arab unity and its simultaneous recognition of the mirage of this ideal coalesced with both U.S. President Woodrow Wilson's championship of the principle of national self-determination and the territorial demands of Britain's war allies to produce the eventual postwar settlement. This process, nevertheless, was nothing like the caricature portrayed by the standard historiography, in which "Middle Eastern countries and frontiers were fabricated in Europe."[14] Rather, it was the aggregate outcome of intense pushing and shoving by a multitude of regional and international bidders for the Ottoman war spoils.

Somewhere between the Hashemite imperial dream of inheriting Turkey-in-Asia in its entirety, the French imperialist ambitions in the Levant, the Jewish quest for a homeland in Palestine, and Britain's regional desiderata; between the Italian and the Greek scramble for much of Anatolia and Rumelia, including the once-proud Ottoman capital of Istanbul, the Armenian and Kurdish yearning for self-determination, and the resurgent, nonimperialist brand of Turkish nationalism under the able leadership of Mustafa Kemal, emerged the modern Middle East as it is known today. It was not like anything that had existed before, it is true, for the millenarian imperial unity characterizing the region from time immemorial had been irrevocably broken. But this did not make the newly established international system less attuned to regional realities, sensibilities, and yearnings than its precursor. Iraq and Jordan, to give one salient example, *were not* "British inventions, lines drawn on an empty map by British politicians after the First World War," as is claimed, but rather a compromise between Hashemite imperial greed and British desire to defer to it while conforming to local realities and forces without antagonizing their anxious French allies.[15]

Even an erstwhile champion of pan-Arabism like the British historian Arnold Toynbee concedes the fundamental difference between the political unity imposed by an empire on its subject peoples and real unity among these constituent elements. "In economic and social terms, the previous unity of these Arab territories under the Ottoman Empire was formal, external, unreal," he wrote. "There was very little of that substantial unity which arises from the constant circulation of goods and people and ideas. In the days when Iraq and Palestine were both painted one colour—the Ottoman colour—on the political map, the Iraqi Arabs and the Palestinian Arabs had really very little to do with one another . . . They were isolated from each other when the territories were all Ottoman provinces."[16]

The only common denominator among these widely diverse populations, apart from broad sharing of language and religion, in themselves remnants from the early imperial Islamic epoch, was their overarching submission to the Ottoman sultan-caliph in his capacity as the religious and temporal head of the worldwide Muslim community. But this meant no general sense of Arab solidarity, not to speak of deeply rooted sentiments of shared history, destiny, or attachment to an ancestral homeland; for even under universal Islamic empires, from the Umayyad to the Ottoman, not to speak of the prolonged periods of fragmentation when the region fell under the simultaneous reign of several empires or kingdoms, there was no unified, linear historical development of the Middle East's Arabic-speaking populations. Rather, there were multitudinous courses of development in the various corners of the imperial order.

This state of affairs explains the total indifference among these populations to the nationalistic message of the secret Arab societies prior to the First World War, as well as their continued loyalty to their Ottoman sultan to the end of the war. Most important, it rebuts the standard historiographical version of widespread yearning for a unified pan-Arab state, or rather empire, in the wake of the First World War. There was no "Arab Nation" at the time, only an intricate web of local loyalties to one's clan, tribe, village, town, religious sect, or localized ethnic minority; *ipso facto* there could be neither general craving for pan-Arab unification nor exasperation with the failure to achieve this objective. Most secret Arab societies did not even call for the destruction of the Ottoman Empire until after the outbreak of war (they wanted instead greater Arab autonomy within the empire). No less important, they articulated not merely the refrain of pan-Arabism, as is universally believed, but even more so the cause of distinct local patriotism: the only message striking some responsive chord among their respective constituents.[17]

The establishment of a vast Arab empire on the ruins of its Ottoman precursor, allegedly denied to the Arabs by the West, has never been a viable option. The conditions were simply not ripe for its emergence at the end of the First World War, and have not ripened ever since. The far-from-perfect solution devised by the postwar settlement was, paradoxically, more in line with regional realities than the chimera of a unified regional order. Indeed, during the eight decades since its establishment, the contemporary nation-state system in the Middle East has proved extremely resilient, withstanding successive challenges to its existence, both by Arab nationalists seeking to "eliminate the traces of Western imperialism" and unify the so-called Arab Nation, and by Islamic fundamentalists attempting to create a regional religious community *(umma)*.

This is neither to suggest that the great powers were driven by the noblest of motives, nor to condone their interference in the Middle East, nor to absolve them of any responsibility for the region's present misfortunes. However, contrary to the conventional wisdom, the post-Ottoman design for the region was no less the making of the local actors than of the great powers. Moreover, the Allies' "original sin," if such was indeed committed, lies not in the breaking of the Middle East's unity but in its over-unification in an attempt to placate the imperial dream of their foremost local allies, the Hashemites. As Winston Churchill, then the colonial secretary, told the House of Commons on June 14, 1921, shortly after presiding over the establishment of the states of Iraq and Transjordan, and the effective limitation of Palestine to the territory between the river Jordan and the Mediterranean:

> Broadly speaking, there are two policies which can be adopted towards the Arab race. One is the policy of keeping them divided, of discouraging their national aspirations, of setting up administrations of local notables in each particular province or city, and exerting an influence through the jealousies of one tribe against another. That was largely, in many cases, the Turkish policy before the War, and cynical as it was, it undoubtedly achieved a certain measure of success.
>
> The other policy, and the one which, I think, is alone compatible with the sincere fulfilment of the pledges we gave during the War to the Arab race and to the Arab leaders, is an attempt to build up around the ancient capital of Baghdad, in a form friendly to Britain and to her Allies, an Arab State which can revive and embody the old culture and glories of the Arab race, and which, at any rate, will have a full and fair opportunity of doing so if the Arab race shows itself capable of profiting by it. Of these two policies we have definitely chosen the latter.[18]

Had the Western powers kept out of Middle Eastern affairs following the collapse of the Ottoman Empire, allowing local forces to run their course, the region would most likely have been transformed into a volatile amalgam of numerous small fiefdoms and kingdoms, mostly antagonistic to one another. As things were, great-power interference ensured the advent of a string of Middle Eastern states that were significantly larger than the political entities that would otherwise have been created, yet substantially smaller than the vast pan-Arab empire envisaged by the Hashemites. It is precisely this unbridgeable gap between the imperial dream and the reality of local patriotism that has created the all-too-familiar, and all-too-tragic, politics of frustration and violence in modern Middle Eastern history.

Abbreviations
Notes
Index

Abbreviations

ADM   Admiralty
CAB   Cabinet
CO   Colonial Office
CZA   Central Zionist Archives
DBFP   Documents on British Foreign Policy, 1919–1939, first series, ed.
       E. L. Woodward and Rohan Butler (London: HMSO, 1960)
FBIS   Foreign Broadcast Information Service
FO   Foreign Office
IO   India Office
NES   Near East Service
PRP   Public Record Office, London
WO   War Office

Notes

Introduction

1. The transcript of the Baker-Aziz meeting was published in five parts by the Iraqi News Agency starting on January 9, 1992. The text was reprinted in FBIS, NES, 92–009, Jan. 14, 1992.

2. Arnold J. Toynbee and Kenneth P. Kirkwood, *Turkey* (London: Ernest Benn, 1926), p. 6. For general studies of the Eastern Question and its various perspectives and interpretations, see M. S. Anderson, *The Eastern Question, 1774–1923* (London: Macmillan, 1966); J. A. R. Marriott, *The Eastern Question: An Historical Study in European Diplomacy,* 2nd rev. ed. (Oxford: Clarendon Press, 1918); A. L. Macfie, *The Eastern Question, 1774–1923* (Essex: Longman Group UK, 1989); Édouard Driault, *La Question d'Orient depuis ses origines jusqu'à nos jours,* 4th rev. ed. (Paris: Felix Alcan, 1909); Stephen Pierce Hayden Duggan, *The Eastern Question: A Study in Diplomacy* (New York: Columbia University Press, 1902); Alfred L. P. Dennis, *Eastern Problems at the Close of the Eighteenth Century* (Cambridge, England: Cambridge University Press, 1901); Max Choublier, *La Question d'Orient depuis le Traité de Berlin,* 2nd ed. (Paris: Rousseau, 1899); Malcolm MacColl, *The Eastern Question: Its Facts and Fallacies* (London: Longmans, Green & Co., 1877); William Gifford Palgrave, *Essays on Eastern Questions* (London: Macmillan and Co., 1872); Allan Cunningham, *Anglo-Ottoman Encounters in the Age of Revolution,* and *Eastern Questions in the Nineteenth Century,* ed. Edward Ingram (London: Frank Cass, 1993).

3. See, for example, Barbara Tuchman, *The Guns of August* (New York: Dell, 1962); Arnold Toynbee, "The Present Situation in Palestine," *International Affairs,* vol. 10 (Jan. 1931), p. 40; Edward W. Said, *Orientalism: Western Conceptions of the Orient,* repr. with a new afterword (London: Penguin, 1995), p. 220; Bernard Lewis, *The Middle East: 2000 Years of History from the Rise of Christianity to the Present Day* (London: Weidenfeld & Nicolson, 1995), pp. 342–343; Farouq al-Shara, "Who Is the Obstacle to Peace in the Middle East?" (public lecture at the Royal Institute of International Affairs, London,

Mar. 4, 1986), p. 1; David Fromkin, *A Peace to End All Peace: The Fall of the Ottoman Empire and the Creation of the Modern Middle East* (New York: Avon, 1990), p. 17.

4. See, for example, George Antonius, *The Arab Awakening* (London: Hamish Hamilton, 1938); Amin Said, *al-Thawra al-Arabiyya al-Kubra* (Cairo: Isa al-Babi al-Halabi, 1951); Suleiman Musa, *al-Haraka al-Arabiyya: Sirat al-Marhala al-Ula li-l-Nahda al-Arabiyya al-Haditha, 1908–1924* (Beirut: Dar al-Nahar, 1970); Abu Khaldun Sati al-Husri, *Yawm Maisalun: Safha min Tarikh al-Arab al-Hadith,* rev. ed. (Beirut: Dar al-Ittihad, 1964); Abdullah Ibn Hussein, *Mudhakkirati* (Jerusalem: Matba'at Bait al-Maqdis, 1945); Zaki Hazem Nuseibeh, *The Ideas of Arab Nationalism* (Ithaca, N.Y.: Cornell University Press, 1956); Zeine N. Zeine, *The Emergence of Arab Nationalism with a Background Study of Arab-Turkish Relations in the Near East,* 2nd. rev. ed. (Beirut: Khayat's, 1966); George Lenczowski, *The Middle East in World Affairs,* 4th ed. (Ithaca, N.Y.: Cornell University Press, 1980), pp. 58–59, 79–87; George Kirk, *A Short History of the Middle East: From the Rise of Islam to Modern Times* (London: Methuen, 1961), chap. 5; Roger Owen, *State, Power and Politics in the Making of the Modern Middle East* (London: Routledge, 1992), especially chaps. 1 and 4; Andre Raymond, "The Ottoman Legacy in Arab Political Boundaries," in L. Carl Brown, ed., *Imperial Legacy: The Ottoman Imprint on the Balkans and the Middle East* (New York: Columbia University Press, 1996), pp. 115–128.
The most formidable critic of this standard historiography was the British historian Elie Kedourie. See, for example, Kedourie, *England and the Middle East: The Destruction of the Ottoman Empire, 1914—1921* (London: Bowes & Bowes, 1956); *The Chatham House Version and Other Middle Eastern Studies* (London: Weidenfeld & Nicolson, 1970); and *In the Anglo-Arab Labyrinth: The McMahon-Husayn Correspondence and Its Interpretations, 1914–1939* (Cambridge, England: Cambridge University Press, 1976).

5. For this widespread misconception see, for example, Feroz Ahmad, "The Late Ottoman Empire," in Marian Kent, ed., *The Great Powers and the End of the Ottoman Empire* (London: Frank Cass, 1996), p. 15; Howard M. Sachar, *The Emergence of the Middle East, 1914–1924* (London: Allen Lane, Penguin Press, 1970), p. 32; Fromkin, *A Peace to End All Peace,* pp. 48–50; John DeNovo, *American Interests and Policies in the Middle East, 1900–1939* (Minneapolis: University of Minnesota Press, 1963), p. 90.

6. L. Carl Brown, *International Politics and the Middle East* (London: I. B. Tauris, 1984), p. 5.

1. Riding the Napoleonic Storms

1. Bernard Lewis, *The Emergence of Modern Turkey* (London: Oxford University Press, 1968), pp. 56–64.

2. Abd al-Rahman al-Jabarti, *Aja'ib al-Athar fi-l-Tarajim wa-l-Akhbar* (Cairo: Lajnat al-Bayan al-Arabi, 1965), vol. 4, p. 285. The Mamluks were slaves, mostly of Central Asian Turkish origins, who came to play an increasingly important role in the running of the Muslim empires. In the middle of the thirteenth century they established their own sultanate, which ruled Egypt and Syria until it was overrun by the Ottoman Empire in 1517. Yet even under Ottoman rule the Mamluks still played a key role in the administration of Egypt.

3. Abd al-Rahman al-Jabarti, *Tarikh Muddat al-Faransis bi-Misr* (Leiden: Brill, 1975), pp. 7–10.

4. For the texts of the alliances see J. C. Hurewitz, ed., *The Middle East and North Africa in World Politics,* 2nd. rev. ed. (New Haven and London: Yale University Press, 1975–1979), vol. 1, pp. 126–133. The Ottoman Empire also signed a defensive alliance against "the common enemy," France, with the kingdom of the Two Sicilies on 14 Chaban 1213/January 21, 1799. For the text of the agreement see Gabriel Efendi Noradounghian, ed., *Recueil d'actes internationaux de l'Empire Ottoman* (Paris: Librairie Cotillon, F. Pichon, 1900), vol. 2, pp. 32–34.

5. It is also important to note that Russian Deputy Foreign Minister Adam Czartoryski's proposal the following year to partition the Ottoman Empire was a contingency plan to secure Russian interests in the event of an Ottoman collapse.

6. Noradounghian, *Recueil,* vol. 2, pp. 70–74.

7. Napoleon to Selim, 10 Pluviôse, Year XIII /Jan. 30, 1805, in Napoleon I, *Correspondance de Napoleon I, publiée par ordre de l'empereur Napoleon III* (Paris: Henri Plon, 1858–1870), vol. 10, no. 8298. See also Napoleon to Talleyrand, June 9, 1806, ibid., vol. 12, no. 10339.

8. Napoleon to Selim III, Nov. 11, 1806; Napoleon to the Ministry of Foreign Affairs, July 28, 1806; Sebastiani to the Sublime Porte, Sept. 16, 1806, in I. de Testa, ed., *Recueil des traités de la Porte Ottomane avec les puissances etrangères* (Paris: Amyot Archives Diplomatiques, 1865), vol. 2, pp. 279–281; Napoleon to Selim, Dec. 1, 1806, *Correspondance,* vol. 14, no. 11338.

9. The sultan also reneged on his 1802 agreement with Russia whereby the latter had gained a say in the appointment of governors *(hospodars)* in the Danubian Principalities of Moldavia and Wallachia.

10. Lewis, *The Emergence,* pp. 72–73.

11. Mustafa IV to Napoleon, 9 Moharrem 1223/Mar. 4, 1808, Testa, *Recueil des traités de la Porte,* vol. 2, p. 308.

12. Napoleon had already recruited Persia to his anti-British coalition in May 1807.

13. Reis Efendi to Sebastiani on 17 zilhidje 1222, in Sebastiani, Feb. 15, 1808, Testa, *Recueil des traités de la Porte,* vol. 2, p. 307.

14. For the text of the 1809 treaty, see Hurewitz, *The Middle East and North Africa in World Politics,* vol. 1, pp. 189–191.

15. Noradounghian, *Recueil,* vol. 2, pp. 86–92.

2. The Greek Tinderbox

1. For the Greek national awakening see, for example, Richard Clogg, *The Movement for Greek Independence, 1770–1821* (London: Macmillan, 1976); Douglas Dakin, *The Greek Struggle for Independence, 1821–1833* (London: B. T. Batsford, 1973); Nikiforos P. Diamandouros, John P. Anton, John A. Petropulos, and Peter Topping, eds., *Hellenism and the First Greek War of Liberation (1821–1830): Continuity and Change* (Thessalonica: Institute for Balkan Studies, 1976); C. M. Woodhouse, *The Greek War of Independence* (London: Hutchinson, 1952); W. Alison Phillips, *The War of Greek Independence, 1821–*

1833 (London: Smith Elder and Co., 1897); Anton von Prokesch-Osten, *Geschichte des Abfalls der Griechen vom Türkischen Reiche im Jahre 1821 und der Gründung des Hellenischen Königreiches* (Vienna: Carl Gerold's Sohn, 1867), 6 vols. For wider developments in the Balkans, see L. S. Stavrianos, *The Balkans since 1453* (New York: Holt, Rinehart, and Winston, 1965).

2. See Foreign Secretary Nesselrode's instructions to the ambassador in Constantinople, Feb. 23/Mar. 7, 1821, in Ministerstvo inostrannykh del SSSR, *Vneshniaia politika Rossii XIX i nachala XX veka: dokumenty rossiiskogo Ministerstva inostrannykh del* (Moscow: Nauka, 1980), series 2, vol. 7, pp. 36–38; Russian circular no. 8, Mar. 18/30, 1821, in Barbara Jelavich, *Russia and Greece during the Regency of King Othon, 1832–1835: Russian Documents on the First Years of Greek Independence* (Tessalonika: Institute of Balkan Studies, 1962), appendix 1, pp. 123–124.

3. For the Greek declaration of independence, see M. S. Anderson, ed., *The Great Powers and the Near East, 1774–1923* (London: Edward Arnold, 1970), p. 30.

4. PRO, proclamation addressed to the Janissary Aghas on May 8, 1821, FO 78/98 (unless otherwise indicated, all British archival source material cited in this book is taken from the PRO).

5. Stratford to Castlereagh, May 1, 1821, encl. in FO 78/98; Stratford to Londonderry, June 12, 1821, FO 78/99/46; Russian dispatch, June 22/July 4, 1821, in Jelavich, *Russia and Greece,* appendix 2, pp. 124–128.

6. Metternich to Stadion, Mar. 26, 1821, in Prince Clemens von Metternich, *Mémoires, documents et écrits divers laissés par le prince de Metternich, Chancelier de cour et d'état. Publiés par son fils le prince Richard de Metternich* (Paris: E. Plon et Cie, 1881), part 2, vol. 3, p. 495.

7. H. W. V. Tempreley, *England and the Near East: The Crimea* (London: Longmans, Green and Co., 1936), p. 53.

8. For the text of the Protocol of St. Petersburg, see Gabriel Efendi Noradounghian, *Recueil d'actes internationaux de l'Empire Ottoman* (Paris: Librairie Cotillon, F. Pichon, 1900), vol. 2, pp. 114–116.

9. For the complete text of the Convention of Ackerman, see ibid., pp. 116–126.

10. Ibid., pp. 130–134.

11. Nesselrode to Lieven, Dec. 25, 1827/Jan. 6, 1828, and Feb. 14/26, 1828, Prokesch-Osten, *Geschichte des Abfalls,* vol. 5, pp. 145–156, 169–176.

12. For the text of the treaty see Noradounghian, *Recueil,* vol. 2, pp. 166–177.

13. Aberdeen to Gordon, Nov. 10, 1829, FO 78/181, nos. 70–74.

14. For the text of the London Protocol of February 3, 1830, see Thomas Erskine Holland, ed., *The European Concert in the Eastern Question: A Collection of Treaties and Other Public Acts* (Oxford: Clarendon Press, 1885), text I.

3. Muhammad Ali's Imperial Dream

1. For general studies of Muhammad Ali, see Afaf Lutfi al-Sayyid Marsot, *Egypt in the Reign of Muhammad Ali* (Cambridge, England: Cambridge University Press, 1984); Abd al-Rahman al-Rafi'i, *Asr Muhammad Ali* (Cairo: Dar al-Ma'arif, 1954); Henry Dodwell, *The Founder of Modern Egypt: A Study of Muhammed Ali* (Cambridge, England: Cam-

bridge University Press, 1931; repr. 1967); M. Sabry, *L'Empire Egyptien sous Mohamed-Ali et La Question d'Orient (1811–1849)* (Paris: Librairie Orientaliste Paul Geuthner, 1930); Rene and George Cattaui, *Mohamed-Aly et L'Europe* (Paris: Librairie Orientaliste Paul Geuthner, 1950); P. M. Holt, *Egypt and the Fertile Crescent, 1516–1922* (Ithaca: Cornell University Press, 1966), pp. 176–192; Khaled Fahmi, *All the Pasha's Men: Mehmed Ali, His Army and the Making of Modern Egypt* (Cambridge, England: Cambridge University Press, 1997).

2. Georges Douin, ed., *Une Mission militaire française auprès de Mohamed Aly, correspondance des Généraux Belliard et Boyer* (Cairo: Société Royale de Géographie d'Éypte, 1923), p. 50.

3. Bernard Lewis, *The Emergence of Modern Turkey* (London, England: Oxford University Press, 1968), chap. 4.

4. See, for example, Ibrahim Pasha to Allush Pasha, Abd. case 236, doc. 66, n.d., in Asad J. Rustum, *The Royal Archives of Egypt and the Origins of the Egyptian Expedition to Syria* (Beirut: American University of Beirut, 1936), p. 33.

5. Ibrahim to Muhammad Ali, Shaban 19, 1248, Abd. case 242, doc. 155, ibid., pp. 54–55.

6. Gabriel Efendi Noradounghian, ed., *Recueil d'actes internationaux de l'Empire Ottoman* (Paris: Librairie Cotillon, F. Pichon, 1900), vol. 2, p. 228.

7. For the English text of the Treaty of Hunkar-Iskelesi, including the secret article, see J. C. Hurewitz, ed., *The Middle East and North Africa in World Politics*, 2nd. rev. ed. (New Haven and London: Yale University Press, 1975–1979), vol. 1, pp. 252–253.

8. See, for example, Nesselrode's circular of 5/17 Aug. 1833, in F. F. Martens, ed., *Recueil des traités et conventions conclues par la Russie avec les puissances etrangères* (St. Petersburg: Ministere des Voies de Communication, 1874–1909), vol. 12, pp. 43–44. In the Russo-Austrian Treaty of Münchengrätz, signed in September 1833, the two powers committed themselves to protecting Ottoman "independence and authority."

9. Palmerston to Campbell, Oct. 26, 1834, FO 78/244. See also Boghoz Bey to Campbell, Sept. 3, 1834, FO 78/246; Barker, Mar. 8, 1830, FO 78/192.

10. On the Palestine revolt see Asad Rustum, ed., *al-Usul al-Arabiyya li Tarikh Suriyya fi Ahd Muhammad Ali Basha* (Beirut: American University of Beirut, 1930–1934), vol. 2, pp. 110–140.

11. Palmerston to Campbell, June 15, 1839, FO 78/372, no. 17; Palmerston to Campbell, Nov. 29, 1838, FO 78/343, no. 30.

12. Boghos Yussuf to Cochelet, Aug. 17, 1840, in Édouard Driault, ed., *L'Égypte et l'Europe: La crise de 1839–1841* (Cairo: Société Royale de Géographic d'Égypte, 1930–1934), vol. 3, pp. 121–123.

13. Hurewitz, *The Middle East and North Africa in World Politics*, vol. 1, p. 272.

14. For the text of the London Convention see Hurewitz, *The Middle East and North Africa in World Politics*, vol. 1, pp. 271–275.

15. On Muhammad Ali's state of mind, see letter by Boghos Yussuf (Muhammad Ali's foreign minister) to Cochelet, Aug. 17, 1840; Muhammad Ali's conversation with Walewski on Aug. 22, 1840 (Walewski's letter of Aug. 24, 1840); and Sami Bey in Procès-Verbal on Sept. 4, 1840, all in Driault, *L'Égypte et l'Europe*, vol. 3, pp. 121–123, 152–156, 215–218; Hodges, Aug. 30, 1840 (see also enclosure, Procès-Verbal), FO 78/406.

16. Grand Vizier to Muhammad Ali, 18, Redjeb 1256, in Driault, *L'Égypte et l'Europe*, vol. 3, p. 232.

17. For the text of the *firman*, see Hurewitz, *The Middle East and North Africa in World Politics*, vol. 1, pp. 276–278.

4. Losing Egypt

1. For British pressures on the sultan, see Stratford, Feb. 22, 1855, no. 148, and Stratford, Mar. 1, 1855, no. 155, both in FO 78/1156.

2. Cited in P. J. Vatikiotis, *A History of Modern Egypt*, 4th ed. (London: Weidenfeld and Nicolson, 1991), p. 73. See also Abd al-Rahman al-Rafi'i, *Asr Isma'il*, 2nd ed. (Cairo: Dar al-Ma'arif, 1948), vols. 1–2; G. Douin, *Histoire du règne du Khedive Ismail* (Cairo: La Reale Società di Geografia d'Egitto, 1933–1941), vols. 1–3; A. Sammarco, *Le règne du Khedive Ismail de 1863 à 1875* (Cairo: Société Royale de Geographie d'Egypte); Pierre Crabitès, *Ismail: The Maligned Khedive* (London: George Routledge and Sons, 1933).

3. Amin Sami, *Taqwim al-Nil* (Cairo: al-Matba'ah al-Amiriyya wa-Dar al-Kutub al-Misriyya, 1916–1936), vol. 3/2, pp. 452–453.

4. Ali Haydar Midhat Bey, *The Life of Midhat Pasha. A Record of His Services, Political Reforms, Banishment, and Judicial Murder. Derived from Private Documents and Reminiscences* (London: John Murray, 1903), p. 65.

5. Letter by Urabi to the Egyptian minister of war, Sept. 9, 1881, CAB 37/6, no. 24, encl. 6. For the reasons behind Urabi's show of force, see also Malet to Granville, Sept. 23, 1881, CAB 37/6, no. 24; Ahmad Urabi, *Kashf al-Sitar an Sirr al-Israr* (Cairo: Matba'at Misr, n.d.), p. 236.

6. Gladstone to Granville, Sept. 12, 13, 16, 1881, PRO 30–29/124. See also Granville to Gladstone, Sept. 14, 1881, add. ms. 44173, fo. 151 (British Library); Malet to Granville, Sept. 21, 1881, FO 78/3324, no. 246.

7. Gladstone to Granville, Jan. 4, 12, 1882, PRO 30–29/160; Jan. 22, 1882, PRO 30–29/125.

8. Wilfred S. Blunt, *Secret History of the English Occupation of Egypt*, 2nd ed. (London: T. Fisher Unwin, 1907), p. 189.

9. Dudley W. R. Bahlman, ed., *The Diary of Sir Edward Walter Hamilton, 1880–1885* (Oxford: Clarendon Press, 1972), vol. 1, p. 271 (hereinafter *Hamilton Diary*); the Earl of Cromer, *Modern Egypt* (London: Macmillan, 1908), vol. 1, pp. 262-264.

10. Lyons to Foreign Office, Apr. 3, 1882, FO 27/2562; Gladstone to Granville, Jan. 31; Apr. 5; May 14, 1882, PRO, 30-29/125; Granville to Malet, May 14, 1882, FO 78/3448.

11. Abd al-Rahman al-Rafi'i, *al-Thawrah al-Urabiyya wa-l-Ihtilal al-Inglizi*, 2nd. ed. (Cairo: al-Bahirah, 1937).

12. Alexander Schölch, *Egypt for the Egyptians! The Socio-Political Crisis in Egypt, 1878–1882* (London: Ithaca Press, 1981), pp. 172–177.

13. Dufferin to Foreign Office, July 2, 1882, FO 78/3398, no. 195.

14. Dufferin to Granville, June 24, 1882, FO 78/3397, no. 168.

15. Ibid.

16. Ibid.; Granville to Dufferin, June 25, 1882, FO 78/3395, no. 302; *Hamilton Diary*, vol. 1, pp. 212, 297.

17. Northbrook to Seymour, July 3, 1882, ADM 116/33; Seymour to Admiralty, July 8, 1882, ADM 116/34; Admiralty to Seymour, July 8, 1882, ADM 116/34; Lyons to Granville, July 5, 6, 1882, FO 27/2574; Granville's draft to cabinet, July 8, 1882, FO 27/2753, PRO 30–29/143.

18. Gladstone to Granville, July 9, 1882, PRO 30–29/126; Granville to Gladstone, July 9, 1882, add. ms. 44174, fo. 160.

19. John Morley, *The Life of William Ewart Gladstone* (London: Macmillan, 1903), vol. 3, p. 82.

20. Gladstone to Granville, July 13, 1882, PRO 30–29/126; *Hamilton Diary*, p. 306.

21. Draft of dispatch from Earl Granville to the Earl of Dufferin, printed for the use of the cabinet, Oct. 27, 1882, CAB 37/9; Queen Victoria to Earl Granville, July 26, 1882, in George E. Buckle, ed., *The Letters of Queen Victoria* (London: John Murray, 1928), vol. 3, 1879–1885, p. 312.

22. Cromer, *Modern Egypt*, vol. 1, pp. 312–320; Rifaat Bey, *The Awakening of Modern Egypt* (Lahore: Premier Book House, 1964), p. 211; Joan Haslip, *The Sultan: The Life of Abdul Hamid* (London: Cassell, 1958), chap. 21.

23. Granville's dispatch to Dufferin, CAB 37/9, p. 15.

24. Memorandum by Colvin, Dec. 12, 1991, CAB 37/7, no. 4.

25. For the logic behind Britain's purchase of the canal shares, see, for example, Derby to Elliot, Dec. 1, 1875, FO 78/2432, no. 386; Derby to Stanton, Dec. 6, 1875, FO 78/2432, no. 108.

26. W. E. Gladstone, "Aggression in Egypt and Freedom in the East," *Nineteenth Century*, 2 (Aug. 1877), pp. 149–166; *Hamilton Diary*, vol. 1, p. 337.

27. *Hamilton Diary*, vol. 1, p. 340.

28. A. J. P. Taylor, *The Struggle for Mastery in Europe, 1848–1918* (New York: Oxford University Press, first pub. 1954; repr. 1971), p. 90.

29. For Dufferin's report see J. C. Hurewitz, *The Middle East and North Africa in World Politics*, 2nd. rev. ed. (New Haven and London: Yale University Press, 1975–1979), vol. 1, pp. 191–194. For Northbrook's mission see CAB 37/13, no. 38, Aug. 9, 1884, and CAB 37/13, no. 44, Oct. 24, 1884.

30. White to Salisbury, May 27, 28, June 27, 28, 1887, FO 78/3998; White to Salisbury, July 10, 12, 17, 19, 1887, FO 78/3999; Cromer, Modern Egypt, vol. 2, pp. 378–380. For the text of the 1887 Convention, see Hurewitz, *The Middle East and North Africa in World Politics*, vol. 1, pp. 453–454.

5. Out of Europe

1. This decision reflected not only the Ottomans' basic sympathy toward France and their wariness of Russia, but also a cold calculation that "a French fleet would beat a Russian fleet even united with a Turkish one." Rose, Dec. 28, 1852, FO 78/895, no. 170.

2. Foreign Office, "Affairs of Turkey. Crimean War, 1854–55. Part V. Eastern Papers. Communications Respecting Turkey, Made to Her Majesty's Government by the Emperor of Russia with the Answers Returned to Them January to April 1853," presented to the houses of Parliament by command of Her Majesty, 1854, pp. 2, 4, 8.

3. Ibid., pp. 4, 8.

4. Ibid., p. 3.

5. Ibid., pp. 6–9, 19–20.

6. On the development of the Ottoman position see Reshid Pasha to Nesselrode, 9 ramazan 1269/June 16, 1853; the note of the Sublime Porte to Western powers, 8 chewal 1269/July 14, 1853; Reshid Pasha to Nesselrode, 14 chewal 1269/July 20, 1853; Protocol of the Balta-Liman Conference, 17 chewal 1269/July 25, 1853; Note of the Sublime Porte, 19 chewal 1269/July 25, 1853; Declaration of the Sublime Porte to the Nation, 21 chewal/July 27, 1853, all in Testa, *Recueil des traités de la Porte Ottomane,* vol. 4/1, pp. 281–283; 292–297; 307–314.

7. On the Russian position see A. de Nesselrode, *Lettres et papiers du chancelier Comte de Nesselrode, 1760–1856* (Paris: Plon, 1904–1911), vol. 10, pp. 225–226.

8. For the European road to the Crimean War, see Luc Monnier, *Étude sur les origines de la Guerre Crimée* (Geneva: Librairie Droz, 1977); Paul W. Schröder, *Austria, Great Britain, and the Crimean War: The Destruction of the European Concert* (Ithaca and London: Cornell University Press, 1972); Bernhard Unckel, *Österreich und der Krimkrieg: Studien zur Politik der Donaumonarchie in den Jahren 1852–1856* (Lübeck and Hamburg: Matthiesen Verlag, 1969); David Wetzel, *The Crimean War: A Diplomatic History* (Boulder: East European Monographs, 1985); John Shelton Curtiss, *Russia's Crimean War* (Durham N.C.: Duke University Press, 1979); Vernon J. Puryear, "New Light on the Origins of the Crimean War," *Journal of Modern History,* vol. 3 (1931), pp. 219–234; H. W. Temperley, "Stratford de Redcliffe and the Origins of the Crimean War," *English Historical Review,* vols. 48 (1933) and 49 (1934).

9. Declaration of the Sublime Porte, 1 moharrem 1270, in Testa, *Recueil des traités de la Porte Ottomane,* vol. 4/2, pp. 7–11; Sublime Porte, 1 moharrem 1270, ibid., pp. 12–13. For the Ottoman ultimatum and the Russian rejection, see Omer Pasha to Gorchakov, 5 moharrem 1270/Oct. 8, 1853, and Gorchakov to Omer Pasha, Oct. 10, 1853, ibid., vol. 4/2, pp. 16–17, 20; Nesselrode's circular of Oct. 31, 1853, and the declaration of Nicholas, Nov. 1, 1853, ibid., pp. 20–21, 22–23.

10. Nicholas to Nakhimov, Dec. 10, 1853, Testa, *Recueil des traités de la Porte Ottomane,* vol. 4/2, p. 33.

11. Reshid Pasha to Stratford de Redcliffe and Baraguay d'Hilliers, 4 rebiul-ewel 1270/Dec. 5, 1853, ibid., vol. 4/2, p. 26.

12. Schröder, *Austria, Great Britain, and the Crimean War,* pp. 200–224.

13. Nesselrode, *Lettres et papiers,* vol. 11, pp. 74–77.

14. A. J. P Taylor, *The Struggle for Mastery in Europe, 1848–1919* (New York: Oxford University Press, 1971), p. 90.

15. See J. C. Hurewitz, *The Middle East and North Africa in World Politics,* 2nd. rev. ed. (New Haven and London: Yale University Press, 1975–1979), vol. 1, pp. 319–322.

16. See telegram and note of Ali Pasha to the *kaimakam* of Moldavia, 3 moharrem 1274/Aug. 24, 1857, and 10 moharrem 1274/Aug. 31, 1857; the circular of Ali Pasha to the Western powers, 3 safer 1274/Sept. 23, 1857, 8 rebiul-ewel 1274/Oct. 28, 1857, and 13 rebiul-akhir 1274/Dec. 1, 1857, in Testa, *Recueil des traités de la Porte Ottomane,* vol. 5, pp. 318–324.

17. Holmes to Elliot, Sept. 28, 1875, encl. in no. 32, in Great Britain, FO, "Turkey,

No. 2 (1876), Bosnia and Herzegovina. Correspondence Respecting Affairs in Bosnia and the Herzegovina"; hereinafter "Turkey, No. 2 (1876)."

18. For Ottoman attempts to crush the uprising, see Safvet Pasha to Musurus Pasha, Aug. 9, 1875, doc. 10; Safvet Pasha to Musurus Pasha, Aug. 22, 1875, doc. 15; proclamation by Server Pasha in Holmes to Derby, encl. 2 in no. 28; promulgation of reforms by Sultan Abdul Hamid on Oct. 3, 1875, encl. in no. 29; Holmes to Elliot, Sept. 28, 1875, encl. in no. 32; Reshid Pasha to Musurus Pasha, no. 54; regulation respecting the functions of the Executive Council, no. 61, all in "Turkey, No. 2 (1876)."

19. Safvet Pasha to Musurus Pasha, Aug. 10, 22, 1875, nos. 11, 15; Holmes to Derby, Sept. 24, 1875, no. 28, in "Turkey, No. 2 (1876)."

20. Shuvalov to Jomini, Oct. 2/14, 1875, no. 102, in R. W. Seton-Watson, ed., "Unprinted Documents: Russo-Turkish Relations during the Eastern Crisis," *Slavonic Review*, vol. 3 (1924–1925), pp. 426–430.

21. Cited in Ali Haydar Midhat Bey, *The Life of Midhat Pasha. A Record of His Services, Political Reforms, Banishment, and Judicial Murder. Derived from Private Documents and Reminiscences* (London: John Murray, 1903), p. 133.

22. For the Ottoman rebuff of the European mediation efforts, see Declaration of the Sublime Porte, Apr. 9, 1877, in Safvet Pasha to Musurus Pasha, no. 519; dispatches from the Turkish government; Protocol of Mar. 31, 1877; Musurus Pasha as communicated to Derby, in Derby to Jocelyn, Apr. 12, 1877, no. 520, all in Great Britain, FO, "Affairs of Turkey (I), 1877."

23. For the full text of the Treaty of San Stefano, see B. H. Sumner, *Russia and the Balkans, 1870–1880* (Oxford: Oxford University Press, 1937), appendix 7, pp. 627–636.

24. Cited in R. W. Seton-Weston, *Disraeli, Gladstone and the Eastern Question* (London: Macmillan, 1935), p. 450.

25. Salisbury to Lady Salisbury, June 24, 1878, as cited in Lady Gwendolen Cecil, *Life of Robert Marquis of Salisbury* (London: Hodder and Stoughton, 1931), volume 2, p. 288.

6. The Young Turks in Power

1. Proclamation by King Nicholas on Oct. 8, 1912, encl. 1, in Count de Salis to Grey, FO 371/1502/45382. See also Lowther to Grey, Oct. 8, 1912, no. 1, p. 1; Bax-Ironside to Grey, Oct. 8, 1912, DBFP, vol. 11, no. 6, p. 4; Bompard to Poincaré, Oct. 8, 1912, no. 88, Ministry of Foreign Affairs, French Republic, *Documents Diplomatiques Français (1871–1914)*, 3rd series (Paris: Imprimerie nationale, 1924–1936), vol. 4, p.fl83 (hereinafter *Documents Diplomatiques Français*).

2. The Ottoman foreign minister to Lowther, cited in Lowther to Grey, Oct. 1, 1912, in DBFP, vol. 9, no. 765, p. 724; Embassy Turkey, communication, Oct. 3, 1912, no. 34; Ministry of Foreign Affairs, French Republic, *Documents diplomatiques. Les affaires balkaniques, 1912–1914* (Paris: Imprimerie nationale, 1922), vol. 4, pp. 26–27; the Sublime Porte's official note to the powers, FO 371/1501/434220; Freiherr von Wangenheim, Oct. 2, 1912, no. 12207, *Die Grosse Politik des Europäischen Kabinette, 1871–1914, Sammlung der*

Diplomatischen Akten des Auswartigen Amtes (Berlin: Deutsche Verlagsgesellschaft für Politik und Geschichte, 1922), vol. 33, p. 151.

3. Letter of a Mohammadan association to the viceroy, Oct. 15, 1912, FO 371/1506/48169.

4. Sazonov to Izvolsky, Nov. 4, 1912, *Mezhdunarodnye Otnosheniia,* second series, vol. 21, no. 157. Not only did Russia *not* attempt to exploit the Ottoman predicament in the Balkans for purposes of self-aggrandizement, but in 1908–1909 it helped convince Austria-Hungary to compensate Turkey for the annexation of Bosnia-Herzegovina and was instrumental in securing a Turco-Bulgarian agreement (June 1909) recognizing Ferdinand as the king of independent Bulgaria in exchange for compensation.

5. Grey to Lowther, Oct. 11, 1912, DBFP, vol. 10/2, no. 16; Lowther to Grey, Oct. 21, 1912, FO 371/1505/47254; Kamil Pasha in Lowther to Grey, Oct. 30, 1912, FO 371/1503/46056. On October 24, Acting Foreign Minister Gabriel Efendi Noradounghian delivered a message to London to orchestrate great-power intervention to stop the war (see FO 371/1502/44983).

6. The Ottoman foreign minister, Nov. 4, 1912, as cited in Lowther to Grey, Nov. 4, 1912, FO 371/1506/48287.

7. For Ottoman attempts to harness great-power support see the Ottoman foreign minister, Nov. 4, 1912, FO 371/1506/48287; Tewfiq Pasha, Nov. 5, 1912, FO 371/1505/47169; declaration made by the Ottoman foreign minister to the ambassadors of Austria, Great Britain, France, Russia, and Germany, Nov. 7, 1912, FO 371/1505/47396; Poincaré to Cambon, Nov. 5, 1912, no. 348, and Poincaré to Fleuriau, Nov. 5, 1912, no. 349, as well as Poincaré's circular to French foreign ambassadors, Nov. 5, 1912, no. 353, *Documents Diplomatiques Français,* vol. 4, pp. 363, 366.

8. Sazonov to Buchanan, in Buchanan to Grey, Nov. 2, 1912, DBFP, vol. 9/2, no. 98, p. 79; Buchanan to Grey, Nov. 8, 1912, FO 371/1505/47589. Interestingly enough, Sazonov rebuffed a British suggestion to consider the possible neutralization of Constantinople. See Grey to Buchanan, Nov. 5, 1912, and Sazonov's response in Buchanan to Grey, Nov. 6, 1912, FO 371/1505/47008 and 47210; Bertie to Grey, Oct. 27, and Grey to Bertie, Oct. 28, both in FO 371/1503/45534.

For the French mediation attempts see in particular Poincaré to the French ambassadors of London and St. Petersburg, Oct. 30, 1912, and Poincaré to the French ambassadors of Berlin, Vienna, and Rome, Oct. 30, 1912, *Documents Diplomatiques Français,* vol. 4, nos. 279 and 284, pp. 291–292, 295. See also, ibid., pp. 310–359; communication from M. Paul Cambon, Oct. 30, 1912, DBFP, vol. 9/2, no. 80, p. 68.

For Austria-Hungary's interests in the crisis see Ludwig Bittner, Alfred Francis Pribramt, Heinrich Srbik, and Hans Vebersberger, chief eds., *Österreich-Ungarns Aussenpolitik von der bosnischen Krise 1908 bis zum Kriegsausbruch 1914* (Vienna and Leipzig: Austro-Hungarian Monarchy, 1916), vol. 4, pp. 769–776.

9. The Bulgarian prime minister in Bax-Ironside to Grey, Nov. 3, 1912, FO 371/1504/46537, and a response by the Bulgarian minister in Buchanan to Grey, Nov. 5, 1912, DBFP, 9/2, no. 129, p. 99; the Ottoman foreign minister, Gabriel Efendi, to Bompard, the French ambassador to Istanbul, in Bompard to Poincaré, Nov. 5, 1912 (no. 357), p. 369, *Documents Diplomatiques Français,* vol. 4, no. 357, p. 369; Poincaré to the French foreign ambassadors, Nov. 5, 1912, ibid., vol. 4, no. 353, p. 366.

10. Ziya Gökalp, *The Principles of Turkism*, Robert Devereux, trans. (Leiden: Brill, 1968).

11. Djemal Pasha, *Memories of a Turkish Statesman, 1913–1919* (New York: Arno Press, 1973), p. 97.

7. The Ottoman Road to War

1. Talaat Pasha, "Posthumous Memoirs of Talaat Pasha," *New York Times Current History*, vol. 15, no. 2 (Nov. 1921), p. 287; Djemal Pasha, *Memories of a Turkish Statesman, 1913–1919* (New York: Arno Press, 1973), p. 97.

2. For the text of the treaty see M. N. Pokrowski, chief ed., *Die Internationalen Beziehungen im Zeitalter des Imperialismus: Dokumente aus der Provisorischen Regierung* (Berlin: Verlag von Reimar Hobbing, 1931), vol. 1/1, pp. 449–450.

3. On the Ottoman-Greek abortive negotiations see Von Mutius, Apr. 29, 1914; Wangenheim to Foreign Office, May 25, 1914, *Die Grosse Politik des Europäischen Kabinette, 1871–1914, Sammlung der Diplomatischen Akten des Auswärtigen Amtes* (Berlin: Deutsche Verlagsgesellschaft für Politik und Geschichte, 1922–1927), vol. 36/2, no. 14578, pp. 770–771, no. 14596, p. 798; von Quadt, May 13, 28, 1914, ibid., nos. 14589 and 14598; Wangenheim to von Bethmann Hollweg, June 17, 1914, ibid., no. 14626, pp. 789–790, 799–800, 823–824.

4. For Enver's own recollection of his Libyan period see *Mudhakkirat Anwar Pasha fi Tarabulus al-Gharb* (Tripoli: 1979).

5. Intercepted cipher telegrams from Enver Pasha, July 10, 15, 26, 27, 1914. Sent by the political resident in the Persian Gulf (Major S. G. Knox) to the foreign secretary to the government of India in the Foreign and Political Dept., Simla, on Sept. 26 and Oct. 1, 1914, FO 371/2144/64214.

6. Wangenheim to Foreign Office, July 21, 1914, in Karl Kautsky, ed., *Die Deutschen Dokumente zum Kriegsausbruch* (Charlottenburg: Deutsche Verlagsgesellschaft für Politik und Geschichte m.b.h., 1919), vol. 1, no. 99, p. 123. On Pallavicini's warning against alliance with Greece, see Wangenheim to Foreign Office, July 23, 1914, ibid., vol. 1, no. 149, pp. 162–163.

7. Wangenheim to Foreign Office, July 22, 1914, ibid., vol. 1, no. 117, pp. 134–136.

8. Ibid.

9. Jagow echoed this view in mid-July: "Turkey could only be regarded as a passive factor for some years to come, due to the poor state of her army. She would be entirely incapable of aggressive action against Russia." Jagow to the ambassadors at Vienna and Istanbul, July 14, 1914, ibid., vol. 1, no. 45.

10. The kaiser's comments on Wangenheim's report of July 23, 1914, ibid., no. 149, pp. 162–163 (emphasis added).

11. Jagow to Wangenheim, July 24, 1914, *Die Deutschen Dokumente*, vol. 1, no. 144, p. 158; Count Wedel (minister in the Imperial Suite) to Foreign Office, July 24, 1914, ibid., no. 141, p. 158; Wangenheim to Foreign Office, July 28, 1914, ibid., vol. 2, no. 285, p. 7; Admiral Alfred P. Tirpitz, *My Memoirs* (London: Hurst and Blacket, 1919), vol. 2, pp. 80–83.

12. Bethmann-Hollweg to Wangenheim, July 28, 1914, *Die Deutschen Dokumente,* no. 320.

13. Wangenheim to Foreign Office, July 30, 1914, ibid., no. 411.

14. The broad contours of the Ottoman-German military collaboration in the event of war were delineated at a meeting in the German Embassy on August 1, 1914, with the participation of Enver, von Sanders, and Wangenheim. For the text of the Ottoman-German treaty see Wangenheim to Foreign Office, Aug. 2, 1914, *Die Deutschen Dokumente,* vol. 3, no. 733; J. C. Hurewitz, *The Middle East and North Africa in World Politics,* 2nd. rev. ed. (New Haven and London: Yale University Press, 1975–1979), vol. 2, pp. 1–2.

For the making of the Ottoman-German alliance of August 2, 1914, see Yusuf Hikmet Bayur, *Türk Inkilabi Tarihi* (Istanbul: Maarif Matbaari, 1953), especially vols. 2 and 3; Kautsky, *Die Deutschen Dokumente;* Maurice Larcher, *La guerre turque dans la guerre mondiale* (Paris: Plon, 1926), pp. 34–36; Talaat Pasha, "Posthumous Memoirs"; Djemal Pasha, *Memories of a Turkish Statesman;* K. Karabekir, *Birinci Cihan Harbine,* repr. ed (Istanbul: Emire Yayinlari, 1998), vols. 1–2; Carl Mühlmann, *Deutschland und die Türkei* (Berlin: Grünewald, Rothschild, 1929); Carl Mühlmann, *Das deutsch-türkische Waffenbündnis im Weltkriege* (Leipzig: Koehler und Ameland, 1940); Mahmoud Moukhtar, *La Turquie, l'Allemagne et l'Europe depuis le traité de Berlin jusqu'à la guerre mondiale* (Paris: Plon, 1924); K. T. Helfferich, *Die Deutsche Türkenpolitik* (Berlin: Ameland, 1921); Ernest Jackh, *The Rising Crescent* (New York: Farrar and Rinehart, 1944); Kurt Okay, *Enver Pascha: Der grosse Freund Deutschlands* (Berlin: Verlag für Kulturpolitik, 1935); Harry N. Howard, *The Partition of Turkey: A Diplomatic History, 1913–1923,* repr. ed. (New York: Howard Fertig, 1966), especially pp. 83–115; Y. T. Kurat, "How Turkey Drifted into World War I," in K. Bourne and D. C. Watt, eds., *Studies in International Diplomacy* (London: Longman, 1967), p. 297; Ulrich Trumpener, "Turkey's Entry into World War I: An Assessment of Responsibilities," *Journal of Modern History,* vol. 34 (Dec. 1962), pp. 369–380; Ulrich Trumpener, *Germany and the Ottoman Empire, 1914–1918* (Princeton: Princeton University Press, 1968), especially pp. 14–61; Ahmed Emin, *Turkey in the World War* (New Haven: Yale University Press, 1930); M. Bompard, "L'entrée en guerre de la Turquie," *Revue de Paris,* vol. 28 (July 1–15, 1921), pp. 61-85, 261–288.

15. Von Moltke to the Foreign Office, Aug. 2, 1914, *Die Deutschen Dokumente,* vol. 3, no. 662; Jagow to Wangenheim, Aug. 4, 1914, ibid., vol. 4, no. 836; von Moltke to the Foreign Office, Aug. 5, 1914, ibid., no. 876.

16. Halil Bey to A. Block, Aug. 9, 1914, as cited in Beaumont to Grey, Aug. 13, 1914, FO 371/2138/42436.

17. For the divisions within the Ottoman government, see, for example, Bayur, *Türk Inkilabi Tarihi,* vol. 3, pp. 71–72; Kurat, "How Turkey Drifted," pp. 299–300.

18. Wangenheim to Foreign Office, Aug. 1, 1914, *Die Deutschen Dokumente,* vol. 3, no. 652; von Mutius (aide-de-camp on duty, Berlin, palace), to Foreign Office, Aug. 2, 1914, ibid., no. 683; Jagow to Wangenheim, Aug. 3, 1914, ibid., no. 712; von Tirpitz to Jagow, Aug. 3, 1914, ibid., vol. 4, no. 775.

19. Djemal Pasha, *Memories of a Turkish Statesman,* p. 118; Bayur, *Türk Inkilabi Tarihi,* vol. 3, p. 76.

20. Hague Convention XIII: Neutral Rights and Duties in Maritime War (1907), articles 3, 13, 14, 21, 24, 25.

21. Mühlmann, *Deutshland und die Turkei*, pp. 101–102; Trumpener, "Turkey's Entry into World War I," p. 377.

22. Arnold J. Toynbee, *Turkey: A Past and a Future* (New York: George H. Dorn, 1917), pp. 28–29.

8. The Entente's Road to War

1. Elie Kedourie, *Politics in the Middle East* (Oxford: Oxford University Press, 1992), p. 93; Malcolm Yapp, *The Making of the Modern Middle East, 1792–1923* (London: Longmans, 1987), p. 266; Feroz Ahmad, "The Late Ottoman Empire," in Marian Kent, ed., *The Great Powers and the End of the Ottoman Empire* (London: Frank Cass, 1996), pp. 15–16. For this standard version see also Ahmed Emin, *Turkey in the World War* (New Haven: Yale University Press, 1930); Feroz Ahmed, *The Young Turks: The Committee of Union and Progress in Turkish Politics, 1908–1914* (Oxford: Clarendon Press, 1969); Joseph Heller, *British Policy towards the Ottoman Empire, 1908–1914* (London: Frank Cass, 1983); Harry N. Howard, *The Partition of Turkey: A Diplomatic History, 1913–1923*, repr. ed. (New York: Howard Fertig, 1966); Frank G. Weber, *Eagles on the Crescent: Germany, Austria, and the Diplomacy of the Turkish Alliance, 1914–1918* (Ithaca: Cornell University Press, 1970).

Interestingly enough, even Ulrich Trumpener, who meticulously documents the extent of Ottoman eagerness for an alignment with Germany, reserves judgment about the motivation behind the Ottoman behavior. See Trumpener, *Germany and the Ottoman Empire, 1914–1918* (Princeton: Princeton University Press, 1968); "Turkey's Entry into World War I: An Assessment of Responsibilities," *Journal of Modern History*, vol. 34 (Dec. 1962), pp. 369–380; "German Military Aid to Turkey in 1914: An Historical Re-Evaluation," *Journal of Modern History*, vol. 32 (1960), pp. 145–149.

2. Grey's minute in Lowther to Grey, Aug. 7, 1908, FO 371/545/27371; Russian ambassador in Berlin to Sazonov, Nov. 8–21, 1913, in B. de Siebert and G. A. Schreiner, eds., *Entente Diplomacy and the World* (London: George Allen and Unwin, 1921), no. 781.

3. Serge Sazonov, *Fateful Years, 1909–1916* (London, England: Jonathan Cape, 1928), p. 136.

4. Ibid., pp. 136–138. For Sazonov's hopeful state of mind following Talaat's visit, see also Graf von Pourtalès (German ambassador to St. Petersburg) to Reich Chancellor von Bethmann Hollweg, May 23, 1914, *Die Grosse Politik des Europäischen Kabinette, 1871–1914, Sammlung der Diplomatischen Akten des Auswärtigen Amtes* (Berlin: Deutsche Verlagsgesellschaft für Politik und Geschichte, 1922–1927), vol. 36, no. 14595, pp. 795–797; Sazonov to Paléologue (French ambassador to St. Petersburg), in Paléologue to Doumergue, Ministry of Foreign Affairs, French Republic, May 17, 1914, *Documents diplomatiques. Les affaires balkaniques, 1912–1914* (Paris: Imprimerie nationale, 1922), vol. 10, no. 242, p. 374.

5. Y. T. Kurat, "How Turkey Drifted into World War I," in K. Bourne and D. C. Watt, eds., *Studies in International Diplomacy* (London: Longman, 1967), p. 294. Kurat's claim that Talaat's proposal was never given any serious consideration by Sazonov owing to his obsessive preoccupation with seizing the straits has been uncritically adopted by others. See, for example, David Fromkin, *A Peace to End All Peace: The Fall of the*

Ottoman Empire and the Creation of the Modern Middle East (New York: Avon, 1990), p. 49; Ahmad, "The Late Ottoman Empire," p. 15.

6. Djemal Pasha, *Memories of a Turkish Statesman, 1913–1919* (New York: Arno Press, 1973), pp. 105–106.

7. M. de Margerie, "Grèce-Turquie et les Iles," July 13, 1914, Ministry of Foreign Affairs—Diplomatic Archives, Intelligence Series, Political and Commercial Correspondence, 1897–1918, vol. 228, pp. 117–123.

8. Beaumont to Grey, Aug. 4, 1914, *Correspondence Respecting Events Leading to the Rupture of Relations with Turkey,* presented to both houses of Parliament by command of His Majesty, Nov. 1914, Cmd. 7628, no. 3, p. 1 (hereinafter "Cmd. 7628—1914").

9. Giers, Aug. 3, 1914, no. 5; Giers, Aug. 4 and 5, 1914, nos. 7 and 8; Tewfiq Pasha, Aug. 6, 1914, in Benckendorff to the Russian Foreign Office, no. 9, in Ministry of Foreign Affairs, *Recueil de documents diplomatiques, négociations ayant précédé la guerre avec la Turquie 19 juillet (1 août)–19 octobre (1 novembre) 1914* (Petrograd: Imprimerie de lÉtat, 1915); Beaumont to Grey, Aug. 3, 1914, Tewfiq Pasha to Edward Grey, Aug. 4, 1914, in DBFP, vol. 11, nos. 598 and 605; Beaumont to Grey, "Cmd. 7628—1914," no. 3, p. 1.

10. Giers, July 23/Aug. 5, 1914, no. 631; Giers, July 23/Aug. 5, no. 632, both in M. N. Pokrowski, chief ed., *Die Internationalen Beziehungen im Zeitalter des Imperialismus: Dokumente aus der Provisorischen Regierung* (Berlin: Verlag von Reimar Hobbing, 1931), vol. 2/6.

11. Sazonov to Giers, Aug. 9, 1914, ibid., vol. 2/6, nos. 1705 and 1779.

12. See Sazonov to Izvolsky and Benckendorff (ambassadors in Paris and London), Aug. 16, 1914, Sazonov to Giers, Aug. 16, 1914, ibid., vol. 2/6, nos. 1924 and 1939; Mallet to Grey, Aug. 20, 1914, "Cmd. 7628—1914," no. 24, p. 8.

13. Buchanan to Grey, Aug. 16, 1914, FO 371/2138/39792; Sazonov to Giers, Aug. 16, 1914, *Die Internazionalen Beziehungen,* vol. 2/6, no. 1924.

14. Grey to Erskine, Aug. 20, 1914, FO 371/2138/42268; Grey to Beaumont, Aug. 7, 1914, "Cmd. 7628—1914," no. 5, p. 2; Churchill to Enver, Aug. 15, 1914, cited in Martin Gilbert, *Winston S. Churchill* (London: Heinemann, 1972), companion vol. 3, part 1, p. 38.

When the Greek ambassador to London asked Grey for clarification of Britain's position regarding the Aegean Islands, the foreign secretary replied: "By Turkish integrity, I meant the state of things when the present war broke out; which included the fact that Italy was in occupation of some of the islands, and would give them back to Turkey on certain conditions" (Grey to Erskine, Aug. 20, 1914, FO 371/2138/42268).

15. Grey to Beaumont, Aug. 16, 1914, "Cmd. 7628—1914," no. 17, p. 5; Grey to Mallet, Aug. 18, 1914, ibid., no. 21, p. 7; Mallet to Grey, Aug. 21, 1914, ibid., no. 27, p. 9; Sazonov to Giers, Aug. 23, 1914, *Recueil des documents diplomatiques,* no. 34.

16. Giers to Sazonov, Aug. 19 and 20, 1914, and Sazonov to Giers, Aug. 21, 1914, *Recueil des documents diplomatiques,* nos. 30–32; Buchanan to Grey, Aug. 21, 1914, FO 371/2138/41796, Aug. 28, 1914, FO 371/2138/44231; Mallet to Grey, Aug. 20, 1914, FO 371/1238/41447; Grey to Mallet, Aug. 22, 1914, "Cmd. 7628—1914," no. 28, p. 9.

17. Beaumont to Grey, Aug. 11, 1914, "Cmd. 7628—1914," no. 9, p. 3; Mallet to Grey, Aug. 18, 1914, ibid., no. 20, p. 6; Mallet to Grey, Aug. 18, 1914, in Gilbert, *Churchill,* companion vol. 3/1, pp. 40–41.

18. Churchill to Enver, Aug. 19, 1914, ibid., pp. 44–45.

19. Grey to Mallet, Aug. 25, 1914, "Cmd. 7628—1914," no. 34, p. 11; Mallet to Grey, Sept. 22, 1914, ibid., no. 112, encl. 1–13, pp. 38–40.

20. Mallet to Grey, Aug. 26, 1914, no. 39, p. 13; Aug. 27, no. 40, p. 14; Cheetham to Grey, Aug. 28, 1914, no. 44, p. 14: all in "Cmd. 7628—1914"; Mallet to Grey, Aug. 28, 1914, FO 371/2138/44220; Gilbert, *Churchill,* vol. 3, p. 198.

21. Gilbert, *Winston Churchill,* vol. 3, pp. 200, 204–205.

22. On August 27, for example, Mallet told the grand vizier of his "apprehensions respecting a raid by *Goeben* and disastrous consequences provoking Quadruple [sic] Entente, which would involve destruction of Ottoman Empire." Three days later he warned Said Halim that British "patience was not inexhaustible, and that [the] consequences of allying themselves [the Ottomans] with our enemies would be serious." A week later, when meeting Talaat, Mallet was equally straightforward. Expressing his exasperation with the Ottomans' complete disregard of the Entente's written guarantee of its integrity, the British ambassador sarcastically commented that he was "personally somewhat relieved, as to guarantee integrity and independence of Turkey was like guaranteeing [the] life of [a] man who was determined to commit suicide." Mallet to Grey, Aug. 2, 7, 30, 1914, Sept. 6, 1914, FO 371/2138. See also Mallet to Grey, Sept. 3, 6, 1914, FO 371/2138/46098 and 46944; Grey to Mallet, Sept. 7, 1914, FO 371/2138/46924.

23. Mallet to Grey, Aug. 23, 27, 31, Sept. 2, 1914, FO 371/2138; Mallet to Grey, Sept. 19, 20, 21, 24, 1914, "Cmd. 7628—1914," nos. 82–84, 90, pp. 27–28, 30.

24. Mallet to Grey, Sept. 10, 11, 15, 1914, FO 371/2138; Grey to Mallet, Sept. 16, 1914, FO 371/2138; Buchanan to Grey, Sept. 10, 1914, FO 371/2138; Grey to Mallet, Oct. 9, 1914, FO 371/2139/56338.

25. Mallet to Grey, Sept. 16, 19, 1914, FO 371/2138; Mallet to Grey, Sept. 20, 1914, "Cmd. 7628—1914," no. 83, p. 27; Grey to Mallet, Sept. 23, 1914, FO 371/2138/52335; Grey to Mallet, Oct. 11, 1914, FO 371/2139/58206.

26. Mallet to Grey, Sept. 27, 1914, "Cmd. 7628—1914," nos. 97 and 98, pp. 32–33; Grey to Mallet, Oct. 4, 1914, ibid., no. 107, p. 36.

27. See, for example, Mallet to Grey, Oct. 5, 6, 7, 10, 11, 12 1914, ibid., nos. 108 and 109, 114–116, 120, pp. 36–37, 40–42.

28. Mallet to Grey, Oct. 15, 16, 1914, ibid., nos. 129, 134, pp. 48–50; Mallet to Grey, Oct. 16, FO 371/2139/66678; Acting Consul-General Heathcote-Smith (Smyrna) to Mallet, Oct. 12, 1914, FO 371/2139/66678 (encl. no 1).

29. H. Bax-Ironside to Grey, Sept. 16, 1914, "Cmd. 7638—1914," no. 131, p. 49; Mallet to Grey, Oct. 23, 1914, ibid., no. 162, p. 68; Buchanan to Grey, Oct. 20, 1914, FO 371/2139/61563; Mallet to Grey, Oct. 22, 1914, ibid., no. 157, p. 66.

30. Mallet to Grey, Oct. 23, 1914, Grey to Mallet, Oct. 24, 1914, FO 371/2139/62834.

31. Mallet to Grey, Oct. 27, 1914, FO 371/2139/64020; Mallet to Grey, Oct. 29, 1914, FO 371/2144/77717; Grey to Mallet, Oct. 28, 1914, "Cmd. 7628—1914," no. 174, p. 71; Mallet to Grey, Oct. 29, 1914, ibid., no. 176, p. 71.

32. Sazonov to Benckendorff, Nov. 1, 1914, FO 371/2145/66389; Grey to Mallet, Oct. 30, 1914, "Cmd. 7628—1914," no. 179, p. 72; Gilbert, *Churchill,* companion vol. 3, p. 216.

9. The Lust for Glory

1. "Our participation in the world war represents the vindication of our national ideal. The ideal of our nation and people leads us toward the destruction of our Muscovite enemy to obtain a natural frontier to our empire, which should include and unite all branches of our race" (Arnold J. Toynbee, *Turkey: A Past and a Future* [New York: George H. Dorn, 1917], pp. 28–29).

2. Yusuf Hikmet Bayur, *Türk Inkilabi Tarihi* (Istanbul: Maarif Matbaari, 1953), vol. 3, p. 198; further addenda to "Report of an Inhabitant of Athlit," circulated on the Nov. 2, 1916, under no. 7977, FO 371/2783/225831, Nov. 10, 1916.

3. Count Johann Heinrich Bernstorff, *The Memoirs of Count Bernstorff* (London: William Heinemann, 1936), p. 154.

4. British intelligence report, FO 371/2783.

5. Djemal Pasha to the French ambassador on Oct. 22, in Mallet to Grey, Oct. 23, 1914, FO 371/2139/62834.

6. For the Turkish expedition against the canal, see, for example, Kress von Kressenstein, *Mit den Türken zum Suezkanal* (Berlin, 1938); Djemal Pasha, *Memories of a Turkish Statesman, 1913–1919* (first pub. in 1922; New York: Arno Press, 1973), chap. 4; Ali Fuad, *Kaifa Ghazawna Misr: Mudhakkirat al-General al-Turki Ali Fuad* (Beirut: Dar al-Kitab al-Jadid, 1962); Cyril Fallas and Sir George F. MacMunn, *Military Operations—Egypt and Palestine: History of the Great War based on Official Documents by Direction of the Historical Section Committee of Imperial Defence* (London: HMSO, 1928–1930), vols. 1–2.

7. On the Gallipoli campaign see, for example, "Historique officiel de l'état-major général turc: La campagne des Dardanelles," trans. M. Larcher, in *Les archives de la grande guerre et de l'histoire contemporaine,* vol. 17 (1929), pp. 129–179; Brigadier General C. F. Aspinall-Oglander, *Military Operations—Gallipoli: History of the Great War based on Official Documents by Direction of the Historical Section Committee of Imperial Defence* (London: HMSO, 1929), vol. 1; Sir Julian Corbett, *Naval Operations in the Great War, based on Official Documents by Direction of the Historical Committee of Imperial Defence* (London: HMSO, 1920–1925), vols. 2–3; General Sir Ian Hamilton, *Gallipoli Diary* (London: Arnold, 1920), 2 vols.; C. Mühlmann, *Der Kampf um die Dardanellen* (Oldenburg, 1927); M. Gilbert, *Winston S. Churchill, 1914–1916* (London: Heinemann, 1971), pp. 219–417; Alan Morehead, *Gallipoli* (New York: Harper, 1956).

8. FO 371/2783, p. 12.

9. The prime minister's statement, Nov. 2, 1915, House of Commons, *The Parliamentary Debates (Official Report), Fifth Series, Volume LXXV, Eigth Volume of Session 1914–15* (London: HMSO, 1916), p. 510.

10. For the Kut debacle see, for example, Sir Charles Townshend, *My Campaign in Mesopotamia* (London: Thornton Butterworth, 1920), vol. 2; F. J. Moberley, *The Campaign in Mesopotamia, 1914–1918* (London: HMSO, 1923–1927); A. J. Barker, *Neglected War: Mesopotamia, 1914–1918* (London: Faber, 1967), pp. 107, 117–120; and Barker, *Townshend of Kut: A Biography of Major-General Sir Charles Townshend, KCB DSO* (London: Cassell, 1967), pp. 154–155.

11. The testimony of Khristofor Mikhailovich Evangulov, in Jacques Kayaloff, *The Fall of Baku* (Bergenfield, 1976), p. 12.

10. Genocide in Armenia

1. For population figures see, for example, Mallet to Grey, Oct. 7, 1914, FO 371/2137/56940; "Turkey: Annual Report, 1913. By the Embassy," FO 371/2137/79138, p. 25.

2. See Fontana to Lowther, Mar. 25, 1913, FO 371/1773/16941; Lowther to Grey, Apr. 5, 10, 1913, FO 371/1773/16736; Admiralty to Foreign Office, Apr. 15, 1913, FO 371/1775/17825.

3. Serge Sazonov, *Fateful Years, 1909–1916* (London: Jonathan Cape, 1928), pp. 140–141.

4. Ironside to Foreign Office, Mar. 3, 1915, and War Office to the Foreign Office, Mar. 4, 1915, FO 371/2484/25073 and 25167; Foreign Office to Ironside, Mar. 9, 1915, FO 371/2484/28172 and 22083.

5. The polemical literature on this issue is immense. See, for example, Talaat Pasha, "Posthumous Memoirs of Talaat Pasha," *New York Times Current History,* vol. 15, no. 2 (Nov. 1921); *Vérité sur le mouvement révolutionnaire arménien et les mesures gouvernementales* (Constantinople, 1916); *Aspirations et agissements revolutionnaires des comites armeniens avant et apres la proclamation de la constitution ottomane* (Constantinople, 1917); Ahmed Rustem Bey, *La guerre mondiale et la question turco-armenienne* (Berne, 1918); Kamuran Gürün, *The Armenian File: The Myth of Innocence Exposed* (London, Nicosia, Istanbul: K. Rustem and Weidenfeld and Nicolson, 1985). Some Western scholars have accepted this apologia. See, for example, Stanford J. Shaw and Ezel Kural Shaw, *History of the Ottoman Empire and Modern Turkey,* vol. II: *Reform, Revolution, and Republic: The Rise of Modern Turkey, 1808–1975* (Cambridge, England: Cambridge University Press, 1977), p. 315.

For the opposite approach see, for example, Haigazn Kazarian, "The Turkish Genocide," *Armenian Review,* vol. 30 (Spring 1977); Richard G. Hovannisian, ed., *The Armenian Genocide in Perspective* (New Brunswick: Transaction Books, 1987); Hovannisian, ed., *The Armenian Genocide: History, Politics, Ethics* (London: Macmillan, 1992); The Permanent Peoples' Tribunal, *A Crime of Silence: The Armenian Genocide* (London: Zed Books, 1985); Navasard Derymenjian, "An Important Turkish Document on the 'Exterminate Armenians' Plan," *Armenian Review,* vol. 14 (1961), pp. 53–55; William Yale, *The Near East: A Modern History* (Ann Arbor: University of Michigan Press, 1958), pp. 230–231.

6. Viscount Bryce, *The Treatment of Armenians in the Ottoman Empire: Documents Presented to Viscount Grey of Fallodon, Secretary of State for Foreign Affairs,* laid before the House of Parliament as an official paper and now published by permission (London: Hodder and Stoughton, 1916), pp. 645–649.

7. Ibid., pp. 649–651; "Annex F: Statistical Estimate Included in the Fifth Bulletin of the American Committee for Armenian and Syrian Relief, Dated New York, 24th May 1916," ibid., pp. YY2; Johannes Lepsius, *Deutschland und Armenian, 1914–1918* (Potsdam: Tempelverlag, 1919), pp. lxv, 256; and Lepsius, *Der Todesgang des armenischen Volkes* (Potsdam: Missionshandlung und Verlag, 1930), pp. 301–304; Aaron Aaronsohn, "Pro Armenia," Nov. 16, 1916, p. 13, The Aaronsohn Archives (Zichron Yaacov, Israel), file 2C/13. See also Aaronsohn, "On the Armenian Massacres: Memorandum Presented to the War Office, London, November 1916," The Aaronsohn Archives, file 2C/14.

8. Bryce, *The Treatment of Armenians,* pp. 641–642; Lepsius, *Der Todesgang des armenischen Volkes,* pp. 301–304.

9. The descriptions in this section are mainly taken from Bryce, *The Treatment of Armenians,* and Aaronsohn, *Pro Armenia.* See also report by Mark Sykes, FO 371/2781/201201.

11. Repression in the Holy Land

1. Owing to the lack of reliable Ottoman demographic data and to latter-day politicization of the Palestine problem, population figures for nineteenth-century Palestine are subject to controversy. For general discussions see, for example, Haim Gerber, "The Population of Syria and Palestine in the Nineteenth Century," *Asian and African Studies,* vol. 13 (1979), pp. 58–80; Alexander Schölch, "The Demographic Development of Palestine, 1850–1882," *International Journal of Middle Eastern Studies,* vol. 17 (Nov. 1985), pp. 485–505; Yitzhak Ben-Zvi, *Eretz Israel Ve-yishuva Bi-yemei Ha-shilton Ha-Ottomani* (Jerusalem: Bialik Institute, 1955). For the Jewish population in Palestine in earlier times, see, for example, Moshe Gil, *A History of Palestine, 634–1099* (Cambridge, England: Cambridge University Press, 1992); Thomas A. Indinopulos, *Jerusalem Blessed, Jerusalem Cursed: Jews, Christians, and Muslims in the Holy City from David's Time to Our Own* (Chicago: Ivan R. Dee, 1991), pp. 93, 101, 109–110.

2. Imperial instruction to the grand vizier, June 28, 1890, as quoted in C. R. Itilhan, *Ittihat ve Terâkkinin Suikastleri* (Istanbul, 1973), p. 199.

3. Raphael Patai, ed., *The Complete Diaries of Theodor Herzl,* Harry Zohn, trans. (New York: Herzl Press and Thomas Yoseloff, 1960), vol. 3, pp. 1128–1129.

4. Reports by Jacobson to Wolffsohn, Dec. 1908—Feb. 1909, Jerusalem, CZA, Z2/7–8.

5. Talaat was not alone in thinking along these lines. Shortly before their downfall in the January coup, Grand Vizier Kamil Pasha, Interior Minister Reshid Bey, and President of the Council Said Pasha were actively lobbying on the Zionists' behalf.

6. Jacobson to Sokolow, Feb. 27, 1913, CZA, Z3/403; Jacobson to Frank, Feb. 28, 1913, Z3/45; Jacobson to P. Nathan, Mar. 2, 1913, Z3/403.

7. Thus according to contemporary British and German sources. See, for example, E. C. Blech (Jerusalem) to Sir Nicholas O'Conor, Nov. 16, 1907, FO 371/356/40321. The Arabic-speaking population of Palestine at the time was estimated at between 600,000 and 700,000. Arthur Ruppin, the head of the Zionist Palestine Office, estimated the Jewish population at the outbreak of the war at the lower figure of 85,000. See Ruppin, *The Jews in the Modern World* (London: Macmillan, 1934), pp. 55, 389. Yet, in his address to the eleventh Zionist Congress in September 1913, Ruppin subscribed to the 100,000 figure.

8. See, for example, intelligence report by Aaron Aaronsohn, "On the Present Economic and Political Conditions in Palestine," Cairo, Apr. 1917, The Aaronsohn Archives, 2d/21; "Conditions of Life in Palestine," July-Aug. 1917, The Aaronsohn Archives, 2d/19.

9. Arthur Ruppin, *Memoirs, Diaries, Letters* (London: Weidenfeld and Nicolson, 1971), p. 153.

10. Moshe Smilansky, *Prakim Be-toldot Ha-yishuv* (Tel-Aviv: Masada, 1978; repr. ed.), p. 182.

11. For Djemal's persecution of the Yishuv in 1917, see, for example, "Conditions of Life in Palestine"; Smilansky, *Prakim,* pp. 182–189; Meir Dizengoff, *Im Tel-Aviv Ba-gola* (Tel-Aviv, 1931), pp. 76–104; Abraham Galante, *Turcs et Juifs* (Istanbul: Haim Razia and Co., 1932), and *Documents officiels turcs concernant les Juifs de Turquie* (Istanbul: Haim Razia and Co., 1931); Hans Peter Hansse, *Diary of a Dying Empire* (Indiana: Indiana University Press, 1955); Rafael de Nogales, *Four Years beneath the Cresecent,* trans. M. Lee (London: Charles Scribner and Sons, 1926); Mordechair Eliav, *Eretz Israel Ve-yishuva Ba-meah Ha-yudtet, 1777–1917* (Jerusalem: Keter, 1978), pp. 451–457.

12. Istanbul and the Arabs

1. Amin Said, *al-Thawra al-Arabiyya al-Kubra* (Cairo: Isa al-Babi al-Halabi, 1951); Suleiman Musa, *al-Haraka al-Arabiyya: Sirat al-Marhala al-Ula li-l-Nahda al-Arabiyya al-Haditha, 1908–1924* (Beirut: Dar al-Nahar, 1970); Zaki Hazem Nuseibeh, *The Ideas of Arab Nationalism* (Ithaca, N.Y.: Cornell University Press, 1956); Zeine N. Zeine, *The Emergence of Arab Nationalism with a Background Study of Arab-Turkish Relations in the Near East,* 2nd. rev. ed. (Beirut: Khayat's, 1966); George Lenczowski, *The Middle East in World Affairs,* 4th ed. (Ithaca, N.Y.: Cornell University Press, 1980), pp. 58–59, 79–87; George Kirk, *A Short History of the Middle East: From the Rise of Islam to Modern Times* (London: Methuen, 1961), chap. 5; Roger Owen, *State, Power and Politics in the Making of the Modern Middle East* (London: Routledge, 1992), especially chaps. 1 and 4.

2. Albert Hourani, *The Emergence of the Modern Middle East* (London: Macmillan, 1981), p. 204.

3. Eliezer Tauber, *The Emergence of the Arab Movements* (London: Frank Cass, 1993), chap. 28. Tauber's is by far the most exhaustive study of pre–First World War Arab societies; it is also among the more generous in terms of citing the total number of Arab activists. Ernest Dawn's earlier study put the total number of activists at 126. See Dawn, *From Ottomanism to Arabism: Essays on the Origins of Arab Nationalism* (Urbana: University of Illinois Press, 1973), pp. 152–153.

4. Ernest Dawn, "The Origins of Arab Nationalism," in Rashid Khalidi, Lisa Anderson, Muhammad Muslih, and Reeva S. Simon, eds., *The Origins of Arab Nationalism* (New York: Columbia University Press, 1991), p. 10.

5. T. E. Lawrence, "Syria: The Raw Material" (written early in 1915 but not circulated), *Arab Bulletin,* no. 44, Mar. 12, 1917, FO/882/26.

6. Ibn Saud to Cox, June 13, 1913, FO 424/239/160; Foreign Office to India Office, June 7, 1913, FO 424/238/152; Foreign Office to India Office, June 18, Aug. 16, 1913, FO 424/139 and 424/239/138; Cox to Ibn Saud, Sept. 11, 1913, FO 424/240/30; DBFP, vol. 10/2, pp. 190–194; report, Dec. 20, 1913, FO 424/251,111–114; Ibn Saud to Trevor, Feb. 26, 1914, FO 424–252/39; Knox, Mar. 15, 1914, FO 371/2123/E12320–1990–44; Grey, Apr. 2, 1914, FO 371/2123/E12320–1990–44; Shakespear's note on Ibn Rashid's affairs, May 21, 1914, FO 371/2124-E29736–1990–44.

7. On Sayyid Talib and his activities see, for example, Crow to Marling, Aug. 28, 1913, FO 195/2451/423; Knox to the foreign secretary to the government of India, Aug. 8,

1914, FO 371/2140/55472; Mallet to Grey, Mar. 18, 1914, in G. P. Gooch and Harold Temperley, eds., *British Documents on the Origins of the War, 1898–1914* (London: HMSO, 1936), vol. 10, p. 827; Suleiman Faydi, *Mudhakkirat Suleimen Faydi: Fi Ghamrat al-Nidal* (Beirut: Dar al-Qalam, 1952); Ahmad Shafiq Pasha, *Mudhakkirati fi Nisf Qarn* (Cairo: Matba'at Misr, 1934), vol. 3, pp. 78–79; Eliezer Tauber, "Sayyid Talib and the Young Turks in Basra," *Middle Eastern Studies,* vol. 25, no. 1 (Jan. 1989), pp. 3–22.

8. Mallet to Grey, Oct. 7, 1914, FO 371/2140/57074. See also consul in Muhammarah to the political resident in the Persian Gulf, Oct. 9, 1914, FO 371/2144, telegram P., no. 138; Oct. 28, 1914, encl. 23, FO 371/2144/64214.

9. Political resident in the Persian Gulf to the secretary to the government of India in the Foreign and Political Department, Simla, Oct. 23, 1914, FO 371/2144, telegrams 1271, 1276; secretary to the government of India in the Foreign and Political Department to political resident in the Persian Gulf, Oct. 24, 28, 1914, ibid., telegrams 963 and 992.

10. Political resident in the Persian Gulf to the secretary to the government of India in the Foreign and Political Department, Simla, Sept. 14, Oct. 11, 23, 30, 1914; first assistant to the political resident in the Persian Gulf to secretary to the government of India, Nov. 3, 1914; secretary to the government of India to political resident in the Persian Gulf, Oct. 24, 28, Nov. 4, 1914; Mallet to the government of India, Oct. 29, 1914; all in FO 371/2144.

11. Sheikh Mubarak of Kuwait to Major S. G. Knox, officiating political resident in the Persian Gulf, Aug. 21, 1914, FO 371/2144/61684 encl. I.

12. Letter from Sheikh Mubarak to Ibn Saud, Oct. 14, 1914 (emphasis added), FO 371/2144,; extract from a letter addressed to Sheikh Mubarak from the emir of Najd (no date, but probably written about Oct. 20, 1914), Dec. 15, 1914, FO 371/2144/82713, encl. See also Arab Bureau (Cairo), "Summary of Historical Documents from the Outbreak of the War between Great Britain and Turkey [in] 1914 to the Outbreak of the Revolt of the Sharif of Mecca in June 1916," Nov. 29, 1916, WO 158/624, pp. 29–30.

13. "Special Notice to be Issued by the Political Resident on the Outbreak of War between Great Britain and Turkey," Oct. 28, 1914, FO 371/2144/64214.

14. For the text of the agreement see J. C. Hurewitz, *The Middle East and North Africa in World Politics,* 2nd. rev. ed. (New Haven and London: Yale University Press, 1975–1979), vol. 2, pp. 57–58.

15. Majid Khadduri, "Aziz Ali Misri and the Arab Nationalist Movement," in Albert Hourani, ed., *Middle Eastern Affairs* (Oxford: Oxford University Press, 1965), p. 155.

16. R. E. M. Russell, "Precis of Conversation with Abd El Aziz El Masri on 16 August, 1914," FO 371/2140/46261; Clayton, "Conversation with Aziz Bey El Masri," Oct. 30, 1914, enclosed in Cheetham to Grey, Nov. 15, 1914, FO 371/2140/177. See also Cheetham to Foreign Office, Aug. 9, 1914, Foreign Office to Cheetham, Aug. 11, 1914, FO 371/1968/37584; Grey to Cheetham, Nov. 14, Dec. 18, 1914, Cheetham to Grey, Nov. 16, 1914, FO 371/2140; *Gazette Extraordinary* as cited in India Office to Foreign Office, encl. 1, Nov. 3, 1914, FO 371/2139/67347; Aziz al-Misri to Kitchener, Feb. 5, 1916, PRO 30/57/48.

17. E. Maucorp, "Sur un entretien avec le Commandant Aziz Bey," Ministry of Foreign Affairs, war 869: note 52, June 7, 1915.

18. Rosslyn E. Wemyss, Jan. 25, 1917, FO 141/825/1198.

19. Aziz Bek, *al-Istikhbarat wa-l-Jasusiyya fi Lubnan wa-Suriyya wa-Filastin khilala*

al-Harb al-Alamiyya (Beirut: Matba'at Sadir, 1937), p. 11. Bek was the head of the intelligence services in the Fourth Army.

20. Cheetham to Grey, November 9, 1914, FO 371/2141; Amin Said, *Asrar al-Thawra al-Arabiyya al-Kubra wa-Mas'at al-Sharif Hussein* (Beirut: Dar al-Katib al-Arabi, 1960), pp. 38–39, 235–236.

21. Suleiman Musa, al-Haraka al-Arabiyya: Sirat al-Marhala al-Ula li-l-Nahda al-Arabiyya al-Haditha, 1908–1924 (Beirut: Dar al-Nahar li-l-Nashr, 1970), p. 107.

13. The "Great Arab Revolt"

1. The foremost exposition of this view is Ernest Dawn's *From Ottomanism to Arabism: Essays on the Origins of Arab Nationalism* (Urbana: University of Illinois Press, 1973).

2. "Correspondence between Sir Henry McMahon, His Majesty's High Commissioner at Cairo, and the Sherif of Mecca, July 1915–March 1916, Presented by the Secretary of State for Foreign Affairs to Parliament by Command of His Majesty," Cmd. 5957, London, 1939, p. 3 (hereinafter—"Hussein-McMahon Correspondence").

3. *Arab Bulletin*, no. 6, June 23, 1916, p. 47, and no. 41, Feb. 6, 1917, pp. 57–58, FO 882/25; McMahon to Grey, Oct. 20, 1915, FO 371/2486/154423; "Intelligence Report," Dec. 28, 1916, FO 686/6, p. 176.

4. Note by Muhammad Mustafa al-Maraghi to Wingate, Sept. 8, 25, 1915, FO 371/2486/127420 and 138500.

5. Grey to McMahon, Nov. 2, 1915, FO 371/2486/163235; a petition to Grey from the "Islamic Society," June 5, 1915, FO 371/2486/72671; *Arab Bulletin*, no. 9, July 9, 1916, pp. 77–78; no. 15, Aug. 10, 1916, pp. 162–165; no. 17, Aug. 30, 1916, p. 195; no. 34, Dec. 11, 1916, pp. 521–525.

6. *Al-Ahram*, June 25, 1916, as cited in the *Arab Bulletin*, no. 7, June 30, 1916, p. 57.

7. See, for example, *Arab Bulletin*, no. 7, June 30, 1916, pp. 57–58; no. 9, July 9, 1916, pp. 78–80; note by Captain G. S. Symes, "Egypt and the Arab Movement," Aug. 14, 1917, FO 141/783/5317.

8. *Arab Bulletin*, no. 15, Aug. 10, 1916, p. 157; no. 22, Sept. 19, 1916, pp. 279–281; no. 25, Oct. 7, 1916, pp. 338–339; no. 26, Oct. 16, 1916, p. 373; Colonel Hamilton (political agent in Kuwait), "Ibn Saud and His Neighbours," *Arab Bulletin*, no. 92, June 11, 1918, pp. 187–192; report by Sir Percy Cox, Dec. 23, 1917, IOR L/P and S/10/388 (P5140), p. 14 (India Office).

9. Vice-Consul McGregor (reporting from Jaffa), Nov. 12, 1912, Fo 371/1507/50271.

10. Colonel Richard Meinertzhagen, *Middle East Diary, 1917–1956* (London: Crescent Press, 1959), p. 7; "Report on the Existing Political Condition in Palestine and Contiguous Areas" by the political officer in charge of the Zionist Commission, Aug. 27, 1918, FO 371/3395/147225, p. 5 (231).

11. *Arab Bulletin*, no. 53, June 14, 1917, p. 263; T. E. Lawrence, *Secret Despatches from Arabia* (London: The Golden Cockerel Press, 1939), pp. 39–40; Joyce to Rees Mogg, Dec. 12, 1916, Joyce Collection, Liddell Hart Military Archives (King's College London).

12. *Arab Bulletin*, no. 66, Oct. 21, 1917, pp. 412–414.

13. Ibid., no. 45, Mar. 23, 1917, p. 128; Lawrence, *Secret Despatches,* p. 23. See also his report in the *Arab Bulletin,* no. 32, Nov. 11, 1916, pp. 477–481.

14. Arab Bureau, "Summary of Historical Documents from the Outbreak of the War between Great Britain and Turkey [in] 1914 to the Outbreak of the Revolt of the Sharif of Mecca in June 1916," Nov. 29, 1916, WO 158/624, pp. 163–167, 194–195, 238–246; report by the War Office, London, Dec. 18, 1917, FO 371/3381/18476; Suleiman Musa, ed., *al-Murasalat al-Tarikhiyya 1914–1918: al-Thawra al-Arabiyya al-Kubra* (Amman: Matba'at al-Quwat al-Musallaha, 1973–1975), pp. 124, 135–136.

15. *Arab Bulletin,* no. 66, Oct. 21, 1917, p. 415; Joyce to Clayton, Sept. 27, 1917, transcription from Aqaba/I/H/77–78 (Joyce Collection).

16. Amin Said, *al-Thawra al-Arabiyya al-Kubra* (Cairo: Isa al-Babi al-Halabi, 1951), vol. I, pp. 110–111; Suleiman Musa, *al-Haraka al-Arabiyya: Sirat al-Marhala al-Ula li-l-Nahda al-Arabiyya al-Haditha, 1908–1924* (Beirut: Dar al-Nahar, 1970), pp. 52–53.

17. Arab Bureau, "Summary of Historical Documents," pp. 145–146.

18. Abdullah Ibn Hussein, *Mudhakkirati* (Jerusalem: Matba'at Bait al-Maqdis, 1945), pp. 105–107; Said, *al-Thawra al-Arabiyya,* vol. I, p. 111; and his *Asrar al-Thawra al-Arabiyya al-Kubra wa Masat al-Sharif Hussein* (Beirut: Dar al-Katib al-Arabi, 1960), pp. 52–53.

19. Djemal to Faisal, Nov. 1917, FO 371/3395/12077; see also David Hogarth's comments in *Arab Bulletin,* no. 74, Dec. 24, 1917, pp. 402–403.

20. For a detailed discussion of this issue, see Chapter 15 below.

21. Joyce to Clayton, Sept. 17, 1917 (Joyce Papers).

22. For Faisal's draft reply and Hussein's response, see Wingate to Balfour, Dec. 25, 1917, FO 371/3395/12077; Musa, *al-Murasalat al-Tarikhiyya,* pp. 154, 156, 158–159; *Arab Bulletin,* no. 75, Jan. 3, 1918, p. 521.

23. T. E. Lawrence, *Seven Pillars of Wisdom: A Triumph* (Garden City, N.Y.: Doubleday, 1935), pp. 554–555.

24. B. H. Liddell Hart, *T. E. Lawrence to His Biographer* (London: Cassell, 1962), p. 142 (recording a conversation with Lawrence, Aug. 1, 1933).

25. Count Johann Heinrich Bernstorff, *Memoirs* (London: William Heinemann, 1936), p. 179.

26. Djemal to Faisal, translation enclosed with Joyce to General Staff, Hijaz Operations, June 5, 1918, WO 158/634; Faisal to Djemal, June 11, 1918, FO 371/3881/146256.

27. Bonn State Archives, IA Türkei 165 43 Pera Telegram, August 22, 1918, "Secret: Report by the German Ambassador on a Conversation with Talaat Pasha"; Musa, *al-Murasalat,* p. 210.

28. T. E. Lawrence to W. Yale, Oct. 22, 1919, in David Garnett, ed., *Letters of T. E. Lawrence* (London: Spring Books, 1964; originally published in 1938 by Jonathan Cape, London), p. 672.

29. Report by T. E. Lawrence, July 30, 1917, FO 686/8.

30. "Faisal's Table Talk," in a report to Colonel Wilson by T. E. Lawrence, Jan. 8, 1917, FO 686/6, fols. 121, 123; Abd al-Razaq al-Hasani, *Ta'rikh al-Wizarat al-Iraqiyya,* part 3 (Sidon: Matba'at al-Ifran, 1939), pp. 189–195.

31. David Hogarth, "Mission to King Hussein," *Arab Bulletin,* Jan. 27, 1918, pp. 22–23.

14. Hussein's Imperial Bid

1. Cited in Christopher Sykes, *Two Studies in Virtue* (London: Collins, 1953), p. 171.

2. The Earl of Oxford and Asquith, *Memories and Reflections, 1852–1927* (London: Cassell, 1928), vol. 2, p. 69.

3. For the text of the Russian demand see "Report of the Committee on Asiatic Turkey," June 30, 1915, CAB 27/1, appendix 1, p. 75.

4. Benckendorff to Sazonov, Mar. 3, 1915, telegram 151, in E. Adamov, ed., *Die Europäischen Mächte und die Türkei während des Weltkrieges. Die Aufteilung der Asiatischen Türkei* (Dresden: Carl Reissner, 1932), p. 12; Raymond Poincaré, *Au service de la France, VI: les tranchées* (Paris: Plon, 1930), p. 94; Christopher M. Andrew and A. S. Kanya-Forstner, *France Overseas: The Great War and the Climax of French Imperial Expansion* (London: Thames and Hudson, 1981), p. 65.

5. Viscount Grey of Fallodon, *Twenty-Five Years, 1892–1916* (New York: Frederick Stokes, 1925), vol. 2, p. 188.

6. "Report of the Committee on Asiatic Turkey," p. 1.

7. For the text of the agreement see J. C. Hurewitz, ed., *The Middle East and North Africa in World Politics*, 2nd. rev. ed. (New Haven and London: Yale University Press, 1975–1979), vol. 2, pp. 22–24, especially articles 8–10. For the negotiations preceding Italy's entry into the war, see, for example, Amedeo Giannini, *L'ultima fase della questione orientale, 1913–1932* (Rome: Instituto per L'Oriente, 1933); Grey, *Twenty-Five Years*, pp. 212–213; Asquith, *Memories and Reflections*, vol. 2, p. 69; R. W. Seton-Watson, "Italian Intervention and the Secret Treaty of London," *Slavonic Review*, vol. 5 (1926), pp. 271–297; W. Renzi, "Italy's Neutrality and Entrance into the Great War: A Reexamination," *American Historical Review*, vol. 73 (June 1968), pp. 1414–1432.

8. Grey to Bertie, Mar. 23, 1915, FO 371/2486/34982; "Report of the Committee on Asiatic Turkey," p. 4.

9. "Report of the Committee on Asiatic Turkey," pp. 4, 29.

10. Kitchener to Grey, Feb. 6, Apr. 4, 1914, and to Tyrrell, Apr. 26, 1914, in G. P. Gooch and H. Temperley, eds., *British Documents on the Origins of the War, 1898–1914* (London: HMSO, 1936), vol. 10, part 2, pp. 827, 830–831; Ronald Storrs, *Orientations* (London: Readers Union Limited, 1939), pp. 129–130. For Abdullah's version see Suleiman Musa, *al-Haraka al-Arabiyya: Sirat al-Marhala al-Ula li-l-Nahda al-Arabiyya al-Haditha, 1908–1924* (Beirut: Dar al-Nahar, 1970), pp. 66–72; and his edited volume, *al-Murasalat al-Tarikhiyya 1914–1918: al-Thawra al-Arabiyya al-Kubra* (Amman: Matba'at al-Quwat al-Musallaha, 1973–1975), vol. 1, pp. 21–22.

11. Ronald Storrs, "Note," Apr. 19, 1914, in Cheetham's dispatch on Dec. 13, 1914, FO 371/1973/87396; Storrs, *Orientations*, pp. 129–130; Kitchener to Grey, Apr. 4, 1914, and Kitchener to Tyrrell, Apr. 26, 1914, in Gooch and Temperley, *British Documents on the Origins of the War*, vol. 10, part 2, pp. 830–831. See also Abdullah Ibn Hussein, *Mudhakkirati* (Jerusalem: Matba'at Bait al-Maqdis, 1945), pp. 71–73; Amin Said, *Asrar al-Thawra al-Arabiyya al-Kubra wa Masat al-Sharif Hussein* (Beirut: Dar al-Katib al-Arabi, 1960), p. 35.

12. FO 371/2139/52598, Sept. 24, 1914; Cheetham to Foreign Office, Dec. 13, 1914, FO 371/1973/87396. For slightly different versions of the message see secretary of state to

viceroy, Foreign Department, Dec. 14, 1914, FO 371/2139/83620; Arab Bureau, "Summary of Historical Documents from the Outbreak of War between Great Britain and Turkey [in] 1914 to the Outbreak of the Revolt of the Sharif of Mecca in June 1916," Cairo, Nov. 29, 1916, WO 158/624, p. 24.

13. Arab Bureau, "Summary of Historical Documents," p. 25; Storrs, *Orientations,* p. 159.

14. For conflicting interpretations of the correspondence see, for example, "Report of a Committee Set Up to Consider Certain Correspondence between Sir Henry McMahon and the Sharif of Mecca in 1915 and 1916," Cmd 5974, London, 1939; "Statements Made on Behalf of His Majesty's Government during the Year 1918 in Regard to the Future Status of Certain Parts of the Ottoman Empire," presented by the secretary of state for foreign affairs to Parliament by command of His Majesty, Cmd. 5964, London, 1939; Elie Kedourie, *In the Anglo-Arab Labyrinth: The McMahon-Husayn Correspondence and Its Interpretations, 1914–1939* (Cambridge, England: Cambridge University Press, 1976); A. L. Tibawi, *A Modern History of Syria, Including Lebanon and Palestine* (London: Macmillan, 1969); and Tibawi, *Anglo-Arab Relations and the Question of Palestine, 1914–1921* (London: Luzac, 1977); George Antonius, *The Arab Awakening* (London: Hamish Hamilton, 1938), pp. 9–10; Isaiah Friedman, "The McMahon-Hussein Correspondence and the Question of Palestine," with comments by Arnold Toynbee and a response by the author, *Journal of Contemporary History,* vol. 5, no. 2 (1970), pp. 83–122, and vol. 5, no. 4 (1970), pp. 185–201; Ernest Dawn, *From Ottomanism to Arabism: Essays on the Origins of Arab Nationalism* (Urbana: University of Illinois Press, 1973), chap. 4.

15. Thus a translation of the word from the unofficial Arabic text in Amin Said, *al-Thawra al-Arabiyya al-Kubra* (Cairo: Isa al-Babi al-Halabi, 1951), vol. 1, p. 131. The official British text, as well as Antonius's translation (p. 414), refers to "the Arab countries." Yet the nature of Hussein's ambitions, as expressed both in his correspondence with McMahon and in his activities throughout the war and in its aftermath, leaves little doubt that what he had in mind was a unified "Arab country"—or more precisely an empire—under his sole rule, rather than a confederation of Arab states, let alone independent and unrelated Arab states.

16. "Correspondence between Sir Henry McMahon, His Majesty's High Commissioner at Cairo, and the Sherif of Mecca, July 1915–March 1916, Presented by the Secretary of State for Foreign Affairs to Parliament by Command of His Majesty," Cmd. 5957, London, 1939, p. 3 (hereinafter "Hussein-McMahon Correspondence"), p. 3.

17. Communication by W. Aubry Herbert, MP, to Lord Kitchener, Oct. 30, 1915, FO 371/2486/164659; T. E. Lawrence, "The Politics of Mecca," sent to the Cairo residency on Feb. 1, 1916, and to the Foreign Office on Feb. 7, FO 141/461, fol. 146.

18. McMahon to Grey, May 14, 1915, FO 371/2486/60357; D. G. Hogarth, "Arabs and Turks," *Arab Bulletin,* no. 48, Apr. 21, 1917, FO 882/26.

19. Note by Reginald Wingate, Aug. 25, 1915, FO 371/2486/138500.

20. Memorandum by Sir Thomas Holderness, Jan. 5, 1915, India Office Records, L/P and S/10/523, p. 53/15; Storrs to Fitzgerald, Sept. 6, 1915, PRO 30/57/47, QQ38 (Kitchener Papers); Grey to Bertie, Mar. 23, 1915, and to McMahon, Apr. 14, 1915, FO 371/2486/34982 and 44598; McMahon to Grey, May 14, 1915, FO 371/2486/60357; India Office to Foreign Office, June 24, 1915, FO 371/2486/83311.

21. Storrs's commentary on Hussein's first letter, Aug. 19, 1914, FO 371/2486/125293.

22. "Hussein-McMahon Correspondence," pp. 2–3; Antonius, *The Arab Awakening*, appendix A, no. 2, pp. 415–416.

23. "Hussein-McMahon Correspondence," pp. 5–7.

24. Ibid., pp. 8–9.

25. Grey to McMahon, Oct. 20, 1915, FO 371/2486/155203.

26. "Hussein-McMahon Correspondence," pp. 9–11.

27. Ibid., pp. 11–12.

28. Ibid., p. 13.

29. Ibid., p. 14.

30. McMahon to Grey, Oct. 26, 1915, FO 371/2486/163832.

31. Storrs, *Orientations,* p. 160.

32. Gilbert Clayton, "Memorandum Regarding Various Conversations Held with a Certain Mulasim Awal (Lieutenant) Mohammed Sherif El Farugi," Oct. 11, 1915, FO 371/2486/157740, and "Statement of Mulasim Awal (Lieutenant) Mohammed Sherif El Farugi," ibid.

33. Eliezer Tauber, *The Arab Movements in World War I* (London: Frank Cass, 1993), p. 113.

34. Clayton, "Memorandum," fol. 227.

35. Ibid., fol. 228.

36. Maxwell to Kitchener, Oct. 12, 16, 1915, FO 371/2486/150309/152729.

37. McMahon to Grey, Oct. 18, 1915, FO 371/2486/153045. See also his telegram on Oct. 26, ibid.

38. Storrs to Fitzgerald, Oct. 12, 1915, PRO 30/57/47, Kitchener Papers, QQ/46.

39. Kitchener to Maxwell, Oct. 13, 1915, FO 371/2486/150309.

40. Comments by George Clerk on Maxwell's letters, Oct. 19, 1915, FO 371/2486/152901.

41. Ibid.

42. McMahon to Grey, Oct. 26, 1915, FO 371/2486/158561.

43. Arab Bureau, "Summary of Historical Documents," p. 78.

15. Dividing the Bear's Skin

1. For the British account of the Nov. 23, 1915, meeting see "Results of Second Meeting of Committee to Discuss Arab Question and Syria," Nov. 23, 1915, FO 882/2; for the French account see Ministry of Foreign Affairs, Series A: Peace, 129.

2. For the British account of the Dec. 21, 1915, meeting see FO 371/2486/196223; for the French account see Cambon to Briand, Dec. 22, 1915, Ministry of Foreign Affairs, ibid.

3. For the text of the Sykes-Picot Agreement, as well as a memorandum by Sykes and Picot accompanying their draft agreement, see CAB 42/11/9. Subsequent quotations are from this same source.

4. "Brigadier-General Macdonough to Sir Arthur Nicolson. (Received January 7)."

5. "Sir T. Holderness to Sir A. Nicolson. (Received January 13); "Note by Sir A.

Hirtzel," Jan. 10, 1916; Captain Hall to Sir A. Nicolson. (Received January 13); all in CAB 42/11/9.

6. See "Arab Proposals. Amended Version," CAB 42/11/9; Nicolson's committee meeting, Jan. 21, 1916, FO 371/2767.

7. For the full text of the modified Sykes-Picot Agreement and the Sazonov-Paléologue and Grey-Cambon-Benckendorff correspondence, see DBFP, vol. 4, pp. 241–251.

8. George Antonius, *The Arab Awakening* (London: Hamish Hamilton, 1938), pp. 248–249.

9. In 1924 *The Last Crusade* was developed into the book *With Lawrence in Arabia* (New York and London: The Century Co., 1924).

10. See in particular Elie Kedourie's *England and the Middle East: The Destruction of the Ottoman Empire, 1914—1921* (London: Bowes and Bowes, 1956), and *In the Anglo-Arab Labyrinth: The McMahon-Husayn Correspondence and Its Interpretations, 1914–1939* (Cambridge, England: Cambridge University Press, 1976).

11. McMahon's letter of Dec. 14, 1915, "Correspondence between Sir Henry McMahon, His Majesty's High Commissioner at Cairo, and the Sherif of Mecca, July 1915–March 1916, Presented by the Secretary of State for Foreign Affairs to Parliament by Command of His Majesty," Cmd. 5957, London, 1939 (hereinafter "Hussein-McMahon Correspondence"), p. 12 (emphasis added). See also his letter from Jan. 25, 1916: "We are greatly pleased to hear of the action you are taking to win *all the Arabs* over to our joint cause, and to dissuade them from giving any assistance to our enemies." Ibid., p. 14 (emphasis added).

12. Albert Hourani, *The Emergence of the Modern Middle East* (London: Macmillan, 1981), pp. 209–210.

13. Viscount Grey of Fallodon, *Twenty-Five Years, 1892–1916* (New York: Frederick Stokes, 1925), vol. 2, p. 236; "Report of the Committee on Asiatic Turkey," June 30, 1915, CAB 27/1, pp. 3, 5.

14. Grey, *Twenty-Five Years,* vol. 2, p. 237.

15. Hussein's letter to McMahon of July 14, 1915, "Hussein-McMahon Correspondence," pp. 3–4.

16. McMahon's letter of Oct. 24, 1915; Hussein's letter of Nov. 5, 1915, ibid., pp. 8, 11.

17. Clayton to Foreign Office, May 3, 1916, FO 882/2; Hogarth to Hall, May 3, 1916, FO 882/14; McMahon to Foreign Office, May 4, 1916, FO 371/2768/84855; David Garnett, ed., *The Letters of T. E. Lawrence* (London: Spring Books, 1964; originally published by Jonathan Cape in 1938), pp. 281–282.

The four documents were McMahon's promises to Hussein of October 24, 1915; the Sykes-Picot Agreement; the British statement to seven Syrian nationalists in Cairo dated June 11, 1917; and the Anglo-French Declaration of November 9, 1918.

18. Hussein's letter to McMahon, Sept. 9, 1915, "Hussein-McMahon Correspondence," pp. 6–7.

19. Kedourie, *In the Anglo-Arab Labyrinth,* p. 155.

20. FO 882/16.

21. Sykes to War Office, Apr. 30, 1917, FO 882/16. For Picot's report of the meeting, see his telegram of May 2, 1917, Ministry of Foreign Affairs, War, 1914–1918, vol. 877.

22. Wingate to Foreign Office, May 7, 1917, reporting Sykes's telegram from Jeddah of the previous day, FO 371/3054/93335; *Arab Bulletin,* no. 50, May 13, 1917, p. 207.

23. For accounts of these meetings see Sykes's telegram of May 24, 1917, FO 371/3054/104269; "Note by Sheikh Fuad El Khatib Taken Down by Lt Col. Newcombe," FO 882/16; Picot's telegram of May 24, 1917, Ministry of Foreign Affairs, War, 1914–1918, vol. 877.

24. Memorandum by Sir Mark Sykes, June 1918, FO 371/3381/107379; "Note by Sheikh Fuad El Khatib." On the basis of his talk with al-Khatib shortly after the meetings, Newcombe wrote that "nothing was written and the Sherif has no copy of the Sykes-Picot agreement: the full text of which he was apparently told yesterday and asked to give a final decision upon at a moment's notice." Note by Lt. Colonel Newcombe D.S.O., May 20, 1917, FO 882/16.

25. Colonel Wilson, interview with King Hussein at British Agency, Jeddah, July 18, 1918, FO 686/9.

26. McMahon's letters of Oct. 24 and Dec. 24, 1915, "Hussein-McMahon Correspondence," pp. 8, 12.

27. McMahon's letter of Oct. 24, 1915, ibid., p. 8.

28. H. W. Young, "Foreign Office Memorandum on Possible Negotiations with the Hedjaz," Nov. 29, 1920, FO 371/5066/14959, especially paragraphs 9–12.

29. "Report of Conversation between Mr. R. C. Lindsay, C.V.O., Representing the Secretary of State for Foreign Affairs, and His Highness the Emir Feisal, Representing the King of the Hedjaz. (Held at the Foreign Office on Thursday, January 20, 1921)," CO 732/3, fol. 366.

Faisal's reasoning was incorporated into Antonius's *The Arab Awakening,* p. 178, almost verbatim.

30. CO 732/3, fol. 366.

31. McMahon to Shuckburgh, Mar. 12, 1922, FO 371/7797/E2821.

32. "Report of a Committee Set Up to Consider Certain Correspondence between Sir Henry McMahon [His Majesty's High Commissioner in Egypt] and the Sharif of Mecca in 1915 and 1916," Mar. 16, 1939, London, Cmd. 5974, p. 9.

33. T. E. Lawrence, "Syria: The Raw Material" (written early in 1915 but not circulated), *Arab Bulletin,* no. 44, Mar. 12, 1917, FO/882/26, pp. 74–75.

34. "Memorandum," Oct. 11, 1915, FO 371/2486/157740.

35. McMahon to Grey, Nov. 20, 1915, reporting Sykes's conversation with Faruqi, FO 371/2486/175418.

36. Maxwell to Kitchener, Oct. 16, 1915, FO 371/2486/152729.

37. McMahon to Grey, Nov. 7, 1915, FO 371/2486/166819. See also McMahon's letter to Grey of Oct. 26, 1915, FO 371/2486/163832.

38. Memorandum by W. Aubrey Herbert, M.P., Oct. 30, 1914, FO 371/2486/164659.

39. Nicolson to Grey, Feb. 2, 1916, CAB 42/11/9.

40. War Committee Meeting, Mar. 23, 1916, CAB 42/11/9.

41. Kedourie, *In the Anglo-Arab Labyrinth,* pp. 87–88.

42. FO 608/107, file 384/16.

43. Kedourie, *In the Anglo-Arab Labyrinth,* pp. 87–88, 211.

44. "Hussein-McMahon Correspondence," p. 8.

45. McMahon to Grey, Oct. 26, 1915, FO 371/2486/163832.

46. "Report of the Committee on Asiatic Turkey," p. 3.

47. Ibid., p. 28.

48. McMahon to Grey, Nov. 19, 1915, FO 371/2486/175418.

49. Hussein's letter of Nov. 5, 1915, "Hussein-McMahon Correspondence," p. 9.

50. McMahon's letter of Dec. 14, 1915, ibid., pp. 11–12.

16. The Balfour Declaration

1. Briand to Paléologue, Mar. 25, 1916, and Paléologue to Briand, Apr. 19, 1916, Ministry of Foreign Affairs, Paléologue MSS 3.

2. Arthur S. Link, trans. and ed., *The Deliberations of the Council of Four (March 24–June 28, 1919), Notes of the Official Interpreter Paul Mantoux* (Princeton, N.J.: Princeton University Press, 1992), vol. 2, p. 163; "Notes of an Anglo-French Meeting Held at the Foreign Office, London, at 3 P.M. on December 23, 1919," in DBFP, vol. 4, p. 599.

3. Herbert Samuel, *Memoirs* (London: The Crescent Press, 1945), pp. 140–141.

4. The Earl of Oxford and Asquith, *Memories and Reflections, 1852–1927* (London: Cassell, 1928), pp. 59–60; M. Brock and E. Brock, eds., *H. H. Asquith: Letters to Venetia Stanley* (Oxford: Oxford University Press, 1982), p. 477.

5. CAB 42/11/9 (emphasis in the original).

6. This is not to say that there was no general awareness within the Foreign Office of the divisions within Jewry over the question of Palestine. After all, the most implacable foe of Zionism in the British cabinet was Edwin Montague, himself a Jew.

7. Minute by Hugh O'Beirne, Mar. 8, 1916, FO 371/2817.

8. Telegram to Bertie (Paris) and Buchanan (St. Petersburg), Mar. 11, 1916, FO 37/2817. See also FO 371/2671/35933.

9. Telegram to Bertie (Paris) and Buchanan (St. Petersburg), Mar. 11, 1916, FO 37/2817; Briand to Bertie, Mar. 21, 1916, FO 800/176; War Committee meeting of Mar. 23, 1916, CAB 42/1/9; FO 371/2671/35933.

10. David Lloyd George, *Memoirs of the Peace Conference* (New Haven: Yale University Press, 1939), vol. 2, pp. 650, 664–665.

11. House of Lords Record Office, Beaverbrook Collection, Lloyd George Papers, F-6-1 (documents 1–16b).

12. Imperial War Cabinet, "Report of Committee on Terms of Peace, 28 April 1917," CAB 21/77.

13. Apr. 3, 1917, CAB 24/9, fos. 306–308.

14. Asquith, *Memories and Reflections,* p. 66.

15. Weizmann to Zangwill, Oct. 19, 1914, in Leonard Stein, ed., *The Letters and Papers of Chaim Weizmann* (Oxford: Oxford University Press; and Jerusalem: Israel Universities Press, 1975), vol. 7, series A, no. 22, pp. 25–26.

16. Graham to Hardinge, June 13, 1917, FO 371/3058; War Cabinet 261, Oct. 31, 1917, CAB 21/58; "Appendix II: Draft Declarations," FO 371/3395, fols. 289–291.

17. Foreign Relations of the United States, *Paris Peace Conference 1919* (Washington, D.C.: Government Printing Office, 1942–47), vol. 4, pp. 163–164 (hereinafter *FRUS—Peace Conference*).

18. Ibid., pp. 161–162.

19. "Memorandum by Mr. Balfour (Paris) respecting Syria, Palestine, and Mesopotamia," Aug. 11, 1919, DBFP, vol. 4, p. 347; Balfour to Curzon, July 2, 1919, ibid., p. 302.

20. "Notes of an Anglo-French Meeting Held at the Foreign Office, London, at 11:30 A.M., on December 23, 1919," and "Notes of an Anglo-French Meeting Held at the Foreign Office, London, at 3 P.M. on December 23, 1919," ibid., pp. 598–599.

21. "British Secretary's Notes of a Meeting of the Supreme Council, Held at the Villa Devochon, San Remo, on Saturday, April 24, 1920, at 4 P.M.," DBFP, vol. 8, pp. 160–162, 168.

22. Ibid., pp. 160–163, 166.

23. Treaty of Sèvres, article 95. For the text of the Treaty of Sevrès see J. C. Hurewitz, *The Middle East and North Africa in World Politics*, 2nd. rev. ed. (New Haven and London: Yale University Press, 1975–1979), vol. 2, pp. 81–89.

17. The Undoing of the Sykes-Picot Agreement

1. Wingate to Foreign Office (enclosing Clayton's letter), Nov. 28, 1917, telegram 1281, FO 371/3054.

2. Cited in David Fromkin, *A Peace to End All Peace: The Fall of the Ottoman Empire and the Creation of the Modern Middle East* (New York: Avon, 1990), pp. 342–343.

3. Minute by H. W. Young, Sept. 20, 1919, FO 371/4183/131671.

4. David Garnett, ed., *The Essential Lawrence* (Oxford: Oxford University Press, 1992; first published in 1951), p. 76.

5. T. E. Lawrence, "Reconstruction of Arabia," Nov. 4, 1918 (memorandum prepared for the Eastern Committee), in Garnett, ed., *The Letters of T. E. Lawrence* (London: Spring Books, 1964; first published in 1938 by Jonathan Cape), pp. 268–269.

6. Ibid.; Minutes of the 37th Meeting of the Eastern Committee of the War Cabinet, Nov. 29, 1918, CAB 27/24 (1918), pp. 148–152.

7. Sykes to Wingate, Mar. 3, 1918, FO 800/221.

8. Mark Sykes, "Memorandum on the Asia-Minor Agreement," Aug. 14, 1917, FO 371/3059/159558.

9. Memorandum by Sir M. Sykes, enclosing the two papers, July 3, 1918, FO 371/3381.

10. H. W. V. Temperley, ed., *A History of the Peace Conference of Paris* (London: Henry Frowde and Hodder and Stoughton, 1924), vol. 6, pp. 140–141.

11. Allenby insisted that "Beirut must remain completely under my control," and he received the Foreign Office's backing to use "tact and judgment" to make sure it did. See Allenby to War Office, Oct. 19, 22, 1918, FO 371/3384/175481 and 175365.

12. On the relationship between Allenby and Faisal see, for example, Allenby to Faisal, Oct. 13, 1918, FO 371/3384/175365; Faisal to Allenby, Nov. 2, 1918, and Allenby's response, FO 371/3384/182643; Allenby to War Office, Oct. 21, 1918, FO 371/3384/177569; FO to Clayton, to be delivered to Faisal, Oct. 12, 1918, FO 371/3384/172123.

13. See, for example, F. Georges-Picot's telegram of Nov. 14, 1918, in E. Brémond, *Le Hedjaz dans la Guerre Mondiale* (Paris: Payot, 1931), p. 308.

14. Clemenceau to Lloyd George, Nov. 9, 1919, in DBFP, vol. 4, p. 521.

15. Fromkin, *A Peace to End All Peace,* p. 257.

16. "Draft Resolutions in Reference to Mandatories," Foreign Relations of the United States, *Paris Peace Conference 1919* (Washington, D.C.: Government Printing Office, 1942–1947), vol. 3, pp. 795–796 (hereinafter *FRUS—Peace Conference).* These principles were subsequently incorporated into Article 22 of the League of Nations' Covenant.

17. Ibid., vol. 5, pp. 3–4.

18. *Lord Riddell's Intimate Diary of the Peace Conference and After, 1918–1923* (London: Victor Gollancz, 1933), entry for Apr. 27, 1919, p. 60; David Lloyd George, *Memoirs of the Peace Conference* (New Haven: Yale University Press, 1939), vol. 2, p. 818.

19. *FRUS—Peace Conference,* vol. 11, pp. 133–134, American Commissioners Plenipotentiary, Mar. 27, 1919.

20. Minutes of the meeting of the Council of Four, Apr. 22, 1919, ibid., vol. 5, p. 112; Arthur S. Link, trans. and ed., *The Deliberations of the Council of Four (March 24—June 28, 1919), Notes of the Official Interpreter Paul Mantoux* (Princeton, N.J.: Princeton University Press, 1992), vol. 2, pp. 137–138.

21. Articles 88, 94, 98. The mandatory was to be selected by the Principal Allied Powers at a later date, though this issue had already been closed at the London and San Remo conferences, where Britain had received the mandates for Palestine and Mesopotamia, and France for Syria and Lebanon.

22. At the same time, the Principal Allied Powers agreed not to object to the voluntary adhesion to such an independent Kurdish State of the Kurds inhabiting the part of Kurdistan that had hitherto been included in the velayet of Mosul.

18. Losing Syria

1. "It is true that in my meeting with Mr. Storrs in the first year at Jeddah, also in my subsequent meeting with the distinguished Sir Mark Sykes, and last year with the eminent Commander Hogarth, I found nothing contrary to, or departing from, the said decisions," Hussein wrote to Wingate on August 28, 1918. "Papers Relating to King Hussein's Version of His Agreements with His Majesty's Government," encl. 1 in no. 1, FO 371/3384/183342.

2. Ibid., encl. 2 in no. 1.

3. "Notes of a Meeting Held at 10 Downing Street, S.W., on Friday, September 19, 1919, at 4 P.M.," in DBFP, vol. 4, pp. 399–403.

4. "Notes of a Meeting Held at 10 Downing Street, S.W., on Tuesday, September 23, 1919, at 12 Noon," ibid., pp. 414–415.

5. For the exchange of letters between Faisal and Hussein see ibid., pp. 411, 424–425, 440–442.

6. "Meeting of Sir Edmund Allenby and the Emir Feisal at the Hotel Victoria, Damascus, on Oct. 3rd, 1918" (extract from letter from H. Chauvel to Lord Allenby, dated Jan. 1, 1936), Allenby Collection, DS 997.58, Liddell Hart Centre for Military Archives, King's College London; "Beirut, Personal Letter to Lady Allenby (Haifa)," Oct. 7, 1918, Allenby Collection, DR 588; T. E. Lawrence, *Seven Pillars of Wisdom: A Triumph* (Garden City, N.Y.: Doubleday, 1935), p. 555.

7. "Secretary's Notes of a Conversation Held in M. Pichon's Room at the Quai

d'Orsay, Paris, on Thursday, 6 February 1919, at 3 P.M.," Foreign Relations of the United States, *Paris Peace Conference, 1919* (Washington, D.C.: Government Printing Office, 1942–1947), vol. 3, p. 891 (hereinafter *FRUS—Peace Conference);* David Lloyd George, *Memoirs of the Peace Conference* (New Haven: Yale University Press, 1939), vol. 2, p. 668.

8. Lawrence, "Minute, March 10, 1919," FO 608/105.

9. "Secretary's Notes of a Conversation Held in M. Pichon's Room at the Quai d'Orsay, Paris, on Thursday, 6 February 1919, at 3 P.M.", *FRUS—Peace Conference,* vol. 3, pp. 889, 890, 892.

10. "Memorandum by the Emir Feisal, 1 January 1919," in FO 608/80; and in David Hunter Miller, *My Diary at the Conference of Paris, with Documents* (New York: Appeal Printing Co., 1928), vol. 4, pp. 297–299.

11. Zeine N. Zeine, *The Struggle for Arab Independence* (Beirut: Khayat's, 1960), p. 50.

12. See reports by Clayton, Oct. 15, 31, 1918, FO 371/3384/173729 and 181781. See also report by Forbes-Adam (Paris), Sept. 26, 1919, DBFP, vol. 4, pp. 439–440; Khairiyya Qasmiyya, *al-Hukuma al-Arabiyya fi Dimashq bayna 1918–1920* (Cairo: Dar al-Ma'arif, 1971), p. 64.

13. Abu Khaldun Sati al-Husri, *Yawm Maisalun: Safha min Tarikh al-Arab al-Hadith,* rev. ed. (Beirut: Dar al-Ittihad, 1964), p. 261.

14. Eliezer Tauber, *The Formation of Modern Syria and Iraq* (London: Frank Cass, 1995), p. 15, sets the number of activists at 169; Khairiyya Qasmiyya, *al-Hukuma al-Arabiyya fi Dimashq bayna 1918–1920* (Cairo: Dar al-Ma'arif, 1971), p. 67, fn. 2, gives the somewhat higher figure of 202. Even the Independence Party (Hizb al-Istiqlal), established in February 1919 as the external and public organ of al-Fatat, included no more than 2,500 activists and some 20,000 sympathizers (Tauber, ibid., p. 50)—hardly a mass movement.

15. "Report by British Liaison Officer on Political Situation in Arabia," Damascus, May 16, 1919, DBFP, vol. 4, p. 264. For the complete memorandum submitted by the congress to the commission see al-Husri, *Yawm Maisalun,* pp. 262–264.

16. "Report of the American Section of the International Commission on Mandates in Turkey, Submitted by the Commissioners Charles R. King and Henry Churchill Crane, Paris, August 28, 1919, 'Confidential Appendix—The Interference of the Occupying Governments with the Commission's Inquiry,'" *FRUS—Peace Conference,* vol. 12, pp. 848–850 (hereinafter "King-Crane Report").

17. Ibid., pp. 780–781.

18. "M. Clemenceau to the Emir Feisal," Apr. 17, 1919; "The Emir Feisal to M. Clemenceau," Apr. 20, 1919; Clayton to Foreign Office, May 21, 1919, reporting a conversation with Faisal the previous day; all in DBFP, vol. 4, pp. 252–253, 265, fn 3.

19. Clayton to Curzon, June 23, 1919, reporting several conversations held by himself and Allenby with Faisal, DBFP, vol. 4, p. 291; Lawrence's minute of May 1, 1919, and Derby to Curzon, Apr. 18, 1919, FO 608/93/360-1-8/7735; Lawrence's minute of May 3, 1919, FO 608/93, fol. 197; Balfour to Curzon, May 5, 1919, FO 608/93/8810; Clayton to Foreign Office, May 21, 1919, DBFP, vol. 4, p. 265, fn 3.

20. Miller, *My Diary,* vol. 1, p. 74; William Yale, "Notes on a Conversation with Emir Faisal on Feb. 13th [1919]," Yale Papers, DR 588.5, Middle East Centre, St. Antony's College, Oxford University.

21. The United States Intelligence Report, Jan. 21, 1919, in Miller, *My Diary*, vol. 4, doc. 246, pp. 260–267; Elie Kedourie, *England and the Middle East: The Destruction of the Ottoman Empire, 1914–1921* (London: Bowes and Bowes, 1956), p. 147.

22. Allenby to Balfour, May 30, 1919, DBFP, vol. 4, p. 256; Balfour to Allenby, telegrams 48 and 49 of May 31, 1919, ibid., p. 259; Clayton to Curzon (reporting Faisal's response), June 15, 1919, ibid., p. 277.

23. Faisal to Lloyd George, Oct. 9, 1919; Lloyd George to Faisal, Oct. 10, 1919; Curzon to Faisal, Oct. 9, 1919, Curzon to Derby, Oct. 16, 1919; all in ibid., pp. 443, 448, 451, 475.

24. Faisal to Lloyd George, Nov. 6, 21, 1919, DBFP, vol. 4, pp. 510–511, 545–546.

25. Clemenceau to Lloyd George, Nov. 9, 1919; "Minute by Mr. Forbes-Adams," Nov. 7, 1919, all in ibid., pp. 510–511, 522, 528–529, 545–546.

26. For the text of the Faisal-Clemenceau agreement, see Vansittart to Curzon, Jan. 17, 1920, no. 416, encl. 1 and 2, ibid., pp. 624–627. See also Derby to Curzon, Jan. 8, 1920; Forbes-Adams to Young, Jan. 12, 1920; Meinertzhagen to Curzon, Jan. 26, 1920, all in ibid., pp. 611–613, 629–630.

27. Husri, *Yawm Maisalun*, pp. 234–236; Ahmad Qadri, *Mudhakkirati an al-Thawra al-Arabiyya al-Kubra* (Damascus: Matabi Ibn Zaidun, 1956), pp. 153, 161, 175–176; Meinertzhagen to Curzon, Jan. 26, 1920, DBFP, vol. 4, pp. 629–630.

28. Meinertzhagen to Curzon, Oct. 21, 1919, DBFP, vol. 4, p. 500.

29. Meinertzhagen to Curzon, Oct. 21, Nov. 10, Dec. 2 (enclosing Clayton's letter), Jan. 13, 1920, DBFP, vol. 4, pp. 495, 523, 565–566.

30. Meinertzhagen to Curzon, Jan. 13, 1920, DBFP, vol. 4, p. 615; Meinertzhagen to Curzon, Feb. 19, 1920 (enclosing Faisal's letter), DBFP, vol. 13, p. 218.

31. For the text of the proclamation of Syrian independence and the attendant correspondence, see al-Husri, *Yawm Maisalun*, pp. 278–288.

32. Al-Said made this claim at a meeting in London with Hubert Young. See Young's report, "Situation in Syria," Apr. 1, 1920, FO 371/5034/E2681.

33. Curzon to Allenby, Mar. 13, 1920, DBFP, vol. 13, p. 225.

34. Allenby to Curzon, Mar. 18, 1920, ibid., p. 231.

35. Curzon to Allenby, Mar. 19, 1920, ibid., pp.fl231–232.

36. Allenby to Curzon, Mar. 20, 1920; Curzon to Allenby, Mar. 22, 1920; "Record by Earl Curzon of a Conversation with the French Ambassador on the Syrian Question," Mar. 30, 1920; memoranda by the French ambassador, Apr. 1, 7, 1920, all in DBFP, vol. 13, pp. 233–235, 237–240, 247–248.

37. A vivid illustration of Faisal's dependence on the Syrian Congress was provided by his encounter with the renowned nationalist thinker Rashid Rida, who in May 1920 became the president of the congress. When Faisal protested against the congress's call to submit his administration to a vote of confidence, claiming that he had created the congress and would concede to it nothing that might impede the functioning of the government, he was bluntly told that, on the contrary, it was the congress that had created him, for he had been one of many generals under Allenby's command, and the congress had made him the king of Syria. *Al-Manar*, vol. 23, no. 5, May 27, 1922, pp. 392–393.

38. See, for example, letter from Faisal to Allenby, mid-Feb. 1920, DBFP, vol. 13, p. 218; Faisal to Curzon, Mar. 28, 1920, ibid., p. 246; Curzon to Hardinge, Apr. 26, 1920, ibid.,

pp. 251–252; official British message to Faisal, Apr. 27, 1920, and Faisal's reply, May 13, 1920, ibid., pp. 252–253, 257–258; Allenby to Curzon, June 9, 1920, enclosing Faisal's response to French Premier Millerand of May 13, ibid., p. 285.

39. "Note from Earl Curzon to French Ambassador," May 18, 1920, and "Note from the French Ambassador to Earl Curzon," May 25, 1920, enclosing Prime Minister Millerand's reply and a proposed joint declaration to Faisal, ibid., pp. 271–272, 278–282. For the text of the ultimatum see "Note adressé le 14 Juillet 1920 par le Gènèral Gouraud Haut Commissaire de la Rèpublique Francaise en Syrie et en Cilicie et Commandant en Chef de l'Armée du Levant à son Altesse Royale l'Emir Faisal," FO 371/5038.

19. A Kingdom for Faisal

1. Ibrahim to Muhammad Ali, Ramadan 13, 1248 (Aug. 10, 1832), Abd. case 243, doc. 85, in Asad J. Rustum, *The Royal Archives of Egypt and the Origins of the Egyptian Expedition to Syria* (Beirut: American University of Beirut, 1936), p. 59; Abd al-Razaq al-Hasani, *Ta'rikh al-Wizarat al-Iraqiyya* (Sidon: Matba'at al-Ifran, 1939), pp. 189–195.

2. "Administration of Mesopotamia" (note by Political Department, India Office, Oct. 1918), FO 371/3381, fols. 185–186.

3. Wilson to Montague, Mar. 21, 1920, FO 371/5071/E2180, fol. 127. See also Wilson to India Office, telegrams 7725 and 8075 of Sept. 15, 27, 1918, FO 371/3381, fols. 183–184; Wilson to Montagu, Feb. 13, 1920, ADD 52455 C, Sir Arnold Wilson Papers (The British Library).

4. "Despatch from Civil Commissioner, Mesopotamia, to Secretary of State for India," Nov. 15, 1919, FO 371/5071/E2180, fols. 132–133.

5. Arnold T. Wilson, *Loyalties, Mesopotamia, Vol. II: 1917–1920* (London: Oxford University Press, 1931), pp. 104, 338; Lady Bell, ed., *The Letters of Gertrude Bell* (New York: Boni and Liveright, n.d.), vol. 2, p. 464.

6. Wilson, *Loyalties,* vol. 2, pp. 115–118, 123.

7. "Conclusions of a Meeting of the Cabinet Held at 10 Downing Street, S.W.1, on Thursday, March 23, 1920, at 11:30 A.M.," CAB 16 (20), fol. 254.

8. House of Commons, *The Parliamentary Debates: Official Report, Fifth Series—Volume 127. Third Volume of Session 1920,* p. 664; *The Parliamentary Debates: Official Report, Fifth Series—Volume 129. Fifth Volume of Session 1920,* p. 2067.

9. Conclusions of the cabinet meeting of Mar. 23, 1920, fol. 254.

10. Gertrude L. Bell, "Syria in October 1919," FO 371/5071/E2180, fol. 135; C. C. Garbett to Montague, Sept. 24, 1920, FO 371/5231/E12841, fols. 23–23A; Lawrence to Churchill, Apr. 15, 1921, forwarded in Allenby's telegram 240 to Curzon, FO 371/6350, fol. 154.

11. *Arab Bulletin,* June 24, 1919, no. 112, FO 882/28; Amin Said, *al-Thawra al-Arabiyya al-Kubra* (Cairo: Isa al-Babi al-Halabi, 1951), vol. 2, part 2, pp. 21–23; Hubert Young, *The Independent Arab* (London: John Murray, 1933), pp. 286–287.

12. David Garnett, ed., *The Letters of T. E. Lawrence* (London: Spring Books, 1964; first published in 1938 by Jonathan Cape), pp. 290–291.

13. Curzon to Clayton, in DBFP, vol. 4, p. 296; "Note by Sir A. Hirtzel," Nov. 3, 1919, FO 371/5071/E2180, fols. 130–131.

14. Wilson to Montagu, Mar. 25, 1920, Wilson Papers, 52455C/1066E (The British Library); Wilson to Hirtzel, Mar. 31, 1920, FO 371/5228.

15. Wilson to Montagu, June 9, 1920, tel. 6948, CAB 24/107, CP 1475, fol. 287.

16. Cabinet, Finance Committee, "Conclusions of a Meeting Held at 10 Downing Street, S.W. on Monday, February 9, 1920, at 5.0 P.M.," CAB 23/20, fols. 177–179; "Appreciation of the Mesopotamia-Persia Situation by Sir Percy Cox," July 24, 1920, FO 371/5231/E13975, fols. 143–144.

17. "Draft of Telegram from Secretary of State for India, to Civil Commissioner Mesopotamia," June 17, 1920, in "Conclusion of a Conference of Ministers Held at 10 Downing Street, S.W. on Thursday, 17th June, 1920, at 11.30 A.M.," CAB 23/22, fols. 218–219; "Conclusions of a Conference of Ministers Held in Mr. Bonar Law's Room at the House of Commons, S.W., on Friday, June 18th 1920 at 11 A.M.," CAB 23/21, fols. 303, 309.

18. Garnett, *The Letters of T. E. Lawrence*, pp. 307–308.

19. "English King for Arabs? Colonel Lawrence on Mesopotamia: Simple Solution: Blunders of British Administration" (article based on an interview with Lawrence), *Daily News* (London), Aug. 25, 1920.

20. H. Garland (acting director, Arab Bureau), "Conversation with Sheikh Abdul Melik El Khatib, Hejaz Agent in Egypt," Aug. 25, 1920, dispatched by Ernest Scott (acting high commissioner, Egypt) to Lord Curzon, Aug. 25, 1920, FO 371/5040/E10953, fols. 7–9.

21. Ibid.

22. Samuel to Foreign Office, tel. 175, Aug. 3, 1920, and Foreign Office to Samuel, tel. 69, Aug. 5, FO 371/5038/E9355, fols. 106–107.

23. Faisal to Lloyd George, Sept. 11, 1920, and "Note to H.B.M.'s Government on the Arab Question: Memo. on Events in Syria, November 1919 to July 1920," FO 371/5040.

24. "The Arab Question," FO 371/5040/E1150, fol. 78.

25. Haddad to Cornwallis, Oct. 8, 1920, FO 371/5065, fol. 17.

26. Curzon to Derby (Paris), Nov. 16, 1920, FO 371/6350, fol. 163.

27. "Appreciation of the Mesopotamia-Persia Situation by Sir Percy Cox," fol. 144.

28. Wilson, *Loyalties*, vol. 2, p. 306.

29. "Mesopotamia—Appointment of Sir Percy Cox as High Commissioner: Instructions of His Majesty's Government," original draft as submitted to the cabinet, Aug. 5, 1920, FO 371/5229, fols. 134–135. See also "Conclusions of a Meeting of the Finance Committee Held at 10 Downing Street, S.W.1., on Thursday, August 12th, 1920, at 5 P.M.," CAB 23/22, Finance Committee 27, fols. 128–131; "Conclusions of a Meeting of the Cabinet, Held at 10 Downing Street, S.W.1., on Tuesday, August 17th, 1920, at 12 noon," ibid., cabinet 49 (20), fol. 124.

30. Cox to Montagu, Dec. 26, 1920, FO 371/6349, fol. 104. See also his telegram from Jan. 2, 1921, ibid., fol. 105.

31. "Conclusions of a Meeting Held at 10 Downing Street, S.W. on Tuesday, 4th January, 1921, at 5.30 P.M.," CAB 23/24, cabinet 1 (21), fols. 4–5. On Faisal's London meetings see "Minute by Secretary of State on the Negotiations with Feisal," Jan. 13, 1921, CO 732/3, fol. 360; "Record of Conversation between Earl Curzon and the Emir Feisal," ibid., fols. 368–369; "Report of Conversation between Sir J. Tilley, K.C.M.G., C.B.,

Representing the Secretary of State for Foreign Affairs, and His Highness the Emir Feisal, Representing the King of the Hedjaz (Held at the Foreign Office on Thursday, December 23, 1920)," ibid., fols. 369–370; "Report of Conversation between Mr. R. C. Lindsay, C.V.O., Representing the Secretary of State for Foreign Affairs, and His Highness the Emir Feisal, Representing the King of the Hedjaz (Held at the Foreign Office on Thursday, January 20, 1921)," ibid., fols. 366–367.

For French pressures see the conversation between de Fleuriau and Sir Eyre Crowe on Jan. 7, 1921, FO 371/6349/E469, fols. 77–78; Curzon to Hardinge (Paris), Jan. 24, 1921, FO 371/6350/E1090/4/91, fol. 165.

32. Lord Curzon, "Instructions to Mr. Cornwallis regarding his Interview with Emir Feisal," Jan. 7, 1921, FO 371/6349/E583, fols. 91–93.

33. "Conversation with Sheikh Abdul Melik El Khatib."

34. Cornwallis, "Note of an Interview with Emir Feisal on 8.1.21," FO 371/6349, fol. 96.

35. "Minute by Secretary of State on the Negotiations with Feisal," fol. 362; Curzon to Allenby, Mar. 22, 1920, DBFP, vol. 13, p. 235; Curzon to Cox (via India Office), Jan. 9, and Cox to Curzon, Jan. 11, 1921, FO 371/6349/E557, fols. 81–83.

36. Curzon to Churchill, Jan. 9, 1921, Churchill to Cox, Jan. 8, 1921, Martin Gilbert, *Winston S. Churchill* (London: Heinemann, 1977), companion vol. 4/2, pp. 1297–1298.

37. Gilbert, *Winston S. Churchill*, pp. 1295, 1300, 1301, 1314.

38. "Conclusions of a Meeting Held at 10 Downing Street, S.W. on Monday, 14th February, 1921, at 12 Noon," CAB 23/24, fol. 80.

39. Lawrence, undated note on a conversation with Faisal, CO 732/3/9836, fol. 402.

40. For the original draft in Lawrence's and Young's handwriting, see "Conference at Cairo—Agenda & Minutes Thereon," CO 732/4/17262, fols. 133–162 (Churchill's draft agenda of Feb. 18, 1921, fols. 134–136; Departmental view on Mesopotamia, fols. 145–154). For the final, slightly revised draft see "Report on Middle East Conference Held in Cairo and Jerusalem, Mar. 12th to 30th, 1921," FO 371/6343, appendix 2, fols. 27–33.

41. For the proceedings of the meeting, see CO 732/3, fols. 409–412. See also "Sherifian Policy in Mesopotamia & Trans-Jordania," an undated internal memorandum for Churchill (c. Feb. 25, 1921), reporting the views of Lawrence and Young, CO 732/3/10127, fols. 418–422.

42. "Report on the Middle East Conference," fol. 66.

43. Ibid.

44. Ibid.

45. Ibid., fol. 67.

46. Churchill to Lloyd George, received at the Colonial Office at 8:30 P.M., Mar. 14, 1921, CO 732/4/17976, fol. 167.

47. Ibid., fol. 171.

48. Lawrence to Churchill, Apr. 15, 1921, FO 371/6350, fol. 154; Cox to Churchill, Aug. 17, 1921, FO 371/6352, fol. 125.

49. Churchill to Lloyd George, Mar. 18, 1921, CO 732/4, fol. 169 (p. 6).

50. Elizabeth Burgoyne, *Gertrude Bell from Her Personal Papers, 1914–1926* (London: Ernest Benn, 1961), p. 157. See also Office of the High Commissioner for Mesopotamia, "Intelligence Report," Apr. 4, 1921, FO 371/6351, fols. 32–33.

51. Montagu, "Note on the Causes of the Outbreak in Mesopotamia," FO 371/5229/E10440, fol. 84; Viceroy of India, "Future of Mesopotamia," Oct. 11, 1920, FO 371/5231/E12756, fols. 10–11; Churchill to Lloyd George, Mar. 18, 1921, CO 732/4/17976, fol. 169; Cox to Churchill, Apr. 17, 18, 1921, Churchill to Cox, Apr. 20, FO 371/6350/E4835, fols. 185–190, 194; Burgoyne, *Gertrude Bell*, pp. 170–171, 212–216, 245; Lady Bell, *The Letters of Gertrude Bell*, vol. 2, p. 590.

52. Office of the High Commissioner for Mesopotamia, "Intelligence Report," May 15, 1921, FO 371/6351, fols. 163–164; "Mesopotamian Intelligence Report No. 12," June 15, 1921, ibid., fols. 114–119.

53. Lady Bell, *Letters of Gertrude Bell*, vol. 2, p. 596; Foreign Office to Marshall, May 24, 1921, FO 371/6351, fol. 21.

54. See, for example, Cox to Churchill, July 9, 11, 12, 31, Aug. 18, 19, 23, 1921, FO 371/6352, fols. 11–14, 24–27, 87–88, 145–149, 152, 166.

20. And One for Abdullah

1. Report by Major Batten, Sept. 10–20, 1920, FO 371/5243.

2. Samuel to Curzon, telegrams 179 and 180 of Aug. 7, 1920, in DBFP, vol. 13, pp. 333–334.

3. "I fear that unless we occupy and establish order in Trans-Jordan the French will go there on the excuse that they are being attacked," warned Hubert Young shortly after Faisal's expulsion from Damascus. FO 371/5038, fol. 40.

4. Hubert Young, "Foreign Office Memorandum on Possible Negotiations with the Hedjaz," CO 732/3, fol. 372.

5. Curzon to Samuel, telegram 80, Aug. 11, 1920, DBFP, vol. 13, pp. 337–338; Curzon to Vansittart, ibid., p. 351.

6. "Palestine—Views of the Department," CO 732/3/9837, Mar. 1, 1921, fol. 406, p. 4.

7. Ibid., fol. 407, pp. 5–6.

8. Lawrence's report on a conversation with Faisal, Feb. 16, 1921, CO 732/3/9836, fol. 402.

9. Suleiman Musa, *al-Haraka al-Arabiyya: Sirat al-Marhala al-Ula li-l-Nahda al-Arabiyya al-Haditha, 1908–1924* (Beirut: Dar al-Nahar, 1970), p. 582; Curzon to Samuel, telegram 70, Aug. 6, 1920, DBFP, vol. 13, p. 331; memorandum by Young, FO 371/5228, fol. 28.

10. "Sherifian Policy in Mesopotamia & Trans-Jordania," Feb. 25, 1921, CO 732/3, fols. 420–421.

11. "Report on Middle East Conference held in Cairo and Jerusalem, March 12th to 30th, 1921. Appendix 17—Palestine: Political and Military," FO 371/6343, fols. 94–96.

12. Churchill to Lloyd George, Mar. 18, 1921, CO 732/4, fol. 170.

13. Lloyd George to Churchill, Mar. 22, 1921, ibid., fol. 171. See also "Conclusions of a Meeting of the Cabinet Held at 10 Downing Street, S.W., on Tuesday, 22nd March 1921 at 11.30 A.M.," CAB 23/24, cabinet 14 (21), fols. 164–165, 167–168.

14. Churchill to Lloyd George, Mar. 23, 1921, CO 732/4, fol. 171.

15. "First Conversation on Trans-Jordania, Held at Government House, Jerusalem, March 28, 1921," FO 371/6343, fols. 99–100, pp. 107–109.

16. Ibid., fol. 99, p. 108; Abdullah Ibn Hussein, *Mudhakkirati* (Jerusalem: Matba'at Bait al-Maqdis, 1945), p. 180.

17. "First Conversation," fol. 100, p. 109.

18. Ibid., fols. 100–101, pp. 110–111.

19. "Second Conversation on Trans-Jordania," "Third Conversation on Trans-Jordania," ibid., fols. 101–102.

20. Letter from Mr. Churchill to Sir Herbert Samuel, at sea, Apr. 2, 1921, ibid., fols. 102–103.

21. From Empire to Nation

1. Kemal Atatürk, *Nutuk* (Ankara: Atatürk Merkez, 1989), 3 vols.; Atatürk, *Atatürk'ün Söylev ve Demechleri* (Istanbul: Kültür Bakanligi Yayinlar, 1980), 2 vols.

2. *A Speech Delivered by Ghazi Mustapha Kemal: President of the Turkish Republic, October 1927* (Leipzig: K. F. Kohler, 1929), p. 16 (hereinafter—*Kemal—Speech*).

3. Ibid., pp. 16–19.

4. Ibid., p. 19.

5. Stanford J. Shaw and Ezel Kural Shaw, *History of the Ottoman Empire and Modern Turkey*, vol. 2: *Reform, Revolution and Republic: The Rise of Modern Turkey, 1808–1975* (Cambridge, England: Cambridge University Press, 1994), p. 342.

6. "Memorandum Concerning the New Organization of the Ottoman Empire," submitted by the Ottoman Delegation to the peace conference on June 23, 1919, in DBFP, vol. 4, p. 650. For Damad Ferid's appearance before the Council of Ten, on June 17, 1919, see *Foreign Relations of the United States, Paris Peace Conference 1919* (Washington, D.C.: Government Printing Office, 1942–1947), vol. 4, pp. 508–512 (hereinafter *FRUS—Peace Conference*).

7. *FRUS—Peace Conference*, vol. 3, p. 872.

8. Lloyd George, *Memoirs of the Peace Conference* (New Haven: Yale University Press, 1939), vol. 2, p. 775; Venizelos to Lloyd George, Feb. 5, 1919, CAB 21/153; *FRUS—Peace Conference*, vol. 5, p. 484.

9. *Kemal—Speech*, pp. 29–31.

10. For the text of the National Pact, see J. C. Hurewitz, ed., *The Middle East and North Africa in World Politics*, 2nd. rev. ed. (New Haven and London: Yale University Press, 1975–1979), vol. 2, pp. 210–211.

11. *Kemal—Speech*, pp. 50, 57–58.

12. See, for example, Meinertzhagen to Curzon, Dec. 2, 1919, enclosing a report by Major J. N. Clayton (Damascus); Calthorpe to Curzon, July 25, 27, 30, Aug. 1, 5, 1919; Lieutenant-Colonel Ian Smith, "Interview with Kemal Bey," Sept. 30, 1919; "Report by Captain Perring (Samsun)," July 29, 1919, all in DBFP, vol. 4, pp. 566–567, 690 fn3, 703, 706, 713, 718–721, 792–794.

13. De Robeck to Curzon, Mar. 25, 1920, ibid., p. 48.

14. Curzon to Sir G. Buchanan (Rome), July 10, 1920, DBFP, vol. 13, p. 99. See also de Robeck to Curzon, June 23, 1920; Curzon to Buchanan, July 30, 1920; Curzon to Webb,

May 26, 1920; Grahame (Paris) to Curzon, June 4, 1920; de Robeck to Curzon, June 4, 23, 26, 1920, all in ibid., pp. 78–81, 89–90, 95, 110–111; E. Brémond, *La Cilicie en 1919–1920* (Paris: Imprimerie Nationale, 1921).

15. Hardinge's comments on de Robeck's to Curzon of June 17, 1920, DBFP, vol. 13, pp. 88–89, fn 2. For French and Italian evasiveness see, for example, Derby to Curzon, June 23, 1920, Buchanan to Curzon, June 25, 1920, ibid., pp. 90–91.

16. "Notes of a Meeting Held at 10 Downing Street, London, S.W., on Friday, March 18, 1921, at 11 A.M.," DBFP, vol. 15, pp. 449–451.

17. Lloyd George, *Memoirs of the Peace Conference*, vol. 2, p. 871.

18. Cabinet: Minutes, Sept. 7, 1922, Cabinet Papers 23/31.

19. Cabinet: Minutes, Sept. 15, 1922, ibid.

20. See, for example, his letter to the *Times* (London), Oct. 8, 1922.

21. For the conference's proceedings see Great Britain, Parliamentary Papers, "Lausanne Conference on Near Eastern Affairs, 1922–1923. Records of Proceedings and Draft Terms of Peace," Cmd. 1814 (1923).

22. Article 28 of the Lausanne Treaty. Turkey would still accept neutral observers of its judicial system, but they would have purely nominal powers.

23. According to the constitution, the Grand National Assembly possessed "legislative authority and executive powers," the latter being exercised by the president and a council of ministers. The principle of the cabinet's responsibility to the Parliament was established. Judicial authority was vested in the tribunals, which were proclaimed independent. The constitution also provided for individual liberty and freedom from discrimination on the basis of religion or race, as well as for the abolition of individual and group privileges. According to Article 69, "All Turks are equal before the law and are expected to conscientiously abide by it. Every kind of group, class, family, and individual special privilege is abolished and prohibited."

Epilogue

1. "Iran's Birthday Party," *Newsweek*, Oct. 25, 1971, pp. 16–17.

2. These effects were mainly manifested in the extraction of territorial concessions from Iraq with regard to the Shatt al-Arab (1975), as well as recognition of Iran's preeminent role by the Gulf monarchies.

3. So were the writings of the early pan-Arabists. Azuri, for example, envisaged his pan-Arab empire as comprising the Fertile Crescent from the Tigris and the Euphrates to the Suez Canal, and from the Mediterranean to the Gulf of Oman. Egypt was specifically excluded from the projected empire because "Egyptians do not belong to the Arab race" (Najib Azuri, *Le Réveil de la Nation Arabe dans l'Asie Turque en Présence des Intérêsts et des Rivalités des Puissances Étrangères, de la Curie Romaine et du Patriarcat Oecuménique* [Paris: Plon et Cie, 1905], pp. 245–247).

4. Abu Khaldun Sati al-Husri, *al-Uruba Awalan* (Beirut: Dar al-Ilm li-l-Malayin, 1955), pp. 11–13; Hisham Sharabi, *Nationalism and Revolution in the Arab World* (New York: Van Nostrand Reinhold, 1966), pp. 3–4.

5. General Nuri al-Said, *Arab Independence and Unity: A Note on the Arab Cause with*

Particular Reference to Palestine, and Suggestions for a Permanent Settlement to Which Are Attached Texts of All the Relevant Documents (Baghdad: Government Press, 1943), p. 8.

6. al-Husri, *al-Uruba Awalan*, p. 12.

7. Aharon Cohen, *Israel and the Arab World* (London: W. H. Allen, 1970), p. 381.

8. Elie Kedourie, *The Chatham House Version and Other Middle Eastern Studies* (London: Weidenfeld and Nicolson, 1970), p. 286; Kedourie, "The Nation-State in the Middle East," *Jerusalem Journal of International Relations*, vol. 9 (1987), p. 3.

9. Michael Howard, *The Lessons of History* (Oxford: Oxford University Press, 1991), pp. 39–40.

10. Ibn Khaldun, *The Muqaddimah: An Introduction to History,* Franz Rosenthal, trans. (Princeton, N.J.: Princeton University Press, 1981), p. 123.

11. "Statements Made on Behalf of His Majesty's Government during the Year 1918 in regard to the Future Status of Certain Parts of the Ottoman Empire," Cmd. 5964 (London: His Majesty's Stationary Office, 1939), p. 4.

12. T. E. Lawrence, "Syria: The Raw Material" (written early in 1915 but not circulated), *Arab Bulletin*, no. 44, Mar. 12, 1917, FO/882/26.

13. *T. E. Lawrence to His Biographers Robert Graves and Liddell Hart* (London: Cassell, 1963), p. 101.

14. David Fromkin, *A Peace to End All Peace: The Fall of the Ottoman Empire and the Creation of the Modern Middle East* (New York: Avon, 1990), p. 17.

15. Ibid.

16. Arnold Toynbee, "The Present Situation in Palestine," *International Affairs,* vol. 10 (Jan. 1931), p. 41.

17. For the classic exposition of the existence of a unified Arab national movement, see George Antonius, *The Arab Awakening* (London: Hamish Hamilton, 1938). See also Zeine N. Zeine, *Arab-Turkish Relations and the Emergence of Arab Nationalism* (Beirut: Khayat's, 1958); Hisham Sharabi, *Arab Intellectuals and the West: The Formative Years, 1875–1914* (Baltimore: John's Hopkins University Press, 1970); Bassam Tibi, *Arab Nationalism: A Critical Enquiry,* Marion Farouk-Sluglett and Peter Sluglett, eds. and trans. (London: Macmillan, 1981); Zaki Hazem Nuseibeh, *The Ideas of Arab Nationalism* (Ithaca, N.Y.: Cornell University Press, 1956); Ernest Dawn, "The Origins of Arab Nationalism," in Rashid Khalidi, Lisa Anderson, Muhammad Muslih, and Reeva S. Simon, eds., *The Origins of Arab Nationalism* (New York: Columbia University Press, 1991), pp. 3–30; Rashid Khalidi, "Ottomanism and Arabism in Syria before 1914: A Reassessment," in Khalidi et al., eds., *The Origins of Arab Nationalism*, pp. 50–69.

18. Martin Gilbert, *Churchill,* vol. IV: *1916–1922* (London: Heinemann, 1975), p. 596.

Index

INDEX